The New Stereo Soundbook

F. Alton Everest
Ron Streicher

TAB BOOKS
Blue Ridge Summit, PA

FIRST EDITION
FIRST PRINTING

© 1992 by **TAB Books**.
TAB Books is a division of McGraw-Hill, Inc.

Library of Congress Cataloging-in-Publication Data

Everest, F. Alton (Frederick Alton). 1909-
    The new stereo soundbook / by F. Alton Everest and Ron Streicher.
       p.   cm.
    Includes index.
    ISBN 0-8306-3904-7   ISBN 0-8306-3903-9 (pbk.)
    1. Stereophonic sound systems.   I. Streicher, Ron.   II. Title.
TK7881.8.E93   1992
621.389′334—dc20   91-29550
                                                         CIP

TAB Books offers software for sale. For information and a catalog, please
contact TAB Software Department, Blue Ridge Summit, PA 17294-0850.

Acquisitions Editor: Roland S. Phelps
Technical Editor: Melanie D. Brewer
Director of Production: Katherine G. Brown
Book Design: Jaclyn J. Boone
Cover design and illustration: Denny Bond, East Petersburg, PA   EL1

To the memory of Richard Heyser

"Stereo is merely an attempt to
create the illusion of reality through
the willing suspension of disbelief."

Contents

Acknowledgment

We gratefully acknowledge the critical reading of the manuscript by Dr. Floyd E. Toole, National Research Council, Division of Physics, Canada, and the helpful suggestions he has given. The authors, however, assume full responsibility for the contents of this book.

Introduction

WHAT IS *STEREOPHONICS*? THE PURPOSE OF THIS BOOK IS TO ANSWER THAT question in both its practical and provocative aspects. By incorporating many of the most recent findings in auditory perception and current developments in surround sound, the concept of stereophonics is expanded from the simplistic one of sound coming out of two loudspeakers to a system yielding total envelopment of the listener in 3-dimensional sound.

Although a previous interest in stereo, or even audio production, on your part would be helpful, it is not essential. The discussions are purposely nonmathematical and are presented in an easily assimilated style, augmented with line drawings and photographs.

In fourteen chapters, the concept and production of stereo sound is explored in all its varied aspects. First, the directional encoding of sounds falling on the ear and how interaural differences in these cues provide spatial texture to the stereo image are made clear. Two chapters are devoted to the philosophical and pragmatic implications of stereo production techniques. Five more chapters examine in detail modern stereo microphone practices. Other chapters are given to a scrutiny of auditory spaciousness, coloration of sound, and optimizing the stereo listening environment.

A unique feature of this book lies in interpreting contemporary advances in stereo through study of contributions by audio pioneers dating back to the early 1930s. By placing stereo in this historical perspective, a survey of the sometimes fragmented efforts of the past provides a basis for understanding current and future developments in the sonic arts.

The essence of stereo lies not in elaborate microphone pickups, nor does it rely on exotic amplifiers or loudspeakers. Rather, the secret resides within us: the amazing process of encoding sound with our bodies and decoding it with our brains. Every sound we hear is directionally encoded by reflections off the folds of our outer ears, by diffraction around our heads, and by reflections off shoulders and torso. The brain then decodes this wealth of information and presents us with a sonic image of the world around us.

In the final analysis, listening is a highly personal experience; like fingerprints, our ears and shape of head are unique to us. No two of us hear a given sound in exactly the same way. Yet we seem to have enough features in common to provide a basis for new and exciting developments in stereophony.

F. Alton Everest
Ron Streicher

1
Early stereophonics

THE WORD *STEREOPHONICS* WAS DERIVED BY COMBINING TWO GREEK
words: *stereo*, which means solid, and implicates three spatial dimensions (depth,
breadth, and height), and *phonics*, which means the science of sound. Thus, to
those with an eye to the future, *stereophonics* can imply *the science of 3-dimensional
sound*.

Because the popular contraction of *stereophonic* to *stereo* is widely understood
and accepted, it will be freely used in this book. This application of the word to
describe systems falling far short of true 3-dimensional reproduction, however,
should not obscure the ultimate Greek meaning of the word.

The goal of engineers is to record and reproduce sound with complete spatial
fidelity. This goal, however, can never be fully attained. Richard Heyser put this
idea in proper perspective by stating: "Stereo is merely an attempt to create the
illusion of reality through the willing suspension of disbelief."

Four terms have been evolved over the years to represent sound reproduction:
monaural, binaural, monophonic, and stereophonic (Fig. 1-1). A one-eared, single-
channel monaural system is shown in Fig. 1-1A, and the binaural system, which
involves a "dummy head" with microphones set into its ears is depicted in Fig.
1-1B. Both of these systems dictate listening via headphones.

If loudspeakers are used, the *monaural* system becomes the *monophonic* system shown in Fig. 1-1C. The common stereophonic system resulting from two
sound transmission channels is shown in Fig. 1-1D.

The common situation of listening through earphones to stereophonic recordings that have been designed for loudspeaker reproduction is illustrated in Fig.
1-1E. The compromise that results will be discussed in later sections. These
modes of reproduction differ in important ways and also will be examined in considerable detail in subsequent chapters.

For now, however, the goal is to avoid confusion of terms. The terms *binaural*
and *stereophonic* have caused confusion for a long time. William B. Snow points out

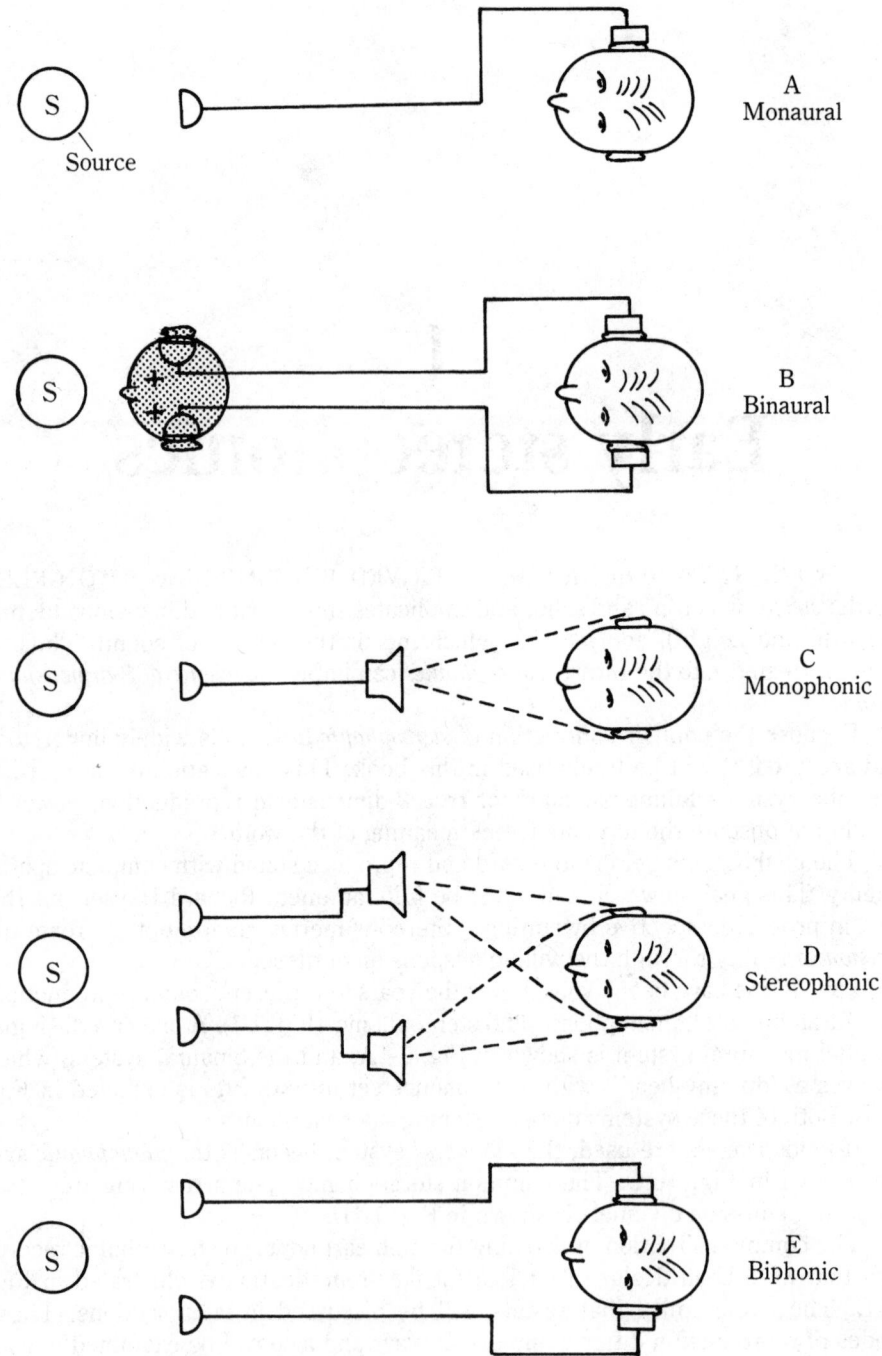

1-1   Classification of the various forms of sound reproduction.

in *Basic Principles of Stereophonic Sound*, that in 1880 Alexander Graham Bell referred to experiments in localization of sound sources as "stereophonic phenomena of binaural audition." This really confuses the concepts (see Reference 1-1).

The single-channel monaural system using a single earphone—or two earphones driven by a common signal—dominated the audio world until adequate power amplification was available to drive loudspeakers. With loudspeaker reproduction the monaural system becomes monophonic or "mono."

The binaural system, utilizing some form of dummy head for the sound pickup, yields realistic reproduction of sonic events. The effect is that the listener's ears are transported to the position of the dummy head. Renewed interest in headphone listening with personal, portable players has spawned significant advances in binaural techniques, which will be discussed in chapter 6.

The first stereo

The first public demonstration of what temporarily will be called stereophonic reproduction took place in Paris at the Exhibition of Electricity in 1881 (see Reference 1-2). At the Paris Grand Opera, ten telephone transmitters, or microphones, developed by Clarence Ader were arranged along the lip of the stage—five on the left and five on the right—as shown in Fig. 1-2. A 3 km cable run connected these transmitters directly to pairs of telephone receivers, also developed by Ader, at the Palace of Industry. One receiver from each pair was connected to a transmitter on the left side, while the other receiver was connected to the corresponding transmitter on the right side. When one receiver was held to the left ear and the other receiver was held to the right ear, the auditor listened to what was happening on the stage through a pair of spaced microphones. The result was astounding. People thronged to the exhibit to experience the startling reality of sounds reproduced from the stage. Even though the microphones and receivers were crude by our standards, they were state of the art at the time, providing sufficient quality to deliver a convincing "stereo" effect. The ability to localize the various sound sources on the stage (solos, choruses, musical instruments, etc.) amazed the crowds of people visiting the exhibit.

The conventional stereophonic arrangements that was shown in Fig. 1-1D uses loudspeakers for reproduction. Direct sound from the right loudspeaker falls on the listener's right ear, while direct sound from the left loudspeaker falls on the left ear. Therefore the sound of each loudspeaker is actually heard by both ears at the same time. This cross-channeling of sound is called *crosstalk*—a term coined by telephone engineers to describe signals from one circuit being picked up by another circuit. Aural crosstalk is always present and is a significant component in stereophonic reproduction. Thus, the Paris demonstration in 1881 was not true stereophonic reproduction because the telephone receivers eliminated this crosstalk. Neither was it a true binaural demonstration because no dummy head was used. Rather, it was more like the contemporary practice of listening to

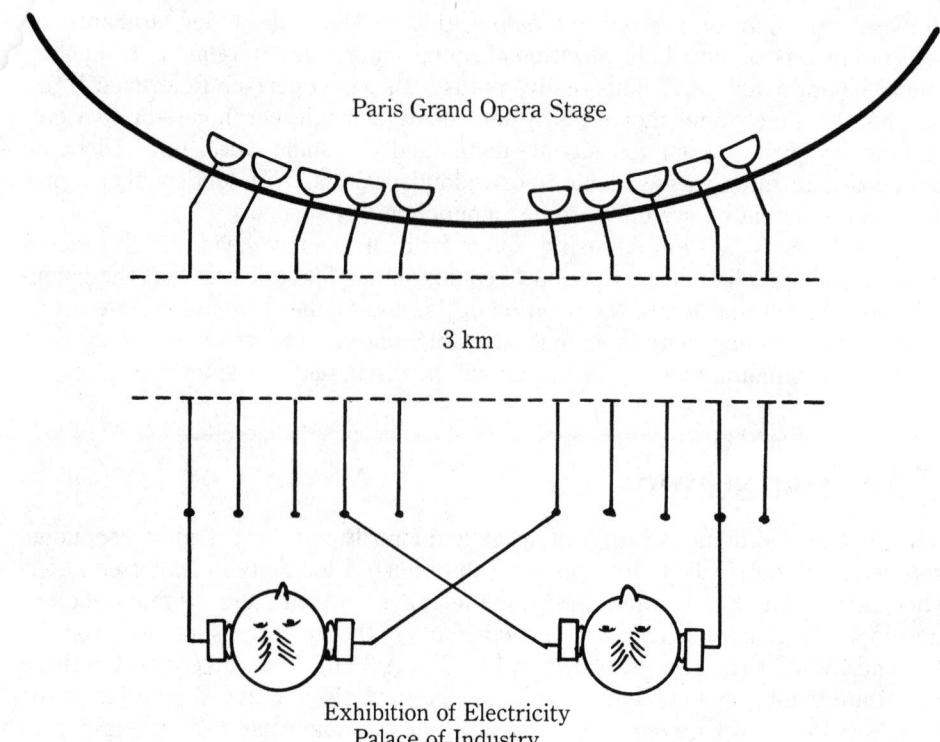

Paris Grand Opera Stage

3 km

Exhibition of Electricity
Palace of Industry

1-2   The first public demonstration of "stereophonic" sound at the Paris Exhibition of
Electricity, 1881. Telephone *transmitters* (microphones) picked up the sound that was
carried by cable to the receiving point, a distance of 3 km.

stereophonic recordings with headphones, which is another special case that
eliminates crosstalk, but with compromise in spatial quality.

Stereo in the 1930s

The 1930s produced significant developments in stereo recording and reproduction. In England the pioneering work of Alan Dower Blumlein (Fig. 1-3) spelled out
in mathematical detail what, decades later, has become common practice. His outstanding contributions are documented primarily in his patents (see Reference
1-3). Most of Blumlein's work in stereophonics was carried out while he was associated with Electric and Musical Industries, Ltd. (E.M.I., now known as Thorn
E.M.I.).

At the same time, equally significant work was being conducted independently at Bell Laboratories in Murrayhill, New Jersey. This is where the three-
channel system of stereophony was developed, which is still in use today. Although
names like Arthur C. Keller, William B. Snow and J.C. Steinberg are found promi-
nently in the early stereo literature, Harvey Fletcher's wise leadership and keen

1-3 Alan Dower Blumlein, whose work in stereophonic sound in England in the 1930s anticipated modern techniques. He was employed by Electric and Musical Industries, Ltd., now known as Thorn E.M.I. Thorn E.M.I., Middlesex, England

1-4 Dr. Harvey C. Fletcher, whose research group at Bell Telephone Laboratories in the 1930s carried on important work in *auditory perspective*, which advanced the field of stereophonics. Brigham Young University

mind cause his name to stand out in early stereo research and development at Bell Labs (see Fig. 1-4).

A half century transpired between the Paris exhibition and the sudden spurt of work in England and in the United States during the 1930s. Due largely to the great depression and World War II, two more decades passed before technology and economics allowed the commercial development of stereo.

Blumlein's contributions

Alan Dower Blumlein was born in Manchester, England, on June 29, 1903. He is well-known in the audio community for the creative nature of his stereo contribution. His scientific contributions are emblazoned in 128 patents, of which only a few are in the field of stereo. In his brief life span of 39 years, Blumlein made basic contributions to wireless theory and practice, telephony, television, and radar, as well as gramophone recording and stereo. His inventions in electronic television camera tubes were enough to place his company's tube on par with RCA's Iconoscope and provide the basis for England's post-war television development.

Blumlein was also in the forefront of airborne radar development, which was a decisive factor in the Battle of Britain of World War II. He died in the crash of a Halifax plane used in his radar research (see Reference 1-4). Blumlein had an exceptionally keen, analytical mind that he enthusiastically applied in many different fields—truly a technical man of all seasons.

The application date on Blumlein's landmark patent, *Improvements in and relating to sound transmission, sound-recording, and sound-reproducing systems*, now a classic source of information, is December 14, 1931 (see References 1-3 and 1-4). In the introduction of this patent, he points out the abilities of the human ear-brain mechanism to discount reverberation and interfering sounds arriving from many directions and to concentrate on a specific, desired sound, which is *psychologically enhanced*. When the desired sound is mixed with the reverberation and produced through a single-channel, the psychological enhancement is lost and confusion results. Blumlein concentrated on the nature of the signals falling on each ear and the differences in magnitude and phase of these two ear signals. Then he described ways to mount pairs of velocity (ribbon) microphones close together and to orient them to produce signals having the desired differences in magnitude and phase to achieve a stereo effect when reproduced. He also described means of recording the signals of both channels in the same record groove—what today is our 45 – 45 degree stereo phonograph disk system.

Part of Blumlein's patent is reproduced in the appendix. Other patents were filed by Blumlein in 1933, 1934, and 1935 that further rounded out his important contributions to stereo.

Fletcher's work at Bell Laboratories

Harvey Fletcher's life spanned from 1884 to 1981. He received his Ph.D. in 1907 at the University of Chicago where he worked with a Nobel Prize winner, Robert A. Millikan, on the famous oil-drop experiment measuring the charge on the electron.

Fletcher and Blumlein, apart from their scientific virtuosity, were quite different. Blumlein, especially in his earlier years, was blunt and rude and had difficulty tolerating any person intellectually inferior to himself. Fletcher, on the other hand, was extremely well-mannered and polished (Fig. 1-4).

Blumlein did his best work within small groups. Fletcher's contributions in stereophony and other fields were made as Director of Physical Research at Bell Laboratories, one of the largest and most respected research institutions in the United States (1933 – 1949). Fletcher was one of the founders of the Acoustical Society of America and won its Gold Medal in 1957. He also received Gold Medals from the Society of Motion Picture Engineers in 1949 and the Audio Engineering Society in 1958, along with the Louis Edward Levy medal for physical measurements of audition in 1924. Fletcher could be considered the mentor of a generation of students of psychoacoustics through his classic books, *Speech and Hearing* (1929) and *Speech and Hearing in Communications* (1953), which summarized in an accessible manner the fruits of his work at Bell Labs.

Harvey Fletcher and his coworkers at Bell Laboratories approached stereophony in a way quite different from Blumlein (see References 1-5, 1-6, and 1-7). They envisioned a large room divided by a wall completely opaque to sound as shown in Fig. 1-5. A sound source, such as an orchestra, was on one side of this wall and the listeners were on the other side. The wall could be considered a per-

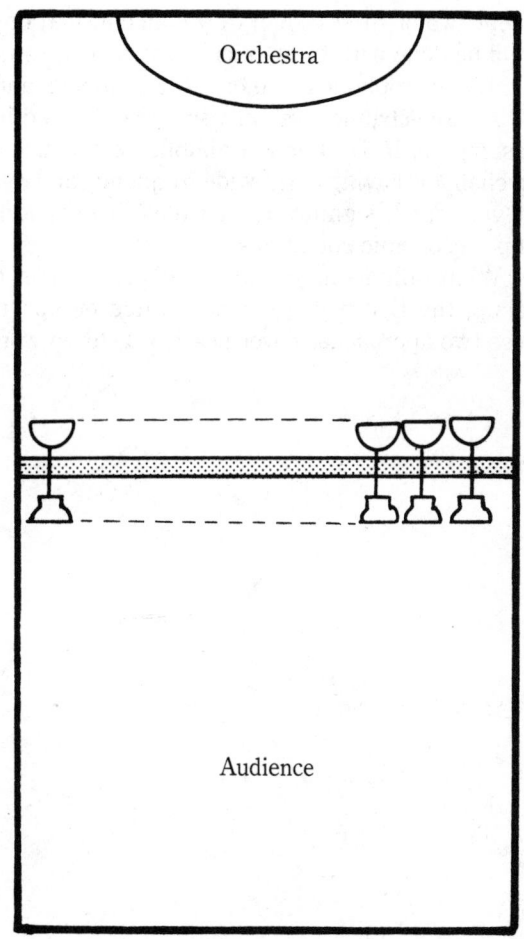

1-5 Researchers at Bell Laboratories envisioned a *wall of sound* covered with microphones on one side and loudspeakers on the other, a sort of infinite-channel system. The horizontal row at the level of the sound sources was judged most important, so rows below and above were eliminated. In this single row—left, center, and right microphones were retained. The three-channel system of stereophony resulting is still in use today.

fect sound barrier and nothing could be heard by the audience. The surface of the wall on the orchestra side was imagined to be completely covered with microphones, and each microphone was connected to a loudspeaker in a comparable position on the audience side of the wall through an amplifier. This changed the wall from being sound-opaque to sound-transparent, at least unidirectionally. The wavefront of sound falling on the microphones would be faithfully reconstructed on the audience side of the partition and perfect, or near-perfect, sound reproduction would result from this "wall of sound."

A sound system comprised of an infinite number of channels is impractical. Therefore, certain modifications were made to enhance the system's practicality.

In stage plays and film dramas most of the action takes place near ground level. Because our ability to locate sound sources in the vertical direction is poor, all microphone/loudspeaker channels can be eliminated except those in one horizontal line at ear height. Fletcher and his coworkers took another bold step in simplifying their reproducing system by eliminating all the channels in that row except two or three. Then they concentrated on experimentally finding out what could be done with these microphones. They studied various combinations of two or three microphones, two or three channels, and two or three loudspeakers.

A three-channel system was demonstrated in 1933 between Philadelphia and Washington. In 1941 another public demonstration was given in New York involving channels having extra-wide frequency and dynamic range. In spite of the interest generated, significant advances in exploiting these new ideas had to await proper economic conditions.

While Blumlein concentrated on single (or coincident-pair) microphone pickup, the Bell workers concentrated on spaced microphone pickup. Together, these two approaches cover nearly all stereo work today, a half century later.

2
How stereo information is conveyed

BEFORE EXPLORING THE PERCEPTION OF SPATIAL SOUND, A FEW BASIC concepts concerning the nature of sound should be reviewed. First, the propagation of sound is relatively slow, compared to light. The speed of sound is only about 1,130 ft/sec or about 770 miles per hour. In aeronautical terms, the speed of sound is Mach-1, or about the speed of a small caliber rifle bullet. Sound travels 1.13 feet in a millisecond, or roughly 1 foot in one-thousandth of a second. The time is takes for sound to travel from a source, such as a person talking or an instrument in a musical ensemble, to a microphone is important and must be considered.

Second, the relationship between the *frequency* of sound and the *wavelength* of the sound should be clearly understood. The diaphragm of a loudspeaker could be likened to a piston driven by a connecting rod as in Fig. 2-1. As the piston moves forward it compresses the air in front of it and as it moves back a partial vacuum, or *rarefaction*, is created. If this pistonlike movement of a loudspeaker diaphragm occurs fast enough, it causes pressure variations to radiate into the surrounding air. The pressure variations are extremely small ripples superimposed on the atmospheric pressure that prevailed at the time of the movement. The number of complete cycles of air pressure compressions and rarefactions per second is called the *frequency* of the sound. The distance an air molecule travels from one pressure peak to the next during one cycle of the piston motion is called the *wavelength* of the sound being radiated.

A *sine wave* is the natural output of a diaphragm driven by the simple harmonic motion of the connecting-rod system. It is called a sine wave because, in mathematical terms, the relative amplitude of the pressure wave is proportional to the sine of the flywheel angle to which the connecting rod is attached. The loudspeaker diaphragm can go through this cyclic movement rapidly—producing a high frequency tone—or slowly—producing a low frequency tone. If the loudspeaker diaphragm is driven by a voice or music signal, more irregular pressure variations result. Irregularity of waveforms results from combining many sine wave tones, such as harmon-

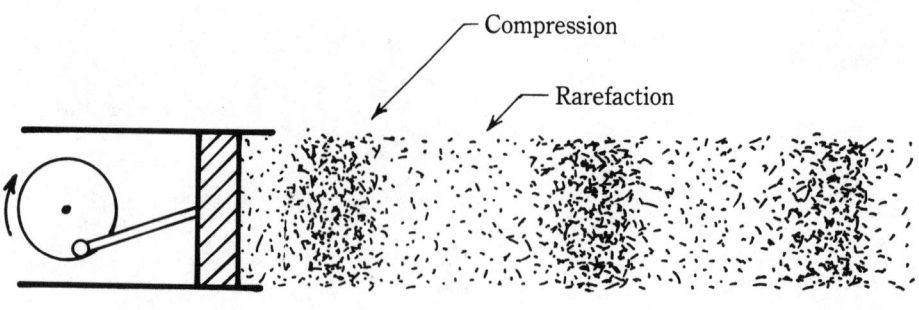

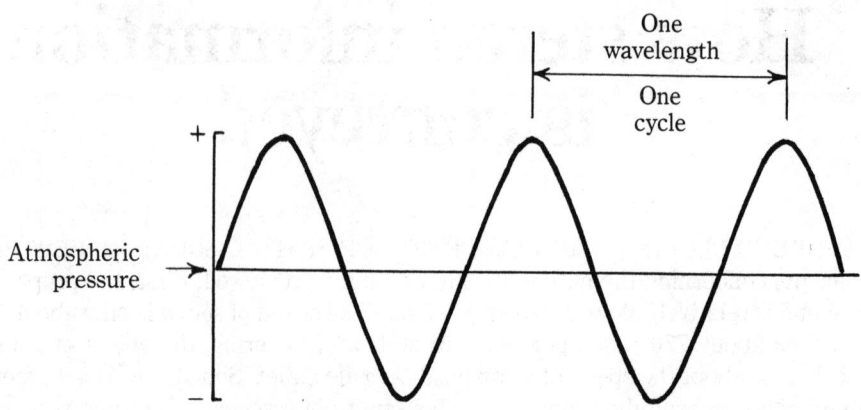

2-1   The reciprocating motion of the piston alternately compresses and spreads out the air particles. If the piston motion is fast enough, sound energy is radiated in the form of compressed and rarified regions in the air. The wavelength of a sound is the distance between successive peaks or successive troughs. These minute changes in pressure constituting the sound wave are superimposed upon the prevailing static atmospheric air pressure.

ics or partials. Pressure waveshapes for low and higher frequency tones and for a typical voice or music signal are shown in Fig. 2-2.

The frequency of a sound is understood as the primary constituent of its pitch in this discussion. In reality, however, other psychoacoustic features are also involved in the perception of pitch.

As previously mentioned, the *wavelength* is the physical distance the sound wave travels during one complete cycle. The wavelength is long for a slow cycle or low frequency of diaphragm movement, and it is short for a fast cycle or high frequency. In musical terms the low frequencies comprise the bass tones, and the higher frequencies comprise the treble tones.

These three important parameters—*frequency, wavelength,* and *speed of sound*—are related as follows:

$$\lambda = \frac{c}{f} \qquad\qquad (2\text{-}1)$$

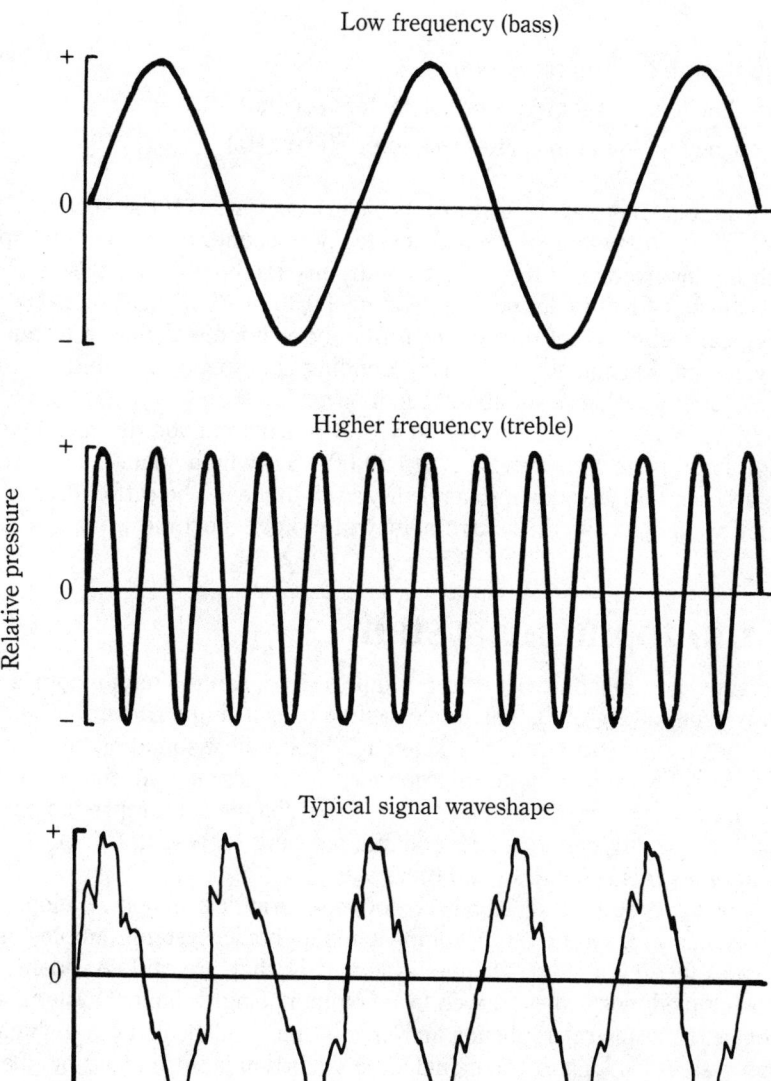

2-2 Three typical periodic waves plotted to the same time scale: A low-frequency sine wave, a sine wave of higher frequency, and a typically irregular speech or music signal.

or,

$$c = \frac{f}{\lambda}$$

(2-2)

or,

$$f = \frac{\lambda}{c}$$

(2-3)

in which,

λ = wavelength in feet (or meters)

c = speed of sound in feet/second (or meters/second)

f = frequency of sound in cycles/second or Hertz (Hz)

For example, the wavelength of a typical bass tone C2, the second C below middle C, has a frequency of about 65 cycles per second, or 65 Hz. The speed of sound in air for average atmospheric conditions is about 1,130 ft/sec. A wavelength of about 17 feet is derived by dividing 1,130 by 65. (Equation 2-1).

A typical treble tone C6, the second C above middle C, has a frequency of 1,046 cycles per second, or 1,046 Hz. Dividing the speed of sound by this frequency yields a wavelength of about 1 foot.

Doubling or halving the number of vibrations per second defines the octave. The audible range is stated as 20 Hz to 20,000 Hz, which spans 10 octaves with wavelength from 65 feet down to as little as 0.5 inches. The difficulties in sound reproduction caused by this extremely wide range become apparent in later chapters.

The monophonic system

To understand stereophonics, it is important to first examine monophonics, or single-channel sound (Fig. 2-3). The mono system uses a single transmission channel between the original source and the listener. The simplest sound pickup in a monophonic system involves a single microphone. A musical sound picked up by one microphone and sent over a single transmission channel to a reproducing system with one loudspeaker can give a reasonably pleasing representation of the music, and for decades this system was all there was.

Technology continues to advance, however, bringing major developments in sound transmission. Other more complex monophonic systems employ multiple microphones feeding a single-channel system, but they are still considered monophonic. Multiple loudspeakers driven by a common, single-channel system, are also monophonic. Multiple microphones and/or multiple loudspeakers in a single-channel mono system can distort the signal. The distortion is introduced by phasing or comb-filter effects, which will be treated in detail in chapter 8.

The stereophonic system

Playing stereophonic signals through two loudspeakers presents an entirely different listening experience than playing a monophonic signal through the same two loudspeakers. In its basic form a stereophonic, or simply a stereo system, uses two related, but nonetheless independent, pickup and transmission channels (Fig. 2-4). The introduction of the second channel brought a quantum jump in the subjective naturalness of the reproduced sound.

Reproduced monaural sounds are somewhat flat and 1-dimensional, lacking much of the spatial texture produced in a live performance. Reproduced two-chan-

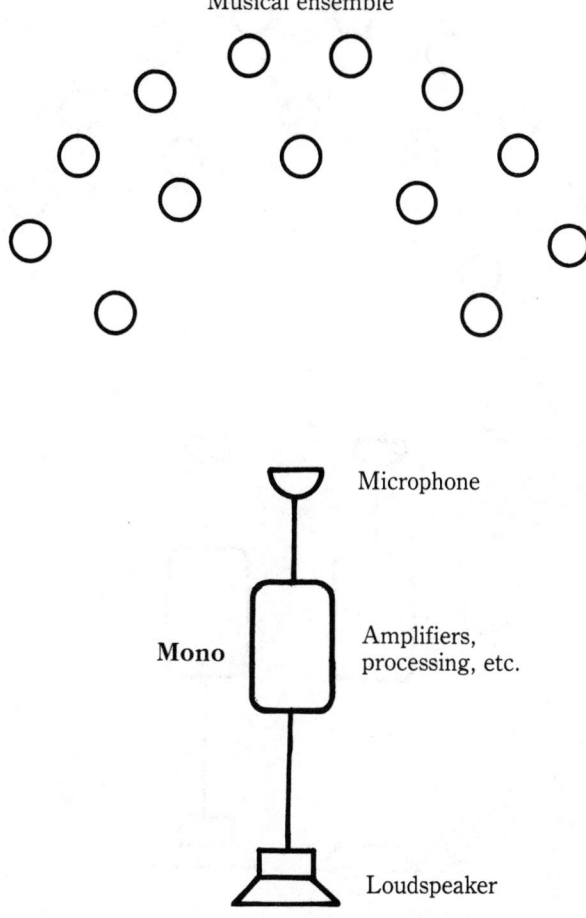

2-3   A typical monophonic recording/reproducing system.

nel stereo signals, however, give a richer, fuller, and more natural perspective to the subject.

The stereo effect relies on certain cues that our ear-brain system can interpret. These cues allow us to perceive not only a more natural reproduction of the musical ensemble, but also some of the spatial characteristics of the music hall itself.

The simplest stereo recording technique involves two microphones set up in front of a source of sound, such as the musical ensemble shown in Fig. 2-5. These could be nondirectional microphones equally sensitive to sound arriving from any direction. The spacing between these microphones is important and will be discussed in detail in chapter 9.

In this example the sound from every instrument in the ensemble is picked up by both microphones as illustrated in Fig. 2-6. Subtle differences in the sound of any instrument are also picked up by each of the two microphones. These differences are the key to understanding the mysterious stereo effect.

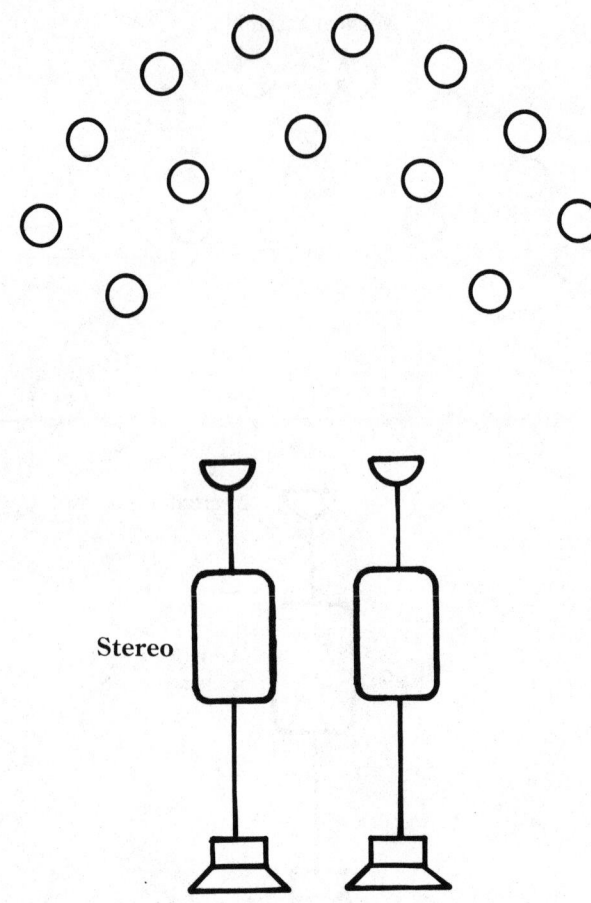

2-4   A typical stereophonic recording/reproducing system involving two channels.

The trumpet illustrated in Fig. 2-7 is closer to the right microphone than the left, so the trumpet sound is of higher intensity in the right channel than in the left. Also, because it is closer, the sound of the trumpet reaches the right microphone a few thousandths of a second earlier than the left. When listened to separately, the right channel sound and the left channel sound are so similar that little, if any, difference could be detected. The differences are there, however, and they are important. These complex differences in intensity and timing between the signals picked up by the two microphones merit careful scrutiny.

Because of the differences in the signals in the two stereo channels the trumpet sounds more realistic when listened to in stereo, and an idea of its relative location and certain impressions of the performance space can be perceived. Sound reflected from distant walls, reverberation, gives the instruments additional richness as the sound decays when the source stops sounding. This tendency of sound to *hang on*

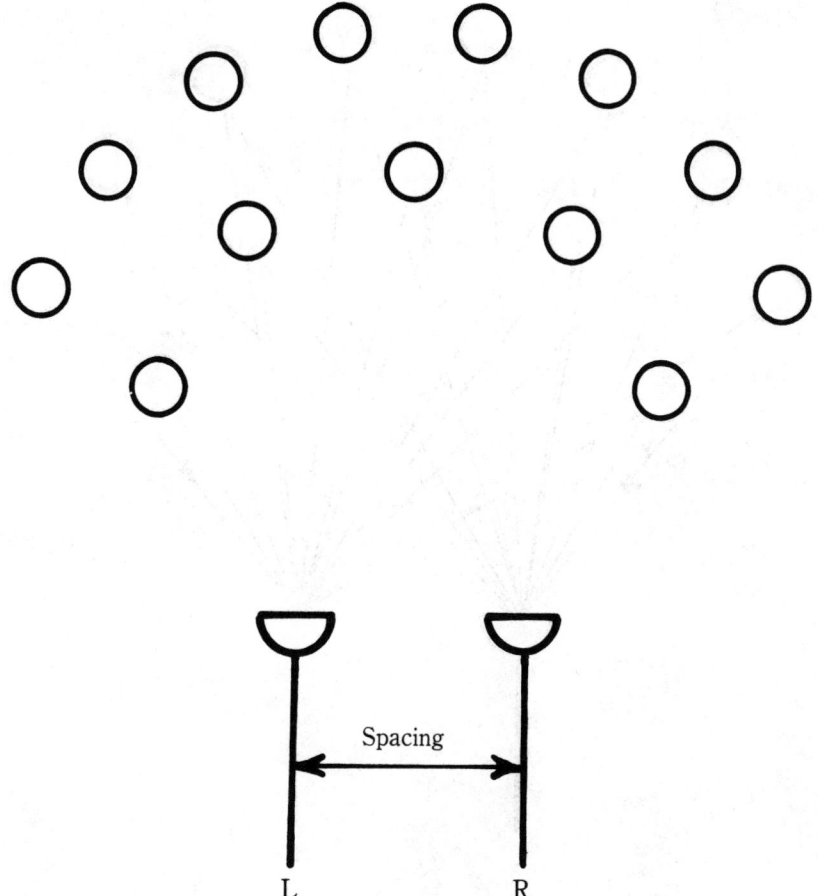

2-5 A musical ensemble picked up by two spaced microphones.

gives a hint as to the size of the room and whether it is *live* or *dead* acoustically. The distance between the trumpet and the microphones also determines the relationship between the direct sound and the reverberant sound. The closer the microphones are to the source, the more the direct sound tends to dominate the weaker, reflected sound—submerging the reverberant effects. Conversely, the further the microphone is from the source, the more the reverberation dominates the sound. When the sound from both microphones is in stereo, a more accurate and complete sonic image of the hall can be preserved.

If a musical instrument is situated exactly along the centerline of the ensemble, as in Fig. 2-8, its sound arrives at both microphones at the same instant and with equal intensity. The sound is then perceived as being in the center. The sounds of all other instruments, however, are different in the left and right channels. Thus, each microphone receives a welter of sounds differing in both intensity and time of arrival (Fig. 2-6). These differences make up the various cues that are

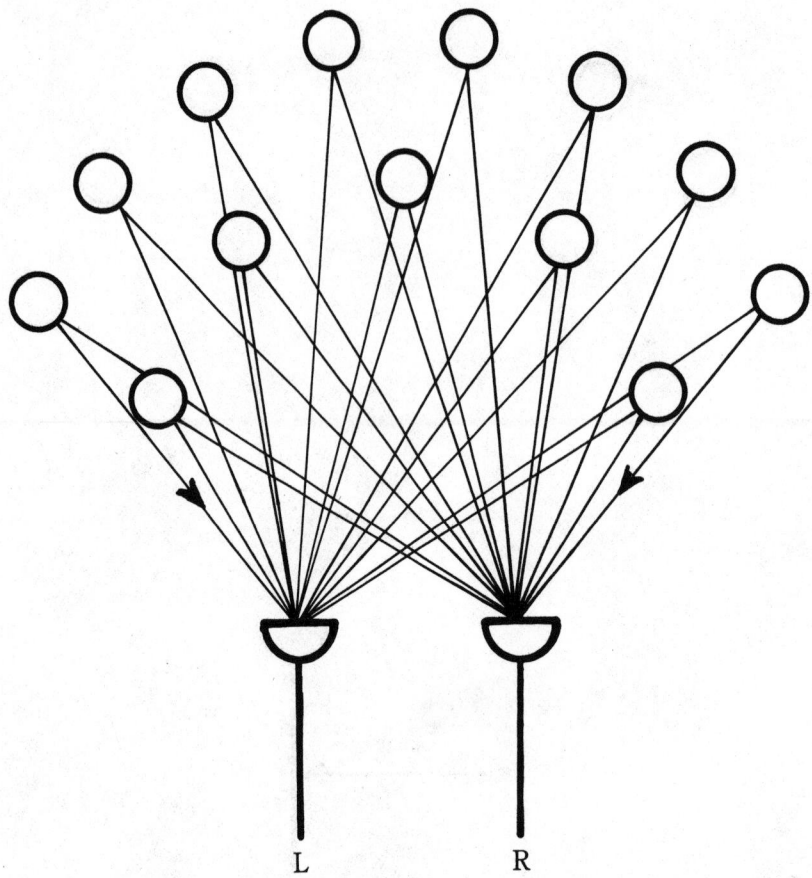

L   R

2-6 The sound of every instrument is picked up by both microphones; however, subtle, but important differences exist between the signals in the two channels.

interpreted by our ear-brain system to give an orderly perception of both the physical arrangement of the instruments in the ensemble and their timbral contrasts.

Intensity effects in stereo

To understand how spatial images are created, intensity cues will be examined first. An instrument, like a violin exactly on the centerline, gives an identical signal in each channel (Fig. 2-9). If the balance control of the stereo reproducing equipment is properly adjusted, a *phantom* image of the violin can be perceived midway between the loudspeakers (Fig. 2-10).

The measure of signal strength is the decibel (dB) because it is convenient to use and it is a logarithmic unit. Our ears respond in an approximately logarithmic

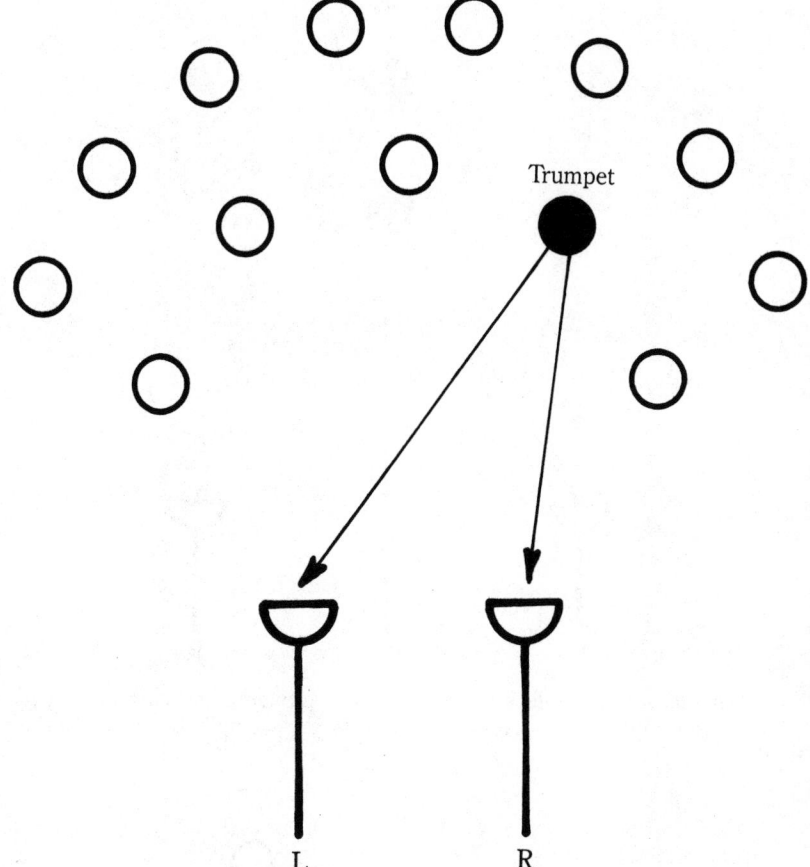

2-7 The sound pressure of the trumpet is slightly higher in the right microphone than the left because it is closer. The trumpet signal also arrives at the right microphone slightly earlier than at the left. These differences in intensity and timing (phase) are basic to the stereophonic effect.

fashion. Table 2-1 illustrates how large numbers expressing sound pressure ratios can be represented conveniently by smaller numbers in decibels.

When the level of the signal to the right loudspeaker is 5 dB higher than the level of the left loudspeaker, the phantom image of the violin sound shifts slightly to the right of center (Fig. 2-11). Increasing the level of the right loudspeaker until it is 10 dB higher than the left causes the phantom image to move further to the right (Fig. 2-12). When the level of the sound from the right loudspeaker is 20 dB higher than the left, the image of the violin sound is moved completely to the right loudspeaker (Fig. 2-13). Conversely, the image of the violin can be shifted completely to the left by increasing the relative level of the left loudspeaker by 20 dB (Fig. 2-14).

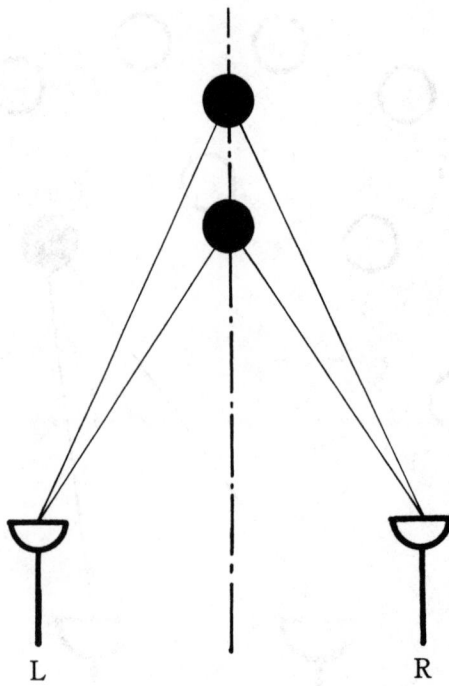

2-8 Sound sources on the centerline between the two microphones arrive with the same intensity and timing. The sound is then perceived as being in the center of the sound-stage.

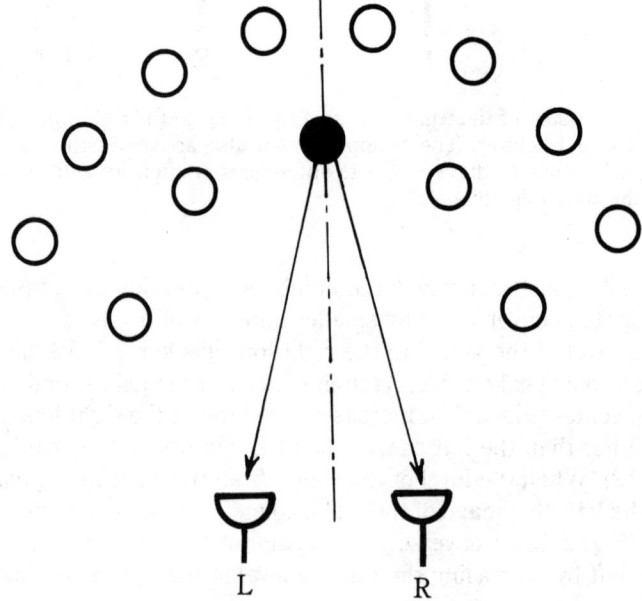

2-9 The sound of a violin directly on the centerline results in a perceived centered image.

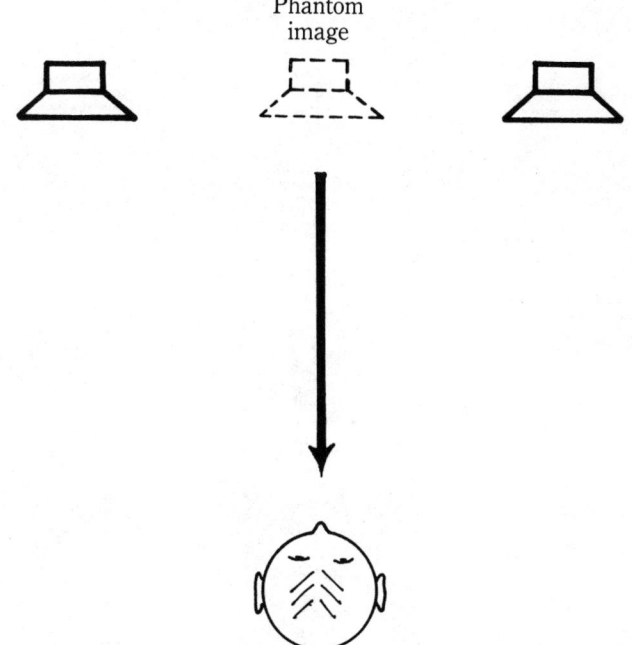

Phantom
image

2-10 If the balance control is properly adjusted, equal signals in the two loudspeakers result in a *phantom image* midway between the two loudspeakers.

Thus, the sonic image of the violinist could be moved at will from right to left or back again, simply by changing the relative intensity of the sound in the left and right loudspeakers. This concept is called *intensity stereo*, because the stereo position is determined solely by the differences in intensity between the two loudspeakers. This is really nothing new; it is what the balance controls on stereo sets have been doing all along. The operator at the mixing console in a recording studio does the same thing by placing mono images at any right-to-left position in the stereo field using a *panoramic potentiometer* or *panpot*.

Table 2-1. The decibel

Ratios of two pressures p_1/p_2	Decibels (dB) $20 \log (p_1/p_2)$
1	0
10	20
100	40
1,000	60
10,000	80
100,000	100
1,000,000	120

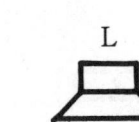
L

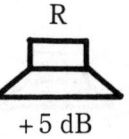
R

+ 5 dB

2-11   Increasing the relative signal level of the right loudspeaker by 5 dB shifts the image slightly away from the centerline in the direction of the louder speaker.

L

R

+ 10 dB

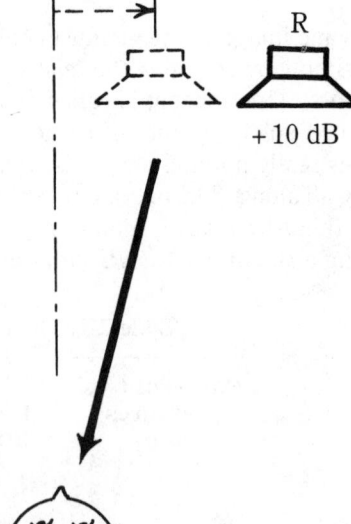

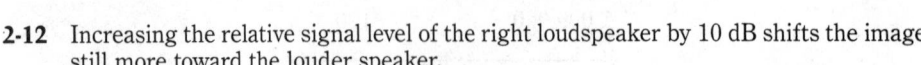

2-12   Increasing the relative signal level of the right loudspeaker by 10 dB shifts the image still more toward the louder speaker.

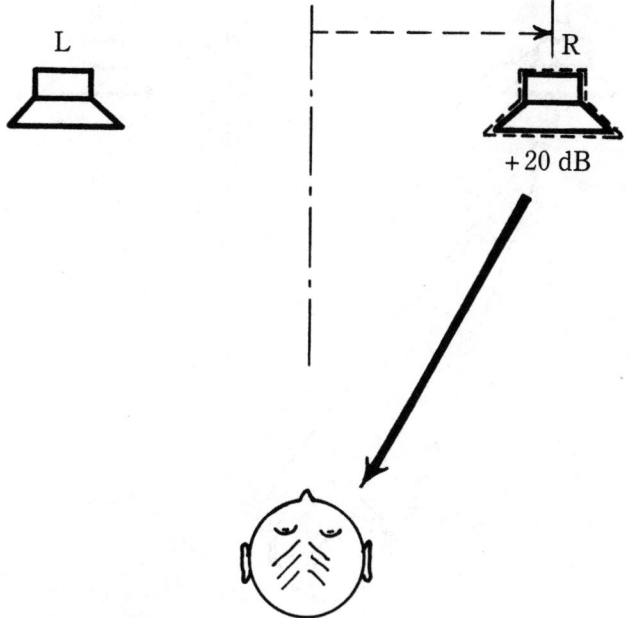

2-13 Increasing the relative signal level of the right loudspeaker by 20 dB shifts the perceived image completely to the right loudspeaker.

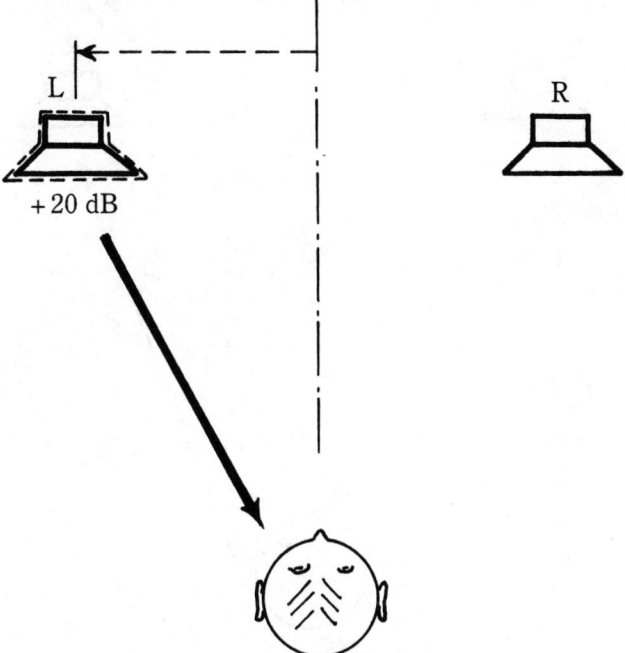

2-14 Increasing the relative signal level of the left loudspeaker 20 dB shifts the perceived image to the left loudspeaker.

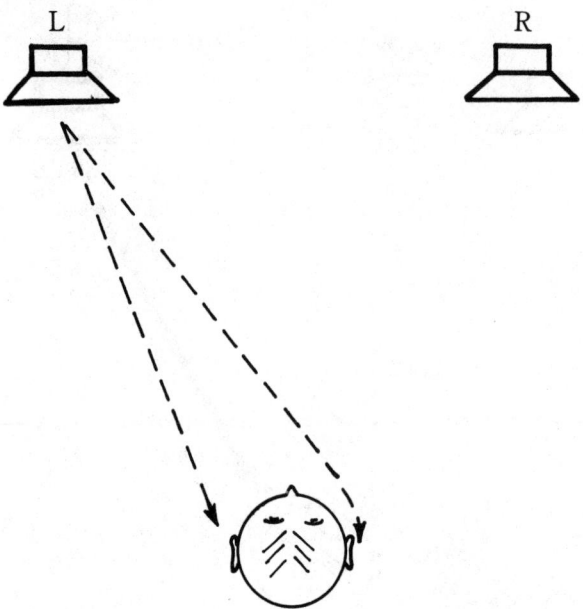

2-15   The intensity of sound arriving at the left ear from the left loudspeaker remains relatively constant as frequency is changed, but the sound to the right ear varies with frequency.

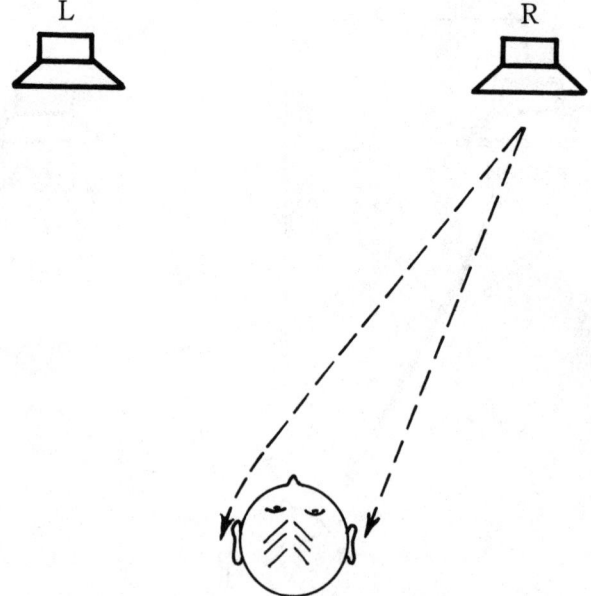

2-16   The intensity of sound arriving at the right ear from the right loudspeaker remains relatively constant as frequency is changed, but the sound to the left ear varies with frequency.

At higher frequencies, the different intensities perceived at the two ears account for most of our ability to differentiate stereo directionality. This is not true, however, at lower frequencies where the intensity of sound at the two ears is almost the same.

The intensity of sound arriving from off-center is constant with frequency at the nearer ear, but the intensity varies at the far ear of the listener; bass tones are higher than treble tones (Figs. 2-15 and 2-16). A tone with a frequency of 4,200 Hz is close to the pitch of the note at the top of the piano keyboard, the fourth C above middle C (Fig. 2-17A). The wavelength of this treble tone is about 3 inches. The size of the human head is a significant obstacle to sound of such short wavelength and therefore casts a sonic shadow on the far side of the head (Fig. 2-17B). This shadow reduces the intensity of the sound in the far ear.

A frequency of 130 Hz, which is close to the pitch of C below middle C, is representative of a bass tone (Fig. 2-18A). The wavelength of this tone is about 8.7 feet. Because the human head is not a significant obstacle to sounds of long wavelengths, the sound readily travels around to the far ear, casting little sonic shadow (Fig. 2-18B).

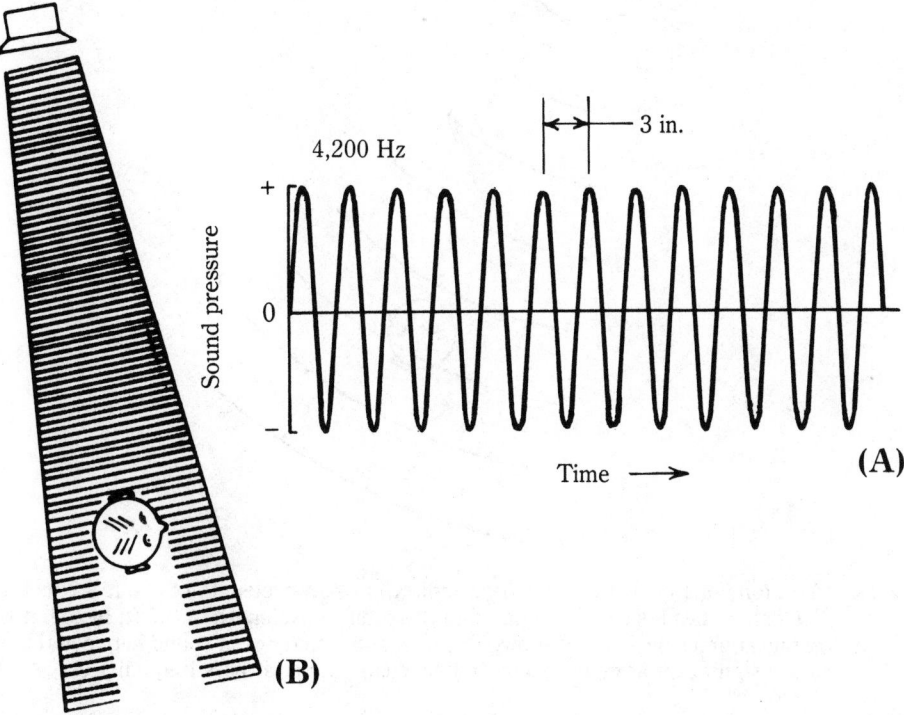

2-17 (A) A tone of 4,200 Hz (about the highest tone on the piano) has a wavelength of about 3″, which is small compared to the dimensions of the human head. (B) The human head is a significant obstacle to sound having a frequency of 4,200 Hz and it will cast a sonic shadow.

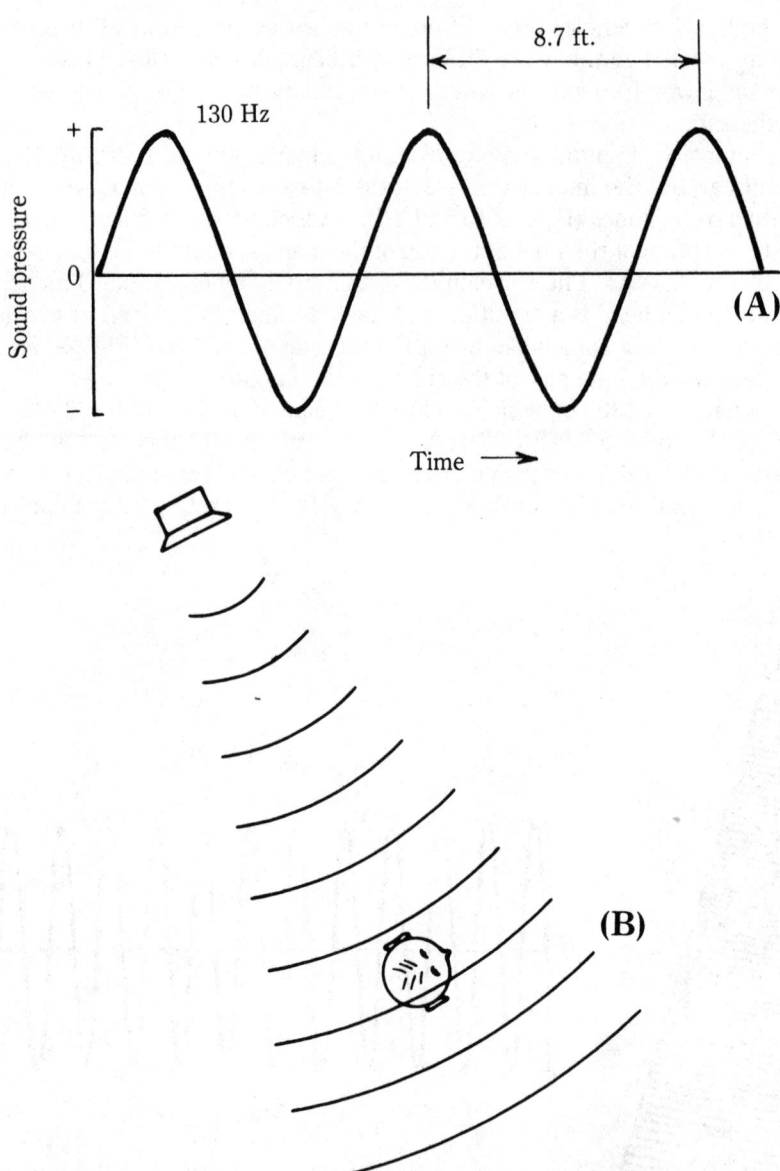

2-18   (A) A tone of 130 Hz (the C below middle C) has a wavelength of about 8.7 feet. (B) The human head is small compared to the sound wavelength of 8.7 ft; hence, it will cast no appreciable sonic shadow. The intensity difference of sound between the two ears is significant at higher audio frequencies, but not at bass frequencies.

Thus, for bass frequencies the signal intensities at the two ears are almost equal. Little or no shadow results from bass sounds, but a distinct sonic shadow accompanies treble sounds. As a result, intensity differences between the two ears are significant at treble frequencies, but negligible at bass frequencies.

Spatial cues are perceived at lower frequencies by the relative time of arrival of the signal at the two ears. As a bass tone wavefront from the left loudspeaker sweeps past the head of the listener, the sound arrives at the left ear shortly before it reaches the more distant right ear, so each ear catches the bass waveform on a slightly different part of its cycle (Fig. 2-19). This time or phase difference is the dominant effect that stereo perception is based on at low frequencies.

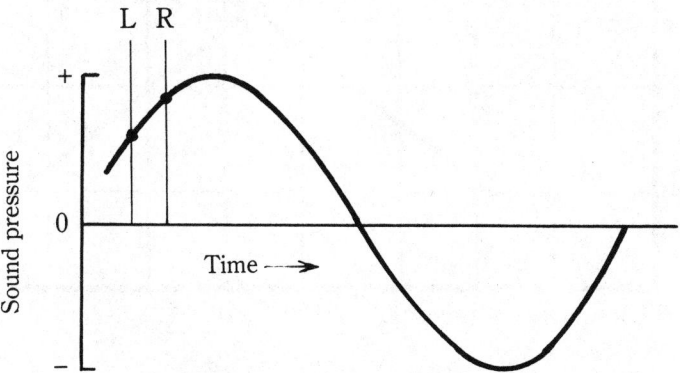

2-19 Spatial cues at bass frequencies depend on the relative time of arrival of the sound at the two ears. The left and right ears catch the bass waveform at slightly different points on the cycle.

Thus, our perception depends equally on two different phenomena for the stereo effect: head shadow or intensity prevails at high or treble frequencies, and the time effect dominates at low or bass frequencies—shown in the graph of Fig. 2-20. Both effects are active in a transition region around 700 or 800 Hz. The wavelength corresponding to the frequency of this crossover region is close to the dimensions of the adult human head.

Time effects in stereo

Also related to the time of arrival of the sound wave at the two ears is another important effect. When the violin soloist is located exactly on the midline between the left and right microphones, the intensity of the sound in each channel is the same (Fig. 2-21). The sound of the violin arrives at both microphones at exactly the same instant, centering the phantom image (Fig. 2-22).

The time of arrival can be changed to isolate the time effect by maintaining the same intensity in both loudspeakers. When the sound in the right loudspeaker is delayed 0.0002 second (0.2 milliseconds or 0.2 ms) by a digital delay device as shown in Fig. 2-23, the phantom image of the violinist shifts slightly toward the left loudspeaker. Delaying the right channel means the sound from the left loudspeaker arrives first at the listener position. The image is shifted toward the loudspeaker from which the earlier sound came. Increasing the delay in the right

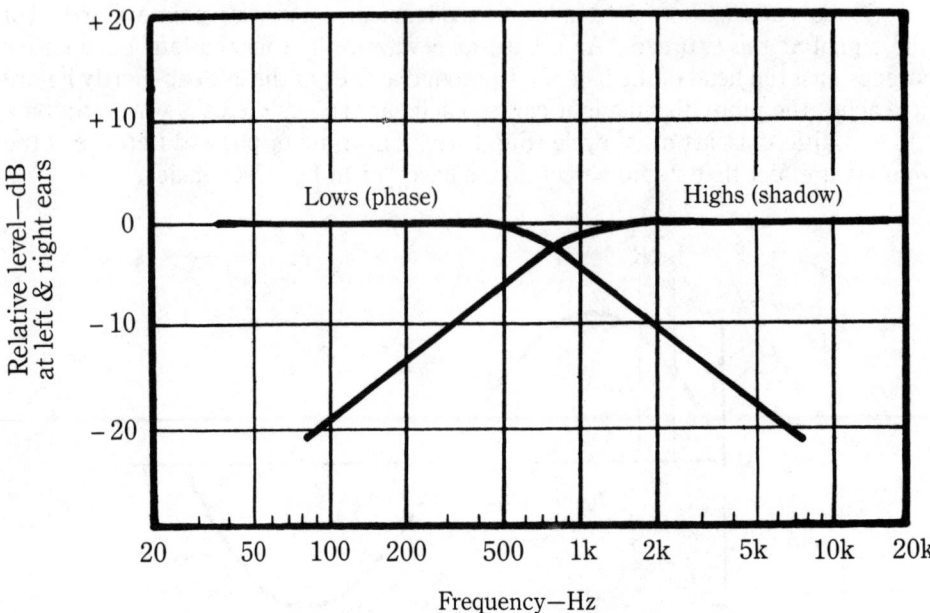

2-20   Perception of stereo spatial cues depends on two entirely different phenomena: time (phase) cues at the lower frequencies and head shadow effect at the higher frequencies. Both effects are present near 800 Hz.

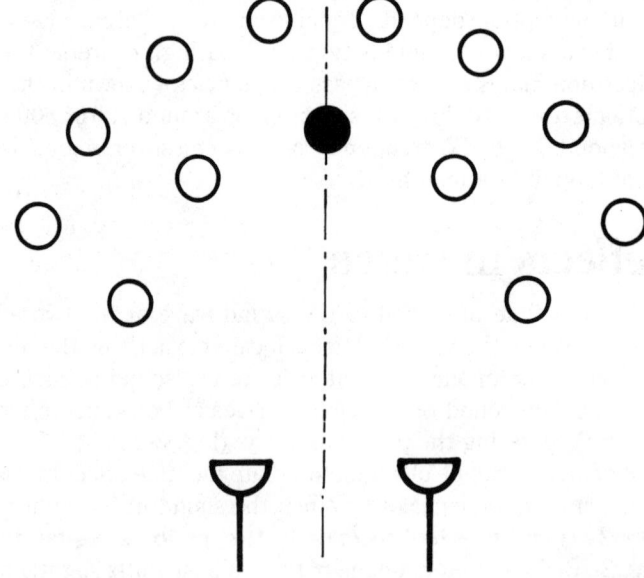

2-21   With the violin soloist precisely on the midline, the intensity of sound in the two channels is exactly the same, and the violin sound arrives at both microphones at exactly the same time.

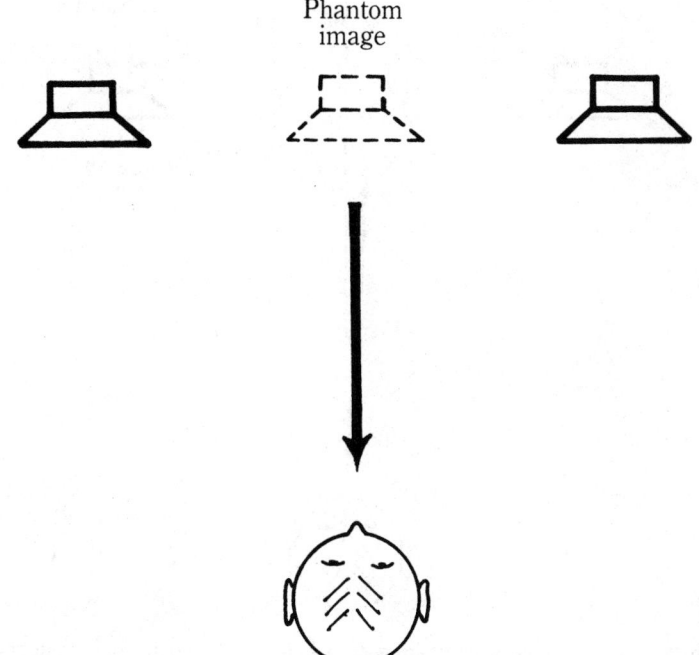

Phantom
image

2-22 The violin soloist on the midline (Fig. 2-21) will produce a phantom image exactly between the two loudspeakers (assuming the balance control has been properly adjusted).

channel from 0.2 ms to 0.5 ms moves the phantom image further toward the left loudspeaker (Fig. 2-24). A delay of 2 ms moves the image of the violinist completely over to the left loudspeaker, even though the intensity remains the same in both channels (Fig. 2-25). Conversely, delaying the sound from the left loudspeaker 2 ms causes the image to shift to the right loudspeaker. These delays do not have to be large—just a few thousandths of a second. Thus, like variations in intensity, the image can be moved at will with time delays.

Stereo timing cues are related to a phenomenon known as *the law of the first wavefront* that states when two coherent sound waves are separated in time by a very short interval (less than 28 ms) the first signal to arrive at both ears with provide directional cues for both ears. This is what happens when listening to conventional stereo. By moving from one position to another a few inches closer to one of the loudspeakers, all of the sound will appear to come from the closer loudspeaker. This places limits on the size of the preferred listening area for proper stereo imaging, which will be discussed more in chapter 14.

So far, two principal agents of stereophonic sound have been explored: differences of intensity and differences in the time of arrival of the two signals. The real secret of stereo, however, is the way the amazing human auditory system interprets these intensity and time cues.

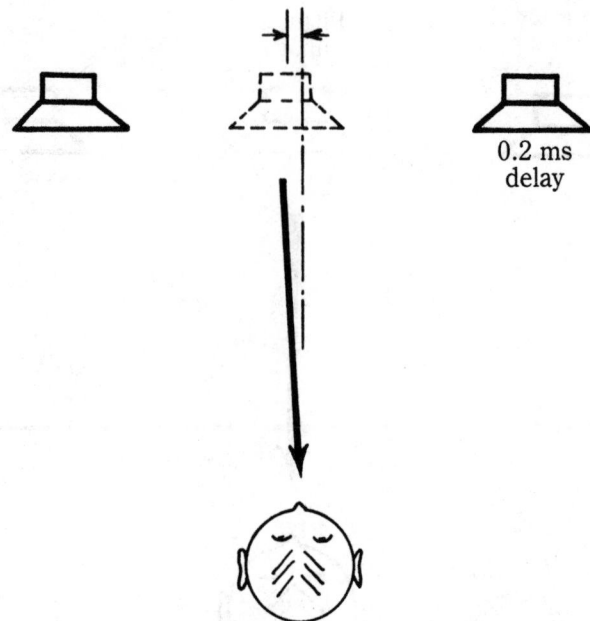

2-23   With the same intensity of violin sound being radiated by both loudspeakers, the phantom image is shifted slightly toward the left loudspeaker by delaying the sound in the right loudspeaker by 0.0002 of a second (0.2 ms).

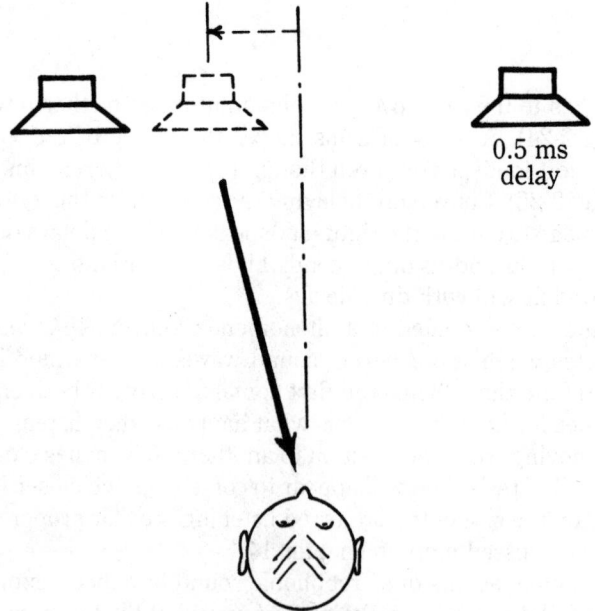

2-24   The phantom image is materially shifted toward the left loudspeaker by delaying the sound to the right loudspeaker by 0.0005 second (0.5 ms).

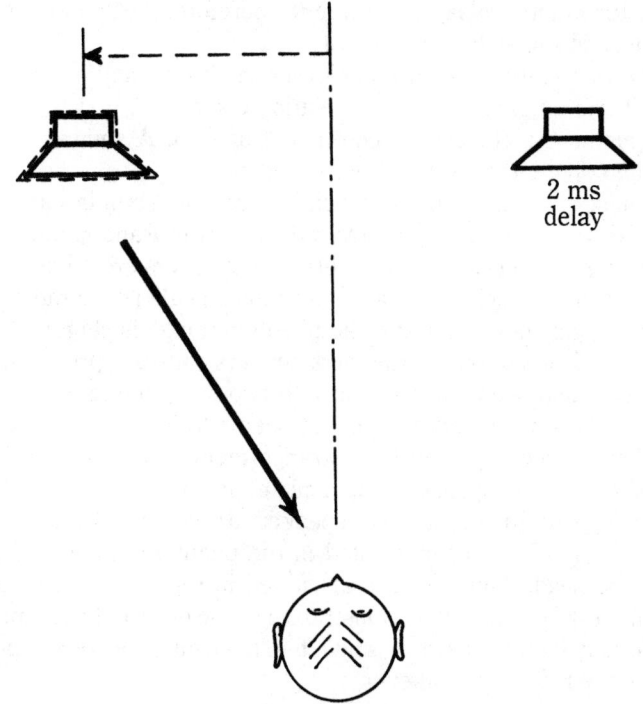

2-25   Delaying the sound from the right loudspeaker by only 0.002 second (2 ms) shifts the phantom image completely to the left loudspeaker. This demonstrates the *law of the first wavefront*, in which the first sound to arrive at the ears determines the perception of direction to the source of sound.

Interaural coherence

As discussed, the sound striking one ear can be slightly different from the sound striking the other ear. Now the concept of interaural (between the ears) coherency is introduced to describe the overall similarity or difference of two sounds.

When a listener faces someone who is speaking, the sound picked up by the listener's left ear is essentially the same as the sound picked up by the listener's right ear. If another person standing off to one side is talking at the same time, the signal reaching the near ear of the listener is quite different from that of the far ear even though both speech signals have somewhat similar spectra. The signals arriving at the two ears from the person directly in front of the listener are *coherent*, while the near and far ear signals from the person at a distant, side position are *incoherent*. Because of this difference in coherency, the ear-brain system is able to concentrate on the coherent signal and ignore the incoherent interference, at least partially.

The sound of one specific instrument in an ensemble is somewhat different when it is picked up by two microphones (Fig. 2-7). The intensities are slightly different and the time of arrival is also different; therefore, the sound at two ears or at two microphones is somewhat incoherent.

Correlation is a mathematical measure of the coherency of two signals. Two completely coherent signals have a correlation coefficient of 1.0; two completely different signals have a correlation coefficient of zero. A sound reflected from a wall is partially coherent with the direct sound.

Random noise is a convenient measuring signal that sounds something like the hissing noise between stations on an FM radio receiver. Random noise signals produced from a single generator feeding both loudspeakers are completely coherent from the "stereo seat" position because both loudspeakers are radiating identical sounds from the same generator and the phantom image is centered.

Reversing the leads to one of the loudspeakers causes a pronounced effect on the sound. The sound seems to split up into two components with different *tone color*, or timbre. A low-pitched component seems to locate near the back of the head of the listener accompanied by a strange feeling of pressure. Also, another component of higher pitch appears as a phantom image between the two loud-speakers. If the leads to the one loudspeaker are corrected (i.e., reversed once more), the random noise is concentrated in the phantom image and perceived in the center of the head. This effect is discussed in regard to the nature of stereo signals in chapter 3. It is a good demonstration of the different perception of coherent and incoherent signals, however, and a test to ensure the correct polarity of the connections to the two loudspeakers.

Spaciousness

A stereo system can convey an impression of the spaciousness of the room where the music was recorded. Spaciousness is based on the concept of coherency between the signals of the two stereo channels. Sound reflected from surfaces in a concert hall is important to perceived spaciousness when the following conditions are met:

- The reflected sound signals are mutually incoherent with the direct sound.
- The reflections have a certain minimum strength.
- The reflections do not arrive more than 50 – 100 ms after the direct sound (or they will sound like echoes).
- The reflections arrive from lateral directions.

These criteria are of primary interest to designers of concert halls because they are the factors that lead to a good stereo recording conveying a sense of hall spaciousness. Auditory spaciousness is examined further in chapter 12.

3
Stereo and the auditory system

PERCEPTION OF THE STEREO EFFECT DEPENDS ENTIRELY ON THE BRAIN'S processing of the acoustical cues received by the ears. The cues generally received by one ear are slightly different than those received by the other. The signals at the two ears are incoherent, to some degree. The signals differ in intensity and timing. The stereophonic edifice rests squarely on these differences, although they are usually extremely small and often difficult to isolate.

What the brain does and how it does it is the province of experimental psychology and physiology. Even a superficial understanding of the way our auditory system interprets stereo cues requires venturing into the psychological and physiological ongoing research and continually refined concepts.

Subjective/objective distinctions

If a rock tumbles down from the heights in the middle of a great uninhabited wilderness, does sound exist if no ear is there to hear it? The physicist would certainly say yes because sound waves can be measured, even from a distance, as they travel out from the point of impact. The psychologist might say no because no human auditory system is present to receive the sound waves. Therefore, it is a matter of definition. Sound could be considered either as a stimulus or a sensation. The stimulus is a physical event, but a living auditory system is necessary to transform the stimulus into a sensation.

Loudness is a subjective term. In the objective realm of the physicist, its *alter ego* would be sound pressure. The two are related, but they are not equal. A musician's pitch has a physical counterpart called frequency. Again the two are related, but they cannot be equated. The musician uses the word *timbre* to describe the richness of tones produced by musical instruments; however, the physicist might prefer the word *spectrum*. Though the subjective and objective concepts might seem to overlap, the distinction between the two outlooks should not be forgotten.

Structure of the ear

Though knowledge of the human auditory system is imperfect, the tantalizing glimpse we have of it is enough to cause a sense of awe and wonder. Even a partial knowledge of the ear's intricate workings is valuable to the practicing musician or engineer.

A highly simplified sketch of the parts of the ear is shown in Fig. 3-1. Sound in the form of vibrations of the air is gathered by the outer ear, or *pinna*. After traveling through the auditory canal the sound-pressure fluctuations cause the eardrum, or *tympanic membrane* to vibrate. In the middle ear, the vibrations of the eardrum activate the three ossicles (*malleus, incus,* and *stapes*) into rocking movement (Fig. 3-2). The mechanical vibrations of the ossicles are transmitted to the fluid-filled inner ear, or *cochlea* (Fig. 3-3). Membrane vibrations of the cochlea agitate the hair cells, which send verve impulses to the brain via the auditory nerve. The membrane, hair cells, and the nerve fibers provide a high degree of selectivity in analyzing the sound as they convert the mechanical movements of the middle ear to neural activity.

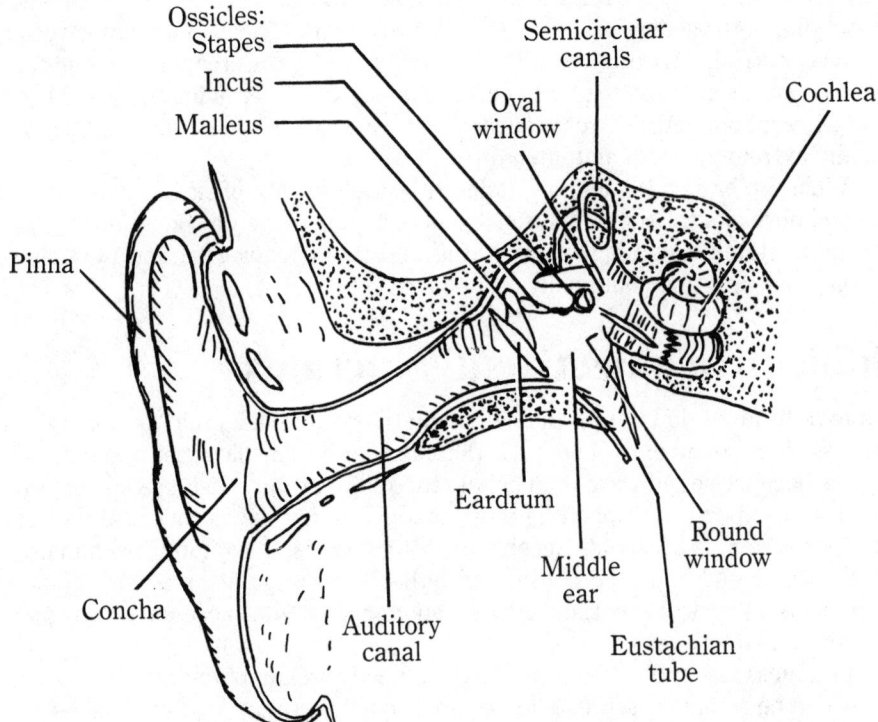

3-1 The sound entering the auditory canal actuates the eardrum. The eardrum movement is conveyed mechanically to the oval window of the cochlea by a linkage of three tiny bones, the ossicles. The movement of the oval window sets the fluid of the inner ear vibrating, which in turn, stimulates the sensitive hair cells that are projections of the auditory nerve.

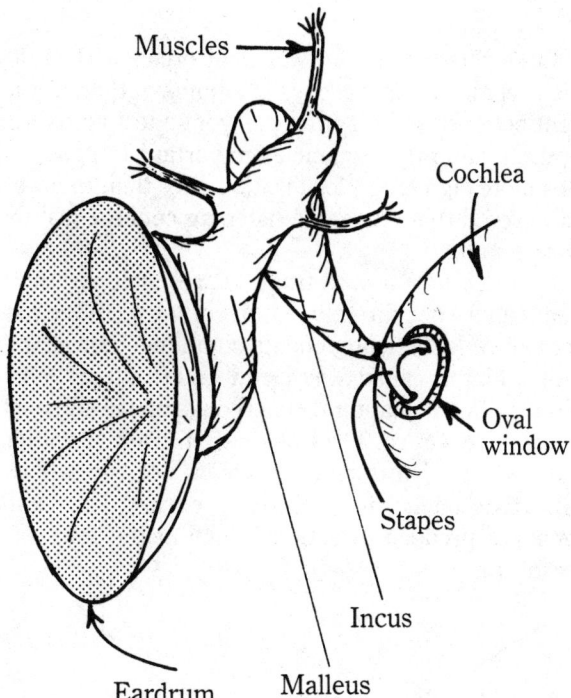

3-2   The three ossicles, the malleus, the incus, and the stapes, mechanically transduce the vibrations of the eardrum to the oval window of the inner ear. In essence, the action of these tiny bones is to provide maximum transfer of energy from the air to the liquid of the inner ear.

Cochlea (unrolled)

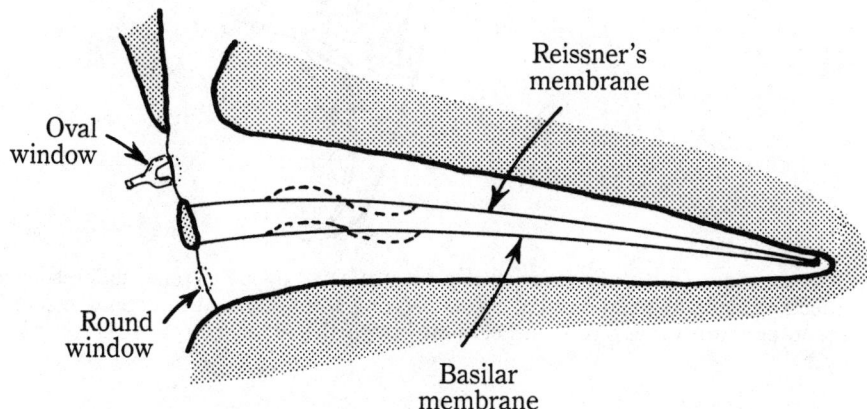

3-3   The vibrations of the oval window by the ossicles give rise to traveling waves in the fluid of the inner ear. These traveling waves stimulate the hair cells on the membranes that transmit impulses to the brain via the auditory nerve.

The pinna

The pinna used to be thought of as a vestigial organ with little or no practical value, but this idea seems obsolete today. The pinna gathers sound and differentiates to some extent between sounds from the front and sounds from the rear. This has slight localization value at frequencies important to speech. Suspicions that the pinna provides more significant localization cues than this were aroused when experimenters discovered that one-eared listening could reveal the direction from which sounds were coming.

Figure 3-4 illustrates how a wavefront, represented by the two sound rays, might enter the ear canal—one directly and the other by reflection off a fold of the pinna. The direct and reflected components come together at the entrance to the ear canal. This combining is called *interference* and results in *comb filtering*, which will be considered in detail in chapter 8. This constructive and destructive interference at the entrance to the ear canal results in significant alterations in sound pressure at the eardrum. The interference effect is not the whole story, however. Resonances within the concha are selectively excited by sounds from specific directions. Resonances produce directional cues in the form of sound pressure changes at the eardrum.

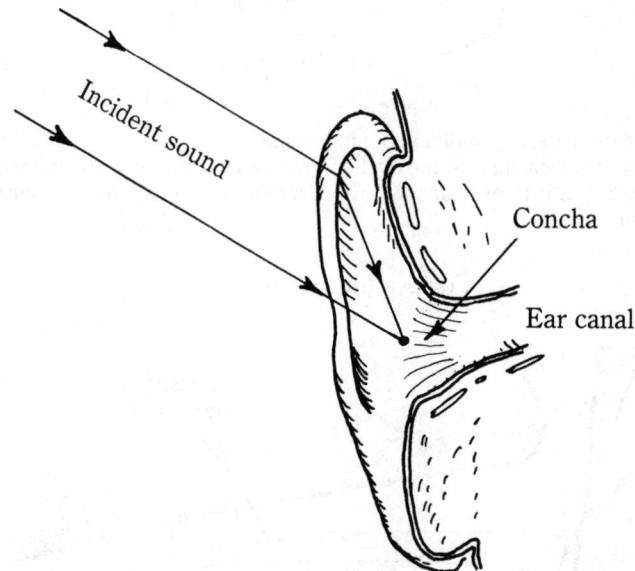

3-4   The sound pressure at the eardrum is greatly affected by interference and resonance effects at the pinna and concha. Sound arriving from different directions results in sound pressure variations at the eardrum, which the brain interprets as directional cues.

The auditory canal

The auditory canal, or *auditory meatus*, could be imagined as a twisted pipe with a changing cross-sectional shape, but acoustically it acts like an organ pipe that is about 3 cm long and 0.7 cm in diameter. The canal is terminated by the eardrum, or *tympanic membrane*. At the frequency at which the canal is a quarter wavelength long, a significant acoustical amplification occurs at the eardrum. This amplification is one of sound pressure only—there is no increase in energy level—but it is useful to pressure actuated devices like the eardrum. Compared to the sound pressure at the entrance to the auditory canal, the sound pressure at the eardrum is increased by this pipe resonance by about 10 dB, or 3-fold in the 2 – 4 kHz region. A further amplification effect occurs due to the diffraction of sound waves around the head. Adding the effects of head diffraction and resonance of the ear canal, a total acoustical amplification of sound pressure at the eardrum could be as much as 20 dB, or 10-fold (Reference 3-1).

The middle ear

The malleus is attached to the eardrum (Fig. 3-2). The vibrations of the eardrum are transmitted to the three ossicles, which transmit them in turn to the oval window of the cochlea. This mechanical action of the hammer, anvil, and stirrup (*malleus, incus,* and *stapes*) transmits the vibrations of the air in the auditory canal to the liquid of the inner ear with maximum efficiency. If airborne sound impinged directly on the oval window of the cochlea, 99.9% of the energy would be reflected, and only 0.1% would reach the fluid of the cochlea. The reason is because air is tenuous and compressible, but the waterlike fluid of the cochlea is dense and incompressible. This remarkable ossicular arrangement, along with other factors such as difference in areas of eardrum and oval window, solves the difficult energy-transfer problem. To the technical person it is a matter of matching the grossly different acoustical impedances of air and liquid by a mechanical system. The person interested in loudspeakers can learn that the eardrum operates as an *acoustic-suspension* system. The *eustachian tube* equalizes static air pressure on both sides of the eardrum. It is normally essentially closed. Therefore the movement of the eardrum is opposed by the springiness of the air trapped in the middle ear.

The inner ear

The stirrup bone, or *stapes* of the middle ear is attached to the oval window of the cochlea, which is part of the inner ear (Fig. 3-2). Vibrations of the eardrum transmitted by the ossicles cause traveling waves to build up on the basilar membrane in the cochlea (Fig. 3-3). The position of the maxima of these traveling waves is a function of frequency. Movements of the basilar membrane excite the sensitive haircells attached to it. When stimulated, the hair cells, or extensions of auditory nerves, send electrical impulses to the brain.

The cochlea is a sound-analyzing mechanism capable of amazing pitch and frequency discrimination. The ear can differentiate between a tone of 1,000 Hz and a tone of 1,003 Hz (a discrimination of 0.3%). This precise distinction between frequency components of music or speech signals requires a narrow peak response with steep sides as shown in Fig. 3-5.

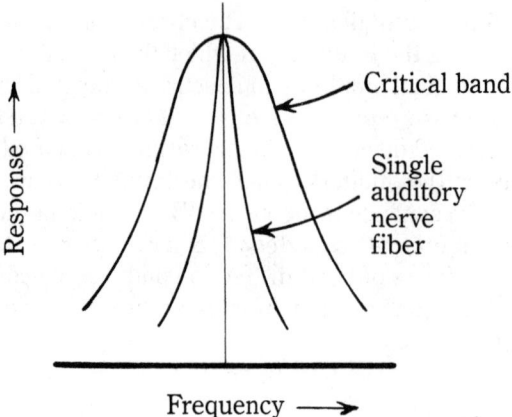

3-5   The cochlea is the sound analyzer of the auditory system. The finest analysis is that provided by the sensitive hair cells. A *tuning curve* of a single hair cell is here compared to that of a so-called *critical band*, which is the auditory filter involved in masking of one sound by another.

Masking and the auditory filters

"I can't hear you when the water's running" is a statement about sound masking. Water sound obscures the sound of the voice, road noise in an automobile can drown out low-level radio music, factory noise can make conversation difficult, and excessive noise from a poorly designed air-conditioning system can degrade the intelligibility of dramatic speech from the stage of a theater.

The American Standards Association has defined masking in two ways:

- The *process* by which the threshold of audibility of one sound is raised by the presence of another masking sound.
- The *amount* by which the threshold of audibility of a sound is raised by the presence of another masking sound.

In early masking experiments it was found that a signal was most easily masked by a noise having significant energy at the same frequency as the signal. H. Fletcher introduced the *critical band* concept suggesting that the auditory system behaves as if it contains a bank of bandpass filters with continually overlapping center frequencies (Reference 3-2). The common audio equalizer has a limited number of bandpass filters spaced in frequency so they overlap at the half-power points or − 3 dB as shown in Fig. 3-6A. The filters of the auditory system are continuous, however, with a complete filter for every audible frequency, suggested in Fig. 3-6B. Selected auditory filters vary in width according to frequency, shown in Table 3-1.

For example imagine a desired signal is a 260 Hz tone, which is close to middle C on the piano, and an interfering (or masking) sound is *white noise* (which has energy uniformly distributed throughout the entire audible band). If an auditory bandpass filter is centered on the 260 Hz tone, according to Fletcher's theory, only

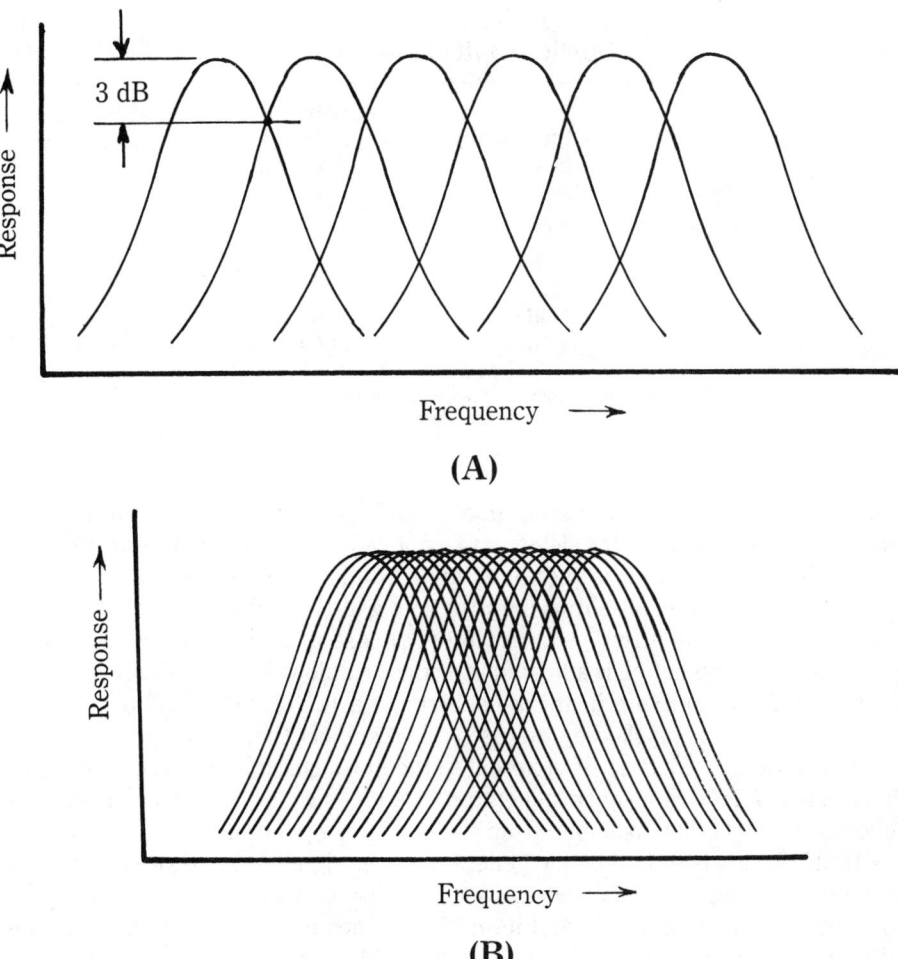

3-6 (A) The characteristics of a standard 1/3 octave filter set of the type used in acoustical measurements. Adjacent filters cross over at the half-power point or at −3 dB. (B) The filter set of (A) is coarse and crude compared to the auditory filters (critical bands) of the human hearing system. Auditory filters are continuous, i.e., a sound of any frequency would encounter an auditory filter centered on it.

the white noise energy passed by that filter will be effective in masking the tone. By increasing the level of the noise, a point will eventually be reached at which the tone is masked and becomes inaudible. At this point all that can be heard is noise.

Binaural unmasking

Binaural interactions are important because the stereophonic illusion depends on the differences of sounds falling on the two ears. A psychoacoustic experiment

Table 3-1.
Auditory filter bandwidths

Center frequency Hz	Width of critical band* Hz
100	38
200	47
500	77
1,000	128
2,000	240
5,000	650

*Calculated equivalent rectangular bandwidths as proposed by Moore and Glasberg, (Reference 3-3)

demonstrating *binaural unmasking* might shed some light on interaural incoherency. In this experiment the listener wears headphones that shut out all sounds except those that pertain to the experiment. Coherent noise produced from one noise signal generator is sent to both the left and the right ears (Fig. 3-7). Then coherent tones set to a frequency of 260 Hz (close to middle-C) are added to the noise and the combination is adjusted to a comfortable volume level (Fig. 3-8). Both the tone and the noise are heard in each ear clearly. Next the level of the tone is decreased until it is masked by the noise. The subject then hears only the noise.

The noise in the left ear is coherent to the noise heard in the right ear because they come from the same noise generator. The tones heard by the two ears are also coherent because they too come from the same tone generator.

If the two leads from the tone generator to the right ear are reversed, the tones in the two ears are made incoherent, but the noise sent to each ear remains coherent (Fig. 3-9). The frequency and level of the tones to each ear remain the same, but reversing the polarity of the tone to the right ear makes the tones incoherent. At the instant the polarity reversal of the right ear tone takes place, the right ear tone, which was previously masked and inaudible, suddenly springs into clear audibility. Making the tones to the two ears somewhat different or incoherent, actually improves the audibility.

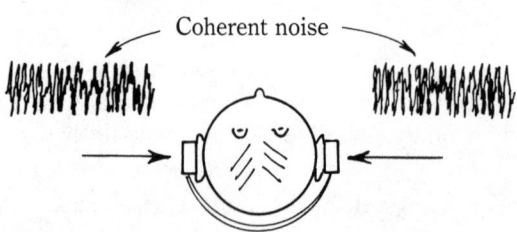

Coherent noise

3-7   Steps in the study of binaural unmasking; coherent noise from the same signal generator is first applied to both left and right headphones.

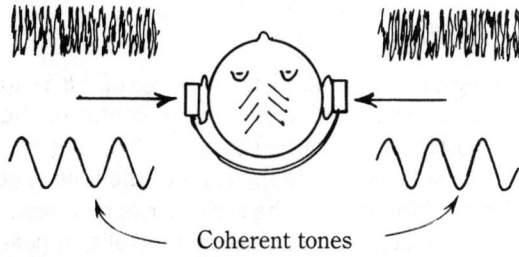

3-8 Coherent tones of 260 Hz (close to middle C) are added to the noise of Fig. 3-7 so that both tones and noise are at a comfortable level. The level of the tone is now decreased until it is just masked by the noise.

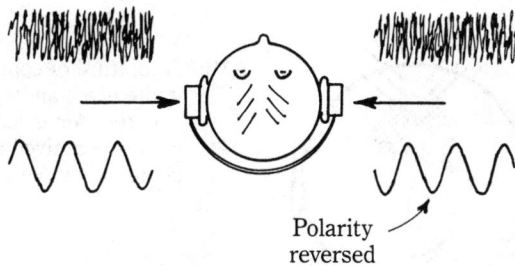

3-9 With the tone just masked by the noise (Fig. 3-8), the two leads from the tone generator to the right ear are simply reversed. As this is done, the tone to the right ear (which was masked) suddenly becomes audible. Introducing an incoherency by reversing the leads improves the audibility of the tone.

The tone in this experiment represents any desired signal—such as speech or music. The noise represents any signals that interfere with hearing the desired speech or music. This experiment would apply to music interfered by air-conditioner noise as the masker, but measurements would be more difficult due to the fluctuation of the music signals.

The amount of binaural unmasking can be measured. Going back to the combined tone and white noise signals sent to the two ears in Fig. 3-8, the tone level again is reduced until the tone is just masked. When the wires connecting the tone generator leading to the right ear are reversed, the tone suddenly becomes audible. Then the tone level is decreased again until it is masked, but this time the amount of the decrease is measured. To overcome the effects of incoherency, the tone had to be reduced about 15 decibels, called the *Binaural Masking Level Difference*, (or BMLD).

This improvement in audibility results simply from introducing a difference in the tones to the two ears, which is astounding. Investigations like this can help us understand how slight differences between the signals to the two ears (interaural incoherencies) are interpreted by the brain to give us stereo image perception.

Perceptual space

Another way of looking at the binaural unmasking effect is to observe that the coherent white noise appears to be located in the center of the head (Fig. 3-10). When the coherent 260 Hz tone is added to the coherent noise, both seem to be located in the center of the head. Again the level of the tone is decreased until it is masked. As the polarity of the tone to the right ear is reversed, the tone suddenly becomes audible and its perceptual image seems to split, appearing in the vicinity of both the left and right ears. At this point the coherent noise image is in the center of the head, and the incoherent tonal image is at both ears as in Fig. 3-11 (Reference 3-4).

Coherent noise
coherent tone

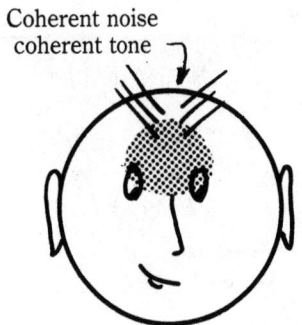

3-10   A mixture of coherent white noise and coherent tones in both ears is perceived in the center of the head.

Coherent noise

Incoherent 260 Hz tones

3-11   A mixture of coherent noise and incoherent tones is perceived as coherent noise in the center of the head, and the incoherent tones near both ears.

Therefore masking appears to be more effective when the masking noise and the masked tone are localized in the same perceptual space within the head. Unmasking only takes place when the images of the two appear in different parts of the head. Coherent sounds seem to be conceptualized in the center of the head, but incoherent sounds form near the ears. Thus the important relationship between coherency and masking can be visualized.

The complete relationship between stereo and the perceptual location of sounds in different parts of the head is obscure. The stereo illusion is based on specific localizable images and highly correlated sounds at the two ears, perhaps differing only in timing or amplitude.

Binaural unmasking vs. frequency

Binaural unmasking works well at 260 Hz, but does it work at other audible frequencies? The results of the same experiment at 4,000 Hz, a high treble frequency near the top of the piano keyboard, indicate that frequency does have a major effect on binaural unmasking. Again white noise is introduced to both left and right earphones (Fig. 3-12). Then a coherent tone with a frequency of 4,000 Hz is introduced to both ears, clearly audible in the white noise (Fig. 3-13). Slowly the level of the tone is reduced until it is masked in both ears. The polarity of the tone to the right ear is reversed, but this time the tone does not spring into audibility; in fact it barely becomes audible (Fig. 3-14). The 15 dB unmasking at 260 Hz shriveled to 2 or 3 decibels at 4,000 Hz.

Also resulting from the change to higher frequency, the coherent noise and the incoherent 4,000 Hz tone localized in the same perceptual space—the center of the head (Fig. 3-15). The loss of the binaural unmasking effect is associated with the loss of the incoherent tone's image shift to the ears.

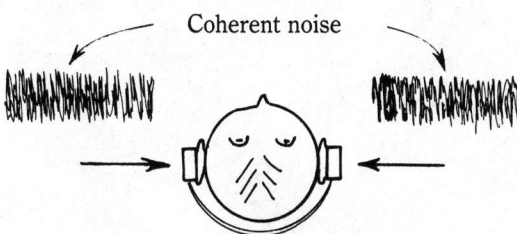

3-12 A repeat of the experiment on binaural unmasking, this time with a frequency of 4,000 Hz. Once again the coherent white noise is applied to both earphones.

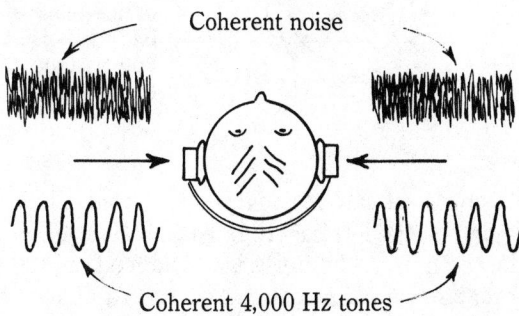

3-13 Coherent 4,000 Hz tones are applied to both earphones at a comfortable level and then reduced until they are just masked by the noise.

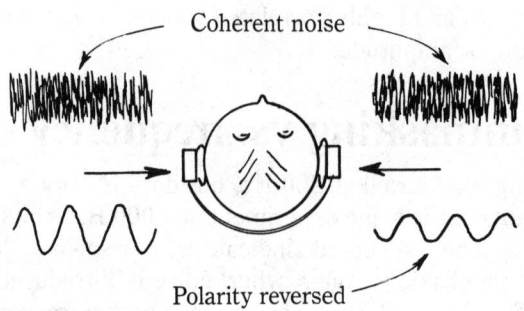

Coherent noise

Polarity reversed

3-14 As the tone is made incoherent by reversing the two leads, it is made audible (i.e., unmasked), but just barely so. Binaural unmasking, so effective at 260 Hz, is of minor effect at the frequency of 4,000 Hz.

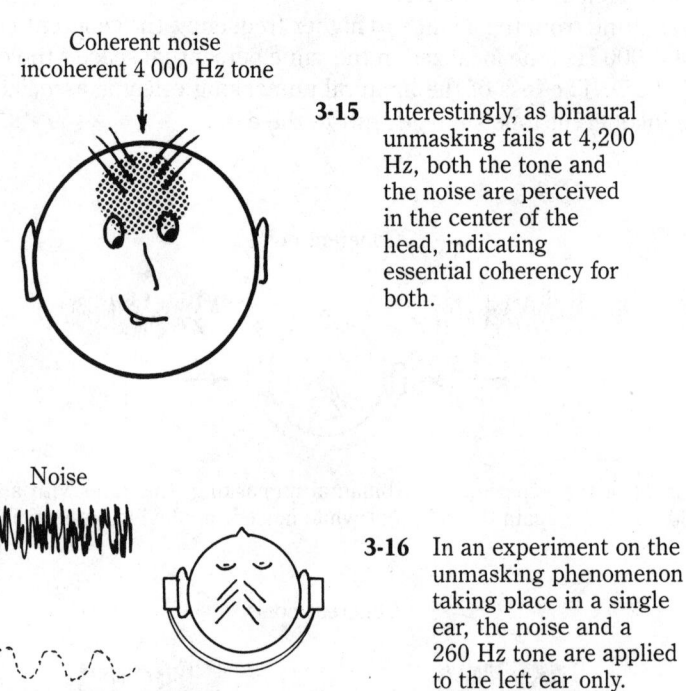

Coherent noise
incoherent 4 000 Hz tone

3-15 Interestingly, as binaural unmasking fails at 4,200 Hz, both the tone and the noise are perceived in the center of the head, indicating essential coherency for both.

Noise

3-16 In an experiment on the unmasking phenomenon taking place in a single ear, the noise and a 260 Hz tone are applied to the left ear only.

260 Hz tone

Unmasking in a single ear can be triggered binaurally. This time the noise and 260 Hz tone are fed only to the left ear (Fig. 3-16). The level of the tone is reduced until it is masked by the noise. The noise is introduced only to the right ear (Fig. 3-17). As the coherent noise is introduced to the right ear, the tone suddenly becomes clearly audible in the left ear. This is further evidence of the interaction between the two ears.

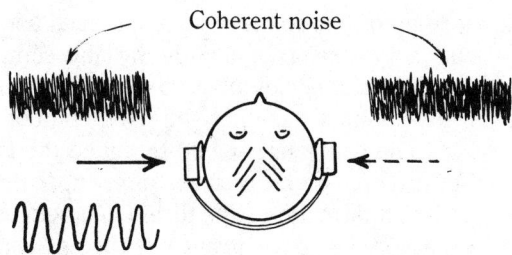

Coherent noise

3-17 In the unmasking in a single ear (Fig. 3-16) the 260 Hz tone is reduced until it is just masked by the noise. As the same coherent noise is introduced to the right ear, the tone suddenly becomes clearly audible in the left ear. This indicates a definite binaural interaction.

The binaural masking effect seems to work better for the lower frequencies. In chapter 2 other low and high frequency spatial localization effects were noted in stereo. At low frequencies our ears respond to time differences, but at high frequencies they compare both intensity and time differences as shown in Fig. 2-20. It is possible that stereo spatial localization and binaural unmasking are related.

Wide band random noise was used as the masking signal for simplicity, but the mask does not have to be a wideband to demonstrate binaural unmasking. The noise in a critical band centered on the frequency of the tone works just as well. At 260 Hz and 4,000 Hz the widths of the critical bands are about 50 Hz and 500 Hz respectively.

Understanding speech in high background noise

Specialists in the field suspect that the same processes that release a desired signal from being masked also help in understanding speech in situations with high background noise. At a party, the human auditory system is capable of picking out and understanding a single voice from a confusing babble of other voices. When facing the talker, the desired speech is coherent in the ears of the listener, while the background noise coming from all directions tends to be incoherent. Thus, the desired signal and the interfering masking noise are perceptually localized in different places in the head. The time and level differences between them trigger the release from masking, which makes the speech intelligible.

When someone speaks in high background noise, attention is focused on what is being said. Subconsciously the two-eared, coherent and incoherent, correlated and uncorrelated magic occurs. It is ready to work at any moment, and it is scarcely thought about.

Transfer functions

The human brain has only sound pressure cues acting on the eardrum to work with when giving a perception of stereo images, localization of sound sources, etc. The eardrum pressure is made up of two components—one fixed and one variable. The fixed component is the auditory canal itself, and the variable component is the sound entering the auditory canal, which carries all of the directional information.

The resonances of the auditory canal, or the fixed component, are described by the curve of Fig. 3-18. The resonances could be called the frequency response of the auditory canal, but research literature uses the term, *transfer function*, which also includes time of arrival information. The difference between the sound pressure transfer function measured at the entrance of the ear canal and that at the eardrum yields the transfer function of the ear canal alone (Fig. 3-18). A first resonance at about 5 kHz and a second resonance at about 10 kHz result from the physical parameters of the ear canal alone. Because these are fixed the transfer function of the ear canal also remains a fixed entity.

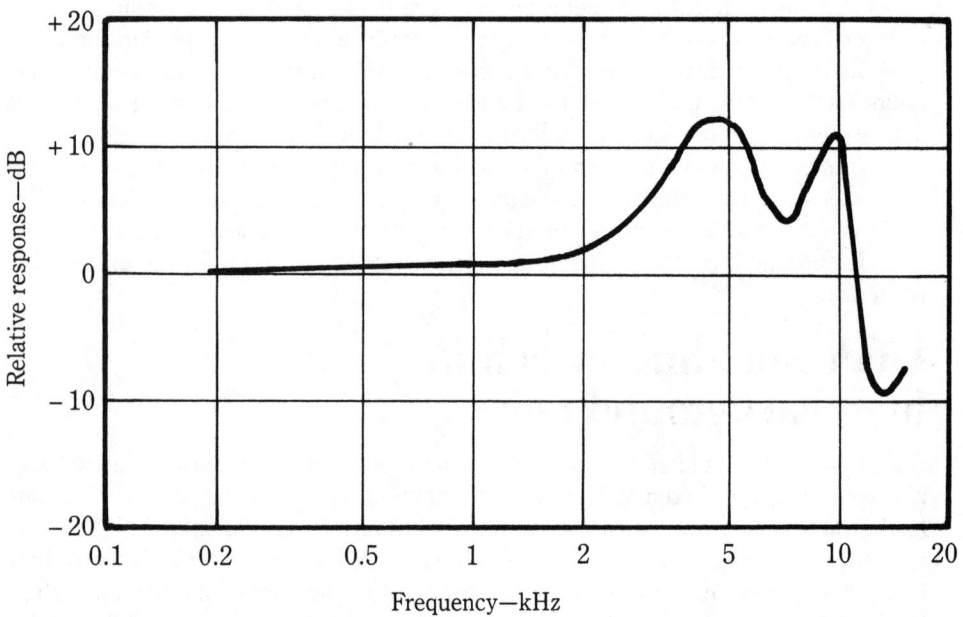

3-18   The auditory canal acts as a resonant pipe. By measuring the transfer function (frequency response) both at the entrance to the canal and at the eardrum and subtracting one from the other, the transfer function of the auditory canal alone is found. The transfer function of the auditory canal is a fixed entity that is superimposed on each of the host of highly variable transfer functions of the outer ear containing directional cues. After Mehrgardt and Mellart, Reference 3-5.

Typical transfer functions of the outer ear are shown in Fig. 3-19, as reported by Mehrgardt and Mellart (Reference 3-5). The sounds falling on the pinna result in a myriad of transfer functions images of different shapes combining at the entrance of the ear canal. Sound source directional information is encoded in these contorted transfer functions.

Sound arriving at the outer ear from directly in front of the listener yields the heavy line transfer function of Fig. 3-19. Sound arriving from 36 degrees to the left of the straight-ahead position yields the transfer function for the left ear labeled *36°*. Sound arriving directly from the left gives the transfer function marked *90°* for the left ear. Combining these highly variable transfer functions at the entrance of the ear canal with the fixed transfer function of the ear canal yields the total sound pressure at the eardrum, complete with all directional cues. This subject is treated in greater detail in chapter 6.

The *0-degree* curve of Fig. 3-19 explains the common practice of *equalizing for presence*. Intelligibility of speech with musical background is improved by an equalization boost in the 2 to 5 kHz region, making the voice more up front and distinct from the musical background.

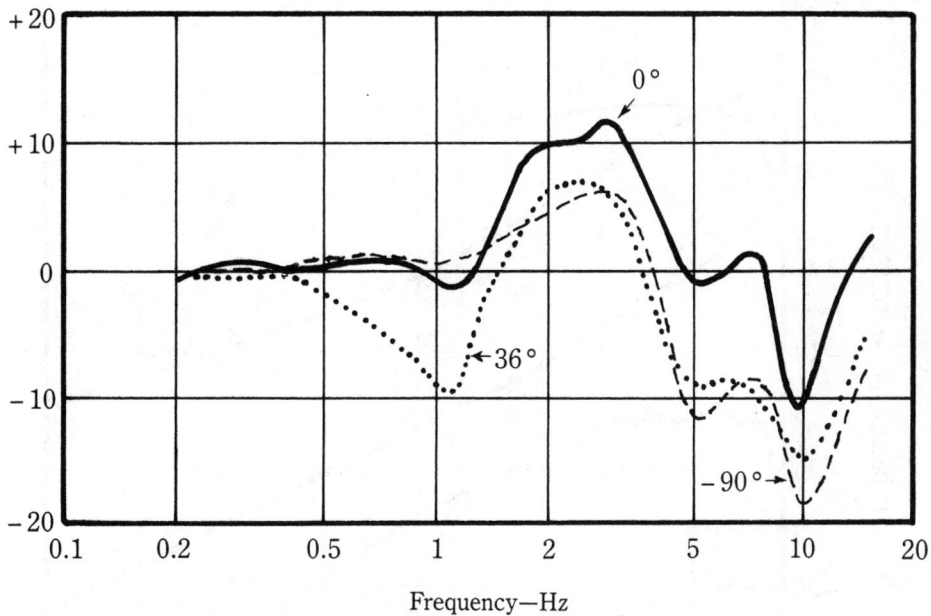

Frequency—Hz

3-19 Typical transfer functions of the outer ear measured between the free field and the entrance to the ear canal. The transfer function for sound arriving from directly in front of the subject (0 degrees), is different from that for sound arriving 36° to the left or from the left (90°). Directional information seems to be encoded in these directionally unique *frequency responses*. After Mehrgardt and Mellart, Reference 3-5.

Effects of reflected sound

Sound travels from a source to a human ear over a direct path. Reflections of the same sound could arrive at the ear over numerous reflected paths. The direct sound arrives first, and a host of reflections arrive later. Each reflection is delayed by an amount of time determined by the distance traveled between the source and the listener's ears. Thousands of reflections are spread out in time and arrive after the direct sound. The human reaction to these reflections depends on the magnitude and the delay. Sometimes the reflections are helpful, but other times they are disastrous.

Many investigations were conducted to study the perceived effect of delayed or reflected sound on a desired signal. The results of some of these studies are summarized graphically in Fig. 3-20 (References 3-6, 3-7, 3-8). All of these experiments used an arrangement of two loudspeakers and a listener—similar to the standard stereo arrangement. The angle between the loudspeakers varied from 45 to 90 degrees. Speech was used as the test signal for these experiments. The studies were conducted under anechoic conditions to minimize extraneous effects.

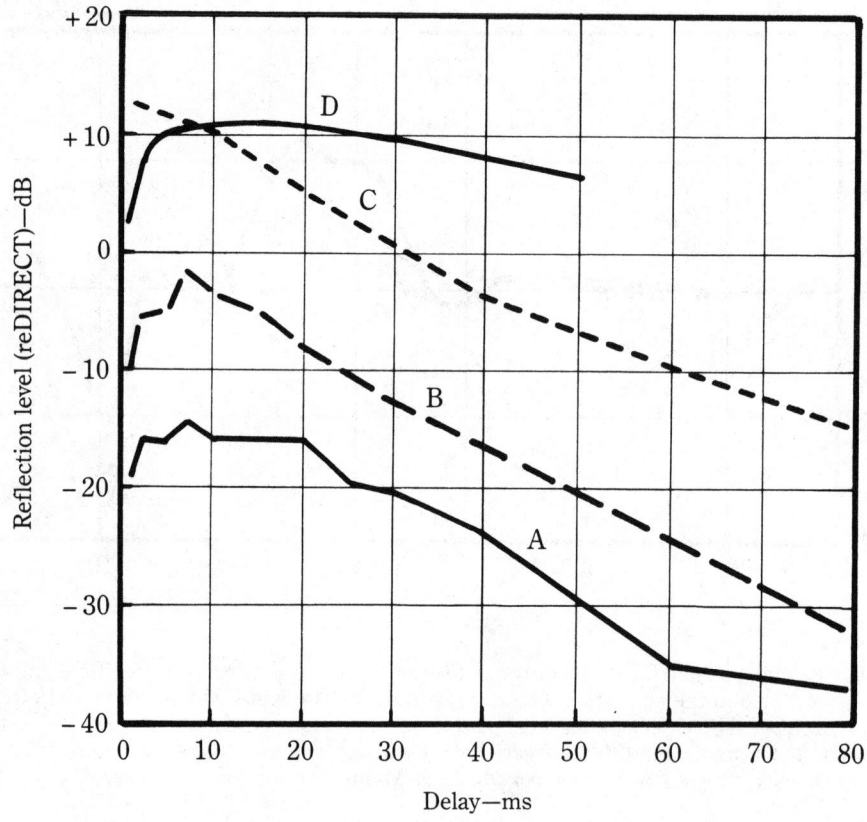

3-20   The results of several investigations on the effects of lateral reflections on the perception of the direct sound in a simulated stereo arrangement. Type of sound: speech, environment: anechoic, angle of lateral reflections: 45 – 90 °. (A) Absolute threshold detection of reflection. After Olive and Toole, Reference 3-6. (B) Image shift threshold. After Olive and Toole, Reference 3-6. (C) Lateral reflection perceived as discrete echo, After Meyer and Schodder, Reference 3-7. (D) Equal loudness of lateral reflection and direct. After Haas, Reference 3-8.

One loudspeaker radiated the direct speech signal. Another loudspeaker, representing the lateral reflection, radiated the same signal delayed by various amounts of time. The effects were documented as the level of the lateral reflection was increased from below threshold.

The level at which the observers first heard something is shown in curve (A) of Fig. 3-20. This was the threshold at which the presence of the reflection was first detectable. A sense of spaciousness was imparted as the reflection level was increased. The effect of lateral reflections in music halls is a sensation of spaciousness added to the music. In the experiment observers experienced an impression of spaciousness, even though they were in an anechoic room. No particular sense of direction was associated with this threshold perceptual effect.

As the level of the reflection was increased by about 10 dB above the threshold of (A), the observers became aware of a change in size or position of the primary auditory image. Curve (B) is a threshold of this new effect.

Curve (C) delineates the threshold of a distinct echo apart from the primary image. This echo was heard along with the direct sound.

Then reflection levels were increased until reflected and direct sounds were equally loud shown in curve (D), which is the well-known Haas curve. Haas reported some interesting observations during this investigation on the effect of a single reflection on speech (Reference 3-8). He found that the level of the delayed sound could be up to 10 dB higher than the direct sound without sounding louder than the direct sound, although the intelligibility of speech was degraded. This effect persisted for delays up to the vicinity of 30 ms. At the same time increased loudness was observed as well as a change in timbre, image shift, and a sense of spaciousness.

Summarizing, Fig. 3-20 pictures the range of perceptual effects resulting from progressive increases in the level of the reflection. Above the threshold of (A) reflections cause a sense of spaciousness. Increasing reflection level even more, another threshold (B) of changes in the auditory image comes into play along with spaciousness. Further increase in reflection level reaches the threshold of discrete echoes at (C). Higher reflection levels reach curve (D), at which the reflection and the direct sound are of equal loudness. These threshold curves are spaced by roughly 10 dB.

Various timbral effects occurred as the reflection level was increased, especially at higher reflection levels, but the spatial and directional perceptions dominate.

Law of the first wavefront

The domination of the earlier sound has been called *the law of the first wavefront*, by Cremer. This concept is extremely important when listening in enclosed spaces filled with a welter of sound reflections. The direct sound from a source in an enclosed space arrives at the listener's ear earlier than sound reflected from surfaces. Therefore the *direction* to the sound source is perceived clearly—even in reverberant spaces. Delays within a 0 – 1 ms range move the sound from the center to the earlier loudspeaker as shown in Fig. 3-21. The law of the first wavefront can be the working equivalent of the precedence effect.

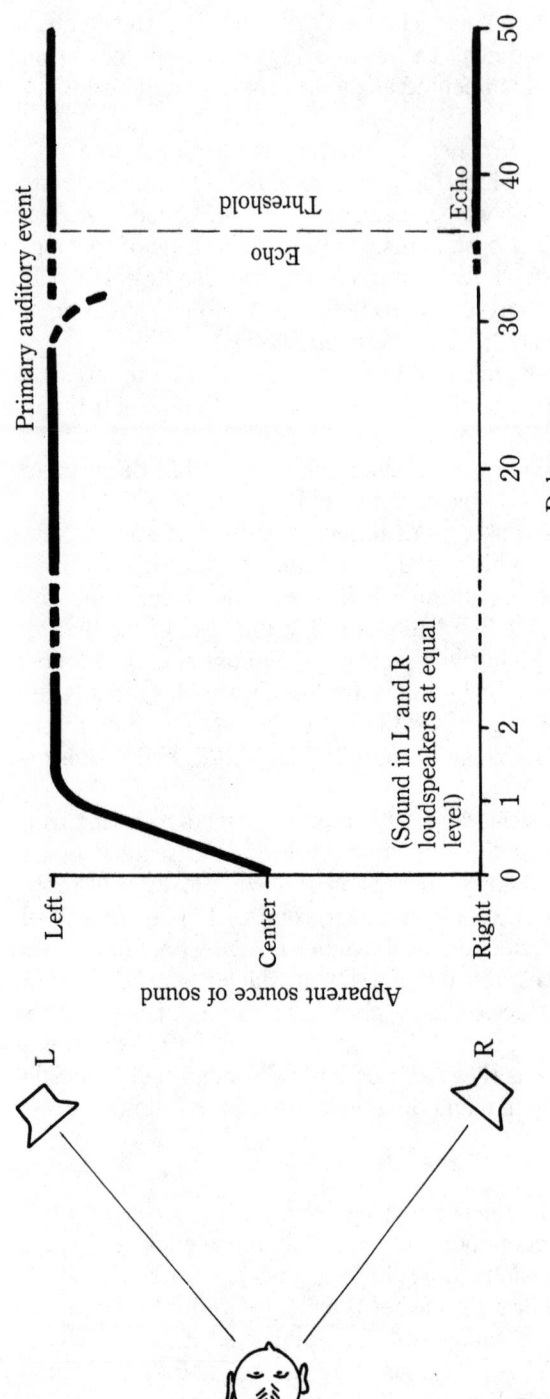

3-21 As the sound to the right loudspeaker is delayed from the center to the left loudspeaker illustrating the law of the first wavefront. As the delay exceeds 35 ms, the sound appears to come from both loudspeakers with a discrete echo.

Echoes

As the sound in one loudspeaker is delayed approximately 30 ms, the delayed sound begins to take the form of a discrete echo. There is a transitional region in which the incipient echo is evident, but not annoying (Fig. 3-21). The echo does not become fully discrete and really annoying until the delay reaches 40 or 50 ms. Beyond this point the echo is definitely both discrete and annoying. This echo threshold is the upper limit of validity of the law of the first wavefront.

A common problem in an auditorium results from sound from the main loud-speakers being reflected from the rear wall or balcony face. The reflected sound often reaches those sitting in seats near the front with a sufficient delay to create a definite echo with accompanying intelligibility problems. For people sitting further back, however, the reflected energy could actually enhance their sound.

Often sound from local supplemental loudspeakers cause the main loud-speakers to sound like an echo because of the differential path length between the two sources and the listener. By delaying the signal to the local loudspeakers, it is possible to achieve an increase in level without the echo.

Effect of reflections on music and speech

Early lateral reflections can help or harm the perception of desired sound. The results of Y. Ando's study documented in *Concert Hall Acoustics*, (1985) considers the effects of lateral reflections on the enjoyment of music, shown in Fig. 3-22A (Reference 3-9). Observers were asked to state whether they preferred the music with or without the spaciousness provided by a single lateral reflection. Half the observers preferred the reflection level and delay indicated by the heavy line. The upper broken line is for 25% and the lower broken line for 75% of the observers preferring reflections of the specified level and delay.

H. Muncie approached a similar problem by asking the observers whether the single lateral reflection interfered with speech (Reference 3-11). The response of half of the observers is represented by the heavy line in Fig. 3-22B. The broken line gives the response of 20% of the observers. The 80% line is off this graph.

The coordinates of Fig. 3-22A and B are identical, inviting the reader to imagine one superimposed on the other for a comparison of the effect of spaciousness on music and speech. The shaded area for music and that for speech interference partially overlap, indicating that some listeners prefer the spaciousness provided by a single lateral reflection for music, but not for speech.

In the average listening room interest in stereo reproduction is focused on reflections delayed in the approximate range of 10 – 20 ms at a level roughly 5 – 10 dB below the direct sound, depending on the geometry and reflecting properties of the surfaces. These figures describe an area of Fig. 3-22A somewhat below the 75% curve. If a 100% curve existed, it might actually include this area, which would indicate that everyone would like the early reflections in this listening room.

Normal reflections from the walls may be ideal for the sound of a live musician in the listening room but intolerable for reproduction of music having spaciousness already recorded with the music.

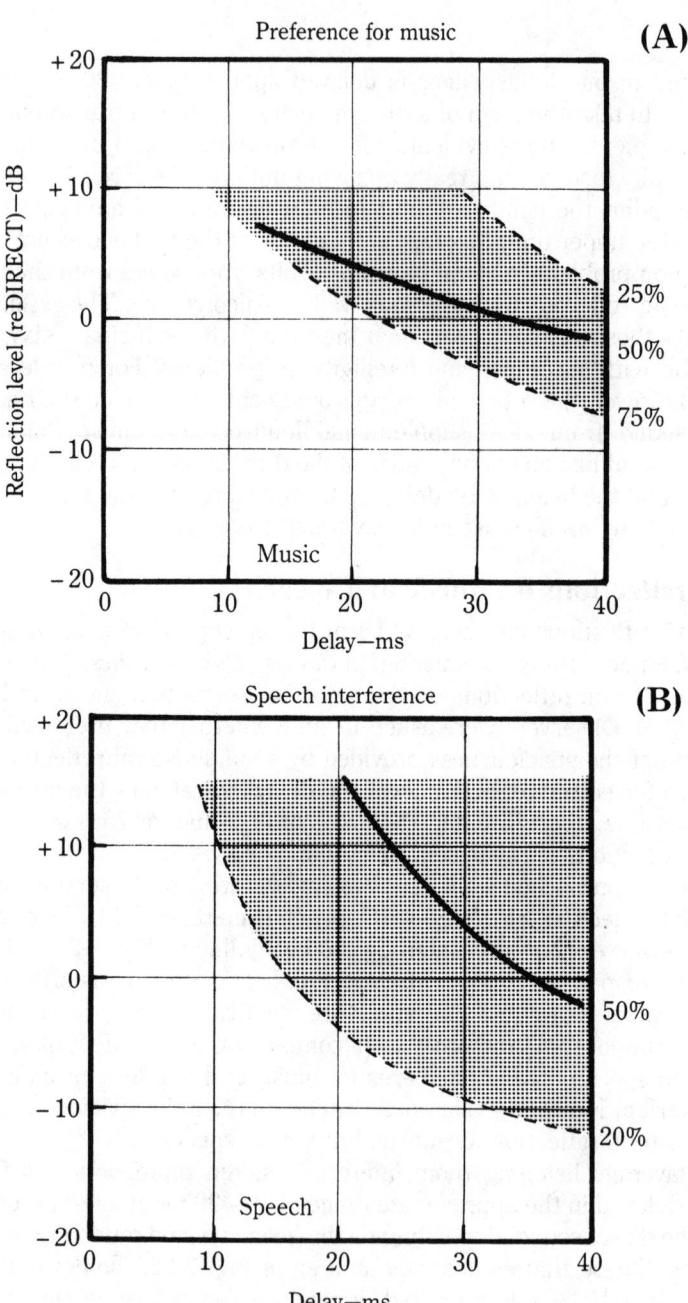

3-22 (A) The results of a study showing the preference for a single lateral reflection on the sound of music. The percentages indicate the proportion of the listeners who preferred the lateral reflection. After Ando, Reference 3-9. (B) The results of a study showing the disturbance of speech by a single lateral reflection. The percentages indicate the proportion of the listeners disturbed. After Muncie, Reference 3-11.

The spaciousness perceived in these tests result from the comb filters produced by combining of lateral reflections with the direct sound. *Combing* is basically a steady-state effect. Music is mostly transients; however, combing of transients results in something interpreted as spaciousness. Ando has demonstrated that people prefer music with spaciousness.

Localization of sound in the median plane

A major emphasis has been the left-to-right localization of sound sources in the horizontal plane. The next natural issue to address is the possibility for a stereo system to yield perceptions of sound arriving from overhead and back or any other point on the hemisphere. The human auditory system is capable of perceiving sound arriving from any direction in the hemisphere. For this to occur appropriate transfer functions must carry the directional information.

The *median plane* is that imaginary vertical plane passing through the head and nose, at right angles to the horizontal plane (Fig. 3-23). The localization of sound perceived by humans is different in the median plane than it is in the horizontal plane. Sound sources in the median plane result in essentially identical signals in the two ears. No time/intensity cues or interaural dissimilarity aids in perception, which characterizes the horizontal plane. Cues resulting from changes in the spectrum of the sound source are evident, however.

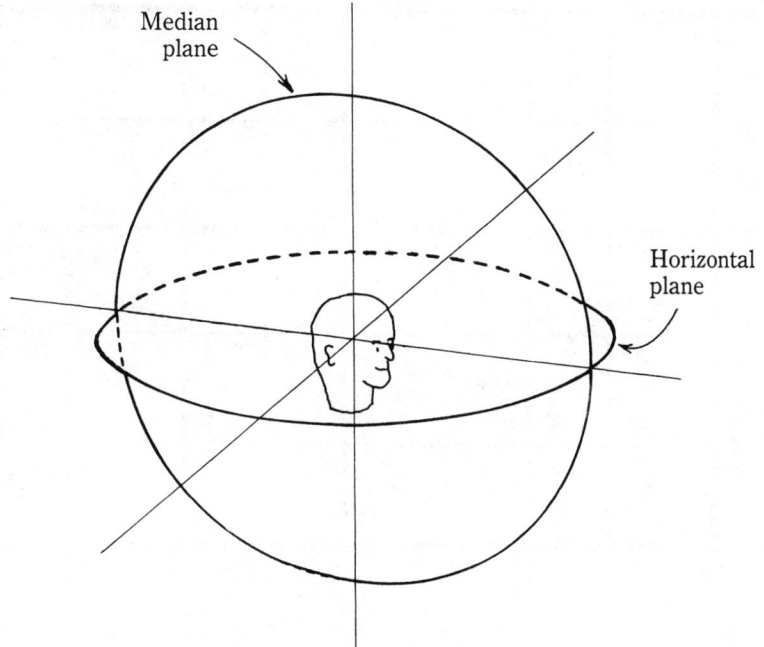

3-23 The median plane is that imaginary vertical plane passing through the center of the head, at right angles to the horizontal plane.

Vertical cues are·produced by changes in the signal spectrum introduced by diffraction at head and pinnae, like the localization of sound in the horizontal plane. Certain frequency ranges of the incoming signal are emphasized or depressed by head diffraction or pinna effects, depending on the direction of arrival. For any 3-dimensional sound reproducing system to work, physical cues must faithfully be recorded and reproduced.

The effectiveness of spectral changes to convey perceptions of sound arriving from points outside the horizontal plane was demonstrated by P.J. Bloom (Reference 3-12). It was suspected that deep notches in the transfer functions at about 10 kHz were cues for specific directions of arrival of the sound (Fig. 3-19). An octave band of noise centered on 8 kHz could simulate sound at the eardrum (Fig. 3-24). A deep and narrow notch was introduced that could be moved about. When listening on headphones to this band of noise and the sharp notch at 8 kHz, the noise appears to come down from above (Fig. 3-25). Shifting the notch to 7.2 kHz changes the apparent direction of the source to a horizontal direction (Fig. 3-26). Moving the notch to a frequency of 6.3 kHz makes the sound appear to come from below (Fig. 3-27). The brain seems to use the position of the notch as a directional cue, apparently confirming a relationship between pinna reflections and the perception of direction.

Blauert summarized many experiments conducted on sound localization in the median plane in his book, *Spatial Hearing*, (Cambridge, 1983) (Reference 3-13).

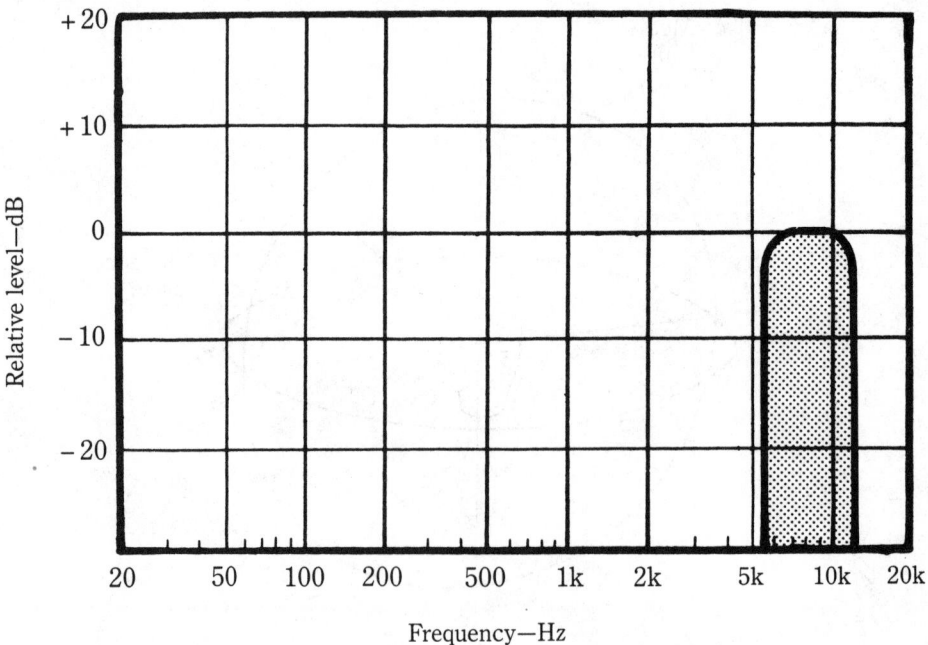

3-24 Spectral changes convey directional information to the ear. To demonstrate this, an octave band of noise is used, which is centered on a frequency of 8 kHz.

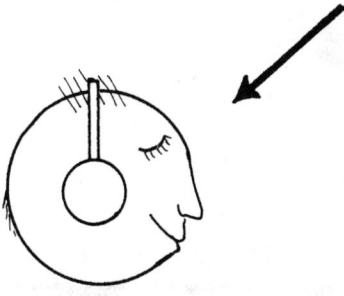

A—notch at 8 kHz

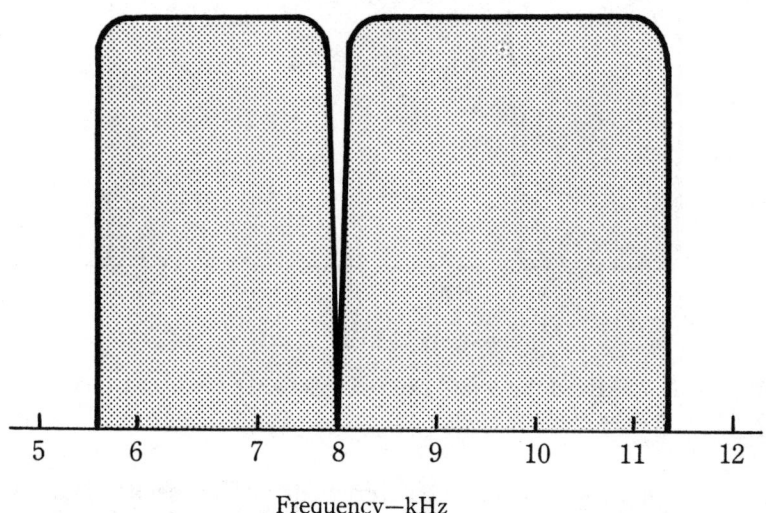

Frequency—kHz

3-25   Listening with headphones to the octave band of noise with a sharp notch at 8 kHz gives the impression that the sound comes from above.

His studies show that the direction of the auditory event depends primarily on the frequency of the signal—not on the direction of the sound source. Figure 3-28 illustrates the correlation between the positions in the median plane and the frequency. Certain redundancy was revealed, for example overhead precepts result from regions near both 500 Hz and 8 kHz, and rear percepts are generated from regions near both 1 and 10 kHz.

In Blauert's characteristically thorough fashion, the subject of sound localization in the median plane was studied formally with many subjects. The signals used were 1/3 octave noise pulses. To simplify an already complex study, the subjects were asked only to judge if the sound appeared to come generally from the foreward, overhead, or rear directions. A statistical study of the data gave the per-

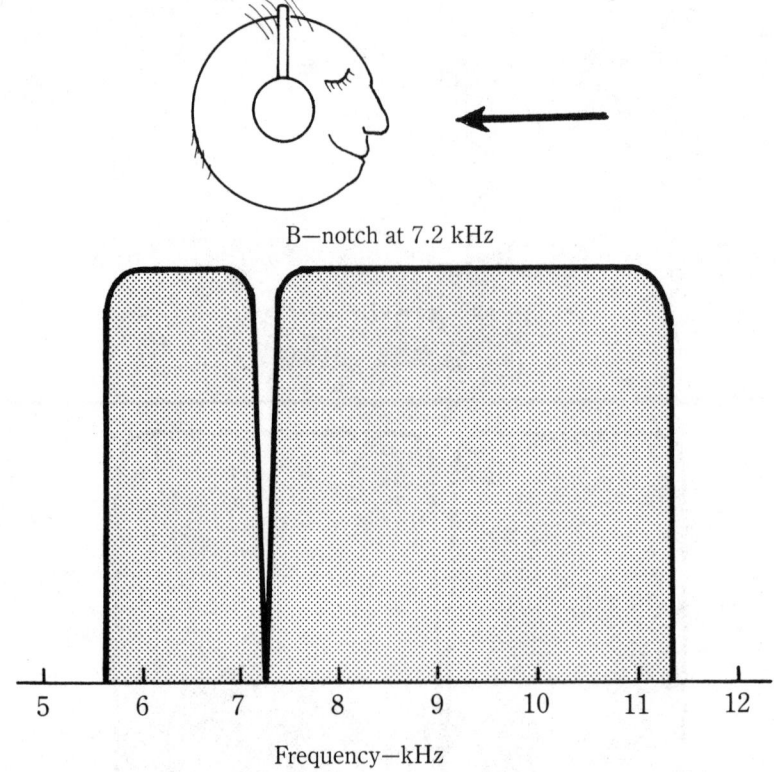

B—notch at 7.2 kHz

Frequency—kHz

3-26 A notch at 7.2 kHz in the octave band of noise gives the impression that the sound comes from a horizontal source.

cent of responses corresponding to each frequency. The results of this study are shown graphically in Fig. 3-29 and can be summarized:

Approximate Frequency Ranges For Directional Bands, Hz

Front	300 – 600	3,000 – 6,000
Overhead	8,000 – 9,000	
Rear	800 – 1,800	9,000 – 15,000

This study suggests the presence of two front, two rear, and one overhead directional bands, though other bands could be revealed with refined measurements. The direction of the auditory event might be correlated with these directional bands on the basis of signal power at specific frequencies.

All of these experiments point to the fundamental importance of the transfer functions. Ample reason now exists to hope for a sound recording and reproducing system that will eventually approximate the ideal and ultimate 3-dimensional meaning of the word *stereo*. It will involve accurately recording and faithfully reproducing the transfer functions of signals from all directions.

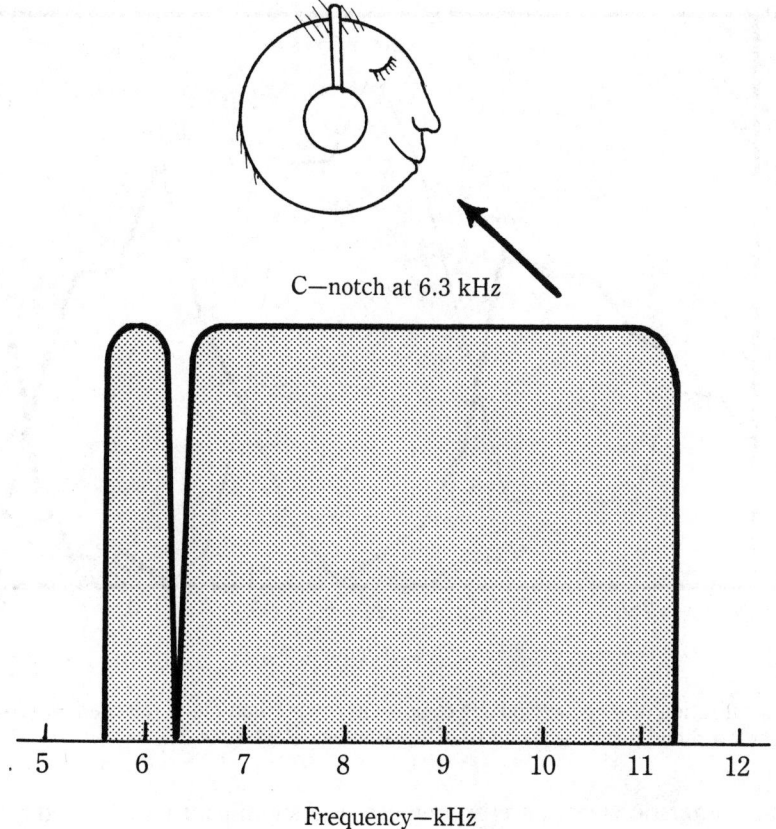

C—notch at 6.3 kHz

Frequency—kHz

3-27 A notch at 6.3 kHz gives the impression that the sound comes from below.

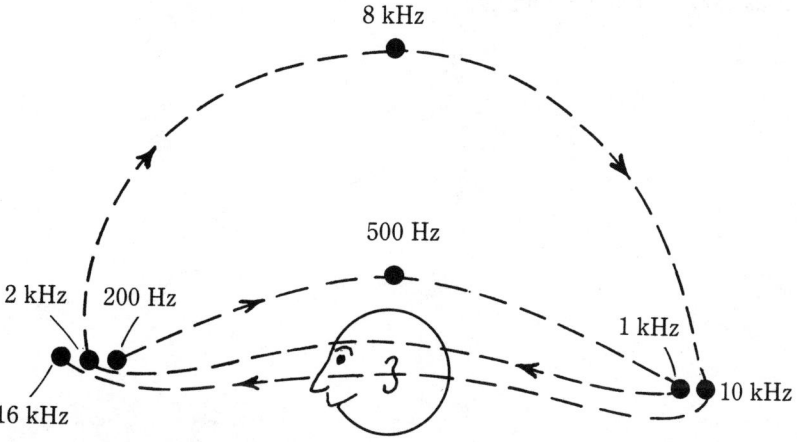

3-28 The apparent direction of tonal signals from loudspeakers in the median plane depends on the frequency of the tone. After Blauert, Reference 3-13.

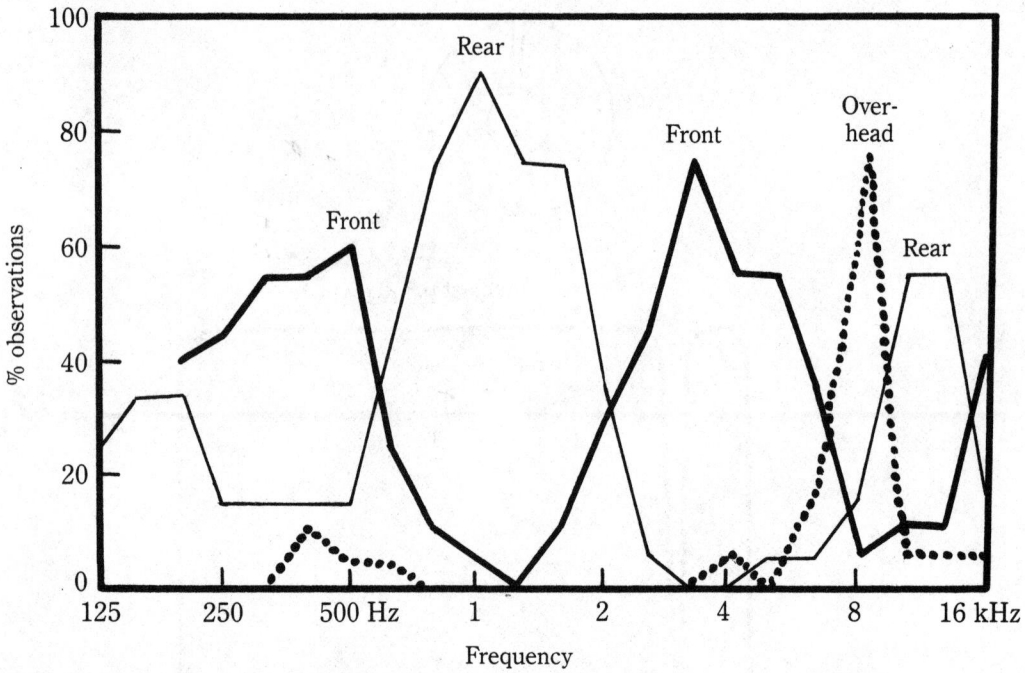

3-29 Localization of ¹/₃ octave pulses of noise in the median plane revealed two front, two rear, and one overhead directional bands. After Blauert, Reference 3-5.

This optimistic view, however, neglects the significant individual differences in the auditory transfer functions. Head, pinna, and ear canal shapes are like fingerprints—no two individuals are identical. Precise pickup, recording, and reproduction techniques are of no avail if the characteristics of the consumer's auditory apparatus vary within wide limits.

4

Philosophical and pragmatic approaches to stereo

THE FIRST THREE CHAPTERS HAVE FOCUSED ON THE VARIOUS PHYSIOLOGICAL, acoustical, and psychoacoustic parameters that form the basis of stereophonic perception. The technical processes employed to produce today's stereo sound through recording and reproduction processes will be discussed in subsequent chapters. These are tangible elements involved in the creation of the stereophonic illusion and are solidly grounded on scientific principles of physics, acoustics, and biophysics.

Before any recording project can begin, however, certain fundamental decisions should be made—decisions that dictate the format, style, and procedures implemented during the recording process. Some of these decisions are limited by the content or style of the subject to be conveyed, for example, music, speech, sound effects, etc. Other more pragmatic factors considered at this stage include: whether the recording/reproduction process is intended to be solely an auditory experience, or will it combine sound and picture; the medium of the recording— commercial record release, radio or television broadcast, film, etc.; the mode of the project (entertainment, documentary, sports or news, etc.); and the anticipated reproduction or listening environment.

These fundamental decisions determine how a recording project is to proceed and many of them are based on more intangible factors such as mood, feeling, and intuition than on scientific fact. Thus science and philosophy must go hand in hand in the creation of the stereo illusion.

The five W's

All writers know that for a message to be communicated the *Five W's* should be addressed: who, what, when, where, and why. These five considerations are equally important to the process of making a recording. After all sound recording is really just another medium of communication—a means of expressing an idea aurally rather than visually.

- *Who* is the listener? Is he/she experienced in the subject of the recording? Is he/she a critical or casual listener?
- *What* is the medium? Will it be reproduced on a cassette or compact disc, radio, television, or a motion picture?
- *When* is he/she listening? Does the listening experience occur in the background or foreground of the listener's attention?
- *Where* is the listening environment? Is it at home, at work, in an elevator, a theater, or in a car?
- *Why* is he/she listening? Is it for the pleasure of the experience, for information content, or simply for entertainment?

The answers to each of these questions contribute significantly to the determination of how the recording should proceed. Some factors can be complementary, while others prove to be mutually exclusive. The technical procedure employed, however, must be compatible with all of these dictates. A producer might decide that more than one answer is appropriate to each of the questions, forcing a compromise between various technical procedures.

Re-creating an event

To initiate the decision-making process, the *flavor* of the recording must be determined. Flavor is intended to convey the essential listening experience a producer, musician, and/or engineer wants to convey to the listener. A recording is an artificial substitute for a live experience—reality—and should never be expected to equal the sensation of *being there*. The best any recording can attain is the simulation of a live experience according to two related, although quite different, philosophies: recreative and creative.

The first philosophy of recording intends to recreate a sonic experience for listeners in their own environment. The purpose of this recreation is to make listeners feel that they are listening to a real event—something that actually happened, or *could have happened*—transferred in time and/or space, and transported into their presence via the recording process. All senses of the event's realism must be captured and retained, so listeners will feel as though they are participants at the event. Concerts, sporting events, news, and documentaries are among the sonic events most appropriate to this recording philosophy.

Technical procedures for recreative recordings generally involve the more *purist* microphone techniques (discussed in chapters 5, 6, 7, and 9). Simple recording methods try to maintain the original ambience of the sonic space and generally offer minimal alteration of the original sonic perspective.

Creating a new event

Creative recordings bring to listeners an experience that never happened in real time, but that the creators of the sonic illusion would like to have happened. The intent is to make listeners participants at this sonic event, even though it might be impossible to achieve in the real world.

When creating a listening experience, applicable recording techniques allow considerably more experimentation—multimicrophone and multitrack procedures are typical. Significant signal processing, synthesis, and artificial ambience are also commonly used to create a new and unique listening experience.

Some believe these two approaches to expressing a sonic image—creative or recreative—are one in the same. This concept stems from the belief that the two are merely alternate means of observing an event and conveying its essence, because the illusion can never equal the reality. In the context of recorded sound, reality is what you make of it. The only true reality is being there.

The listener's perspective

The listener's aural *viewpoint* of the recording also can be described by two contrasting sonic perspectives. In the listener's perspective, however, the differences between the approaches are more distinct than the styles of creating a listening experience. These two aural perspectives can be called *You are there* or *They are here*, in which "you" refers to the listeners and "they" are the performers.

With *You are there*, the intent is to generate an aural perspective that will transport the listeners into the same sonic environment as the event—or to put listeners into the audience, as it were. This approach is appropriate to almost any form of real-sonic event, especially concerts, sporting events, dramatic or documentary presentations, environmental scenes, and the like.

On the other hand, *They are here*, attempts to bring the sonic event to the listeners—*and reproduce it in the listening environment*. This approach is only plausible when the sonic event could logically occur in this listening space. Hence, a baseball game, large symphony orchestra, or World War II would not be convincing, while a ping pong match, a string quartet, or a boxing match might be.

The two-by-two matrix

The style of the reproduction can be related to the viewpoint by placing them both into a matrix. If the top is labeled according to philosophy and the sides according to perspective, it is possible to derive four distinct approaches to the recording and reproduction of a sonic experience. These approaches are the logical result of the experience itself (Table 4-1).

Both *You are there* and *They are here* recordings can be either recreative or creative, depending on the sonic illusion desired. The various technical means to accomplish these styles differ from one to another, which can be seen by expanding the contents of the matrix to include some of the relevant production techniques employed for each approach (Table 4-2).

The matrix implies that although four initial directions of a recording project can be followed, within each are several alternate routes the producer or engineer could also pursue. Once the primary course is determined, however, it should be

Table 4-1. The two-by-two matrix

	Re-creative	Creative
YOU ARE THERE		
THEY ARE HERE		

Table 4-2. The two-by-two matrix
(Expanded to show technical aspects of each mode)

	Re-creative	Creative
YOU ARE THERE	Simple techniques: Blumlein or Coincident XY; Near-coincident; Spaced; Ambisonics; preservation of natural ambience; minimal enhancement of original acoustics	Multi-microphone and/or multi-track techniques; special effects processing; synthesis; creation of artificial ambient space; "Anything Goes . . ."
THEY ARE HERE	Coincident microphones or close multi-microphone techniques; little natural ambience in the recording; close, intimate sound	Multi-microphone and/or multi-track techniques; special effects processing; synthesis; little ambient space; deliberate placement of sonic elements; "Anything Goes . . ."

followed to its final destination. Sudden or abrupt deviations from the chosen course might lead the listener to conscious or subliminal confusion and thereby destroy the illusion. In the theater if the lighting becomes noticeable the essence of the play is lost. The same concept holds true for the sonic illusion. If the listener becomes aware of the technique, the intended content will not be conveyed.

Technical considerations

Various technical constraints inherent to the recording and reproduction medium also play an important role when determining the processes to use. These considerations are practical restrictions of the recording format, for example: amplitude, dynamics, phase, spectrum, and distortion.

Amplitude

The amplitude limitation relates to the absolute signal level inherent with the recording and playback medium. Recording techniques intended for digital audio production allow significantly greater freedom of choice to the recording engineer than techniques used for cassette or AM radio broadcast—where the signal level and dynamic range are significantly more restricted.

Dynamics

Related to amplitude, the *dynamic range* of a recording refers to the extremes between loud and soft. Like absolute amplitude, these extremes also must be considered in context with both the sonic material and the listening environment. For a recording to equal the impact of a live concert, the playback must be at a sound pressure level near to the volume the listener would experience in the concert hall. This is limited in the practical world where the problems of home playback equipment, consideration for neighbors, and other factors restrict the playback volume to a more conservative level. A recording must be able to preserve the impression—even if not the full extent—of the dynamic range of the original, or else the emotional impact is diminished. After all, a full symphony orchestra, a heavy-metal band, or even a competent singer can easily overpower the acoustical capacities of a small apartment.

Phase

When considering the integrity of the stereo image, the technical factor most important is phase coherency between the channels. If the production introduces contradictions between the amplitude and phase cues in the stereo signal, serious image confusion could result. Therefore it is important to retain consistent amplitude and coherent phase response throughout the entire recording/reproduction process, regardless of the medium of distribution.

Although amplitude, spectrum, and dynamic range can all be compromised to some degree without causing serious deterioration of the stereo image, improper attention to phase coherency during the original recording process will produce a flawed recording from the outset. Therefore, the implementation of proper microphone techniques is crucial during the original recording stages, and these should complement the style of the recording and the demands of the distribution medium.

Spectrum

Spectrum is a technical term that describes the waveform texture of all individual sounds—defining their sonic identity. *Timbre* is another, more musical name for spectrum. Although the two terms are not identical, they are closely related because the preservation of spectrum is essential to the presentation of timbre. Throughout the recording and reproduction process, careful preservation of the spectral integrity of the sound is necessary to maintain the illusion for the listener.

Distortion

Distortion is the primary enemy of spectrum. Distortion creates unwanted alterations in the sonic fidelity of the audio chain. It can affect any or all of the other factors involved, and its insidious effects can be introduced anywhere in the long progress from performer to listener.

Distortion can be linear or nonlinear. Linear distortion simply produces changes in the amplitude and phase response of the audio signal without adding anything to it. Nonlinear distortion creates new, unwanted components and adds them to the audio signal. These components can be either harmonically or nonharmonically related to the original signal and are audible even at relatively low levels compared to the original signal. Thus, nonlinear distortion is considered much more annoying to the listener than linear distortion.

Although these technical considerations are not inherently part of the philosophy of the recording process, they should be considered during the earliest planning stages because they interact with philosophical factors. It is useful to compare the technical parameters with various distribution formats by placing them into two columns, as in Table 4-3. These are not meant to imply parallel comparisons, however.

Table 4-3. Technical considerations of recorded formats

Technical	Format
• Amplitude Response (i.e., frequency response; amplitude spectrum)	• Analog Tape (reel-to-reel or Cassette)
• Phase Response (i.e., phase spectrum)	• Phonograph record (LP)
• Dynamic Range	• Digital Compact Disc or tape
• Residual Noise (Signal-to-Noise ratio)	• Broadcast (AM, FM, TV)
• Non-linear distortion (i.e., harmonic, intermodulation, transient, etc.)	• Film (magnetic, optical, digital)

Recording formats

Each of the recording formats listed in Fig. 4-3 sets its own technical limitations on the recording/reproduction process. As an example, the cassette format places greater constraints on the technical capabilities of a recording than a compact disc or a phonograph record. All technical parameters—amplitude, phase response, dynamic range, distortion, and spectral content—have narrow limits and should be considered when producing an original recording intended for cassette distribution.

However, if the same recording is released as a medium that does not pose these restrictions, such as a compact disc, the original recording should not be compromised for the sake of the cassette. Make the initial recording suitable for the compact disc and then use this full range recording to produce another, more restricted master suitable for cassette duplication.

A less obvious comparison is drawn when considering a compact disc recording that will subsequently be broadcast. Usually the constraints of the broadcast medium are imposed by the broadcast facility. The broadcast chain incorporates signal processing devices to restrict dynamic range, spectrum, etc., so the original compact disc recording is preserved unaltered.

Suppose the recording is to be made by the broadcast facility's own production staff, initially for air, but reserving the option for subsequent release as a compact disc. Should the recording be made preserving full spectrum, with maximum separation and dynamic range, or should the recording team constrain these factors to suit the limitations of the broadcast medium? The decision is made by the program's producer, who might choose to tailor the original recording to suit the broadcast medium, and thereby limit further use of the material; or he/she might choose to retain the options for future use of the recording, and leave any technical reductions in the hands of the broadcast engineer. Both attitudes are valid, but the decision must be made at the outset.

Sonic and visual images

When assessing the impact of television on the dwindling radio audience, someone once said: "Yes, but radio has better pictures."

The point of this statement was that the visual images presented by television (or film) dictate precisely what we will see, and therefore constrain our imaginations. To the audio component of the program these constraints correspond to media-imposed restraints, in that they dictate what the sonic perspective must be. The recording engineer is no longer free to create an autonomous sonic image. *You are there* becomes the only possible attitude, and *you*, the listener, are limited to being a spectator of the event, instead of a participant.

When producing sound with pictures (television or film) severe restraints are placed on the sound department to maintain a sonic perspective that will complement the visual image. (Chapter 13 discusses more fully the various perspectives available for sound with pictures.) If the sound editor wishes to withhold editorial decision over the sonic image until the picture has been cut, this dictates certain microphone and recording techniques which can afford a degree of flexibility during the rerecording mix.

The law of compromises

Again, the basic approach to making a stereo recording must be decided at the outset of the project. This approach is determined by the several, often competing, technical and philosophical factors involved. This decision process acknowledges the "Law of Compromise," inherent throughout the world of audio.

This law, though it is not written anywhere, is universally imposed nonetheless, and dictates that any decision with regard to the production or reproduction of a recorded experience must result from a choice among compromises. What is best for one set of circumstances will likely sacrifice others. It is the charge of the producer to select from among these compromises those that will be the most beneficial—or viewed from the obverse, the least damaging—to the final product. Although this might seem like a cynical viewpoint, it is merely pragmatism. Illusion or reality—you can't have both.

5

Two-microphone stereo techniques

"STEREO DOES NOT EQUAL MONO TIMES TWO." THIS MESSAGE APPEARED on the title slide of a workshop conducted by Randall Hoffner of NBC at a convention of the Audio Engineering Society. Although this axiom might seem somewhat humorous, at first, its underlying meaning merits serious consideration.

As expressed in previous chapters, conveying stereo information requires a minimum of two transmission channels and two loudspeakers. Further, our hearing perception system relies on differences in the information received and conveyed by our two ears. Two signals, two transmission paths, and two ears—so far, so good. It has also been emphasized that the correlation between these two signals determines how a listener will perceive the sense of stereo space within a recording. It is this interaural correlation that makes stereo more than suit the simultaneous transmission or reproduction of two monophonic audio signals.

An analogy can be made to our visual perceptions. When covering one eye and looking out a window, one can still discern lateral images. Determining the distance between various elements in the scene, however, is a different matter. Human vision is stereoscopic—different information from each eye is required to perceive depth.

Similarly, plugging one ear still allows sounds from all around to be heard, but the ability to determine precisely where a sound originated becomes difficult. As with the eyes, two ears are required to provide the minutely differing cues essential for determining spatial information in the surrounding soundfield (see chapters 2 and 3).

Inverse square law

The intensity of a sound decreases as distance from the source increases. In a free field, like an open or unenclosed space such as outdoors, spherical divergence prevails. The inverse square law dictates that the intensity of a sound falls off as the square of the distance because the intensity of sound is energy per unit area.

The nature of the inverse square law is shown in the diagram of Fig. 5-2. As sound is emitted from the source, S, the concentration of energy over surfaces A_1, and A_2 is equal. If $R_2 = 2R_1$, the area of A_2 is equal to four times that of A_1, so the acoustic intensity (sound energy per unit of area) at A_2 is only one fourth that at surface A_1. Because intensity is proportional to pressure squared, the sound pressure at A_2 is half that at A_1. Sound pressure is easier to measure than intensity. Audio engineers interpret the inverse square law as resulting in a 6 dB sound-pressure reduction for each doubling of the distance. In terms of loudness, a 6 dB reduction in pressure represents roughly a decrease in loudness by somewhat less than one-half.

It is important to reiterate that the inverse square law applies only in a free field or nonreverberant environment. In enclosed spaces, such as indoors, true spherical divergence rarely prevails because sound tends to build up due to room reflections. Loudspeaker directivity might also be involved. Indoors, the reduction in sound pressure might be only 3 or 4 dB for a similar doubling of distance.

The monophonic sound system

In a monophonic sound system, sound is picked up and reproduced via only one channel. In its simplest form, such a system would include one microphone, one transmission channel, and one loudspeaker (Fig. 5-1). Ignored for the moment is what happens when a monophonic signal is played back through the two loudspeakers of a conventional stereo system.

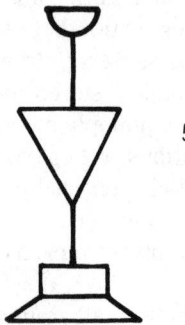

5-1   The basic monophonic signal chain, comprised of a single microphone, amplifier channel, and loudspeaker.

If a microphone responds equally to sounds coming from any direction, it is *omnidirectional*. A monophonic sound system using this microphone responds uniformly to a broad sound source, no matter what direction the sound originates from. The only distinctions the system recognizes are intensity differences as discussed above. These differences along with the relationship between the direct and indirect sound components, cue the monophonic listener to the distance the sound source is from the microphone pickup, and the size and character of the performing space.

Thus a monophonic system will reproduce faithfully the entire sound source, but without conveying any sense of direction. All sounds arriving at the microphone are transmitted and reproduced through one loudspeaker. Reproduced in

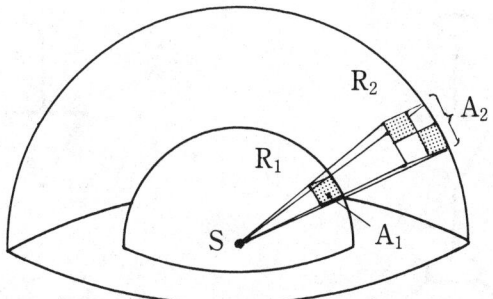

5-2 The inverse square law. As sound energy is emitted from the source, *S*, it radiates outward in a spherical pattern, the same sound energy flowing through areas A1 and A2. If $R_2 = 2 \times R1$, then $A_2 = 4 \times A_1$. (The surface area of a sphere varies with the square of the radius.) The inverse square law states that sound intensity decreases as the square of the distance from the source (i.e., sound pressure decreases as the first power of the distance).

this way, an entire symphony orchestra is constricted into a common space, with no spatial differentiation between the strings, winds, brass, or percussion sections. Furthermore, any sense of depth is compressed—although instruments further back sound somewhat more distant, they do not seem nearly as remote as they do when they are heard live.

In addition, almost all sense of space—the environment in which the performance is taking place, all ambience and reverberation—is compressed into the primary sound and will come from the same direction. Like listening through a small opening in the wall of a concert hall, the *flat* sound conveys little information to the listener about the size of the orchestra or the space in which it performs. The result is unnatural—if someone were inside a hall listening to a live performance, sound would come from all directions, not just through one small hole in the wall.

The conventional stereo system

A conventional stereo system requires two transmission channels and two loudspeakers. Like the monaural system, these transmission channels could also be fed by only two omnidirectional microphones—one connected to each channel (Fig. 5-3). This simple system would provide many of the essential cues necessary to convey spatial localization and depth. At the same time, however, it would include some misinformation that could cause the listener to perceive an inaccurate aural image. These stereo signals can be achieved by other methods, and some are more faithful to the original sound source than others.

The phantom center image

When stereo is reproduced via two loudspeakers, the listener can hear only two possible sources of sound: one left and one right. A full stereo panorama can be conveyed, however, using *phantom* images. All sounds heard between the two

5-3 The basic stereophonic signal chain, comprised of two microphones, amplifier channels, and loudspeakers.

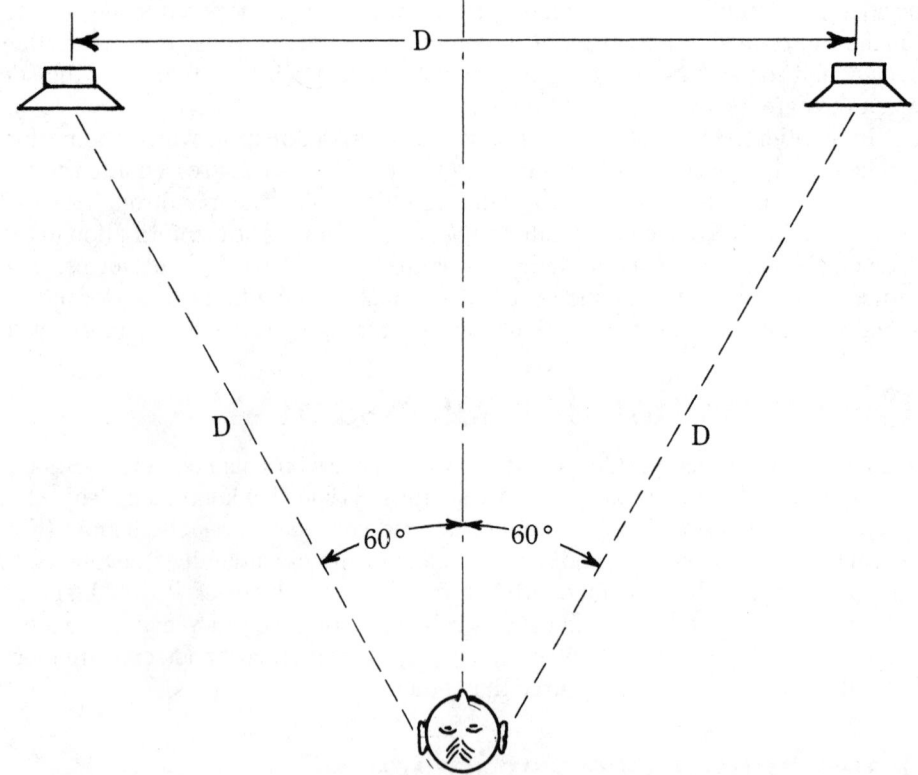

5-4 The recommended arrangement of a stereophonic playback system requires that the listener be positioned along a line perpendicular to and bisecting a line between the two loudspeakers. The listener should then be situated so an equilateral triangle is formed by the two loudspeakers and the listening position.

loudspeakers are *phantom* images—they are not *solid* signals, but the result of our hearing perception process. The position of these images is determined by a combination of sound energy reproduced by the two loudspeakers together.

A basic stereo reproduction system is shown in Fig. 5-4. The listener is situated along a line that is perpendicular to, and bisects, the line between the two loudspeakers. The optimum angle from the listener to either loudspeaker is approximately 60°, so the listener and the loudspeakers are at the corners of an equilateral triangle.

If identical signals are introduced into both loudspeakers, equal sound energy will be radiated by each and the listener will perceive the sound as if it were coming from a point exactly between the two loudspeakers. Because the listener is equally distant from each loudspeaker and equal intensity signals are produced by them, no intensity or time-of-arrival differences are perceived from the listening position. It was shown in chapter 2 that this condition corresponds to a sound coming from directly in front of the listener. This condition is analogous to a situation when the sound subject is equidistant from both microphones, as in Fig. 5-5. Any effects of room acoustics, or other interfering factors, are ignored in this discussion.

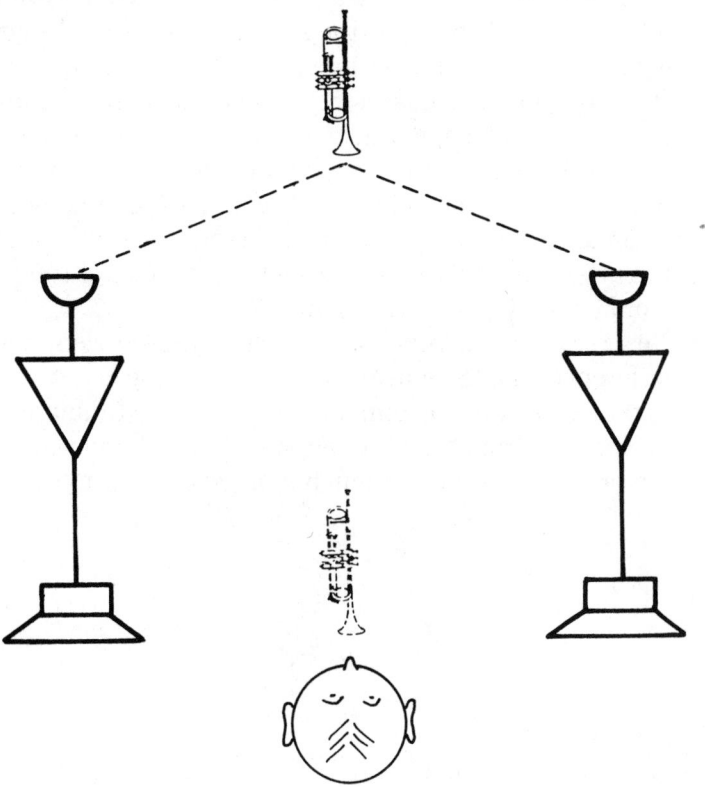

5-5 The sound of a trumpet tends to come from a *phantom center* point between the two loudspeakers if the instrument is located at a point equidistant from the two microphones.

A dramatic comparison between the sense of space and increased realism conveyed via stereo, as contrasted with monophonic signals can be evidenced in the following experiment.

- Place three loudspeakers in a row, as shown in Fig. 5-6A, and connect them to a sound system via a switching array, shown in Fig. 5-6B. Carefully balance all levels, so the sound output from the center loudspeaker is equal to the combined output of the left and right loudspeakers.
- If a monophonic signal is reproduced equally through both the left and right loudspeakers, it will *appear* to come from a center position between the two loudspeakers—a phantom center. Only slight differences should be heard when switching between the center, loudspeaker, and back again to the left and right loudspeakers. Again the effects of room acoustics are being ignored. In actuality, the effect of room acoustics on phantom imaging can be significant.
- Now, if a truly stereophonic signal is reproduced, however, a significant difference should be heard when comparing the two stereo loudspeakers to the center (mono sum) loudspeaker. The dramatic difference between monophonic and truly stereophonic sound reproduction is what makes the process of stereo so much more satisfying to the listener.

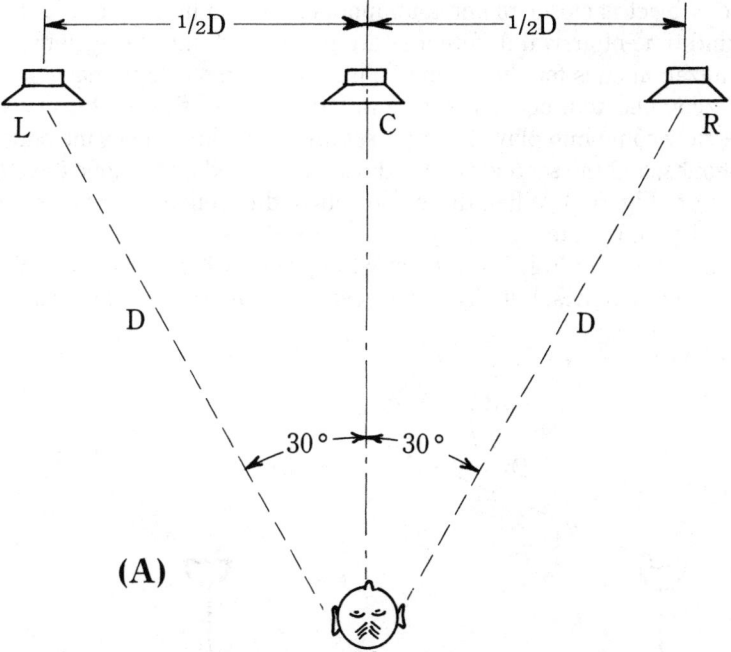

(A)

5-6 (A) An experimental setup where a center loudspeaker is added to a conventional two-loudspeaker stereo playback system. The three loudspeakers should be connected as shown in (B). The values of R_1 and R_2 should be chosen such that the sound pressure level from the center speaker is equal to the combined sound pressure from the left and right loudspeakers. By switching between the center speaker and the stereo pair, the sonic difference between a *hard* center and a *phantom* center easily can be heard.

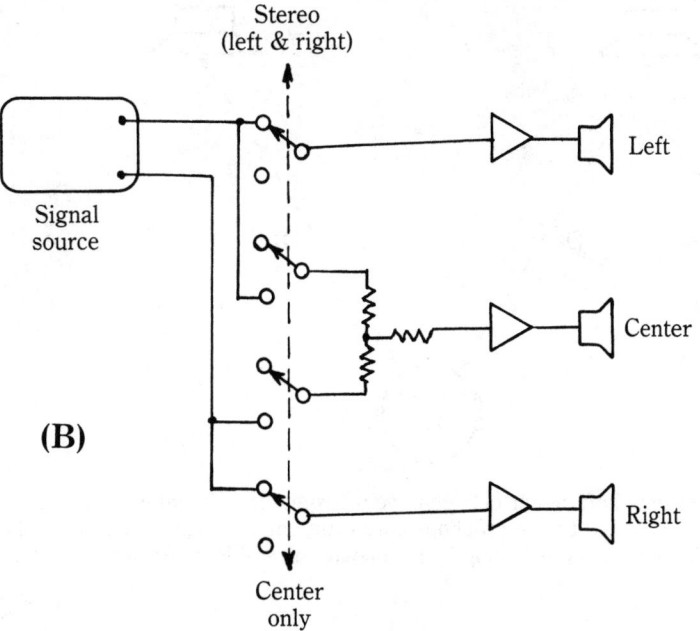

(B)

If the sound subject is closer to one microphone, the conditions are different. Both intensity and time-of-arrival differences are introduced into the system, producing dual localization cues for the listener. This condition starts to make stereo perception more complicated, because two conflicting sets of these intensity and time differences now come into play. The first set are those differences introduced into the microphones, and the second set are those introduced by the loudspeakers during reproduction (Fig. 5-7). When these two sets of differences interact, distortion of the stereo image results.

In the example shown in Fig. 5-7, a trumpet is placed where it is not equidistant from the two microphones, but slightly off-center, to the right. (The terms *left*

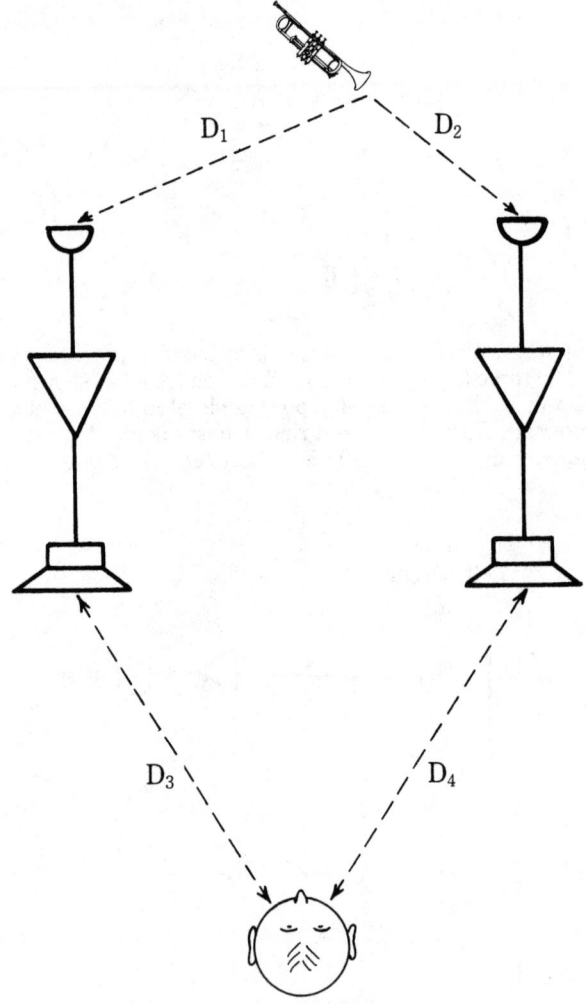

5-7   If a trumpet is located off-center between two microphones, the intensity and time-of-arrival differences at the two microphones are different from those that are radiated from the two loudspeakers, resulting in a somewhat unstable image for the listener.

and *right* relate to the listener's perspective.) Thus, the sound from the trumpet arrives at the two microphones at different times, corresponding to the different distances, D_1 and D_2. When reproduced via the two loudspeakers, these two signals reach the listener via two additional paths, D_3 and D_4. As a result the sound from the trumpet to the listener's ears will have traveled two different transmission paths: D_1 and D_3 for the left channel, and D_2 and D_4 for the right. If D_3 and D_4 are equal, the original time and intensity differences between the trumpet and the two microphones will be maintained. However, if D_3 is not equal to D_4, two additional time-of-arrival differences result for the listener, and the compounding of these time-of-arrival differences skews the stereo image unnaturally toward the closer loudspeaker. (Due to the law of the first wavefront, if the listener is not centered between the two loudspeakers, this shift of image location will happen to some degree with any stereo signal). The greater the distance from the centerline results in a more significant effect on center imaging.

The hole in the middle effect

The *hole in the middle* effect results when the two microphones of a stereo pair are spaced more than a few feet apart, as in Fig. 5-8. Due to the inverse square law, sound sources located closer to the microphones dominate, while sounds from more distant sources are considerably reduced in level. In Fig. 5-8, the instruments in the middle, relatively far from the microphones, suffer from this effect. As a result, the middle instruments tend to be heard rather weakly—little sound seems to come from between the loudspeakers. The instruments that should sound in the center will be clustered together instead with the outer instruments around the two loudspeakers. Furthermore, the sound will appear somewhat unnatural or *phasey*, due to comb-filter effects (see chapter 8).

In the 1930s experiments were conducted by Bell Laboratories to remedy these problems. By implementing a third, center transmission channel, they filled in the hole in the middle, and restored a more defined central image. This image is no longer considered a phantom image, because of the discrete transmission channel (Fig. 5-9). Although adopted only briefly in the 1950s for home-stereo systems, the center channel became the foundation of all motion picture sound systems currently in use throughout the world. It is now finding its way back into home multi-channel, surround sound systems (see chapter 13).

Reverberation

An important difference between monophonic and stereo reproduction systems stems from their treatment of the reverberation in the recording space. *Reverberation* is the random sound that surrounds the listener in a live concert hall experience. It is comprised primarily by a multitude of lateral reflections reaching the listener from all directions—all delayed in time relative to the direct sound signal. Reverberation is generated when the direct sound from the source is reflected by the numerous surfaces of the space, such as walls, ceiling, floor, etc. Reverberation

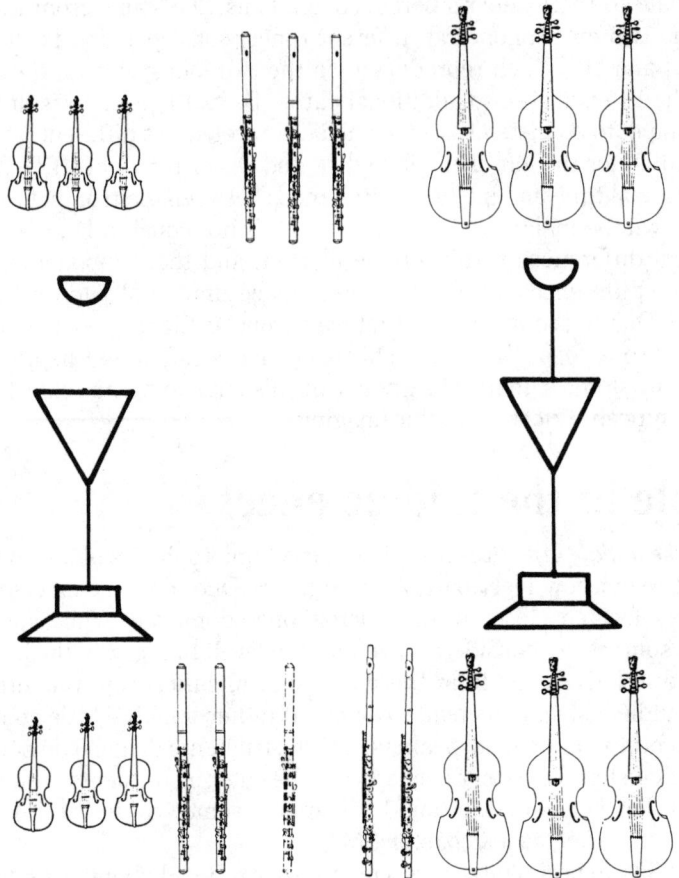

5-8 When the microphones are widely spaced, the sound of any instruments located in the center, between the two microphones, tends to be *compressed* into the two loud-speakers, creating a *hole-in-the-middle* effect.

gives a specific characteristic sonic signature to every performance space, and is one of the most important reasons why all concert halls sound different.

Critical distance

The effects of reverberation can be related to another concept in sound, *critical distance*. When a sound source is heard in an enclosed space, both direct sound (sound arriving in a direct path from the source) and indirect sound (sound reflected from the walls, ceiling, etc.) are heard. The relative balance between the direct and indirect (or reverberant) sound largely determines how clearly the source can be perceived. The more direct the sound is, the more distinct and articulate the source will be. The more reverberation that is heard, the more *muddy* the impression of the source will be. (Other terms frequently used to convey these impressions are *wet*, *live*, or *distant* for highly reverberant sounds, and *dry*, *dead*, or *present*, for nonreverberant sounds.)

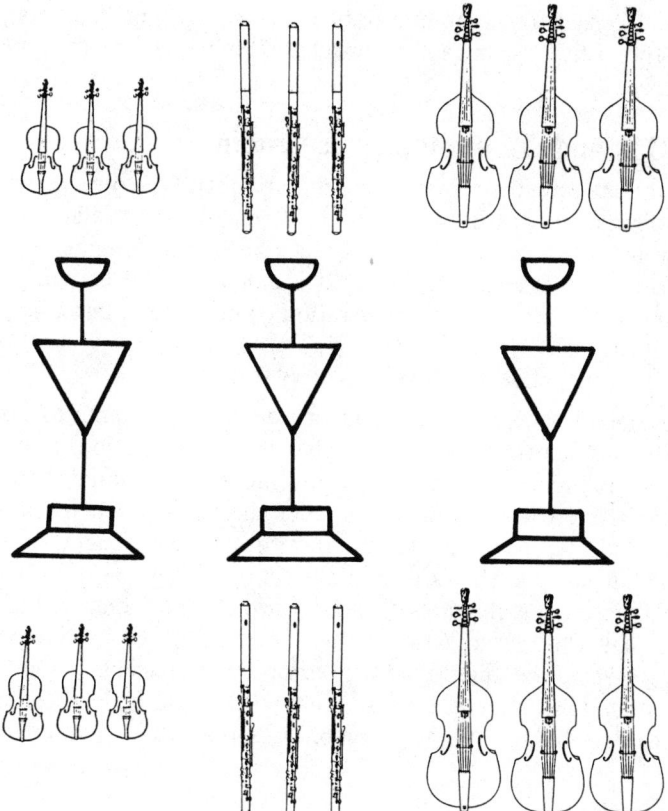

5-9 By adding a third signal chain to Fig. 5-8, a solid center image can be maintained.

The critical distance from the sound source is a position where the total energy content of the direct sound received is equal to the total energy content of the reverberant sound.

Ideally, a listener or microphone should be located within the critical distance from the source to achieve a sound that is articulate, with a good sense of *presence*. Critical distance is particularly important in speech, because excessive reverberation makes words unintelligible. Reverberation could be dominated by reflections from the sides and behind the listener, and great effort is made by both acoustical designers and recording producers to keep reverberation in proper balance so it does not overwhelm the direct sound.

Listening from a position beyond the critical distance is less satisfying. The sound is indistinct, with reverberation masking the clarity and articulation of the subject.

The difference between a human listener and a microphone is extensive. The brain makes a significant difference regarding the effects of reverberation on the listening experience. The microphone cannot discriminate between direct and indirect sound by any means other than its inherent directional pattern. The human auditory system focuses the listener's attention on the direct sound, even in the presence of a significant amount of reverberation. Some listeners prefer to sit well beyond the critical distance of a concert hall to enjoy a more *enveloping* musical experience.

Reverberation and the monophonic system

Monophonic sound systems combine reverberation with the direct sound signal, so little or no distinction can be perceived between them. Because only one loudspeaker reproduces the composite signal, the reverberation emanates from exactly the same place as the direct signal. This is not a natural listening experience, because in most real situations, reverberation comes from all around the listener.

Reverberation and the stereophonic system

Stereophonic sound systems, on the contrary, enable the listener to easily and naturally differentiate between the direct signal and reverberation. Stereo offers the sound a chance to breathe, and thus provides more *space* around the direct sound. This produces a more natural experience for the listener. Surround sound techniques, discussed later in chapter 13, increase this sense of spaciousness by providing additional speakers to the sides and behind the listener.

Various recording techniques provide different methods of controlling the amount and quality of reverberation in stereo recordings. Sometimes it is done as the recording takes place, directly in the performance space, and sometimes reverberation is created by artificial means. Whatever the method, stereo listeners can tolerate more reverberation in their recordings than their monophonic counterparts.

Stereo perspectives vs. multiple microphone systems

In subsequent chapters, several different approaches to stereo microphone techniques are presented. In general, these fall into two categories: minimalist stereo, and multiple-microphone stereo. Both approaches are valid and have their proper applications. The two techniques are sometimes combined, although this might seem contradictory at first.

The difference between a two-microphone perspective and a mix of several microphones is distinct. A basic two-microphone technique can accurately *capture* the basic sonic impression of the performance, but might still lack some of the intimate, subtle details of the ensemble or space. In this instance, supplemental microphones might be necessary to provide subtle reinforcement for what could be deficient in the main pickup. One might wonder if this is a two-microphone or a multimicrophone pickup. Although this might be considered merely a semantic argument, the authors contend that this situation is really a two-microphone pickup, because the other microphones are merely supplemental to the main pickup, and would not be seriously missed if removed from the mix.

In this context, a multimicrophone pickup exists when each microphone contributes significantly to and is an essential part of, the complete sound perspective. Remove any single microphone, and something disappears from the mix.

This fundamental question is given considerable examination as the book progresses. Chapters 6, 7, and 9 present the basic two-microphone perspectives, and chapter 10 discusses multimicrophone techniques. What matters in the final result, however, is the sound as perceived by the listener. Does the sonic perspective convey the intentions of the creators as described in chapter 4? How this question is answered is the secret to the illusion of stereo—and the reality.

Super stereo

The type of stereo discussed thus far—and again throughout much of the remainder of this book—should be called conventional stereo, because it only hints at what the full 3-dimensional meaning of the word *stereo* implies (see chapter 1). Conventional stereo is concerned only with the sound within a limited region along the horizontal plane, bounded by, or slightly exceeding, the two loudspeakers. Some aspects of *super stereo* are examined in chapter 12, and the various surround-sound and multidirectional activities are discussed in chapter 13, prompted by the inherent limitations of conventional 2-dimensional stereo.

This provokes the question: "Is there hope for true 3-dimensional sound from two-channel systems—sound that can live up to the original meaning of stereo?" Strong evidence exists to support the belief that all the spatial cues necessary for 3-dimensional stereo can be transmitted via a two-channel system, when properly produced. Manfred Schroeder, an outstanding researcher in the field, stated ". . . because we have only two ears . . . *two* loudspeakers should suffice to evoke all the proper perceptions of acoustic space—*provided* the sound waves radiated from the two loudspeakers are 'tailored' in such a way as to produce, at the listener's eardrums, pressure waves indistinguishable from those that the ears would have received in a free field set up by the desired sources (including sources to the rear, overhead, and to the extreme sides)." (See Reference 5-1.)

Tailoring sounds properly is most certainly a difficult task, but encouraging signs exist today. One approach is to record the sound for the two channels directly at the eardrums of a real or simulated human head. Another possibility is offered by special, electronic processing during either recording or later in the reproduction of the distributed medium.

At first, the thought of using just two microphones to pick up all the signal nuances necessary to evoke, on playback, all the proper perceptions of 3-dimensional space, including sounds from the rear half of the listener's hemisphere seems incomprehensible. Admittedly, the task is not easy. The secret is in preserving the original transfer function shapes (chapter 3), or using processing to simulate them (chapter 6). Schroeder called this "a kind of super stereo," but until many technical heights are scaled, the embellishments of conventional stereo cannot be improved.

6

Binaural recording and reproduction

THE BINAURAL SYSTEM REQUIRES THE TRANSFER FUNCTIONS REPRODUCED at the listener's eardrums, such as sound pressure amplitude and timing variations with frequency, to be identical to those that the sound sources would produce at a listener's eardrums at the point of pickup. Achieving this ideal—the faithful transduction and transmission of these transfer functions, from all sound sources to the eardrums of the listener—is an intrinsically complex problem that becomes easier to understand when broken down into basic elements.

A transfer function could be represented as a graph of the sound pressure amplitude and timing variations with frequency constantly changing in time. Because speech and music are primarily transient sounds, any view of transfer functions must be a momentary snapshot.

The transfer functions associated only with the source are illustrated in Fig. 6-1. The violin sound is characterized by a certain timbre, or spectrum, that can be represented by a graph illustrating its sound pressure and timing variations plotted against frequency. This transfer function is altered as it travels the direct path to the listener. For example, it is reduced in amplitude by inverse-square divergence—the farther it goes the weaker it gets. If the distance is great, the higher frequency components of the sound could be further decreased significantly by absorption in the air. Altered somewhat by these transmission factors, the direct sound strikes the ear of the listener.

The violin sound also strikes the ear of the listener through reflections from the ceiling, the rear and side walls, and many other surfaces. Each of these reflected components must be represented by its own discrete transfer function altered in specific ways by divergence, reflection losses, etc. Describing just the sound from a single instrument, the violin, requires many transfer functions, making up many discrete components of sound falling on the listener's ear. Multiplying this by a hundred instruments in the symphony orchestra, each with its distinctive timbre and complex room reflection pattern, and then multiplying again by two—

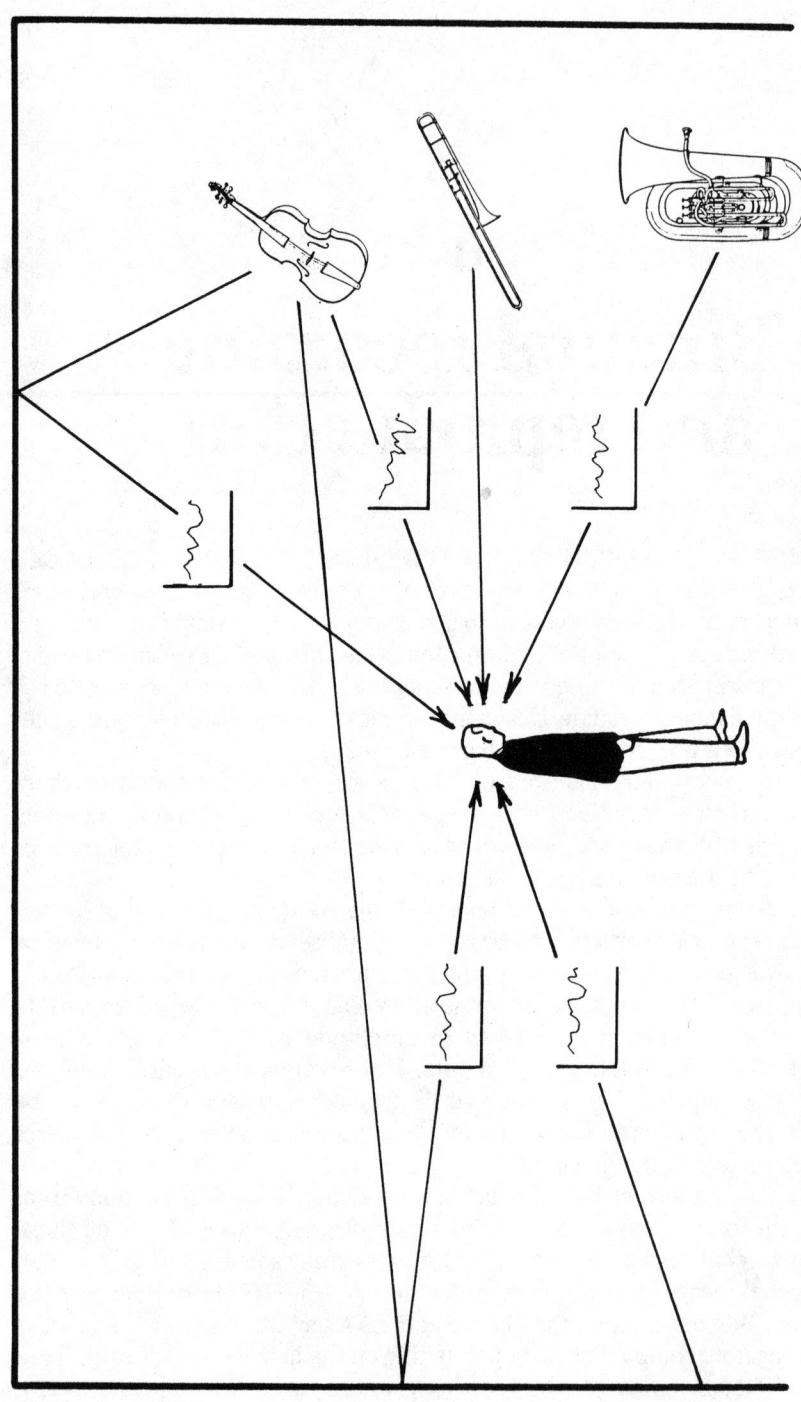

6-1   A transfer function representing a specific source of sound is significantly altered by the medium and by reflections as it travels to the listener. Such transfer functions are subjected to further changes as they are directionally encoded by head diffraction, pinna reflections, etc. The resonances of the auditory canal, a fixed entity, also affect the shape of the encoded transfer functions at the eardrum but the brain is able to *see through* the fixed effect and concentrate on the important directional cues.

because all these transfer functions are similarly applied to both ears—places a tremendous burden on the human ear/brain mechanism to elicit an intelligible sonic experience.

The interrelationship of the various transfer functions is outlined in Fig. 6-2. The transfer function of each element of the complex source is subjected to transmission effects that vary with distance traveled, reflection losses that vary with the angle of incidence, and other similar factors.

The sound components represented by the host of transfer functions strike the ears of the listener (Fig. 6-2). Each one strikes the left pinna, for example, at a different angle and enters the opening of the ear canal. Here reflected and direct components interact and concha resonances are stimulated. Sound rays are also reflected from the shoulders and torso of the listener and are refracted around the head, which acts as an obstacle to the sound. All of these direct, reflected, and diffracted components are combined at the opening of the ear canal.

The concha is the entrance to the ear canal (see Fig. 3-1). Both the concha and the ear canal exhibit resonances. The ear canal transfer function remains fixed, stamping its signature on all the variable directional cues from the pinna to the eardrum. If the microphones of the dummy head are placed at the entrance to the ear canal, its binaural signals would include all the transfer functions of the pinna and concha. These transfer functions change with source direction, but have only the listener's ear canal transfer function to traverse.

All of the transfer functions considered so far vary with angle of incidence on reflecting walls, ceiling, etc. The transfer functions also vary with angle of incidence on pinna, concha, shoulder, torso, and head. All are combined at the entrance to the ear canal.

One transfer function that does not change with angle is that of the ear canal. The ear canal of each ear acts as an acoustic transmission line of fixed characteristics, terminated by the eardrum. The transfer function of this ear canal (see Fig. 3-18) is imposed upon every other transfer function traveling through it (see Fig. 3-19). The air pressure and timing variations actuating the eardrums are the composites of all the many transfer functions of the outside world, plus those of the ear canal itself.

These transfer functions are just the external, airborne, physical stimuli acting on the eardrums of the listener. The mechanical action of the bones of the middle ear carries the delicate vibrations to the fluid of the inner ear where they are changed to electrical impulses. The auditory nerve carries the impulses to the brain where the perception of the acoustic event is formed.

In spite of all the changes in timbre induced by directional encoding, the violin sounds like a violin whether it is near or far, directly in front of, to the extreme left or right of, or even behind the listener. Blindfolded, the listener can easily identify the sound as that of a violin and tell accurately where the violin is located.

Requirements of the dummy head

By the time the transfer function representing the direct sound of the violin reaches the eardrum of the listener, it is encoded to carry two types of information:

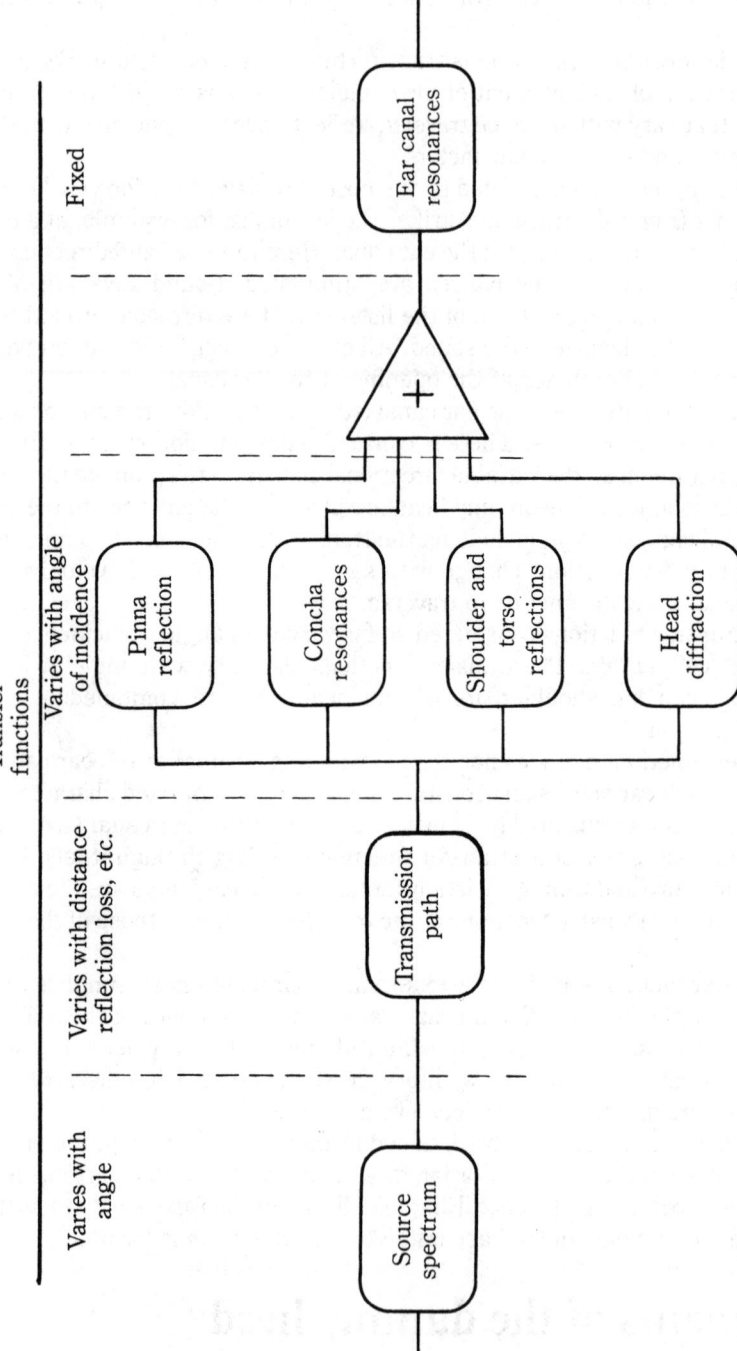

6-2   Each sound source has a spectrum (frequency response or transfer function) that is a function of direction. The sound waves of this source spectrum traveling toward the listener, or microphone are decreased in intensity by spherical divergence and are changed at each reflection depending upon the characteristics of the reflecting surface. As the source transfer functions altered by transmission effects reach the listener, they are directionally encoded by reflections from the pinna, shoulders, and torso, and by diffraction around the listener's head. The shape of the encoded transfer functions is further changed by resonances in concha and ear canal. The brain seems to neglect the fixed ear canal effects, giving directional percepts on the basis of the complex sound pressure changes at the eardrum.

the inherent spectrum of the violin sound itself, and the directional encoding of the spectral shape by reflection and diffraction of the sound by the listener's body. The faithful recording system must record both of these components accurately and artificially. In a binaural system, recording the spectral shape faithfully is achieved with an anthropomorphic manikin using microphones set into each ear with the microphone diaphragm at the eardrum position, or preferably, at the entrance to the ear canal.

Recording with the microphone diaphragm at the entrance to the ear canal relies on the listener's ear canal to complete the transmission path. Care must be exercised to avoid passing the sound through the ear canals twice—once in the dummy head and a second time in the ear of the listener. Reflections from the head, shoulders, and torso of the manikin must emulate those from a human body. The dimensions and surface-reflection characteristics therefore must be adjusted to those of an average human.

Directional encoding of the sound picked up by the microphones in the dummy head results from:

- Pinna reflections
- Concha resonances
- Shoulder reflections
- Torso reflections
- Diffraction around the head

The effect of each of these is a function of the angle of sound arrival, and serves as the agents of the spectrum alterations of the sound. In other words, the shape of the transfer function of the violin is altered to include the directional cues.

Dummy head recording

In chapter 1 the word *stereo* implies the existence of three dimensions. Conventional stereo produces sound images confined largely to the horizontal plane. Binaural systems, however, eventually promise full 3-dimensional sound.

The pickup of binaural recording (Fig. 1-1B) is a pair of microphones embedded in the ears of a dummy head to simulate the ears of the human head. The output of the left microphone is amplified (Fig. 6-3) and applied to the left earphone as the right microphone output is amplified and applied to the right earphone. This process virtually transports the listener's ears to the position of the dummy head. Full effects can be faithfully reproduced and the naturalness of binaural sound images is startling.

The accuracy of the head simulation determines the ultimate accuracy of the spatial image. If the eardrums of the listener are actuated by pressure and timing variations from the headphones identical to those that would actuate the listener's eardrums if in the exact position of the dummy head, perfect reproduction of the sound source and the surrounding environment would result.

Binaural reproduction by headphones

Headphones are commonly used for stereo and binaural reproduction with personal, portable radios, and cassette or compact disc players. Unfortunately, the availability of true binaural recordings is limited, so conventional stereo recordings dominate this form of listening. This popular form of headphone listening, well suited for binaural recordings, ironically is used almost exclusively with stereo recordings. Spatial distortion results when stereo recordings made expressly for loudspeaker reproduction are heard through headphones.

Listening to binaural recordings with headphones has many advantages (Fig. 6-3). Sounds picked up by the left microphone of the dummy head are transmitted solely to the left earphone of the listener. Sounds picked up by the right microphone are transmitted solely to the right earphone. Any sound the right microphone picks up from a source on the left is simply the sound that the right ear would normally hear. Everything is natural and normal, and no artifacts of crosstalk or interference are introduced.

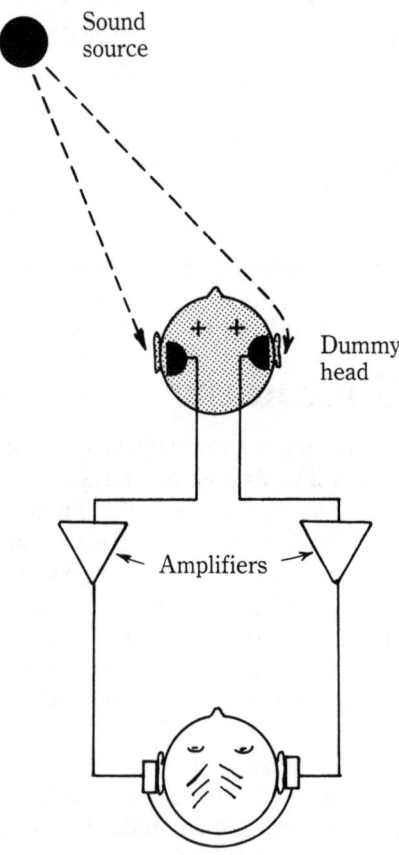

6-3   The pickup for binaural recording is a pair of microphones mounted near the concha position in the pinnae of a dummy head. Sounds picked up by these microphones are directionally encoded by the pinna reflections and head diffraction of the dummy head. The pickup by left and right microphones, amplified and reproduced by earphones, give the perception that the listener's ears are actually at the location of the dummy head microphones.

Binaural reproduction by loudspeakers

Earphones guarantee the left-right integrity of the sounds presented to the ears. In Fig. 6-4 an entirely different situation prevails. The left and right loudspeakers are not coupled directly to the left and right ears of the listener. The width of the radiation pattern of the loudspeakers and the directional properties of the pinnae result in both a desired and an undesired component of sound heard by each ear. A sound source to the left of the dummy head, for example, sends a spurious component to

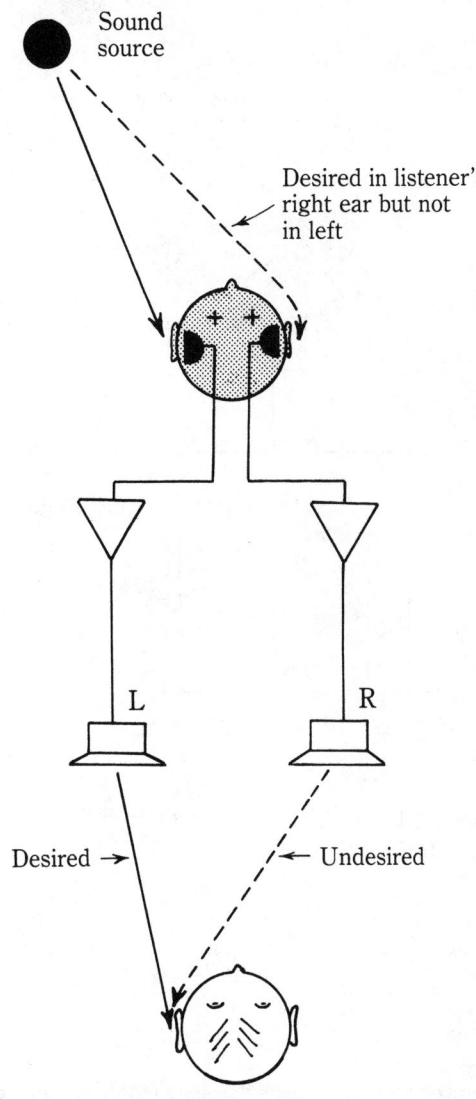

6-4 Binaural signals reproduced by loudspeakers are distorted by crosstalk. An example of crosstalk is the undesired signal to the left ear from the right loudspeaker. The effects of this crosstalk can be electronically cancelled.

the left ear of the listener via the right loudspeaker, which is not strictly part of left-channel sound (Fig. 6-4). In Fig. 6-5 a sound source to the right of the dummy head sends a spurious component to the right ear, which is not rightfully a part of the right-channel sound.

If loudspeakers are used to reproduce dummy-head binaural signals, the left ear of the listener hears an unwanted component from the right loudspeaker and

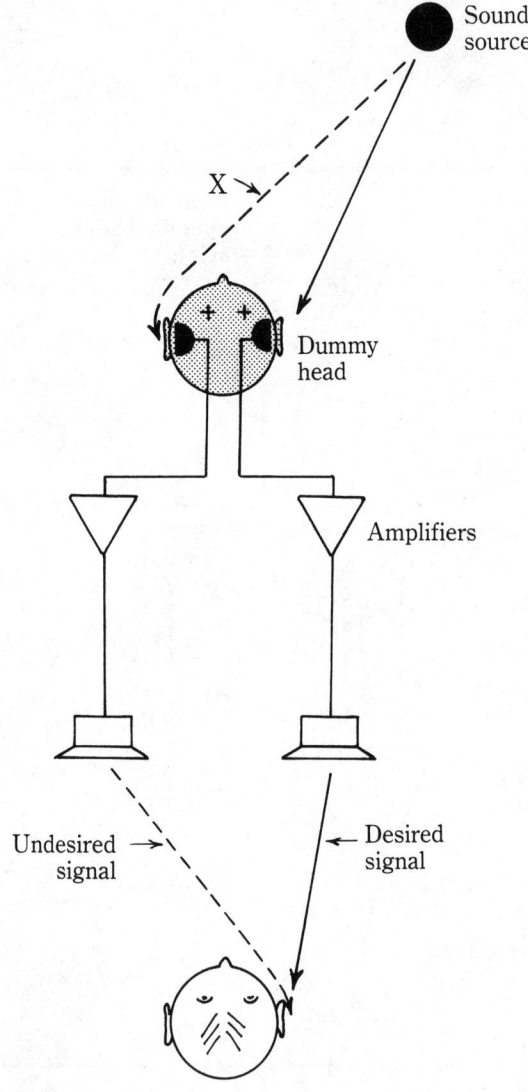

6-5   Binaural signals reproduced by loudspeakers are distorted: for example, the undesired signal from the left loudspeaker to the right ear. These reproduced crosstalk effects should not be confused with the desired signal X picked up by the left ear of the dummy head intended for the left ear of the subject.

the right ear hears an undesired sound from the left loudspeaker. This *crosstalk* devastates loudspeaker reproduction of binaural sound from a basic dummy head pickup system as both imaging and frequency response are degraded.

This loudspeaker crosstalk should not be confused with the far-ear pickup of the dummy head (see *X* in Fig. 6-5). In human listening, both ears are involved in the perception of sound from any direction. The far-ear pickup of a dummy head is conducted to the corresponding far-ear earphone as in human hearing. A crosstalk problem occurs only when the loudspeakers *leak* spurious information to both ears.

Avoiding crosstalk with headphones

Because the use of headphones obviously eliminates crosstalk, why has the use of headphones for high-fidelity binaural listening been so limited? Many reasons other than the quality of reproduction and inconvenience limit the binaural system. Headphones of high quality are available but expensive, and headphone cords restrict the freedom of movement. Also, the perceived image is usually jammed into the space between the two earphones, an image inside the head instead of a wide, spacious, and external sound stage. This effect is the result of standing waves and resonances set up between the eardrum and the membrane of the earphone and in the irregular cavities between the earphone and the pinna. Such standing waves and resonances alter the shape of the composite transfer function destroying the open, free-field perception (Figs. 3-18 and 3-19). The listener is unable to associate an external location to the sound, and the only remaining location is inside the head resulting in the *musical hat* effect.

Avoiding crosstalk with a barrier

Binaurally recorded material could be played through normal stereo loudspeakers with full binaural spatial effects if crosstalk were eliminated. Crosstalk problems can be treated in other ways besides headphones. The simplest, most graphic, and perhaps the most awkward way is the use of a solid barrier shown in Fig. 6-6. Bock and Keele used such a device in their research on the effect of crosstalk on stereo reproduction (Reference 6-1). Small monitoring loudspeakers, placed so the high-frequency radiators are closest to the plywood barrier, minimize the effect of reflections off the barrier. Such a setup eliminates crosstalk for listening to binaural, dummy-head material on loudspeakers but promises little for general application.

Cancellation of crosstalk electronically

Cancellation of crosstalk with electronic circuits was first proposed by Atal and Schroeder (References 6-2, 6-3). In conventional two-loudspeaker stereo, the image of the sound sources is usually restricted to the space between the two loudspeakers. Images overhead, to the rear, and extreme sides are not accurately positioned. Schroeder said two loudspeakers *should* be sufficient to reproduce sounds from any direction, though (see Reference 5-1). The electronic approach described

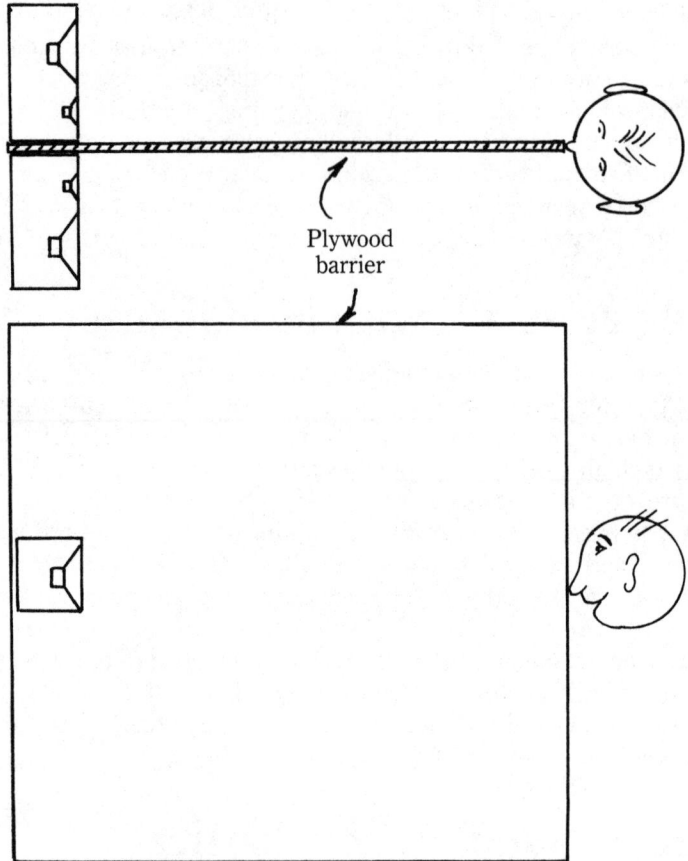

6-6 One effective but impractical way to eliminate crosstalk in listening to binaural signals with loudspeakers is the use of a plywood barrier.

by Atal and Schroeder was tested and the results were encouraging. The resources of a mainframe computer were required to perform the test, however, which limits application of the basic idea.

Bauer, Damaske and others have attempted to solve the crosstalk cancellation problem with simple filter circuits (Fig. 6-7, References 6-4, 6-5). Applying these simple circuits to the improvement of the stereophonic image and to transaural listening has yielded some success; however, true 3-dimensional stereo has remained ephemeral until recent years.

The promise of *super-stereo* electronics

Complexities of the overall listening process might seem to make the goal of a two-loudspeaker, 3-dimensional binaural system unattainable. That goal has not been attained, but systems approaching it exist and improvements keep coming.

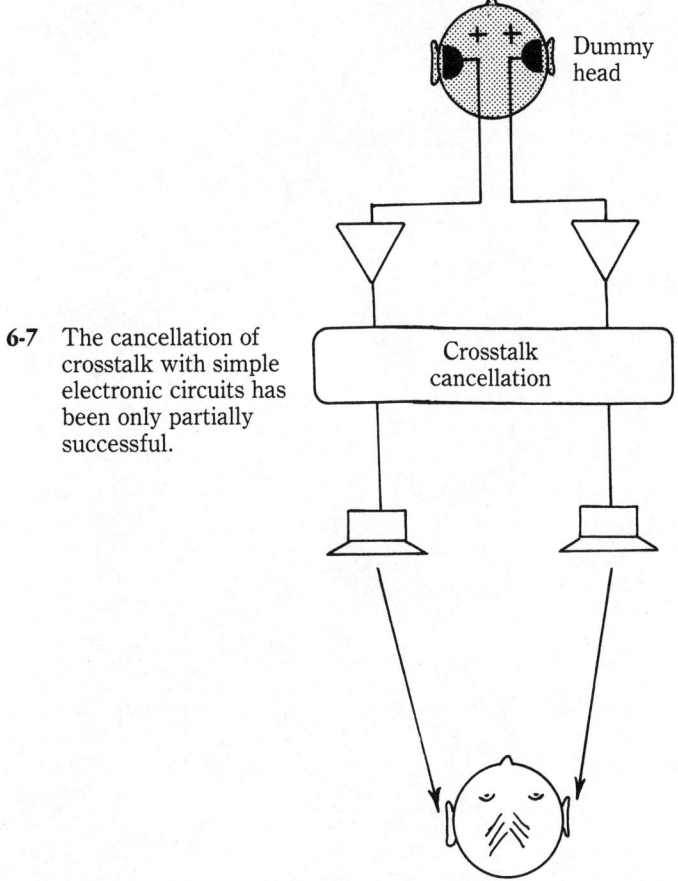

Dummy head

6-7 The cancellation of crosstalk with simple electronic circuits has been only partially successful.

Crosstalk cancellation

Atal and Schroeder mathematically calculated and specified the full requirements necessary for the system in their visionary patent filed in 1962 and issued in 1966 (References 6-2, 6-3). In a simplified form, their scheme was to introduce transfer functions between the binaural head and the loudspeaker reproduction, shaped in amplitude and timing so the crosstalk signals are canceled (Fig. 6-7). This scheme is shown schematically in Fig. 6-8. Every element in this schematic is calculated from only two experimentally determined transfer functions: function X, between the loudspeaker and the listener's far ear, and function Y, between the loudspeaker and the listener's near ear. These X and Y complex transfer functions (amplitude and timing as functions of frequency) are measured between a loudspeaker in an anechoic or dead room and the right and left eardrums of a human listener. All of the complex transfer functions represented by boxes A and B in Fig. 6-8 are calculated from the X and Y pair.

One complicating factor is that the crosstalk canceling signal also *talks-across* to the other ear and must be canceled. This new canceling signal crosses back to the original ear, and so on.

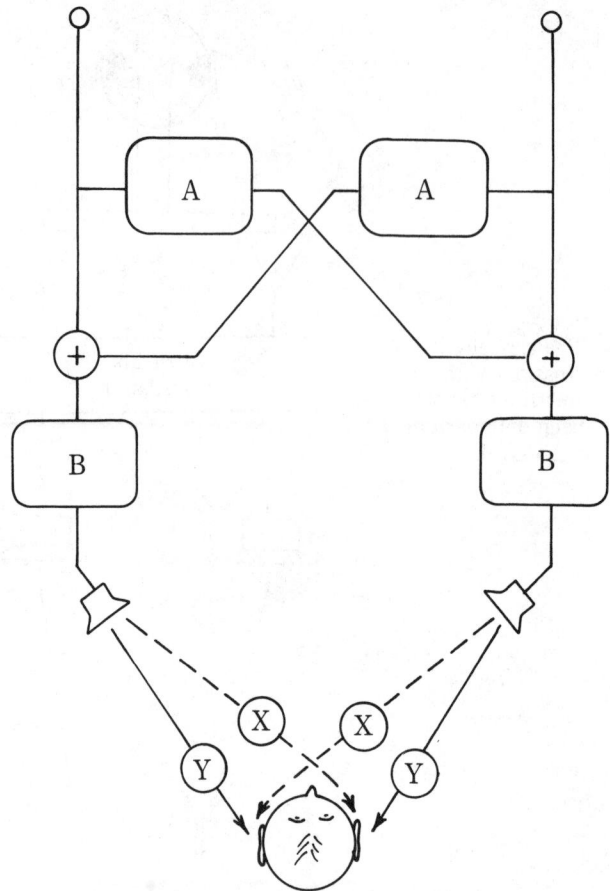

6-8   Faithful reproduction of binaural head signals by loudspeakers has been mathematically defined by Atal and Schroeder. The *A* and *B* elements of their circuit can be obtained from complex transfer functions *X* and *Y* measured between the loudspeaker and the listener's ear in an anechoic chamber.

Atal and Schroeder first implemented this scheme in a powerful, mainframe computer, performing finite impulse response filtering for the cancellation of crosstalk. The results demonstrated the accuracy of the basic mathematical model.

Cooper and Bauck demonstrated that the use of minimum-phase filters in *shuffler* formation can simplify the realization of the crosstalk-canceling filters (Reference 6-6). Developments like this should hasten the application of the Atal-Schroeder crosstalk-canceling scheme for consumer equipment.

Dummy head developments

"Every few years binaural recording seems to undergo a renaissance, each time becoming a little better but, each time, eventually falling from fashion," (Toole,

Reference 6-7). This statement accurately appraises past history—whether or not the trend continues remains to be seen. Interest in more faithful recording and reproduction of sound has never been so great, however, especially the spatial fidelity of sound. Steady progress in dummy-head research is occurring. The central position occupied by the dummy head in binaural recording and reproduction requires a glance at the early and later developments in dummy heads.

Informal approaches to dummy heads

Some experimenters, amazed at hearing their first binaural recordings, have struck out on their own with limited resources (Reference 6-8). Aware of the compromises involved, store-window manikin heads of plastic or plaster are often pressed into service. Diffraction around the head might be duplicated reasonably well, but directional cues from the pinnae would be only as accurate as the pinnae contours and surface. In spite of the deficiencies, the sounds recorded from such heads can be remarkably convincing.

Using the experimenter's own head by mounting a small electric condenser microphone at the entrance to each ear canal is far better. Sennheiser supplies a stethoscope-type device that holds the microphones in place (Fig. 6-9). In this way real pinnae and real head factors are recorded with the ear canal transfer function supplied by the listener.

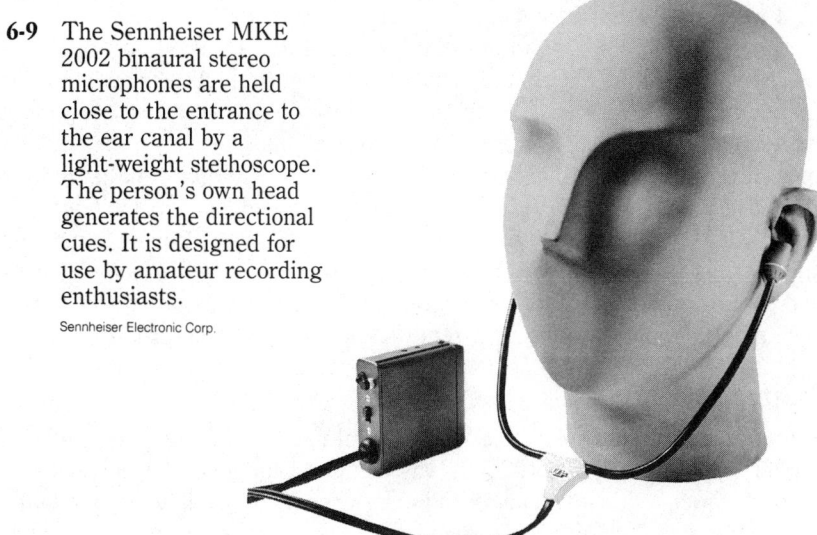

6-9　The Sennheiser MKE 2002 binaural stereo microphones are held close to the entrance to the ear canal by a light-weight stethoscope. The person's own head generates the directional cues. It is designed for use by amateur recording enthusiasts.

Sennheiser Electronic Corp.

The Neumann head

The Neumann artificial head was designed to make head-related binaural recordings of studio quality and has had wide professional usage (Fig. 6-10). The dimensions of the head are equivalent to the dimensions of the human head, with special

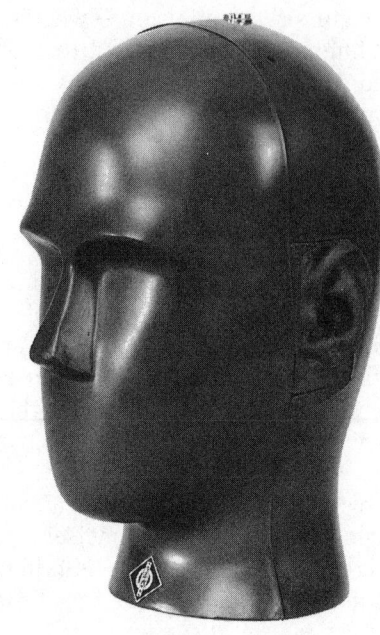

6-10   The Neumann KU 81i artificial head was developed for head-related binaural recording. Particular attention has been given to exact simulation of the pinnae.

Georg Neumann & Co.

attention to the accuracy of the pinnae. The microphone diaphragm is located mid-concha, 4 mm into the ear canal.

The improved model has pinnae that closely imitate the human pinnae. The pinnae are made of a material that also has texture and reflective properties closely matching human tissue. The head is equalized to yield the flattest response in a diffused field, i.e., sound arriving in random directions.

Some differences of opinion have been voiced as to whether equalizing for free-field (sound arriving with no reflections) or diffuse field is the best way to go. Advocates of the latter base their case on subjective evaluation of tonal quality. Normal hearing takes place in diffuse-field conditions, with both direct and reflected sound involved. The whole argument might be specious because the differences are small and variation in listener's hearing might be greater.

The Kemar manikin

The Kemar manikin (Knowles Electronics Manikin for Acoustic Research), shown in Fig. 6-11, appeared around 1975. It was designed for research purposes, especially those associated with hearing aids (Reference 6-9). Head, ear canal, and pinna dimensions and shapes have been carefully matched to the average human head. In addition, the pinnae are easily exchangeable to permit the study of ear size effects. The head is mounted on a torso to emulate torso reflections.

The manikin has a 1/8-inch-thick Plastisol *flesh* over a polyester glass fiber skull, artificial pinnae, and ear canals. The interior of the manikin is coated with 1/4-inch lead-pellet-filled resin to provide mass and reduce coupling of the manikin to acoustic fields. All dimensions are slightly greater than the average human to

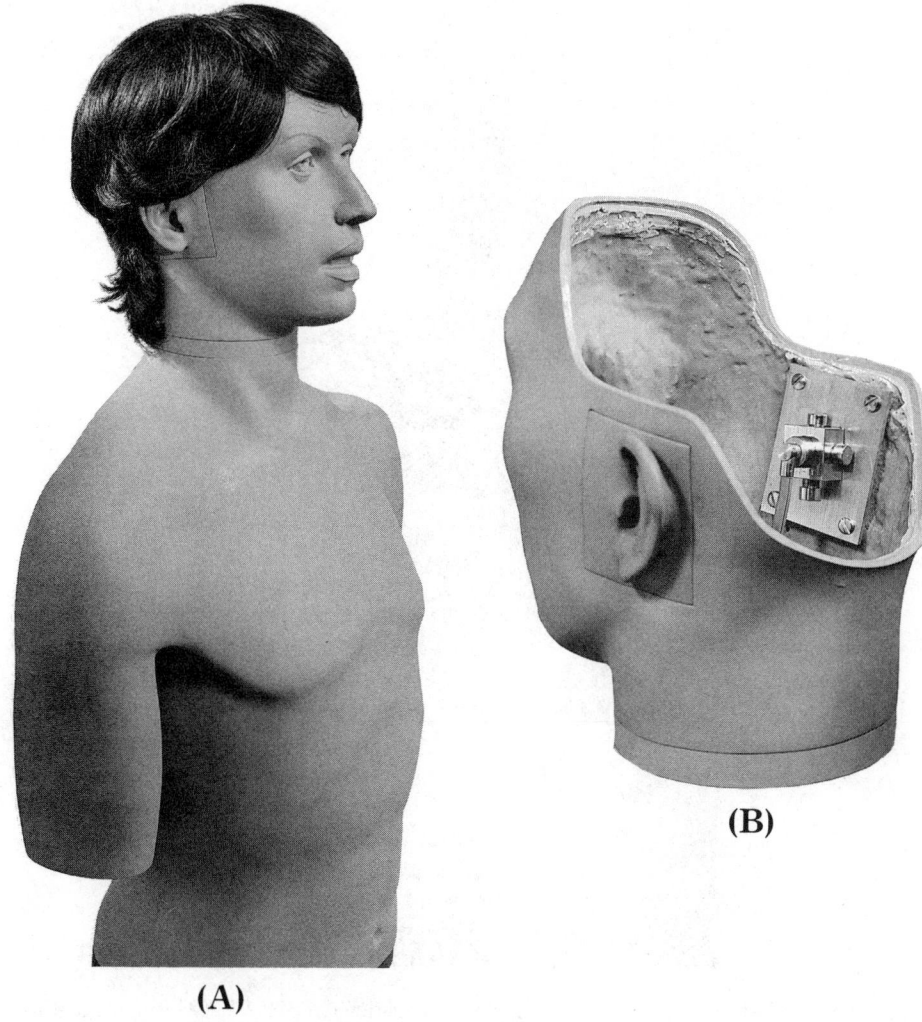

(A)

(B)

6-11 The Kemar Manikin was designed for research purposes. It has been used widely in hearing aid studies. The pinnae are exchangeable to study effects of pinna size. The torso supplies torso reflections. <small>Industrial Research Products, Inc., a Knowles Company</small>

match the average dimensions of the original seven astronauts of the NASA Mercury Program, but are within 4% of the average male and female.

The Aachen head

The Aachen head is a product of the latest research and digital modeling techniques, developed by Head Acoustics GMBH of Aachen, Germany, and is one of the most advanced binaural systems extant (Fig. 6-12 and References 6-10 through 6-13). The initial application for the Aachen head was the measurement of vehicle noise, but the system is quite adaptable to recording for loudspeaker playback.

6-12 The Aachen Head, produced by HEAD Acoustics GmbH, West Germany, features full digital signal processing. It is suitable for high-quality binaural recording and its signals can be reproduced by loudspeakers with essentially full binaural effect. A binaural mixing console makes possible the conversion of mono signals into spatial signals that can then be mixed with binaural signals from the head. Sonic Perceptions, Inc.

Head Acoustics also offers an external ear simulator or electronic artificial head. This simulator is an electro-acoustical device capable of transforming any monaural input signal into two head-related ear signals. Signals recorded with conventional microphones can be translated into ear signals of an average test person for playback of any chosen direction. In this way, monaural signals can be processed for mixing with binaural signals. Head Acoustics also developed a mixing console for mixing binaural signals.

The B&K Head and Torso Simulator

The most recent addition to the list of available dummy heads is the Brüel & Kjaer Head and Torso Simulator (Fig. 6-13). Its mathematically-describable surfaces replicate the geometry of a median adult human head and torso. The ear simulator consists of a removable silicone-rubber pinna coupled to an ear canal. A mouth simulator enables the head and torso simulator to speak. This device is designed primarily for testing telephones, headsets, hearing aids, hearing protectors, and the like, and it can be adapted for binaural recording.

A ghostly dummy head

Greisinger reported opposition to the appearance of dummy heads in recording venues (Reference 6-14). The grisly sight of a vaguely anthropomorphic head hanging by a string behind and above the conductor is disconcerting to the musicians, the conductor, and the audience. His firm, Lexicon, built a simplified *Kunstkopfgeist*, or artificial ghost head, with the usual pinnae and microphones mounted on a U-shaped sheet of clear plastic, with an open back, a forehead, but

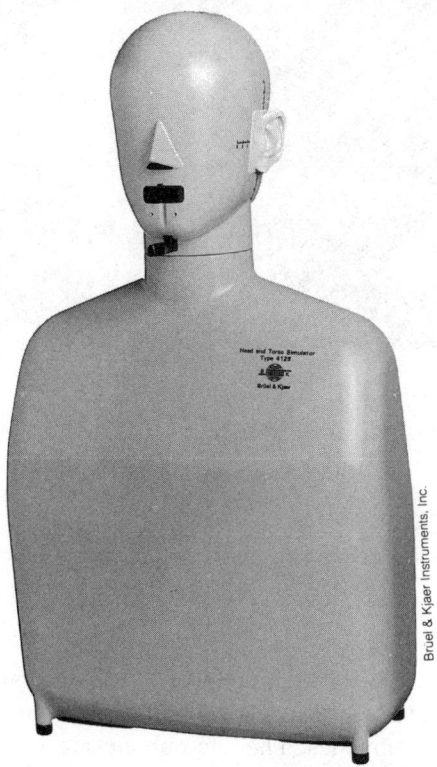

6-13 The Brüel & Kjaer Type 4128 Head and Torso Simulator is designed especially for acoustic and electroacoustic measurements but is also useful for binaural recording.

no chin. In spite of such abbreviations, it localizes vertically as well as the more complete head and has a smooth frontal localization as well.

Quasi-binaural devices

A spherical dummy head was developed in Germany by Gunther Theile, with neither human features nor pinnae. The microphones are mounted flush with the surface of the sphere and are used without special equalization. This highly simplified dummy head gives results surprisingly close to those of the more detailed heads.

Crown International offers a quasi-binaural microphone designated as Stereo Ambient Sampling System (SASS) (Fig. 6-14). This system includes a monocompatible, near-coincident microphone array, available with either the less expensive pressure zone microphones or omnidirectional studio microphones.

6-14 A quasi-binaural device, the Stereo Ambient Sampling System™ (SASS™) is a monocompatible, near-coincident microphone array. U.S. patent 4658931. Crown International

Several spaced-microphones-with-baffle-between have been offered commercially and many others have been assembled by experimenters. Bang and Olufsen at one time offered two figure-eight ribbon microphones with a barrier, while others use pressure microphones. The microphone spacing is approximately 6.5-inches. The barrier is disc-shaped, about 11 inches in diameter with absorbent material applied to both surfaces to minimize the effect of reflections. This barrier could be imagined as a human head with the microphones spaced the distance between human ears. The performance of the spaced microphone with barrier is inferior to dummy heads.

Binaural sound processing

Human ears respond to an infinite number of points on a hemisphere. Dummy heads also respond to sound from all these possible directions as a binaural recording is made. One might ask if it is possible to combine a monaural signal (sound effects, reverberation, accent microphone output, etc.) with a binaural signal as it is recorded with a dummy head. Combining them without binaural processing of the mono signal does not work. Passing the mono signal through an infinite number of ear-related transfer functions representing all the points on the hemisphere is impractical. The practical approach is to determine experimentally the minimum number of directions for the processing of the mono signal that results in a signal that sounds acceptable when mixed with the dummy head binaural signal.

If a mono reverberation signal is mixed with music recorded with a dummy head, the directions in space that dominate 3-dimensional reverberation must be considered. The people that developed the Aachen head found that for simulating a modest-sized hall, reverberation processed for three bands the forward direction (± 15 degrees), from the right (+ 45 to + 90 degrees), from the left (– 45 to – 90 degrees), and vertically in 5-degree steps produces a realistic reverberation when mixed with binaural music. With 2-degree horizontal resolution, the infinite number of possible points on the hemisphere, each with its distinctive outer-ear transfer function, is reduced within the restricted bands to a number that can be handled by digital means. Processing of this general type permits the mixing with the original binaural signal of mono sound effects, mono reverberation, accent microphone signals, etc. It is even possible to synthesize a convincing 3-dimensional binaural signal from a series of monaural recordings.

Marketing of binaural audio

In the search for higher quality recording and reproduction of sound, there is general agreement that Schroeder's *super stereo* idea with its emphasis on head-related transfer functions offers the greatest promise. A flurry of measurements of head-related transfer functions resulted from this general consensus. The availability of probe microphones and time-delay spectrometry has facilitated such measurements of pinnae and ear-canal transfer functions in both academic and corporate laboratories (Fig. 6-15). Measurements on many individuals confirmed significant variations of head-related transfer functions, for comparable directions, from one person to the next. Some have even claimed that ear transfer functions are as unique to the individual as fingerprints.

Such variations of transfer functions among the general public guarantee perceptual variations among individuals listening to the same sounds. This poses problems in marketing binaural devices to consumers. Devices based on transfer functions of the average person must give the proper percepts to individuals having ear transfer functions differing greatly from that average. Another fundamental problem is the conflict between visual and auditory cues such as the apparent movement of the sound source as the head is moved. Imagine the orchestra flying back and forth as one's head is shaken.

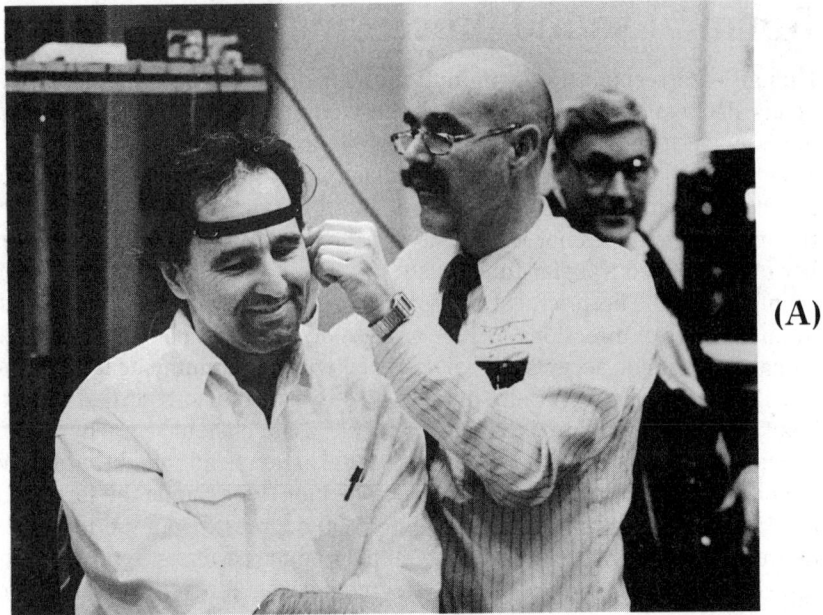

(A)

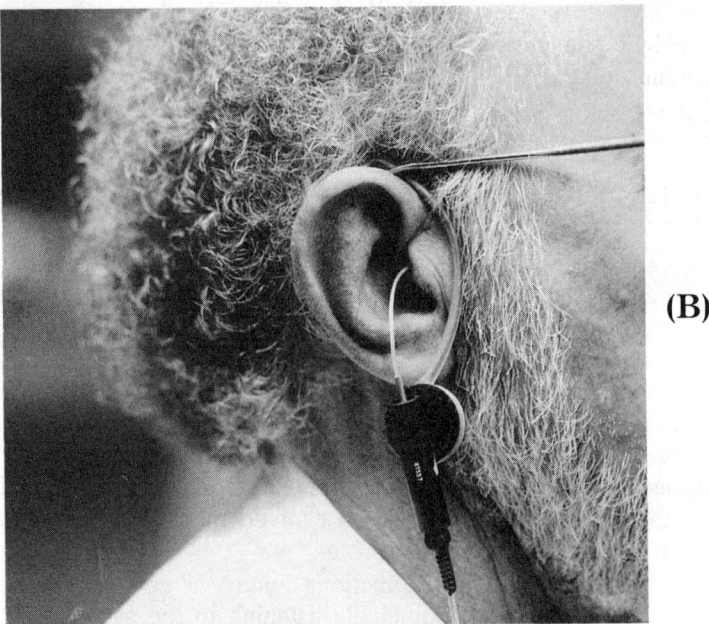

(B)

6-15   (A) Interest in head-related recording at Syn-Aud-Con Seminars has included measurements of ear transfer functions by use of time-delay spectrometry. Dr. Mead Killion of University of Indiana is inserting a probe microphone in Dr. Peter D'Antonio's ear with Don Davis looking on. (B) A probe microphone arranged for measuring the combined pinna transfer function and auditory canal transfer function near the surface of the eardrum. Synergetic Audio Concepts

7

Coincident-microphone techniques

CHAPTER 3 EXAMINED WHY INTERAURAL INCOHERENCE IS IMPORTANT for proper perception of stereo imaging. When considering stereo microphone configurations, however, the term *coherence* has a different connotation. In this context phase coherence results from preserving only intensity cues and excluding any phase, or time of arrival, cues between the two microphones of the stereo pair. To avoid confusion that might result from using these different meanings for the word *coherence*, the term *phase integrity* is used in this chapter.

Intensity stereo

If the microphones of a basic stereo pair are placed as close together as possible—so any differences in the time of arrival of sounds are kept to a minimum—the pickup is called a *coincident pair*. Such a stereo pickup could be configured using two directional microphones, as shown in Fig. 7-1. The microphones are placed one immediately above the other, so their diaphragms are essentially coincident with respect to the horizontal plane. (As discussed in chapter 5, conventional two-channel stereo is concerned only with lateral perspective. Although some minor phase errors will be introduced between the two channels from sound arriving along this vertical displacement, these errors are not significant and could generally be ignored, provided this vertical spacing is kept small.) The microphones are angled symmetrically on either side of the midpoint of the stereo soundstage, so that each microphone emphasizes half, or one side, for example, of the stereo image. Because the acoustical input of the two microphones differs only in intensity, as determined by the direction of arrival of the sound, these coincident microphone techniques often are called *intensity stereo*.

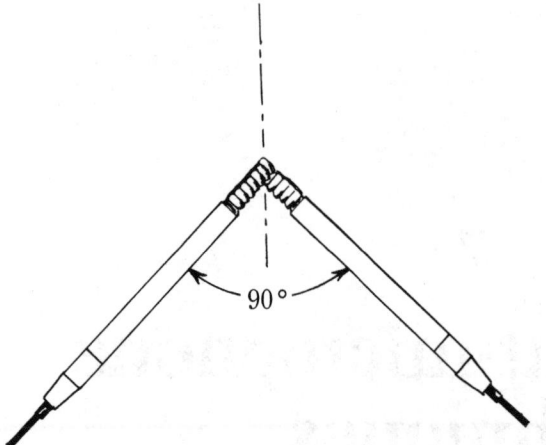

7-1 Arrangement of microphones for a coincident pair, also known as *intensity stereo*. The microphones are crossed, so the right microphone records the left audio channel, and the left microphone records the right audio channel.

Monophonic compatibility

With intensity stereo there are virtually no comb-filtering effects due to phase cancellation if the signals between the two microphones are subsequently combined to produce a monophonic signal (see chapter 8).

Mono compatibility is an important consideration for any program that will be broadcast over radio or television. Since the beginning of stereo media, a concern for *backward* compatibility with monophonic reproduction systems has existed. Music stores in the late 1950s had to stock two different versions of each record: one monophonic and one stereo. Early stereo radio broadcasts were carried via two different stations—one for each channel—until the compatible FM multiplex system currently in use was developed.

Broadcasters still need to maintain monophonic compatibility, because even today the majority of people who listen to radio do so via monophonic sets. Similarly with television audio, the vast majority of receivers only produce mono sound. Despite the proliferation of multiplex movie houses in almost every community, most of the motion picture audiences are still listening to a monophonic sound reproduction system.

Thus, any producer wishing to present a quality-sounding program to the entire audience must pay attention to mono compatibility. Failure to do so results in degradation of the stereo image, the mono timbre, or both.

The choice of the polar pattern, the angle between the principal axes, and the position of the two microphones relative to the sound source determines the character of the stereo image.

The Blumlein technique

The British inventor Alan Blumlein was introduced in chapter 1. Much of today's practice has evolved from his pioneer work in stereo. Blumlein postulated the use

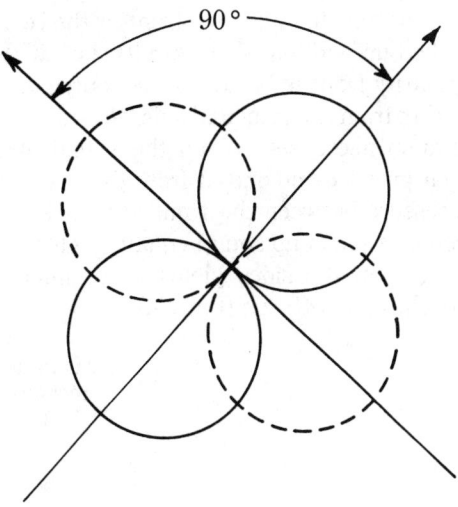

7-2 A Blumlein pair of crossed bidirectional microphones. A 90° angle is required so the principal pickup axis of each microphone is precisely aligned with the null axis of the other.

of two microphones, each having a bidirectional (figure-eight) pattern, angled so their principal axes were at 90° to one another (Fig. 7-2).

Bidirectional microphones

To understand Blumlein's idea, the characteristics of the bidirectional microphone should be examined (Fig. 7-3). Regardless of the electrical method used by the microphone to generate its output, the true bidirectional microphone is, perhaps, the most responsive of all types to the direction of sound wave arrival, because it responds to the pressure gradient on either side of its diaphragm. Sound arriving

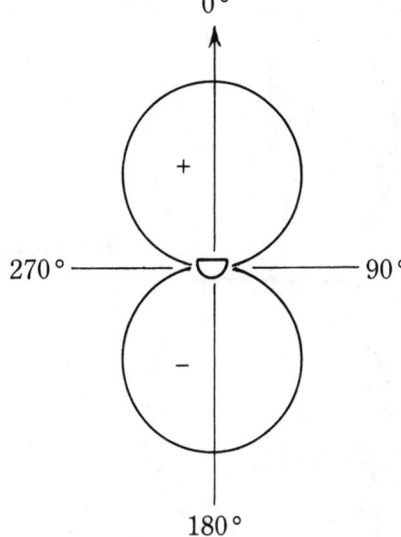

7-3 Polar response diagram of a bidirectional microphone.

directly on-axis to either the front or the rear of the microphones (0° or 180°) will be picked up with equal sensitivity, i.e., with equal magnitude, although of opposite polarity front to back. As the source of sound moves around the microphone, departing from the principal axis, the difference in pressure on the two sides of the diaphragm decreases. When the sound arrives directly from the sides (90° or 270°) it produces no output from the microphone, because no difference exists in the pressure between the front and back of the diaphragm (Fig. 7-4). Thus, the microphone picks up sound equally well from either the front or back, but sound arriving from the sides yields lower microphone output as the point of origin approaches 90° off-axis (Fig. 7-5).

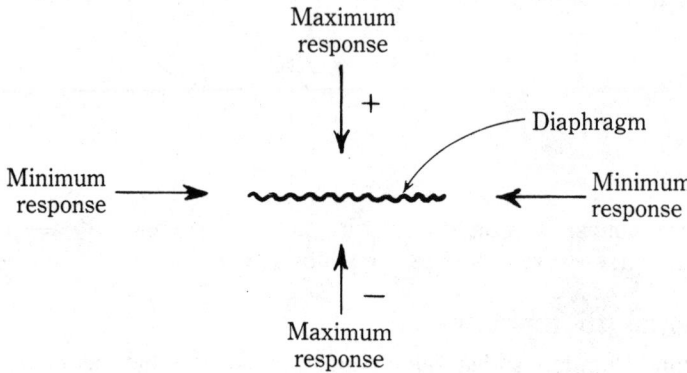

7-4   The bidirectional microphone responds to the pressure gradient (i.e., the difference in pressure) between the front and back of the diaphragm. Maximum output occurs when sound arrives directly from the front or rear of the microphone. Minimum response occurs when sound arrives directly from the sides, because there will be no difference in pressure on the two faces of the diaphragm.

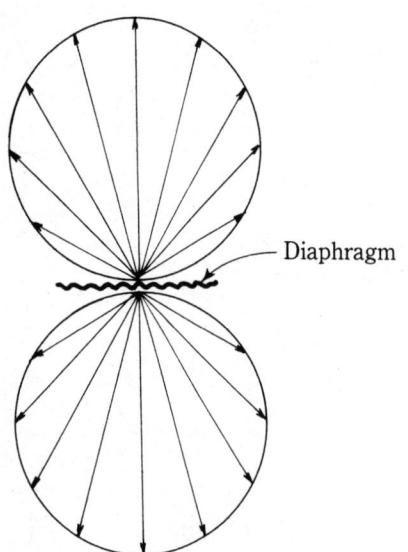

7-5   Output of a bidirectional microphone decreases as the source of sound moves from directly in front or rear around to the sides. The polarity of the front and rear lobes is of equal sensitivity, but opposite polarity.

Absolute polarity

Again, the rear lobe of a bidirectional microphone is of opposite polarity to the front lobe (Fig. 7-3). When a sound pressure wave moves outward from its source, it creates a series of compressions and rarefactions in the air. These series can be considered also as positive and negative pressure waves, relative to a fixed point in space—such as a microphone. (Compressions are positive pressure, and rarefactions are negative pressure.) The bidirectional microphone's electrical output corresponds to these changes in pressure by producing positive and negative electrical signals respectively for signals arriving from the front (0°). Sound waves arriving from the rear (180°) produce electrical signals of equal amplitude, but with opposite polarity. The concept of absolute polarity states that a positive electrical signal is produced by a positive pressure wave, and for a negative pressure wave a negative signal is produced. This concept is true for all other directional polar patterns as well.

Because the movement of air is so minute with sound waves, it is hard to visualize absolute polarity with microphones. An easy experiment can verify this principle using loudspeakers (Fig. 7-6). In the illustration, a flashlight battery is connected through a switch to a loudspeaker. If the positive terminal of the battery is connected to the positive terminal of the loudspeaker, the cone moves outward, creating a positive pressure wave when the switch is closed. Positive pressure results from positive voltage, and absolute polarity is defined. This procedure is a common method for determining the polarity of a loudspeaker and is recommended for verifying the hookup in a stereo playback system.

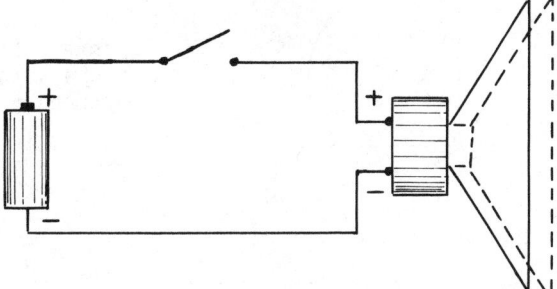

7-6 A simple experiment to observe the effects of absolute polarity: If positive voltage from the battery is applied to the positive terminal of the loudspeaker, the cone will move outward, compressing the air. This is analogous to the situation at the other end of the audio chain, where a compression results in a positive voltage at the positive output terminal of the microphone. The entire audio system should be configured so that absolute polarity is maintained throughout: a compression produces positive voltage, which in turn, ultimately results again in positive air pressure.

Testing the absolute polarity of the other elements in the recording and reproduction chain is more difficult, because inverting amplifier stages could be introduced at any point along the way. Unfortunately, no standards exist for maintaining absolute polarity throughout the signal chain.

The ability to hear the effect of polarity is controversial, and no definitive evidence has been determined yet. Whether or not the audibility of absolute polarity differences is possible, it is nonetheless important to maintain proper polarity throughout the entire audio chain. Careful attention, therefore, should be given to sounds that arrive from the rear quadrant of the bidirectional microphone.

Blumlein stereo

Alan Blumlein conceived the idea of arranging two bidirectional microphones as in Fig. 7-2, so the axis of maximum sensitivity of one was directly aligned with the axis of minimum sensitivity of the other. Thus, optimum pickup of each half of the stereo soundstage could be achieved with maximum separation between the two signals. The left-oriented microphone, for example, is insensitive to sounds coming from the right, and vice versa.

For the moment, ignore the contribution of the rear lobes in the stereo signal, and concentrate only on sounds arriving from the front of the microphones (Fig. 7-7). Sound arriving along the 0° axis of the pair results in an equal response from both microphones, because it is 45° off-axis from each. A phase coherent signal results that ultimately will provide a strong *phantom* center image from the two loudspeakers (refer to chapter 5).

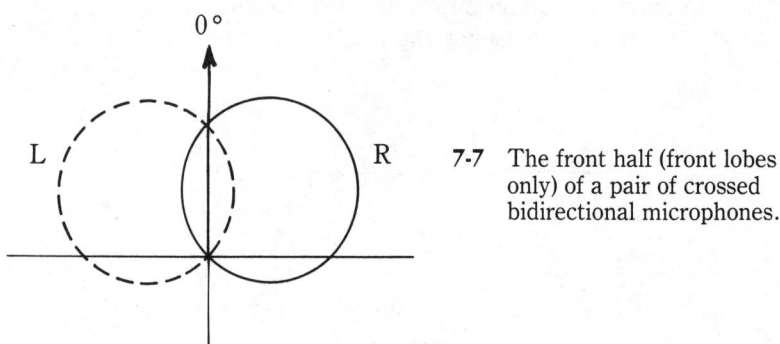

7-7   The front half (front lobes only) of a pair of crossed bidirectional microphones.

As the source of sound moves off-axis from the center toward the right, the output of the right microphone increases, while the output of the left decreases (Fig. 7-8). At a position exactly 45° off-axis from center, the output of the right microphone is at its maximum, while the output of the left microphone is zero, because the sound arrival is now aligned with the null of that microphone. Corresponding output relationships occur for sounds arriving from the left.

Thus, for sound arriving from 45° left to 45° right, the output of the microphone pair varies solely according to the *intensity* differences at the microphones. Voltage differences are generated between the two channels that accurately track the vector differences of the sound-arrival angle. Corresponding signals are conveyed for reproduction by the loudspeakers. In this way, the Blumlein system produces what many consider the most *accurate* representation of the original stereo soundstage for sounds arriving from in front of the stereo pair.

7-8 Sound arriving at the microphones of Fig. 7-7 from an angle of 45° will produce maximum output from the right microphone and minimum output from the left microphone.

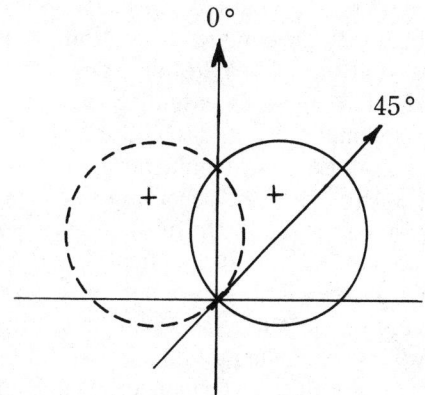

Because sound in a *real* space is not limited to only the front quadrant, however, the effect of the rear lobes of the microphones must be considered. Pickup from the rear quadrant is equal in sensitivity, although it is of opposite polarity to the front. Therefore, this pickup must be examined to determine its contribution to the stereo signal (Fig. 7-9). In most concert situations the rear lobes of a Blumlein pair will be positioned so they respond to sounds from the hall and the audience. Thus, they contribute to the sense of ambience surrounding the primary sound source. The rear lobes are the source of most of the reverberation heard in a recording.

7-9 The rear half (rear lobes only) of a pair of crossed bidirectional microphones. The channel orientation is crossed: the right microphone is output to the left channel, and vice versa.

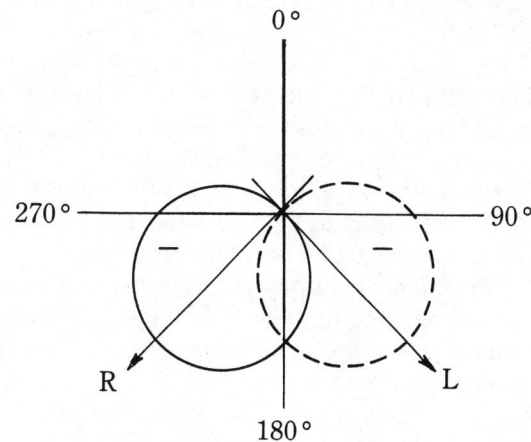

The distinction between ambience and reverberation is subtle, but nonetheless important. Ambience describes the inherent sonic character of a particular environment or space and the sounds that exist in the space as a natural state of its being. Examples include the sound of air conditioning, background noises, and other natural sounds that comprise the general sonic texture. Reverberation is the result of spatial effects on the direct sound source and the numerous reflections that sound makes on its journey around the environment and back to the listener. Together, ambience and reverberation contribute an important element of the *sonic illusion*, and should be carefully considered. Keeping them in proper balance with the principal signal is essential. Too much reverberation makes the recording *muddy* and indistinct, and too little reverberation causes a *dry* or lackluster quality in the sound. Excessive ambience can overpower or distract the listeners' attention from the subject of the recording (for example environmental noises, such as air conditioning systems, traffic, audience sounds, etc.). Proper placement of the microphones is the only practical way to control this relationship. By positioning the microphones so they are within the critical distance from the sound source, a direct-to-reverberant relationship can be maintained. Final critical placement is achieved by experimentation and careful listening.

In a favorable performance space, the contribution of the rear lobes of the Blumlein pair can be appreciated. In an unfavorable environment that produces too much reverberation or excessive noises, however, the results are less pleasing, and another technique for making the recording is recommended.

The contribution of the rear lobes to the stereo perspective will be reversed from the actual left/right forward presentation. The rear lobe of the left microphone aims at the right side of the audience, and vice versa (Fig. 7-2). Although of little significance with ambience or reverberation, this crossing of channels may be of importance when part of the direct sound field (for example, antiphonal choirs or principal action in a radio play) is located to the rear of the stereo pair.

Finally, the soundfield as a whole or at least in the horizontal plane, is important in the Blumlein pickup. Although the principal sound generally comes from the front, much of it is reflected by the walls and ceiling of the performance space back to the sides and rear of the microphones. With large or broad subjects, some of the direct sound source can be picked up from the sides of the microphone pair (Fig. 7-10). With a Blumlein pair, sounds arriving within the side quadrants are picked up by the positive lobe of one microphone and the negative lobe of the other, resulting in an out-of-phase situation between the two channels. This pickup produces ambiguous localization and a hollow sound for the stereo listener, and a *phasey*, disconcerting sound for the mono listener. Unless this condition is desired as a special effect, it should be avoided.

The Blumlein technique, originally proposed in the 1930s, is not the most common microphone technique used today, because it is best suited when both the sound source and the performance spaces are favorable. In reality, however, such ideal conditions are not often present. Recording engineers and producers encounter the common problem of uninteresting or unpleasant acoustics within modern performance spaces. Because the Blumlein technique faithfully reproduces these poor acoustics and blends them into the stereo image, other techniques must be employed to control their influence in the recording.

Other polar patterns

The bidirectional microphone operates on a pressure gradient principle—it responds to *differences* in air pressure on opposite faces of its diaphragm. Another

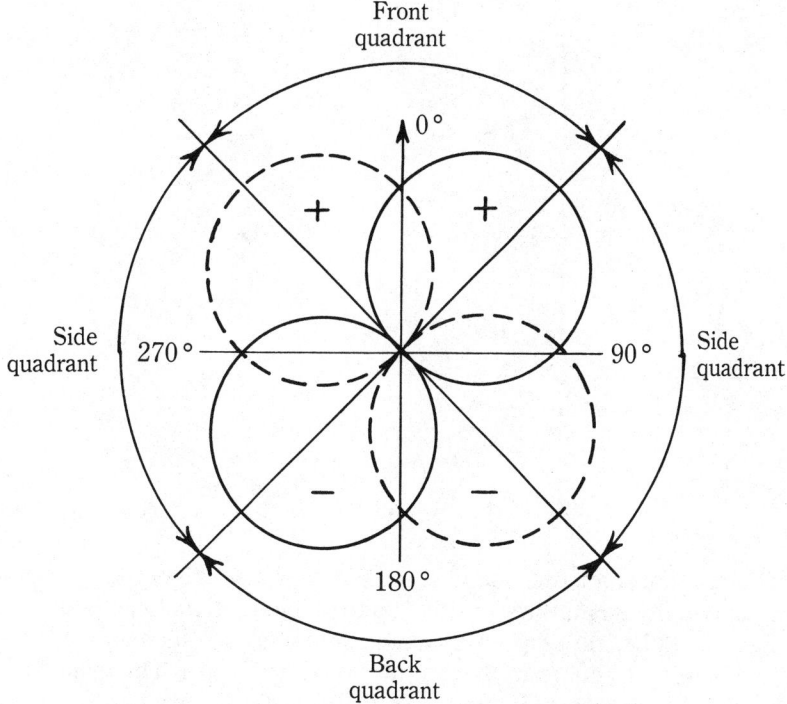

7-10 The overall pickup pattern of a crossed bidirectional (Blumlein) microphone pair. The front and back quadrants are in-phase between the two stereo channels, but the two side quadrants are out-of-phase between the two channels, because the positive lobe of one microphone interacts with the negative lobe of the other.

fundamental type of microphone, the *pressure pickup*, has a diaphragm that vibrates in response to the actual fluctuations of air pressure, which make up sound waves. These minute fluctuations are superimposed on the relatively great static atmospheric pressure prevailing at the time. The pressure microphone responds only to these changes in absolute pressure associated with the sound wave, resulting in a nondirectional pickup. This type of microphone is *omnidirectional*.

Any polar response is dependent on the wavelength of the sound relative to the size and shape of the microphone. In general, all microphones tend to become more directional at higher frequencies and less directional at lower frequencies. How accurately the microphone maintains its polar response over the entire audio frequency range is an important factor in determining its overall quality.

The most common directional microphone is the *cardioid*. The term *undirectional* is sometimes used, but is misleading because it implies the microphone will respond to sound coming from only one direction.

The polar pattern of the cardioid microphone is shown in Fig. 7-11. Its response is greatest to the front (0°), with reduced response to the sides (90° and 270°), and essentially none from the rear (180°). The first such microphone pattern was achieved by combining the output of an omnidirectional microphone with

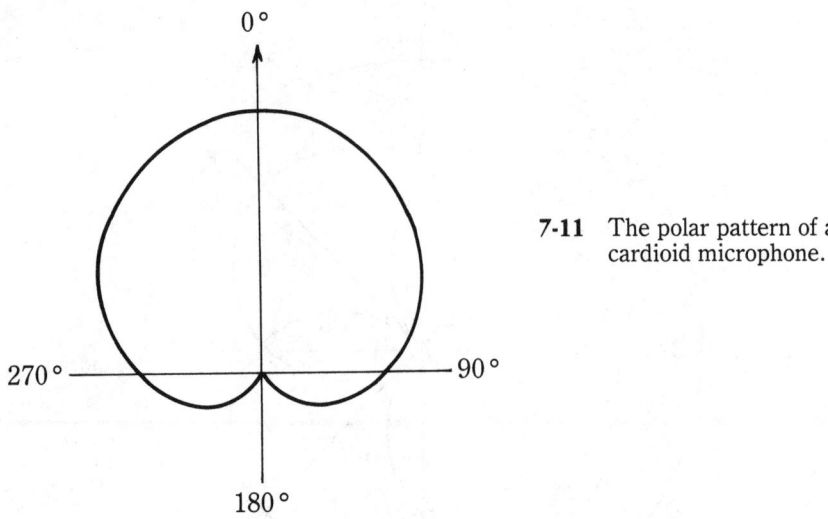

0°

270°   90°

180°

7-11   The polar pattern of a
cardioid microphone.

that of a bidirectional microphone (Fig. 7-12A). Because the output of the omnidirectional microphone is always positive and the bidirectional has both a positive and a negative lobe, the signals combine producing an increase in sensitivity toward the front and a decrease toward the rear (Fig. 7-12B). The result is a heart-shaped pattern, called the cardioid (Fig. 7-12C). With a perfect cardioid the output at 180° would be zero; however, this ideal has never been achieved in the real world. Many good approximations exist, that have become a staple element in the recording engineer's toolkit.

Several variations on the cardioid have been developed, and each has its own particular polar pattern shown in Fig. 7-13. The degree of pickup from the sides and rear can vary greatly from one polar pattern to the next, and each type has its particular applications in sound recordings.

XY stereo techniques

In Fig. 7-1, two directional microphones are arranged as a stereo pickup. This arrangement is sometimes referred to as an *XY* stereo configuration.

When the microphones are cardioids, the response is primarily to the front half of the soundfield (Fig. 7-14). By eliminating the rear lobes of the bidirectional microphones, the pickup of unwanted sound from the rear—ambience, reverberation, a noisy audience, etc.—is greatly reduced. This reduction not only benefits the clarity of the stereo image, but it is crucial for the derived monophonic signal, where excess reverberation or noise easily complicates or confuses the sonic texture.

As with the Blumlein technique of crossed bidirectional patterns, crossed cardioids provide a strong sense of lateral spread across the stereo soundstage. Because this technique also results solely from differences in intensity between the microphones, the two signals have phase integrity—resulting in a highly accurate and stable image for the listener. Because the microphones pick up little from the

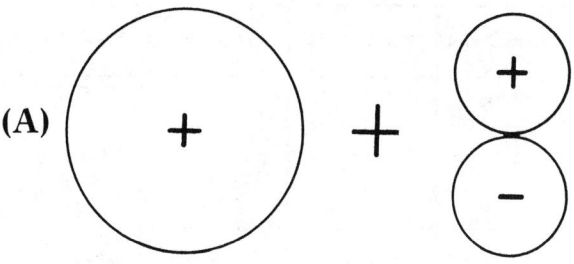

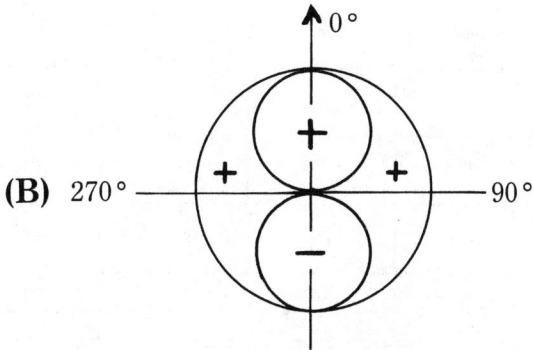

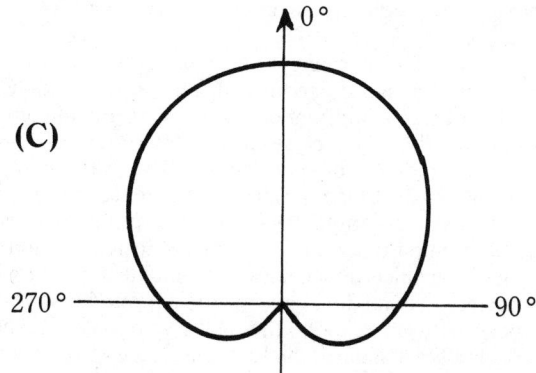

7-12 Derivation of the cardioid microphone by summing an omnidirectional with a bidirectional microphone. (A) An omnidirectional microphone and a bidirectional microphone with equal absolute output signal levels. (B) The effect of superimposing these two patterns on one another. The positive lobe of the bidirectional adds to the positive output of the omnidirectional increasing the total output, while the negative lobe of the bidirectional combines with the omnidirectional to reduce the total output. (C) The resulting polar pattern is a cardioid microphone, with full response at 0°, reducing by about 6 dB at 90° and 270°. In theory, there is no output at 180°; in reality, however, there is some output, but it is greatly reduced.

CHARACTERISTIC	OMNIDIRECTIONAL	BIDIRECTIONAL	CARDIOID	HYPERCARDIOID	SUPER–CARDIOID
POLAR RESPONSE PATTERN					
POLAR EQUATION $F(\theta) \propto$	1	$\cos\theta$	$1/2(1+\cos\theta)$	$1/4(1+3\cos\theta)$	$.37+.63\cos\theta$
PICKUP ARC 3 dB DOWN $(\theta 3)$	360°	90°	131°	105°	115°
PICKUP ARC 6 dB DOWN $(\theta 6)$	360°	120°	180°	141°	156°
RELATIVE OUTPUT AT 90° (dB)	0	$-\infty$	-6	-12	-8.6
RELATIVE OUTPUT AT 180° (dB)	0	0	$-\infty$	-6	-11.7
ANGLE AT WHICH OUTPUT = 0 (θ_0)	—	90°	180°	110°	126°
RANDOM ENERGY EFFICIENCY (RE)	1 0 dB	.333 −4.8 dB	.333 −4.8 dB	.250 ① −6.0 dB	.268 ② −5.7 dB
DISTANCE FACTOR (DSF)	1	1.7	1.7	2	1.9

① MINIMUM RANDOM ENERGY EFFICIENCY FOR A FIRST ORDER CARDIOID
② MAXIMUM FRONT TO TOTAL RANDOM ENERGY EFFICIENCY FOR A FIRST ORDER CARDIOID

7-13 The common first order microphone polar patterns: omnidirectional, bidirectional, cardioid, hypercardioid, and supercardioid. The polar equations given define the specific relationship of the omnidirectional and bidirectional components of each. The general formula for this polar equation is $f(\Theta) = A + B\cos\Theta$, where A and B describe the ratio of the omnidirectional and bidirectional components, and $A + B = 1$. This proves that by appropriate combining of the omnidirectional (scalar) and bidirectional (vector) components, any polar pattern can be achieved. This concept is of primary importance for microphone designers, and is also critical to the understanding of how microphone patterns combine to produce stereophonic images. The two characteristics, random energy efficiency and distance factor, describe how the various polar patterns relate to the total sound environment. Taking the omnidirectional pickup as the standard, the Random Energy Efficiency is a measure of relative sensitivity of that pattern to the reverberant (random energy) field; the Distance Factor tells how much farther from the sound source the pattern can be placed to achieve the same direct-to-reverberant sound ratio as the reference omnidirectional. After Eargle.

rear, they can be located further from the sound source and still maintain a good direct-to-reverberant ratio. This is advantageous when the ensemble is large or sightlines are critical—such as live performances or video presentations.

Although other polar patterns could be used for XY pickups, the most common configuration uses cardioid microphones, angled between 60° and 135°, shown in Fig. 7-14. The angle determines the *width* of the stereo image, and is suggested by the actual width of the soundstage relative to the placement of the microphones. Because the polar pattern of a good cardioid microphone provides uniform frequency response to about 90° off-axis, the resulting stereo image can encompass a broad span.

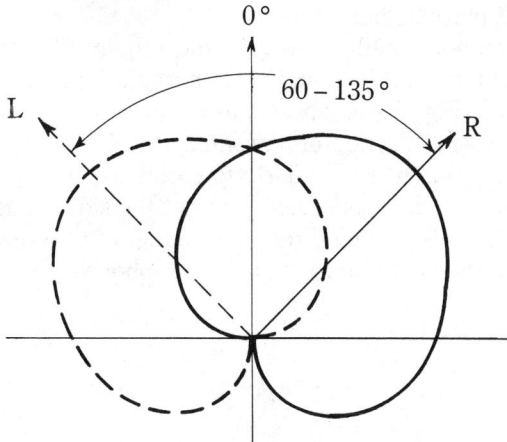

7-14 An *XY Stereo* pair of crossed cardioid microphones. The choice of angle between the two microphones is determined by the size of the sound source and the placement of the microphone pair.

A major benefit of all coincident techniques is that the angular fidelity of the pickup closely matches the original source. Lateral position within the reproduced sound stage is independent of the distance the sound subject is from the microphones, because the intensity differences between the two signals are determined primarily by the polar pattern of the microphones. Thus, a person talking at a position 45° off the centerline will reproduce a sonic image at that angle, whether the speaker is 2 feet or 20 feet away from the microphones.

Matching the microphones

Attention should be given to the polar frequency response of the microphones used to configure an *XY* pair (Fig. 7-14). Because the principle axes of both microphones are aimed away from the main body of the sound stage, the off-axis frequency response of the microphones primarily determines the timbre of the pickup. Any erratic, off-axis response will result in coloration of the sound. This response can be unflattering to the principle sound source, but could prove even more devastating to background or peripheral sounds, such as the reverberation in musical performances, or the environment and sound effects in dramatic productions.

When the subject moves with respect to the microphones, as with dialogue, sound effects, or action scenes, the timbre of the sound changes with position and these changes will be more noticeable to the listener than if the subject is stationary.

The overall response of each microphone in the pair should be matched closely. Because the pickup is heavily dependent on polar response, any differences between the response of the microphones will affect the stability of the pickup. If the left microphone of a stereo pair suffers from reduced high-frequency response, the right channel would favor higher pitched sounds. For example, if a flute were located in the center of an ensemble, its reproduced stereo image would pull to the right as it plays higher up the scale.

If cardioid microphones fail to provide the required pickup due to distant placement problems, a more directional pattern might be used, such as hypercardioid or supercardioid (Fig. 7-15). These can often be used at a greater distance, yet still provide increased rejection of unwanted sound from outside the principal soundstage. They are configured similarly to cardioids, but with a slightly more narrow angle, due to their decreased sensitivity at the sides. Their rear lobes provide some pickup of sounds coming directly from the rear, however, but this is considerably less pickup than with bidirectional microphones.

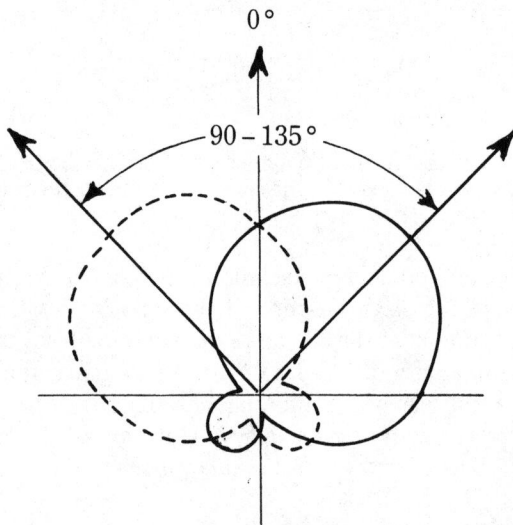

7-15   An *XY Stereo* pair of crossed hypercardioid microphones. The angle between them ranges from 90° to 135°.

The mid/side technique

Alan Blumlein proposed many theories about stereo production, in 1934, but perhaps his most innovative ideas concerned a form of hybrid pickup. It was not until the 1950s, however, that this approach was adapted in a practical way. At the time the Danish State Radio was beginning to experiment with stereo radio programming, a microphone system was needed which would provide good monophonic and stereo signals at the same time. One of their engineers, H. Lauridsen, made use of the new technology in multiple-pattern condenser microphones to configure a high-quality stereo pickup that relied on two different polar patterns. Lauridsen's theory, following Blumlein's earlier ideas, projected that if a single microphone is positioned to provide a proper, well-balanced monophonic pickup, then only the directional information lacking in the mono signal need be added to create a stereophonic image for the listener.

The concept of this ingenious mid/side technique is simple. The *mid* signal is the discrete monophonic pickup provided by a single microphone, aimed with its principal axis aligned with the center of the sound source (Fig. 7-16). Although original experiments used a cardioid microphone (shown in Fig. 7-16), in practice, any polar pattern can be used.

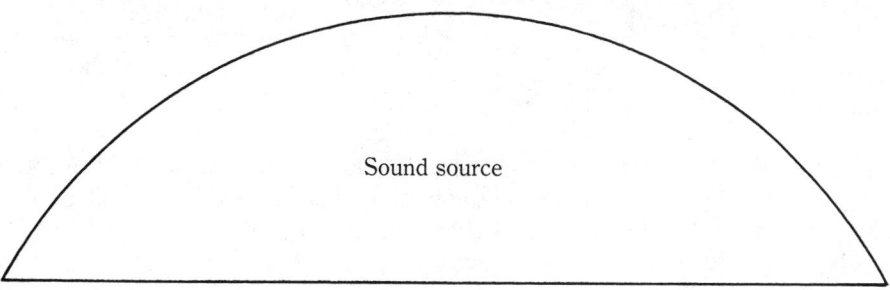

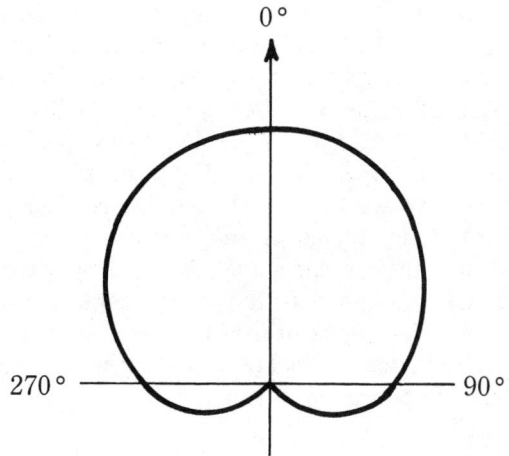

7-16 The mid microphone of a mid/side stereo pickup is aimed directly on-axis to the center of the sound source.

The directional *side* information is provided by a bidirectional microphone aimed laterally so its axis of minimum pickup (90°) is aligned with the principal axis of the mid microphone (Fig. 7-17). The side microphone is positioned vertically coincident with the mid microphone, to reduce any horizontal time-of-arrival differences between the two microphones. Because the two lobes of the side

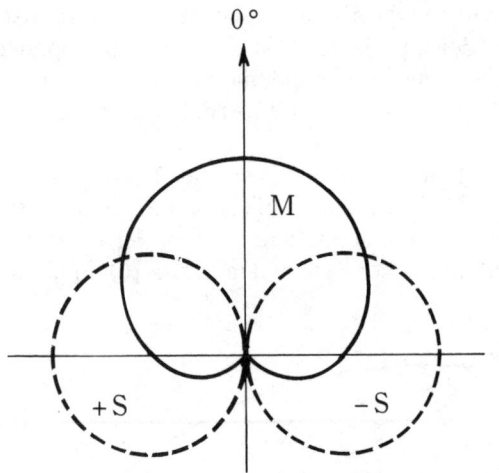

7-17   The basic configuration of a mid/side stereo pickup: the mid microphone is aimed at the 0° axis. The side microphone is a bidirectional, with its null plane aligned with the principal axis of the mid microphone. By convention, the positive lobe of the side microphone is oriented to the left side of the stereo soundstage.

pickup are aimed left and right, and the null is aimed directly toward the sound source, the signal from this microphone contains primarily directional and ambient (or reverberant) information. Little direct sound is included.

These two signals are not yet stereo, however. The stereo signal is accomplished in a special way, using an electronic *matrix* (Fig. 7-18). By combining the signals from the mid and side microphones together, two new signals can be created: *mid + side* and *mid – side*, or $M + S$ and $M - S$ (Fig. 7-19). To make this explanation more clear, an omnidirectional microphone is used as the mid signal in the following discussion. In Fig. 7-12, a cardioid pattern was achieved by combining omnidirectional and bidirectional patterns. This is exactly what happens in the *MS* matrix: the mid and side components are combined to produce a new signal for each stereo channel. Figure 7-19A shows that by *adding* $M + S$, a cardioid signal aimed to the left is produced. (By convention, the positive lobe of the side microphone is generally oriented toward the left side of the stereo soundstage.) In Fig. 7-19B, a right-facing cardioid is created by *subtraction* (i.e., adding with inverted polarity) of the side signal from the mid signal, $M - S$. This results in two signals, one from the cardioid oriented to the left, the other from the cardioid to the right; this is, in fact, a discrete stereo signal. It is important to repeat that the resultant stereo pickup is comprised of two cardioid patterns, derived from the combining of the omnidirectional mid and bidirectional side patterns.

Advantages of the *MS* technique

Why bother with *MS*, when two cardioid microphones can be used? This question is understandable because it does require more effort to accomplish stereo via the mid/side technique, than by conventional XY methods. The extra effort of using the *MS* technique instead of two microphone aimed left and right is rewarded by several advantages.

First, because *any* polar pattern can be used for the mid microphone, an infinite variety of polar patterns can be created for the resulting equivalent XY pair.

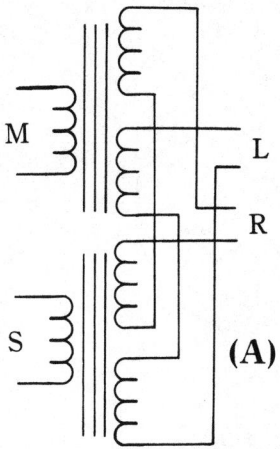

7-18 (A) A simple transformer array to combine the mid and side signals into conventional left (mid plus side) and right (mid minus side) signals. (B) A basic mid/side matrix circuit using active components.

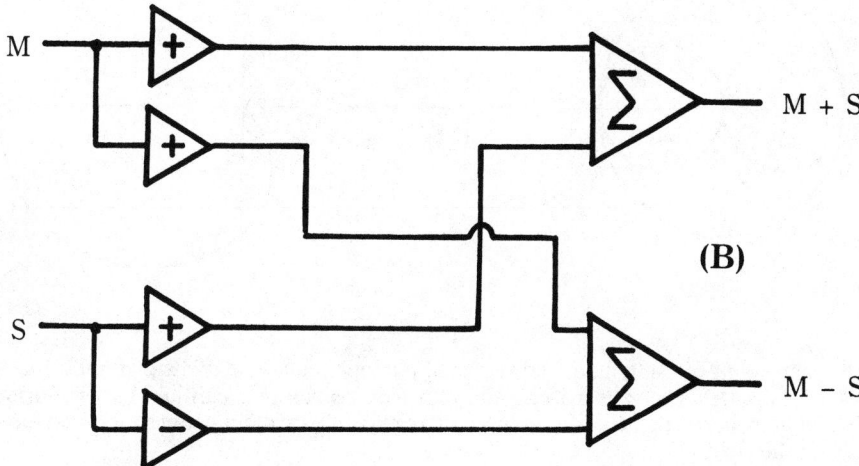

Thus, the choice of polar pattern is not restricted to an omnidirectional microphone or a cardioid (Fig. 7-20). In all cases, however, the side microphone *must* remain a bidirectional

By varying the amount of the *M* and *S* components in the matrix, using a mid/side balance control, the *effective width* of the resulting stereo image can also be changed, (Fig. 7-21). For example, if more mid than side signal is used, the image will be narrow, and if more side than mid signal is used, the image will be broad. Thus, the width of the stereo signal over a wide range can be adjusted fully (Fig. 7-22). At extremes of the balance control, monaural signals result. If the side component is set to zero, the left and right outputs will be identical and in-phase; this is the output of the mid microphone. If the mid component is set to zero, the left and right outputs will be identical, but out-of-phase; this is the output of the side microphone.

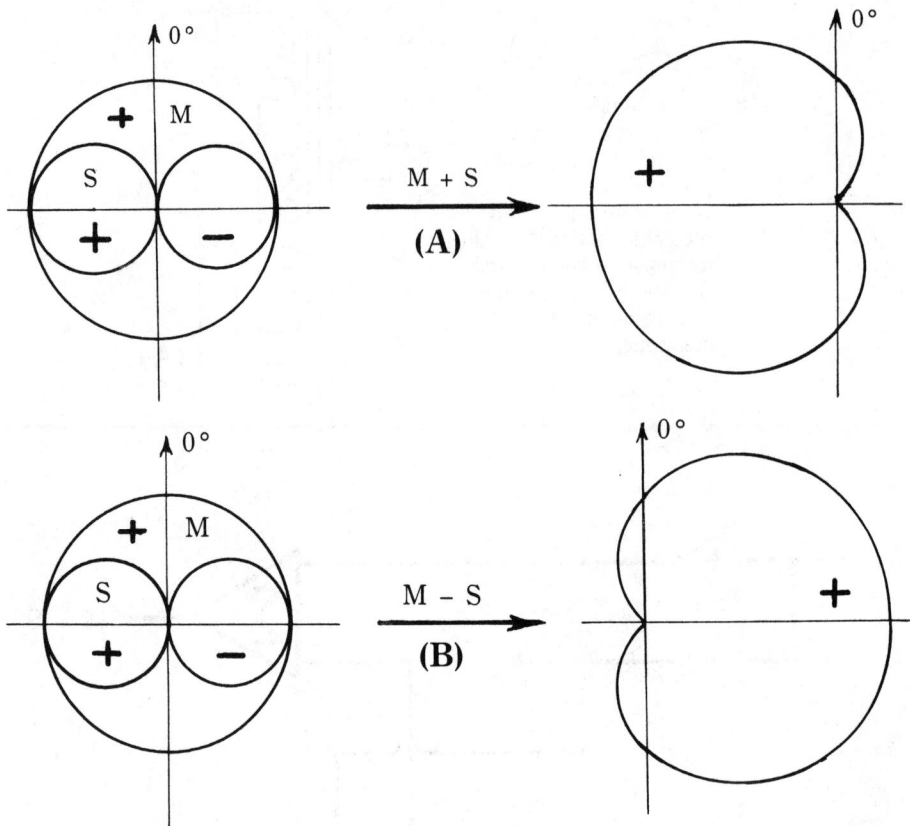

7-19 The result of using an omnidirectional microphone as the mid signal for a mid/side pickup. (A) After the matrix, mid plus side results in a cardioid pattern, oriented directly to the left. (B) Mid minus side results in a cardioid pattern, oriented directly to the right.

Because both the polar pattern of the mid microphone and the effective angle of the resulting XY pair can be varied, the mid/side technique is capable of providing an infinite variety of stereo perspectives (Fig. 7-23, Reference 7-1). An active matrix device for creating these various perspectives is shown in Fig. 7-24.

While the mid/side technique has achieved extreme versatility in the stereo image, it still preserves absolute monophonic integrity. This preservation occurs because when the two stereo signals are combined, only the mid component remains: $(M+S) + (M-S) = 2M$. The contribution of the side microphone is completely eliminated. Therefore MS techniques surpass even the XY techniques in preserving monophonic compatibility—an important consideration for broadcasters. The elimination of the side component automatically reduces the reverberation or ambience in the stereo signal for monophonic listeners, thus also providing the mono signal with increased clarity.

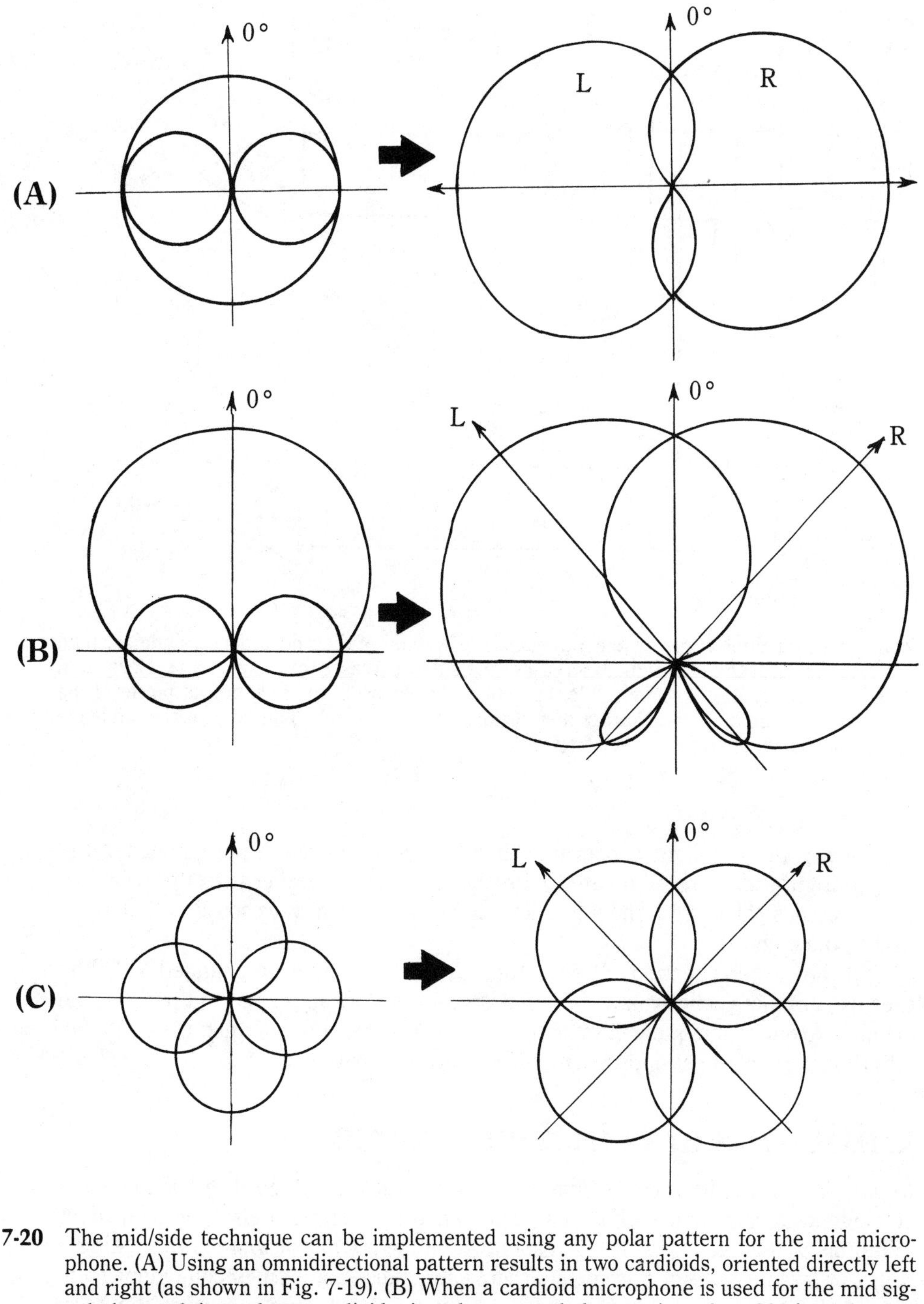

7-20 The mid/side technique can be implemented using any polar pattern for the mid micro-phone. (A) Using an omnidirectional pattern results in two cardioids, oriented directly left and right (as shown in Fig. 7-19). (B) When a cardioid microphone is used for the mid sig-nal, the result is two hypercardioid microphones, angled approximately ±66° from the cen-terline. (C) When a bidirectional microphone serves as the mid signal, the result is a Blumlein pair—crossed bidirectionals at ±45°.

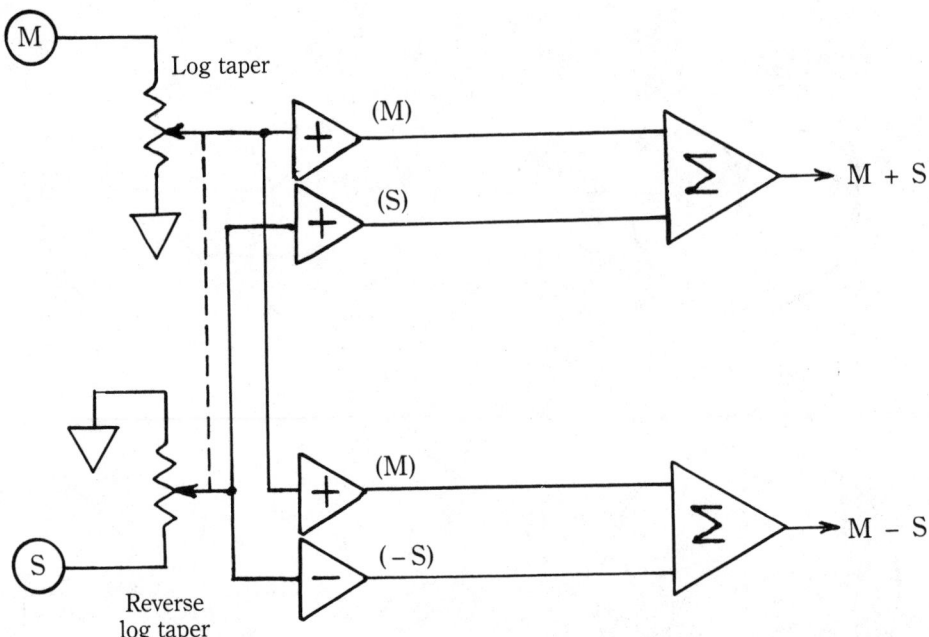

7-21   An adjustable mid/side matrix, where the amount of the mid and side signals can be varied. As the mid signal increases, the side decreases, and vice versa. Because a dual concentric (log/reverse-log) potentiometer is used, the total output power of the matrix remains constant at any setting of the control. This allows the mid/side matrix to function as a stereo width control.

Finally, the problems concerning the off-axis response of microphones in the *XY* configurations are eliminated with the *MS* technique, because the principal pickup comes solely from the mid microphone, which is always set directly *on-axis* to the sound source.

So the earlier question "Why bother with *MS*?" might be changed to "Why ever use anything other than *MS*?" This is a matter for engineer and producer to decide. No one technique will work for every situation, and circumstances will dictate the approach most appropriate for any given situation.

Criticisms of coincident stereo

Much has been written concerning the sonic advantages—and disadvantages—of coincident microphone techniques. The most frequent criticism of coincident microphone techniques is that the sound produced is *dry* or *analytical*, lacking a sense of spaciousness achieved by other techniques. Sometimes coincident techniques also are chastised for having a too *narrow* image, that is *confined* between the two loudspeakers (References 7-2, 7-3, and 7-4).

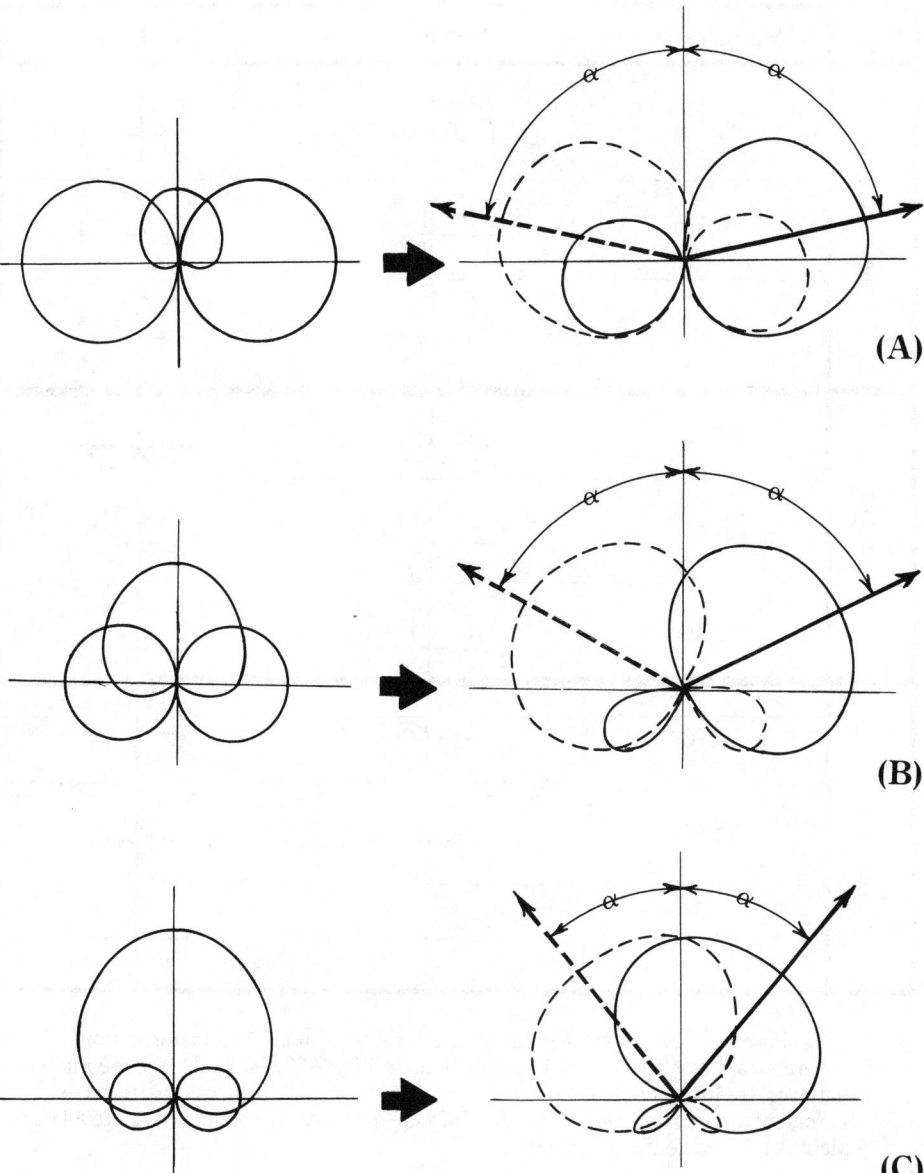

7-22 The *MS* to *XY* transformation is shown using a cardioid pattern for the mid microphone, and three ratios of mid to side signals. (A) *M:S* = 30:70; (B) *M:S* = 50:50; (C) *M:S* = 70:30. The angle *a* between the resulting *XY* pair is derived from the equation $\alpha = \arctan[(1 - A) \div A(1 - B)]$, where *A* is the proportion of the mid microphone's contribution to the *MS* matrix, and *B* expresses the decimal fraction of the omnidirectional to bidirectional component of the polar pattern of the mid microphone (Reference 7-1). In this instance, where the mid microphone is a cardioid, *B* = 0.5 (refer to Fig. 7-13).

Mid	Mid/side ratio	Sum	Difference
Omnidirectional	30:70		
	50:50		
	70:30		
Cardioid	30:70		
	50:50		
	70:30		
Bidirectional	30:70		
	50:50		
	70:30		

7-23 This shows just nine of what is an infinite variety of mid/side transformations. Three different ratios of mid to side are shown (as in Fig. 7-22) for each of three mid polar patterns—omnidirectional, cardioid, and bidirectional. The derived patterns depicted in this figure are shown separated for the sake of clarity. In reality, these are all equivalent *XY* coincident configurations.

For some people the coherent precision of the coincident microphone techniques, particularly *MS*, simply sounds too analytical, or too correct. Though the soundstage might be accurately reproduced it might be simply insufficient to satisfy their sonic and/or emotional desires. They desire something more: "spaciousness."

One means of alleviating this objection is to manipulate the low frequency equalization of the difference signal—the left minus right—of the stereo pickup. According to Griesinger, "Coincident and near coincident techniques with spatial equalization can also deliver excellent spaciousness, and in addition provide accurate directional imaging and depth." (Reference 7-3)

7-24 The MS-38 is an active mid/side matrix converter with stereo width control.

Another method to increase spaciousness is to introduce some incoherence into the stereo pickup by creating some time delay between the two channels. Achieved by either electronic means, called *shuffling*, or physically, by introducing a slight spacing between the microphones, the result is claimed to add a sense of space to the recording (see chapter 9). Whether this *space* is considered phase distortion (comb filtering, as discussed in chapter 8) or sonic enhancement lies fully in the ear of the listener.

Subjective evaluation

Thus far the various microphone techniques discussed have omitted one significant factor in the evaluation process—the spaces in which sound is recorded and subsequently reproduced. The environment of the recording is critical to the sound of the recording, because microphones in a room encode the stereo signal, which is subsequently decoded via loudspeakers in an entirely different room.

Subjective choices are the foundation of creating a stereophonic image; these cannot be expected to satisfy all listeners under all circumstances. The concepts behind the creation of stereo imagery are presented here. It is up to you as a performer, a recording engineer, a producer, or simply a listener, to determine what various techniques are appropriate to serve both illusion and reality.

8
Audibility of reflections

COLORATION IS A TERM USED TO DESCRIBE THE DETERIORATION IN THE audible quality of a sound signal. The term comes from an analogy to light. The energy of white light is distributed throughout the electromagnetic spectrum, as the energy of music and speech signals is distributed throughout the sound spectrum. If the distribution of light energy is changed, the color of the light changes. A change in the sound spectrum can result in an audible change in the quality of the sound, and this change is called a *coloration* of the sound—or a change in timbre of the sound.

Most people agree that a flat frequency response, or transfer function, of a system gives the highest subjective quality of sound through a system, though it is debatable. A flat response characteristic of a system will not introduce a coloration of its own, however.

Adjusting a tone control or equalizer of a high-fidelity system can introduce an intentional and potentially desirable audible change in sound quality, sometimes termed a coloration of the sound. This term, however, is usually reserved for the unintentional degradation in sound quality.

Effects of reflected sound

Sound from a source reaches the listener, or microphone, first over a direct path; this is the shortest route from source to listener. Sound reflected from walls or other objects arrives later because the sound travels farther. In other words, the reflections are delayed relative to the direct sound.

Numerous psychoacoustical investigations were conducted that relate directly to conditions in the typical home or commercial listening room. These tests used one loudspeaker for the primary sound and another for the delayed, or reflected, sound in an approximation of the conventional stereo arrangement, with the

123

observer in the *stereo seat*. Most of the work was done under anechoic conditions, such as a *dead* room, to avoid extraneous effects. Therefore, the results can be applied with confidence to the common stereo situation.

Threshold perceptions

In any effect to be studied, the first appearance of that effect (its threshold) is a definite, basic starting point. For example, how audible is a reflection from a side wall? Figure 8-1 shows the results of one such measurement—the absolute threshold for the perception of a delayed reflection using pink noise as the signal. The threshold varies somewhat with the magnitude of the delay. For each delay, the level of the reflection is increased gradually until it is barely heard. Repeating the process for many delays, the threshold curve of Fig. 8-1 is found. In the shaded area beneath this curve, the reflection is not heard, but above the line the reflection is heard. The higher the level of the reflection above the threshold, the more prominent its effect (Reference 8-1).

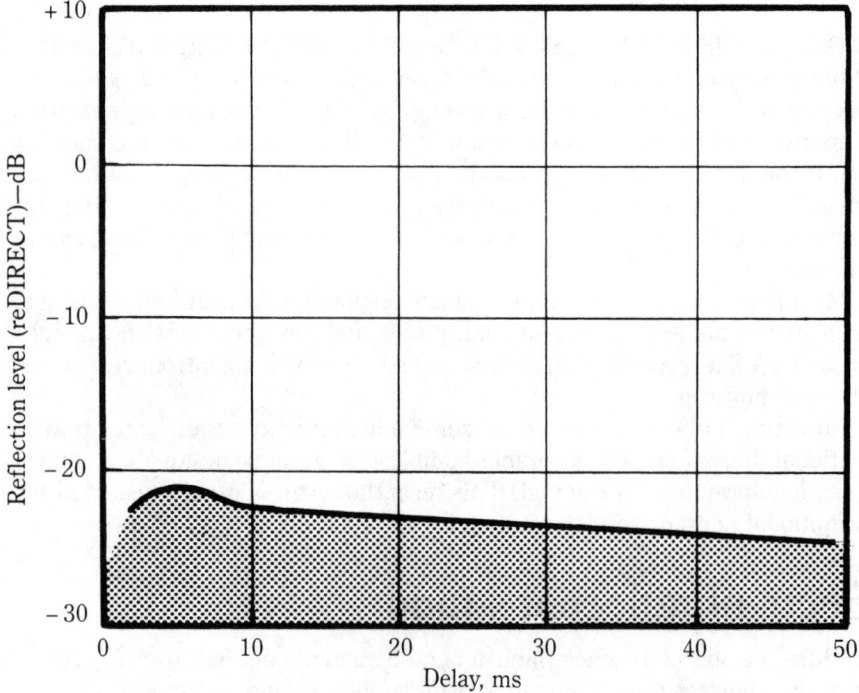

8-1   Absolute threshold for a single lateral reflection using pink noise for a signal. After Olive and Toole, Reference 8-1.

If you are unfamiliar with graphs of this nature, the minus signs on the vertical scale might seem strange. The vertical scale represents the ratio of the reflection's sound level to that of the direct, primary sound. In other words, if the reflection is equal to the direct sound, the ratio is represented by 0 dB. *Minus 10 dB* means that the reflection is 10 dB below the direct; *minus 20 dB* indicates that the reflection is 20 dB below the direct, etc.

Adding a sense of spaciousness and a broadening of the image are the most general effects for reflection levels above threshold. These generally are considered desirable.

Thresholds of other effects occur above this threshold of absolute audibility of the reflection. A threshold for image shift or spreading of the image is found about 10 dB above the absolute threshold (see Fig. 3-20). By increasing the level of the reflection another 10 dB, a third threshold is reached at which the reflection begins to take on the character of a discrete echo.

Audibility of reflections of different signals

The threshold of audibility of Fig. 8-1 holds for pink noise whose spectrum falls off with frequency at a rate of 3 dB/octave. It is pink because the low frequency (red) end is emphasized. This noise is a very convenient, steady source that gives results close enough to speech and music to justify its use in many tests. The question arises, does the absolute threshold for other types of signals vary significantly from that of pink noise?

Figure 8-2 shows threshold measurements made on several different types of signals. The threshold of audibility for pink noise is represented by curve A and is repeated from Fig. 8-1. The threshold for *castanets*, a sharp impulsive sound, is shown in curve B. The threshold for speech, illustrated in curve C, is higher than the noise curve for delays less than 40 ms. A comparison of curves A and C shows how well pink noise represents speech in acoustical or psychoacoustical measurements (Reference 8-1).

The sound of a full symphonic orchestra is graphed by curve D. For this sound, it was necessary to raise the level of the reflection to within 10 dB of the direct, primary loudspeaker sound before the reflection was barely audible. In the listening room a reflection of the symphony-orchestra sound with a level of – 15 dB would not be heard. Reflection levels between – 10 and 0 dB are necessary for listening room spaciousness to be added to the sound; however, this is not necessarily desirable. The spaciousness of the concert hall is part of the sound originally recorded, which is reproduced as part of the signal. For an accurate reproduction of this sound, more spaciousness in the listening room probably would not be desirable (Reference 8-2).

Audibility and reflection angle

Reflections of sound from the loudspeakers come toward the listener from all directions. The floor and the front wall reflections (behind the loudspeakers) are approximately 30° from the listener's median plane, both below and above the horizontal plane. The side wall reflections are at least 30° from the forward direction. Rear reflections and multiple reflections come from almost every direction. Is the ear equally responsive to reflections from all of these directions?

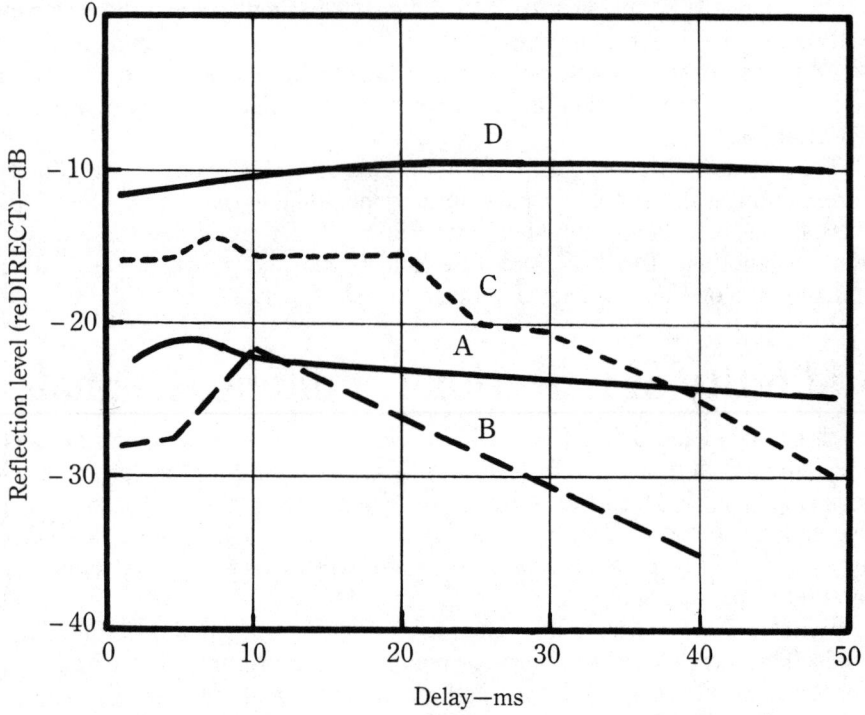

8-2   Effect of type of signal on the threshold of audibility of a single lateral reflection. After Olive and Toole, Reference 8-1.

A. Pink noise, after Olive and Toole, Reference 8-1
B. Castanets, after Olive and Toole, Reference 8-1
C. Speech, after Olive and Toole, Reference 8-1
D. Music, after Schubert, Reference 8-3 cited by Olive and Toole.

The basic threshold curve of Fig. 8-1 is repeated again in Fig. 8-3 as curve A. The curve was made with loudspeakers separated by a 65° angle and will be considered a point of comparison representing the normal stereo setup. A vertical 60° angle represents reflections from the ceiling shown in curve B. This ceiling reflection, curve B, is close to curve A. In other words, reflections from the ceiling have the same effect as lateral reflections from the side walls.

Even though side and ceiling reflections have the same effect, curve C in Fig. 8-3 shows that reflections coming from the same direction as the direct, primary sound are more difficult to hear by 5 – 10 dB. The masking effect of the direct sound is greater when the reflection comes from the same direction. In other words, reflections from all angles have roughly the same effect, except for the reflection coincident with the direct sound (Reference 8-1).

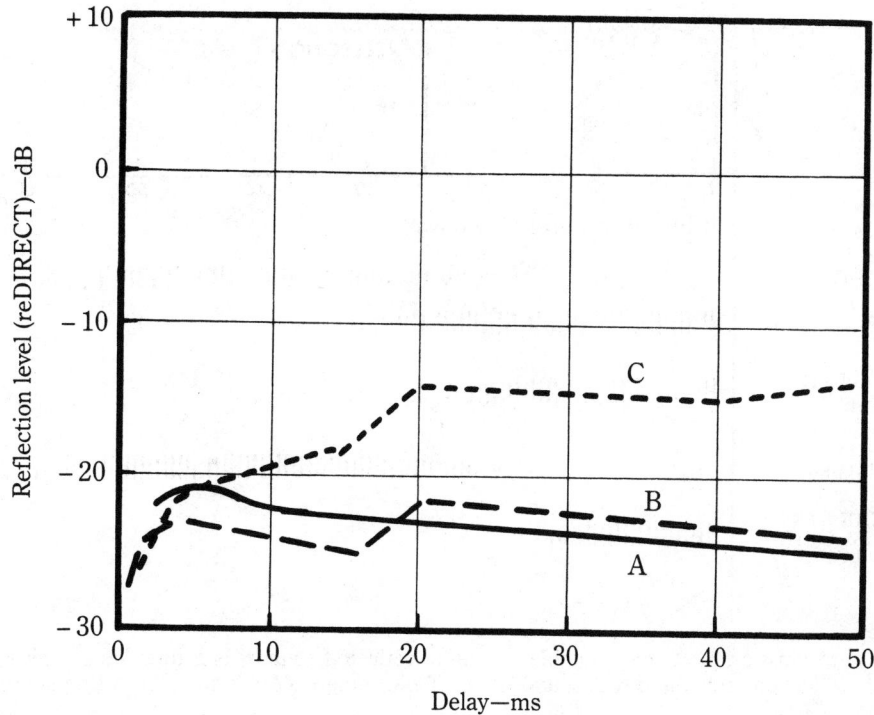

8-3   Effect of direction of reflection on the threshold of audibility of a single lateral reflection.

A. Lateral, 65°, after Olive and Toole, Reference 8-1
B. Vertical, 60°, after Olive and Toole, Reference 8-1
C. Primary and reflected sounds from same direction. After Olive and Toole, Reference 8-1.

Audibility and reflection spectrum

Although it is convenient to conduct psychoacoustical tests by simply delaying the direct signal to get the reflection signal, does the spectrum of the reflection affect the results? Many effects can change the spectrum of the reflection, for example loudspeaker directionality. The high frequency response of the loudspeaker toward the side wall is much lower than that on axis; thus all lateral reflections have spectra differing from that of the direct sound. Further, the absorption characteristics of rugs, drapes, sculptured foam, glass fiber, etc., are all different, and all such surfaces change the spectrum as the sound is reflected. Many factors guarantee that the reflection spectrum is significantly different from the direct sound (Reference 8-1).

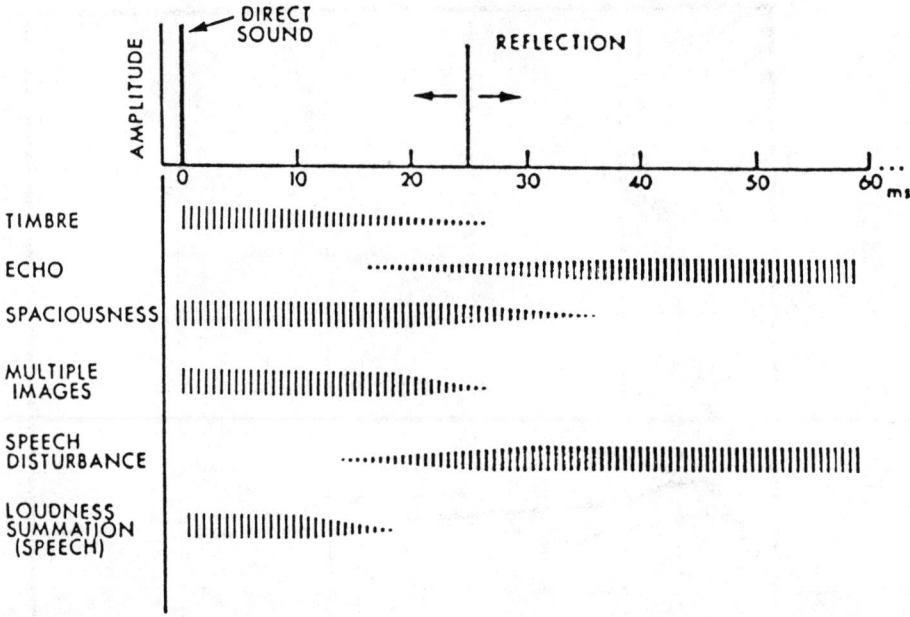

8-4 An illustration of some audible effects of reflected sounds as a function of delay of reflection after the direct sound. After Toole, Reference 8-2 and Audio Engineering Society.

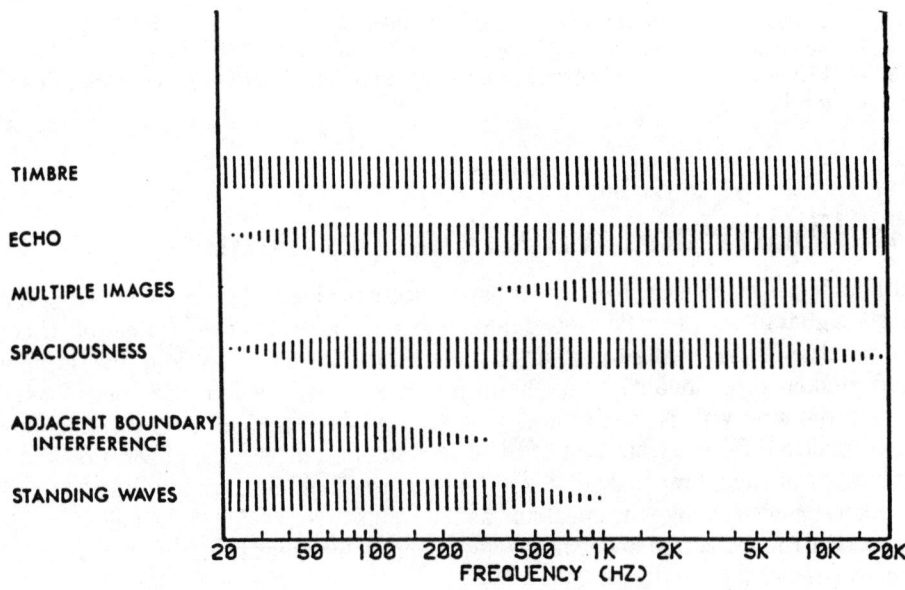

8-5 An illustration of some audible effects of reflected sounds as a function of frequency. Toole, Reference 8-2 and Audio Engineering Society.

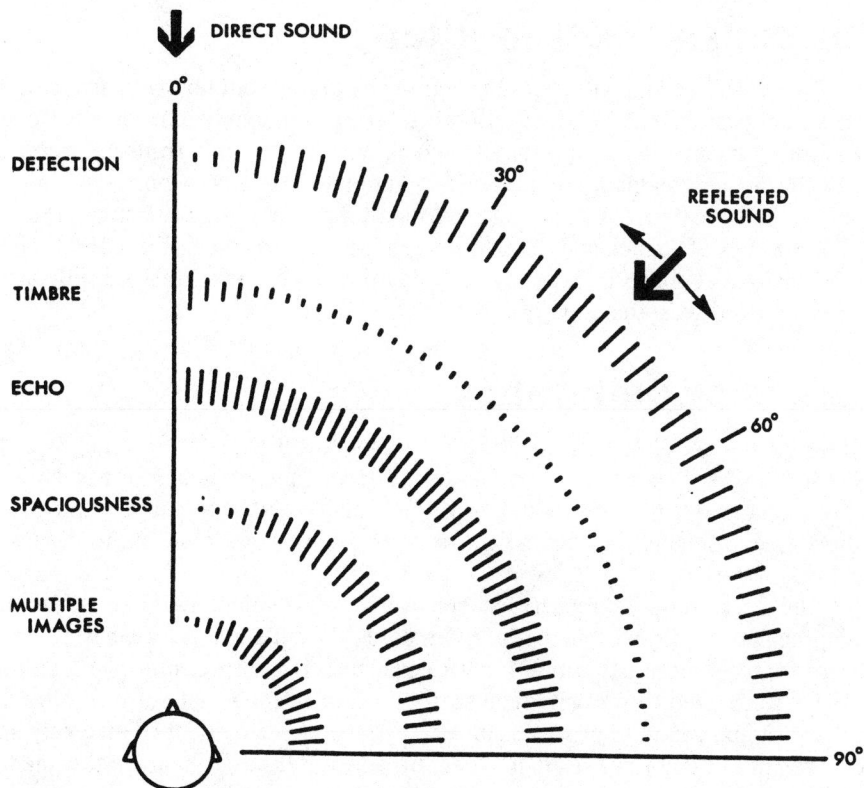

8-6 An illustration of some audible effects of reflected sounds as a function of angle of incidence upon a listener. Toole, Reference 8-2 and Audio Engineering Society.

Audible effects of reflected sounds

Figure 8-4 shows graphically the various audible effects of reflected sound as a function of delay between direct and reflected component (Reference 8-2). Figure 8-5 depicts the various audible effects of reflected sound as a function of frequency (Reference 8-2). Figure 8-6 illustrates the variations of some audible effects of reflected sounds as a function of angle of incidence upon a listener (Reference 8-2).

In summary, the audibility of single reflections has been examined for several variables. Audibility varies greatly with changes in the amount of delay between the direct and the reflected sounds. The type of signal, such as pink noise, speech, castanets, orchestra, etc., also greatly affects audibility. Angular separation between direct and reflected sounds has a minor effect on the audibility of reflection, except when the two are coincident; the reflection then tends to be suppressed. The general effect of reflected sounds is illustrated in Figs. 8-4, 8-5, and 8-6.

Why consider comb filters?

The term *comb filter* has been widely used in the popular audio press as an explanation of delayed reflection effects. Comb filtering is a steady-state phenomenon. It has limited application to music and speech, which are highly transient phenomena. With transient sounds, the audibility of a delayed replica is more the result of successive sound events. A case might be made for proper application of combing to brief snatches of speech and music that approach steady state, but already there is an etymological impasse. The study of the audible effects of delayed reflections is better handled with the generalized threshold approach.

What is a comb filter?

A filter changes the shape of the frequency response or transfer function of a system. An electronic circuit used to shape the frequency response of a system to achieve a certain desired end could be a filter. It also could be a system of pipes and cavities used to change an acoustical system, such as in some microphones to adjust the pattern.

In the early days of multitrack recording, experimenters were constantly developing new, different, and distinctive sounds. *Phasing* and *flanging* were popular words among these experimenters (Reference 8-4). At first multiple-head tape recorders were used to provide delayed replicas of sounds that were then mixed with the original sound to produce some unusual and eerie effects. Currently special electronic circuits are used to generate these delays. Whatever the means, these audible colorations of sound are the result of comb filters.

Tonal signals and comb filters

A 500 Hz tone is shown as a line on a frequency scale in Fig. 8-7A. All of the energy concentrated in this pure tone is located at this frequency. Figure 8-4B shows an identical signal except it is delayed by 0.5 ms in respect to the signal of A. The signal has the same frequency and amplitude, but the timing is different. Consider both A and B as acoustical signals combining at the diaphragm of a microphone. Signal A could be a direct signal and B a reflection of A off a nearby sidewall. What is the nature of the combined signal the microphone puts out?

Because signals A and B are pure tones, such as simple sine waves, both vary from a positive peak to a negative peak 500 times per second. Because of the 0.5 ms delay, these two tonal signals will not reach their positive or negative peaks at the same instant. Often along the time axis both are positive, or both are negative, and at times one is positive while the other is negative. When the sine wave of sound pressure representing signal A and the sine wave of sound pressure representing signal B combine (with due respect to positive and negative signs) they produce another sine wave of the same frequency, but of different amplitude. In this *linear* system, a system through which a signal can pass without change in waveshape, no new frequencies are generated. If combining took place in a nonlin-

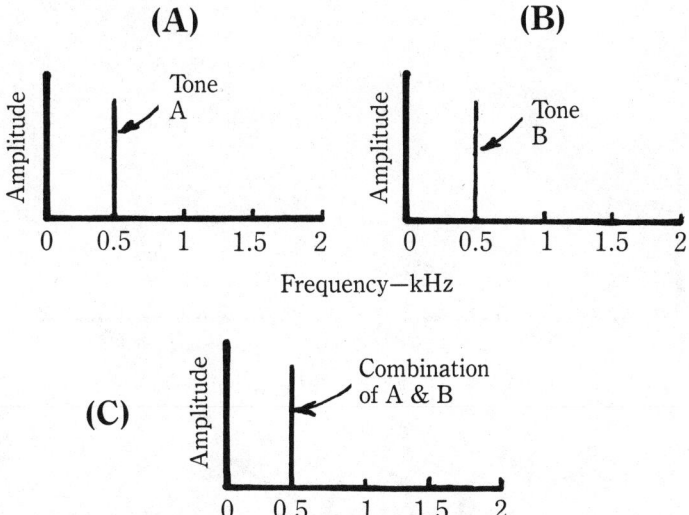

8-7 Tonal signals and comb filters; (A) a sine wave having a frequency of 500 Hz, (B) another sine wave of 500 Hz that is delayed 0.5 ms from *A*, and *C* is a summation of A and B. The 500-Hz signal and its delayed counterpart reach their peaks at slightly different times, but adding them together simply yields another sine wave; there is no comb filtering.

ear system either new frequencies, or sidebands would be created or, if signals A and B were of different frequency, beats would be produced. None of these produce what is called comb filtering.

The sine wave is the simplest of all waveshapes. Fourier has shown that any waveshape, for example music or speech, can be broken down into a series of sine waves of different amplitudes, frequencies, and timings—no matter how complex they are. Only a sustained musical tone approximates a sine wave, and because music is mostly transient, sustained tones are rare.

Combing of music and speech signals

The spectrum of Fig. 8-8A can be applied to an instantaneous slice of music, speech, or any other signal having a distributed spectrum. Figure 8-8B is identically the same spectrum but delayed 0.1 ms from Fig. 8-8A. Figure 8-8C is the acoustical combination of the A and B sound pressure spectra at the diaphragm of the microphone. The resulting overall response of Fig. 8-8C appears like a sine wave, but combining spectra is different from combining tonal signals. This sine-wave appearance is natural and is actually a sine-wave shape with the negative loops made positive.

Combing of direct and reflected sound

How the 0.1 ms delay in Fig. 8-8 was obtained was not specified. It could have been from a digital-delay device, or it could have been a reflection from a wall or

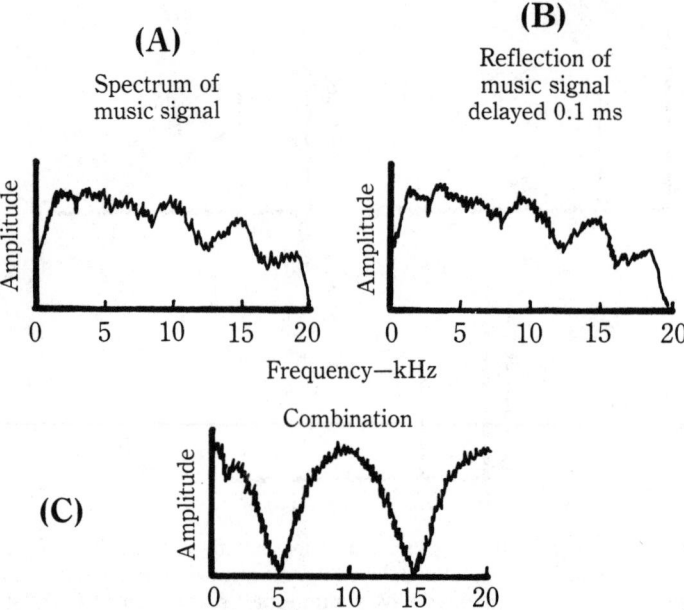

8-8 Combing of signals having distributed spectra; (A) instantaneous spectrum of music signal. (B) a replica of *A*, which is delayed 0.1 ms from *A*. (C) a summation of *A* and *C* showing typical comb filtering.

other object. The spectral shape of a signal will be changed somewhat upon reflection, depending on the angle of incidence, the acoustical characteristics of the surface, etc.

A reflection delayed 0.1 ms will have traveled (1,130 ft/sec) (0.0001 sec) = 0.113 ft further than the direct signal. This difference in path length, only about $1^{11}/_{32}$ inch, could result from a grazing angle with both source and listener, or microphone, close to the reflecting surface. Greater delays are expected in more normal situations such as those of Fig. 8-9. The spectrum of Fig. 8-9A is from a noise generator. This is a "shhh" sound similar to the between-station noise of an FM radio receiver. Random noise of this type is used widely in acoustic measurements because it is a continuous signal, its energy is distributed throughout the audible frequency range, and it is closer to speech and music signals than sine or other periodic waves. In Fig. 8-9B, this random noise signal drives a loudspeaker, which faces a reflective surface; a microphone is then placed at varying distances from the reflective surface.

In Fig. 8-9B, the microphone diaphragm is placed about 0.7 inches from the reflective surface. Interference takes place between the direct sound the microphone picks up from the loudspeaker and the sound reflected from the surface. The output of the microphone shows the comb-filter pattern characteristic of a 0.1 ms delay.

Placing the microphone diaphragm about 3.4 inches from the reflective barrier, as in Fig. 8-9C, yields a 0.5 ms delay, which results in the comb-filter pattern

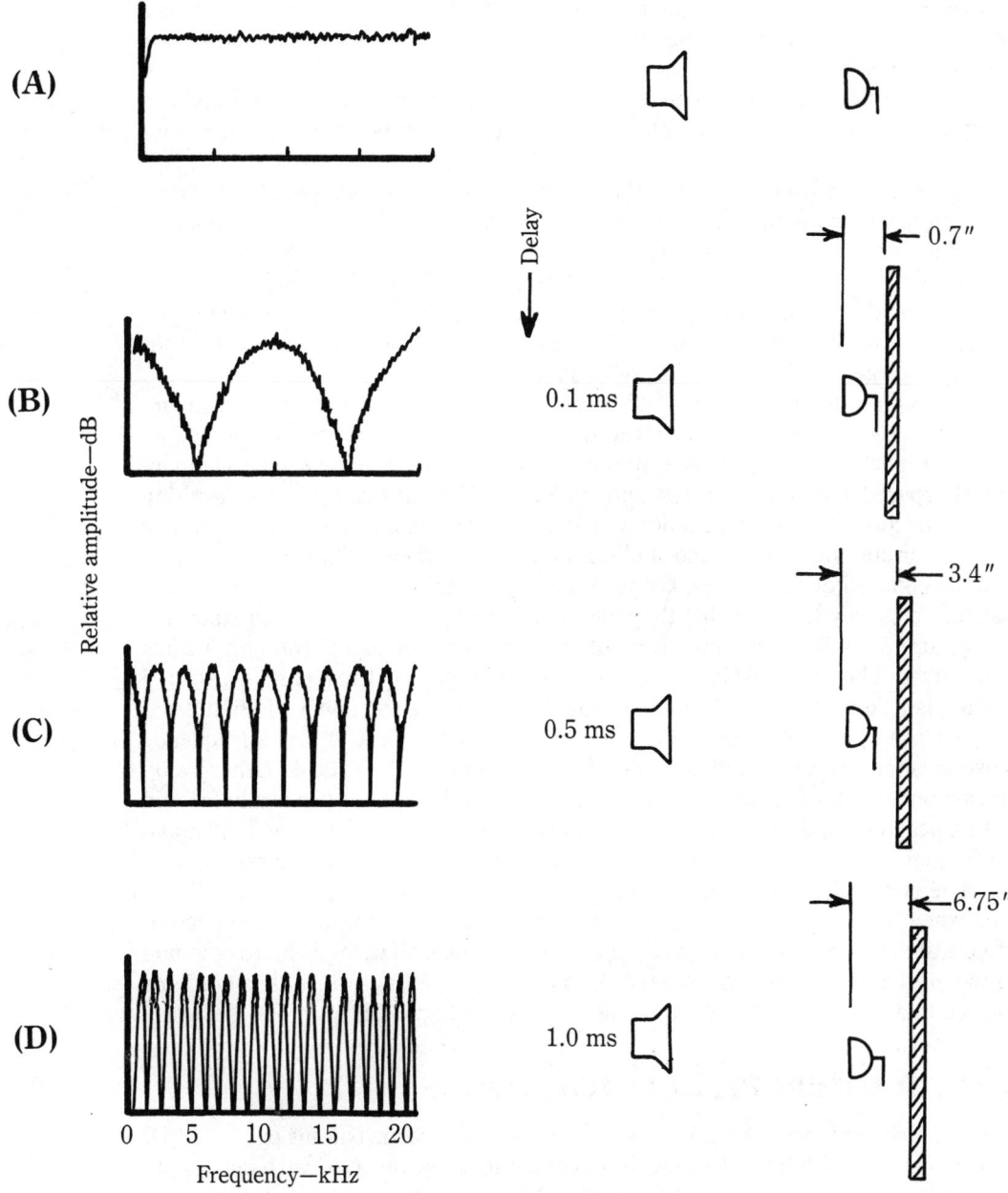

8-9 A demonstration of comb filtering in which direct sound from a loudspeaker is acoustically combined with a reflection from a surface at the diaphragm of a microphone. (A) No surface, no reflection. (B) Placing the microphone 0.7 in from the surface creates a delay of 0.1 ms and the combination of the direct and the reflected rays shows cancellations at 5 and 15 kHz and every 10 kHz. (C) A delay of 0.5 ms creates cancellations much closer together. (D) A delay of 1 ms results in cancellations even more closely together. If t is taken as the delay in seconds, the first null is $1/t$ and spacing between nulls or between peaks is $1/2t$.

shown. Plotted on a linear frequency scale, the pattern looks like a comb—hence the name *comb-filter*. Increasing the delay from 0.1 to 0.5 ms has increased the number of peaks and the number of nulls five-fold.

In Fig. 8-9D, the microphone is 6.75 inches from the reflective barrier giving a delay of 1.0 ms. Doubling the delay has doubled the number of peaks/nulls once again.

Increasing the delay between the direct and reflected components increases the number of constructive and destructive interference events proportionally. Starting with the flat spectrum of Fig. 8-9A, the far-from-flat spectrum of B is distorted by the presence of a reflection delayed only 0.1 ms. An audible response change would be expected. One might suspect the distorted spectrum of D might be less noticeable because the multiple, closely-spaced peaks and narrow notches tend to average out the overall response aberrations.

Reflections following closely after the arrival of the direct component are expected in small rooms because the dimensions of the room are limited. Conversely, reflections in large spaces would have greater delays, which generate more closely-spaced comb-filter peaks and nulls. Thus, comb-filter effects resulting from reflections are more commonly associated with small room acoustics. The size of various music halls and auditoriums renders them relatively immune to audible comb-filter distortions, because the peaks and nulls are so numerous and packed so closely together that they merge into an essentially uniform response.

Figure 8-10 illustrates the effect of straining a music signal through a 2 ms comb filter. The relationship between the nulls and peaks of response are related to the piano keyboard as indicated. Middle C, (C4), has a frequency of 261.63 Hz, and is close to the first null of 250 Hz. The next higher C, (C5), has a frequency close to twice that of C4 and is treated favorably with a +6 dB peak. Other Cs up the keyboard will be either discriminated against with a null or especially favored with a peak in response—or something in between. Whether viewed as fundamental frequencies or a series of harmonics, the timbre of the sound suffers.

The comb filters illustrated in Figs. 8-8, 8-9, and 8-10 are plotted to a linear frequency scale. In this form the *comb* appearance and visualization of the delayed effects are most graphic. A logarithmic-frequency scale however, is more common in the electronics and audio industry. A comb filter resulting from a delay of 1 ms plotted to a logarithmic frequency scale is shown in Fig. 8-11.

Comb filters and critical bands

Is the human auditory system capable of resolving the perturbations of Fig. 8-9D? The resolution of human hearing is circumscribed by the critical band tuning curves of the inner ear. The critical bandwidths at representative frequencies are recorded in Table 3-1. For example, the average critical bandwidth of the human auditory system at 1,000 Hz is about 128 Hz. A peak-to-peak comb-filter frequency of 125 Hz corresponds to a reflection delay of about 8 ms (1/0.008 = 125 Hz), which corresponds to a difference in pathlength between the direct and reflected components of about 9 feet (1,130 ft/sec × 0.008 sec = 9.0 ft). This situation is plotted in Fig. 8-12B. To illustrate what happens for greater delays, Fig. 8-12C is

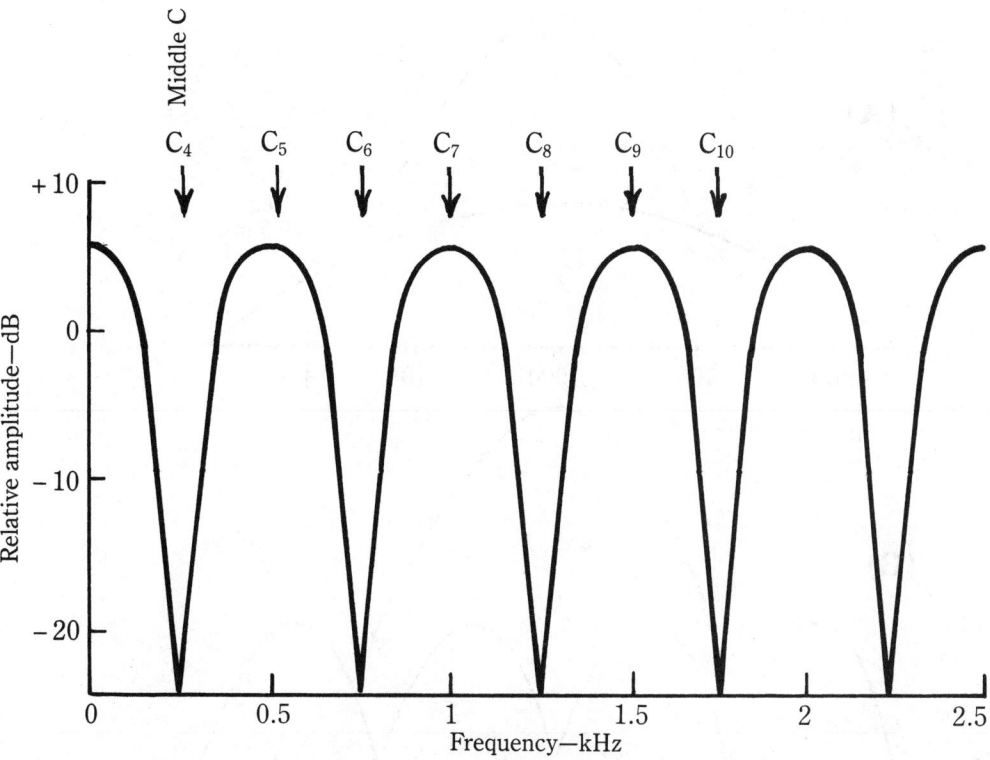

8-10 Passing a music signal through a 2 ms comb filter affects the components of that signal as indicated. Components spaced one octave can be boosted 6 dB at a peak or essentially eliminated at a null, or can be given values between these extremes.

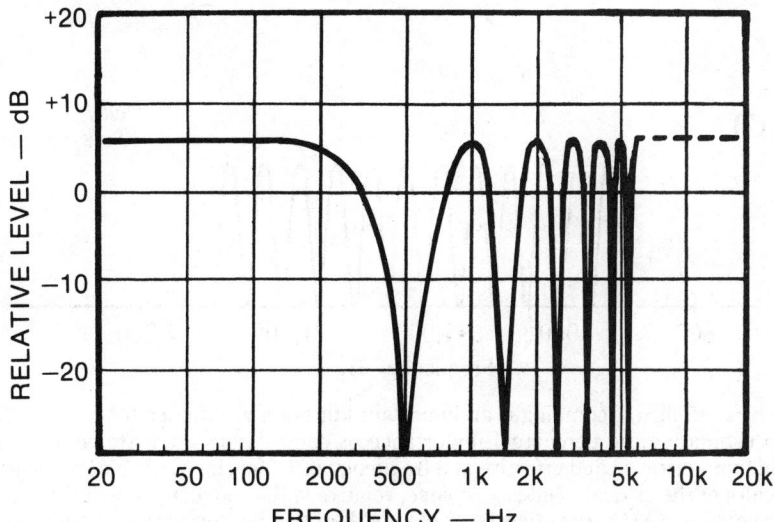

8-11 Up to this point all comb filters have been plotted to a linear scale to demonstrate the origin of the term *comb*. Plotted to the more convenient and familiar logarithmic scale aids in estimating the effects of a given comb on a given signal.

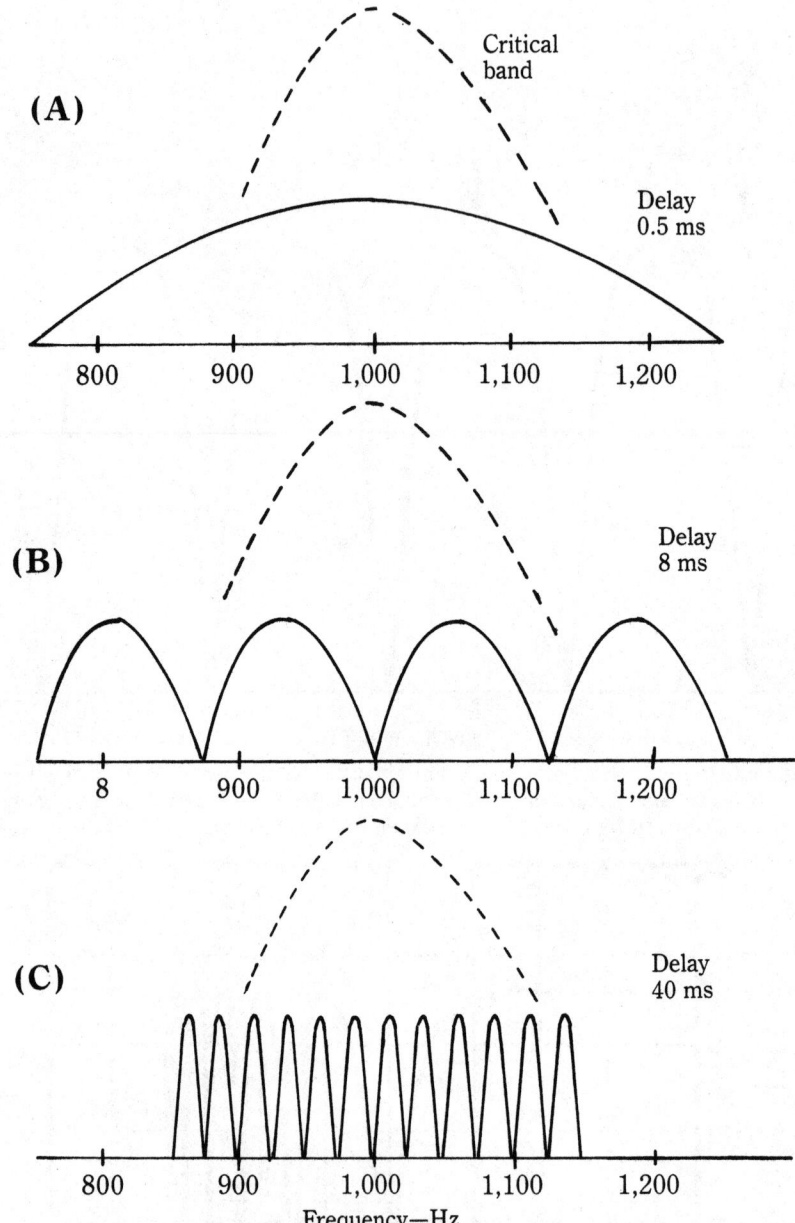

8-12 The audibility of combing is an important but not a well-understood factor. To assist in estimating the perceptual importance of comb filters, they are compared to the auditory critical band effective at a frequency of 1,000 Hz. (C) At a delay of 40 ms the width of the critical band is so coarse, relatively, that no analyzing of the comb filter is possible. (A) On the other hand the width of the auditory critical band is comparable to the comb peak at 0.5 ms delay. (B) is an example in between *A* and *B*. This would seem to confirm the observation that in large spaces (long delays) comb filters are inaudible, while they often are very troublesome in small spaces (short delays).

sketched for a delay of 40 ms. Shorter delays are represented by Fig. 8-12A for a delay of 0.5 ms.

The relative courseness of the critical band cannot analyze and delineate the numerous peaks and nulls resulting from a 40 ms delay (Fig. 8-12C). Therefore, the human ear would not be expected to interpret response aberrations resulting from 40 ms combing as a coloration of the signal. On the other hand, the combing resulting from the 0.5 ms delay (Fig. 8-12A) could be delineated by the ear's critical band at 1,000 Hz resulting in a perceived coloration of the signal. Figure 8-9B illustrates an intermediate example in which the ear is marginally able to analyze the combed signal. The width of the critical bands of the auditory system increases rapidly with frequency. It is difficult to imagine the complexity of the interaction between a set of critical bands and a constantly changing music signal, with diverse combing patterns from a host of reflections. Only carefully controlled psychoacoustical experiments can determine if the resulting colorations are audible.

Coloration and spaciousness

A reflected wave reaching the ear of a listener is always somewhat different than a direct wave. The characteristics of the reflecting wall vary with frequency. By traveling through the air, both the direct and reflected components of a sound wave are altered slightly, due to the air's absorption of sound, which varies with frequency. The amplitudes and timing of the direct and reflected components differ. The ears respond to the frontal, direct component somewhat differently than to the reflection from the side. The perception of the reflected component is always different than the direct component. The amplitudes and timing will be related, but with an interaural correlation less than maximum.

Weakly correlated input signals to the ears contribute to the impression of spaciousness. If no reflections occur, such as when listening outdoors, there is no feeling of spaciousness. If the input signals to the ears are right, the perception of the listener is that of being completely enveloped and immersed in the sound. The lack of strong correlation is a prerequisite for the impression of spaciousness.

Combing in stereo microphone pickups

Because two microphones separated in space pick up a sound at different times, their combined output will be similar to the single microphone with delayed reflections. Therefore, spaced microphone stereo-pickup arrangements are susceptible to comb-filter problems. Under certain conditions the combing is audible, imparting a *phasiness* to the overall sound reproduction, interpreted by some as room ambience. It is not ambience, however, but distortion of the time and intensity cues presented to the microphones. It is evident that some people find this distortion pleasing, so spaced microphone pickups are favored by many producers and listeners.

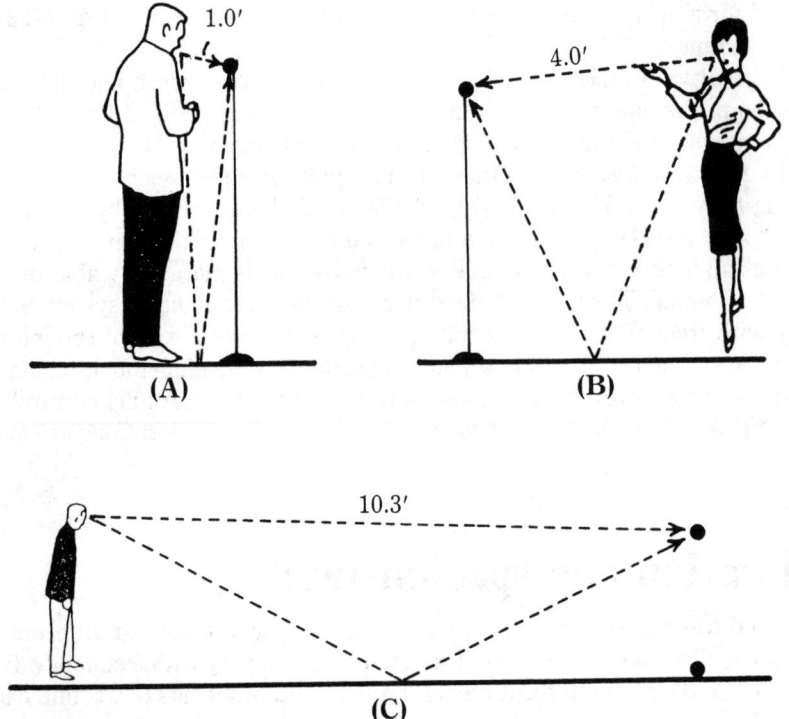

8-13   Common microphone placements compared with respect to production of comb filters (see Table 8-1). (A) Reflection 20 dB down, minimum comb-filter problems. (B) Reflection only 8 dB down, comb-filter problems expected. (C) Reflection almost same level as direct, comb-filter problems certain. A microphone on the floor of (C) would reduce the difference in path length between direct and reflected components (and the combing) to almost zero.

Common comb-filter producers

Figure 8-13 illustrates three microphone placements which produce comb filters. A close source-to-microphone distance is shown in Fig. 8-13A. The direct component travels 1 ft and the floor-reflected component travels 10.1 ft (see Table 8-1). The difference between these (9.1 ft) means the floor reflection is delayed 8.05 ms (9.1 ft/1,130 ft/sec = 0.00805 sec). The first null is therefore at 62 Hz with subsequent null and peak spacing of 124 Hz. The level of the reflection is – 20 dB with reference to that of the direct component (20 log 1.0/10.1 = – 20 dB).

Similar calculations for Fig. 8-13B and *C* are included in Table 8-1. In *A* the direct component is 10 times stronger than the floor reflection. The effect of the comb filter would be negligible. Figure 8-13C has a reflection almost as strong as the direct, and the comb-filter effect would be maximum. Figure 8-13B is intermediate between *A* and *C*.

Table 8-1. Comb-filter situations
(Refer to Fig. 8-13)

Fig. 8-13	Path length, Ft.		Difference		First null $1/2t$	Pk/null spacing $1/t$	Refl. level
	Direct	Refl.	Ft.	(t) ms.	Hz	Hz	dB
A	1.0	10.1	9.1	8.05	62	124	−20
B	4.0	10.0	6.0	5.31	94	189	−8
C	10.3	11.5	1.2	1.06	471	942	−1

A microphone is shown on the floor in Fig. 8-13*C*. A floor bounce would occur, but the difference between the direct and reflected path length would be small. Therefore, the comb filter effect would be essentially eliminated.

Comb filters in stereo listening

In the standard stereo listening arrangement the input signals to each ear come from two loudspeakers. These signals are displaced in time with respect to each other because of the loudspeaker spacing; the result is the generation of comb-filters. Blauert indicated that comb-filter distortion is not generally audible (Reference 8-5). The auditory system has the ability of disregarding these distortions as the perception of timbre is formed. This is called *binaural suppression of colorations of timbre*, however, no generally accepted theory exists to explain how the auditory system accomplishes this (Reference 8-5). Distortion can be heard by plugging one ear; however, this destroys the stereo effect. Comparing the timbre of signals from two loudspeakers producing comb-filter distortion and one loudspeaker (that does not) will demonstrate that stereo comb-filter distortion is barely audible. The timbre of the two is essentially the same. Furthermore, the timbre of the stereo signal changes little as the head is turned.

9

Spaced microphone stereo techniques

IN THE EARLY DAYS OF THE DEVELOPMENT OF STEREOPHONIC TECHNIQUES, researchers experimented with two different approaches. Alan Blumlein focused on coincident microphone techniques in England. At the same time, in the United States, spaced microphones were used for experimental recordings of the Philadelphia Orchestra by Arthur Keller, Harvey Fletcher, William Snow, and others at Bell Laboratories (Reference 9-1).

Time-of-arrival (phase) effects are important in the preservation of directional cues for accurate stereo imaging. The research work done at Bell Laboratories cannot be slighted, however, because it has led to contemporary mixing engineers at well-respected recording companies such as Telarc, Delos, RCA, and London regularly using spaced microphone techniques.

Near-coincident microphone arrays

The natural spacing between the two ears on the human head has engendered several stereophonic experiments. Binaural pickup, in it simplest manifestation, specifically requires that headphones be used for reproduction (see chapter 6). Most other microphone techniques, however, are intended for loudspeaker playback.

By placing the two microphones relatively close together, much of the phase integrity discussed in earlier chapters can be preserved; therefore, these *near-coincident* configurations are still largely dependent on intensity differences for their stereophonic information. The spacing between the microphones, however, introduces phase differences that can be significant to the sound produced from the system.

When compared to the truly coincident pickups discussed in chapter 7, near-coincident techniques provide an increased sense of *space* around the performers; this is similar to adding *air* or providing a more open sound. This effect is due solely to the phase anomalies (i.e., comb filters) introduced by the time-of-arrival differences between the two microphones. This phasiness often is considered pleasing and a favorable improvement over the more analytical, dry sound produced by coincident techniques. When creating the audio illusion, however, there can be no gains without realizing corresponding losses. In this case, the losses involve a compromise of the solidity and stability of the central region of the stereo image, accompanied by a decrease in monophonic compatibility due to the comb filter effects discussed in chapter 8. Because in near-coincident techniques the spacing between microphones is relatively small, only the upper frequencies (generally above 1,000 Hz) are affected, and sonic degradation due to these phase-related effects is minimal. These upper-frequency phase anomalies create the *airiness* frequently praised when these techniques are used.

The O.R.T.F. technique

This microphone configuration, named for the French national broadcasting agency, *Office de Radiodiffusion-Télévision Française*, was developed for producing pleasing stereo while maintaining adequate monophonic compatibility. The principal axes of the two cardioid microphones in this configuration are angled away from each other at an included angle of 110°, with capsules separated by 17 cm. (Fig. 9-1). This array closely resembles the interaural spacing and angular reception of the ears on an average adult human head.

Because two directional microphones such as cardioids are used at this angle and spacing, the O.R.T.F. technique still provides intensity differences between the stereo channels. At low frequencies, the signals from the two microphones are virtually phase coherent. With minimal phase differences becoming apparent only at higher frequencies, the comb filter effects are tolerable, producing a pleasing *air*

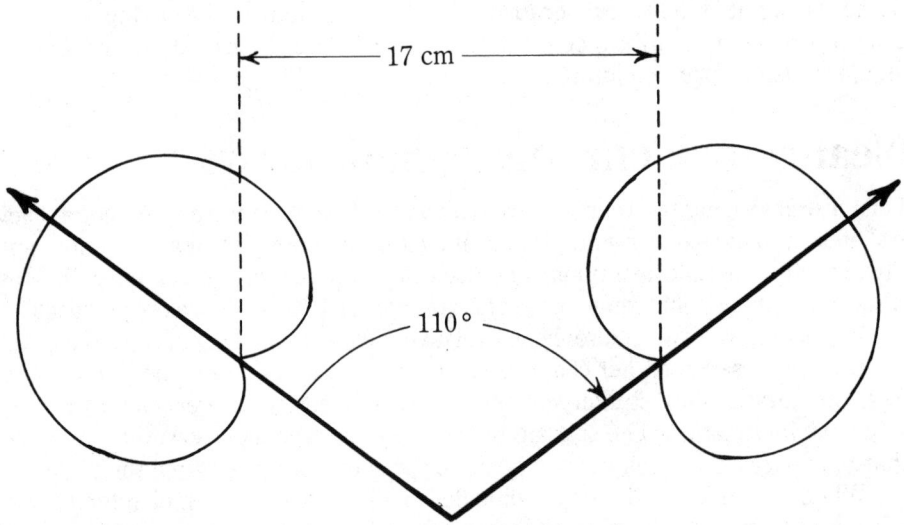

9-1 The O.R.T.F. (Office de Radiodiffusion Télévision Française) stereo microphone array. Configured with two cardioid microphones, spaced 17 cm, and angled outward at 110°.

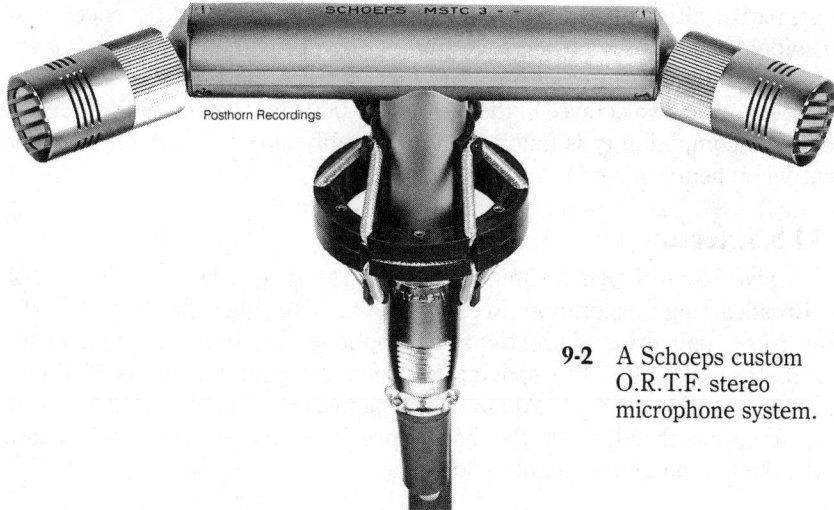

9-2 A Schoeps custom
O.R.T.F. stereo
microphone system.

around the subject. It is this sense of openness that makes O.R.T.F. one of the
most widely used microphone pickups in Europe (Fig. 9-2).

The N.O.S. technique

Developed by engineers at Netherlands Radio, the N.O.S. array (*Nederlandsche
Omroep Stitching*) also uses two cardioid microphones set at an angle of 90°, with a
capsule spacing of 30 cm (Fig. 9-3). The narrower angle still provides intensity

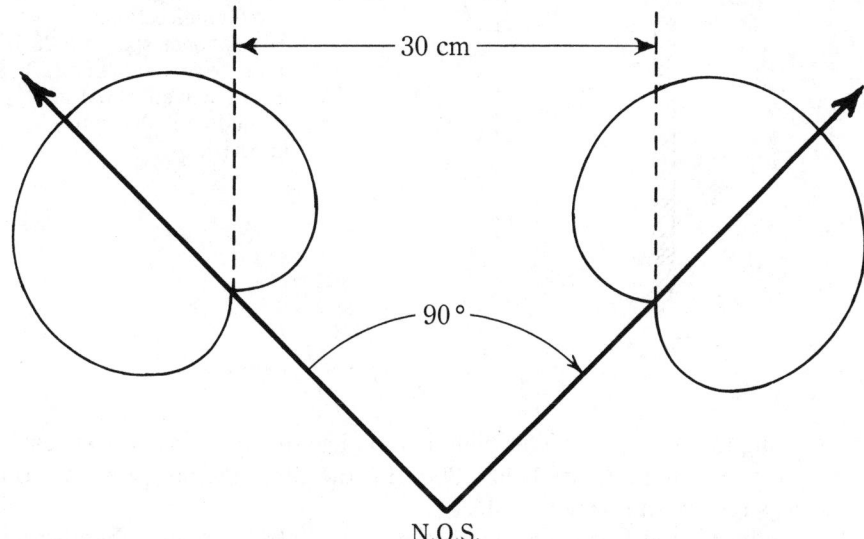

9-3 The N.O.S. (*Nederlandsche Omroep Stitching*) stereo microphone array. Configured
with two cardioid microphones, spaced 30 cm apart, and angled outward at 90°.

cues primarily, although the wider spacing produces phase differences that become evident at lower frequencies, beginning at approximately 250 Hz, or around Middle C. This point differs from the O.R.T.F. technique, where audible comb filter effects occur two octaves higher, around 1,000 Hz. Due to comb-filter effects, monophonic compatibility is much more noticeably affected, although it is not as evident when heard in stereo.

The O.S.S. technique

The *Optimal Stereo Signal* technique was proposed first by Jürg Jecklin of the Swiss Broadcasting Corporation (Reference 9-2). Also called the Jecklin Disk, this system uses a pair of omnidirectional microphones separated by an acoustically opaque baffle (Fig. 9-4). The spacing between the microphones is 16.5 cm; the diameter of the disc is 28 cm. Again, this spacing is an approximation of an average adult human head, with the baffle providing some acoustical separation between the two omnidirectional pickups.

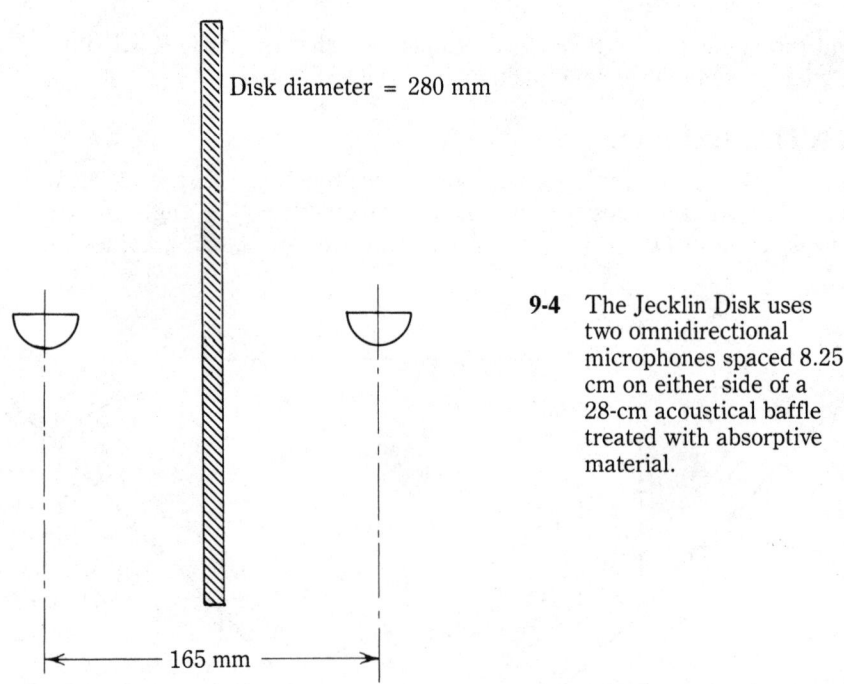

Disk diameter = 280 mm

9-4   The Jecklin Disk uses two omnidirectional microphones spaced 8.25 cm on either side of a 28-cm acoustical baffle treated with absorptive material.

165 mm

According to the inventor: This combination has the following properties:

1) In the frequency range below 200 Hz, the disk has no influence. Both microphones receive the same signal.

2) With increasing frequency, diffraction occurs at the edge of the disk with an increasing effect of separation of the two microphones.

3) The polar response of the OSS microphone is omnidirectional, which is sat-

isfactory for rooms with either r.. minal or too short a reverberation time.'' (Reference 9-2)

This approach is an attempt to bridge the gap, between binaural and stereo techniques. i.e., between headphone and loudspeaker reproduction. It works fairly well for both, but it also presents some compromises that prevent it from being technically correct for either technique. Due to the recent interest in personal stereo portables, however, this microphone technique has inspired further research to develop stereo microphone systems that will serve successfully both headphone and loudspeaker listening (Fig. 9-5 and Reference 9-3).

9-5 The Schoeps model KFM-6U stereo microphone, based on the theories of Gunther Thiele. Posthorn Recordings

The Stereo Ambient Sampling System

The S.A.S.S. array was developed by Michael Billingsley for Crown International, Inc. (Reference 9-4). The product was designed to give highly localized stereo imaging for loudspeaker reproduction. The monocompatible, near-coincident array allots, an omnidirectional microphone capsule for each channel, mounted near, or flush with, a boundary approximately 12.7 cm square. The two boundaries are angled left and right of center. The sound diffraction of each boundary creates a directional polar pattern aimed left and right of the center, much like a coincident or near-coincident array. The capsules are *ear-spaced* 170 mm apart (Fig. 6-14), separated by an acoustical baffle. The polar patterns of the boundaries and the spacing between capsules were chosen to provide natural perceived stereo imaging. As a near-coincident array, the S.A.S.S. array forms stereo images by a combination of spacing, isolating, and shaping of the directional pattern of otherwise omnidirectional capsules used to create time and spectral differences between channels (Reference 9-5).

This product was a unique implementation of the boundary effect achieved by placing a pressure-responsive (omnidirectional) pickup within a pressure boundary surface. With the S.A.S.S., two pressure-zone microphones are employed to produce the stereo array. Because the pressure boundary surfaces are relatively small, a 6 dB increase results only in the mid- and high-frequency directional, or hemispheric, response of the pickup due to the buildup of pressure at the reflecting boundary surfaces. At the same time, the pickup retains the generally even polar response and extended low-frequency response inherent to the omnidirectional microphones used.

Arrangement of microphones

The specific arrangement of microphones is always a matter of taste, which is determined by the specific application at hand. Therefore, restricting oneself to a strictly defined angle or spacing is a self-defeating exercise. The generic category of near-coincident techniques can encompass any configuration of two microphones spaced a short distance apart; the choice of polar pattern and included angle is determined by the situation. If reasonable care is given to the configuration and placement of a near-coincident array, the resulting sound quality of the pickup most often will be satisfactory. Therefore, this is a generally safe approach to producing a stereo recording. If setup time is short or no sound check is possible, a near-coincident microphone pickup will almost always produce a good balance and perspective; it might not be spectacular, but it should not be bad either.

Widely spaced microphones

The experiments at Bell Laboratories in the 1930s led first to the *wall of sound* approach discussed in chapter 1, which for practicality was reduced to two or three widely spaced microphones. Spaced microphone techniques are sometimes called A-B stereo, as opposed to the term XY associated with coincident techniques. Because omnidirectional microphones supposedly receive sound equally well from all directions, they were the ideal choice for implementing spaced techniques (Fig. 9-6). With this arrangement, the inverse square law is important when determining the left-right stereo image. Sounds originating closer to each microphone are reproduced louder than those further away; and tend to *cluster around* the respective loudspeakers when played back. Time-of-arrival effects also play an important role, contributing to both the determination of the lateral placement of the elements within the stereo image and the production of other phase-related phenomena. Once the microphones are separated by an appreciable distance, (more than 25 feet), discrete echoes possibly could be perceived as the soundwave travels between the two pickups.

Lateral imaging

Chapter 2 discussed the effects of level and time-of-arrival differences on the perception of lateral imaging. A common signal emanating more loudly from one loudspeaker of a stereo pair tends to sound like it is coming primarily from that loudspeaker. Similarly, the law of the first wavefront dictates that when a signal

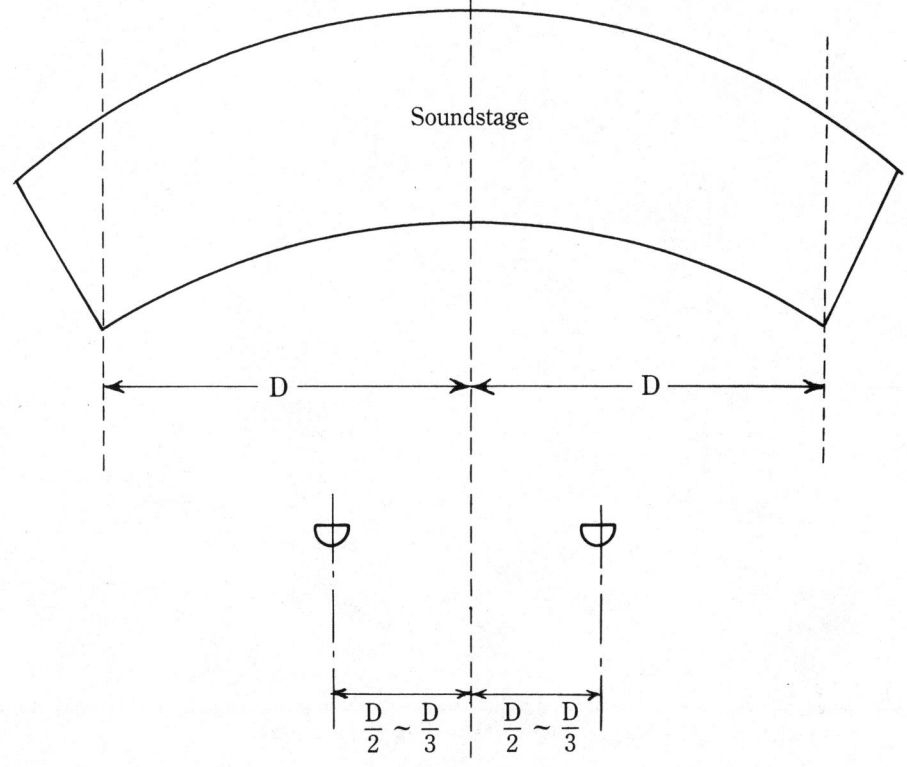

9-6 General arrangement for spaced omnidirectional microphones, showing that the spacing between the two microphones is $1/3$ to $1/2$ the width of the sound stage.

arrives at a listener from two different directions separated slightly in time, the signal that arrives first will determine the direction of the perceived source.

If a trumpet player is centered between two microphones, the distance (D_1) and amplitude (A_1) between the trumpet and each of the microphones is equal, resulting in signals with equal time-of-arrival (T_1) and amplitude (A_1) at the ears of the listener (Fig. 9-7). This produces a phantom image of the trumpet in the center, between the two loudspeakers.

If the trumpet player moves away from the center position, toward one of the two microphones, the situation changes considerably (Fig. 9-8). Due to the inverse square law, the trumpet will be significantly louder at the right microphone (A_4), moving its image toward the right loudspeaker. Because it is also closer to the right microphone, the sound is reproduced slightly sooner from the right loudspeaker, and the law of the first wavefront causes it to be heard from that speaker. Thus, these two effects combine to determine the lateral imaging of sounds placed between the two microphones of a spaced pair.

Only sounds originating exactly on the centerline between the microphones will sound like they are centered between the loudspeakers. Chapter 2 demon-

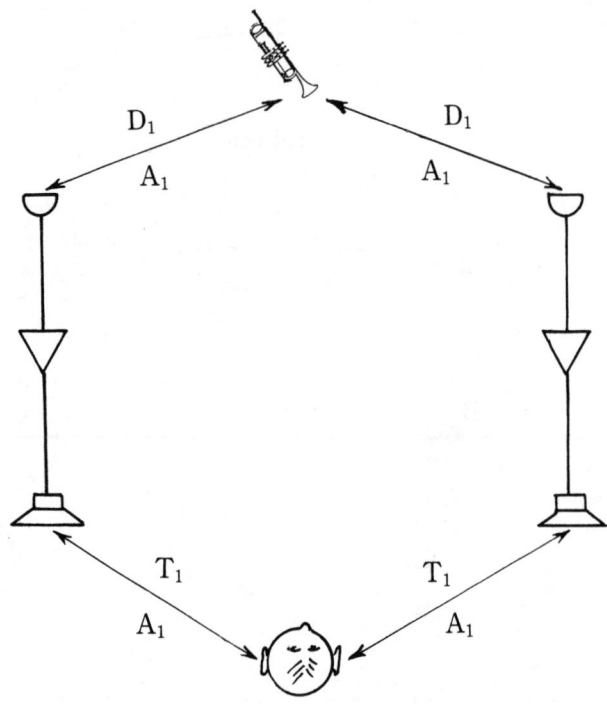

9-7 If a trumpet is centered between the two microphones, the time of arrival and amplitude of its reproduced signal will be equal for the listener.

strated that it takes as little as a one or two millisecond of time difference to move a signal almost completely to one loudspeaker or the other. Thus, even slight movement away from that centerline causes significant shifts in the reproduced imaging. Coupled with the change in intensity and timbre of the sound as it is closer to one microphone than the other, this time difference causes stereo imaging with spaced microphones to degrade rapidly, and collapse around the two loudspeakers, with little or no sound coming from the center of the soundstage. For this reason, a third microphone often is added to the array (Fig. 9-9). Placed at the midpoint between the left and right microphones and mixed equally into each channel, this microphone fills in the hole in the middle and creates a more stable center image.

Phase-related problems

Chapter 8 discussed the problems encountered when a signal is picked up and reproduced via two different path lengths and the comb filter effects that result. This is the case with widely spaced microphones. Elements of the sound source that are not exactly located along the centerline are reproduced with varying amounts of time delay between the two channels—resulting in comb filtering when reproduced via two loudspeakers. These effects are more pronounced when the two stereo channels are combined into a monophonic signal, because phase cancellations are always more audible when the summations are electrical rather than acoustical.

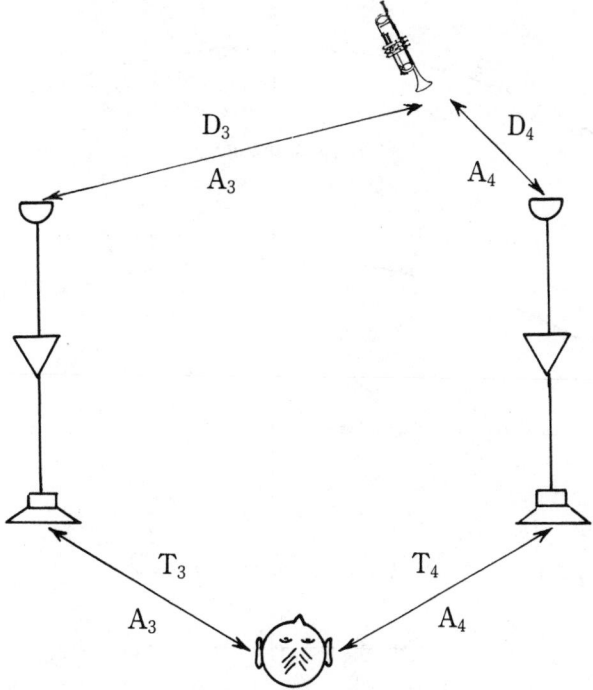

9-8   If the trumpet is closer to the right-channel microphones, the inverse square law will produce unequal levels at the ears of the listener. This, together with the shorter time of arrival, will cause the sound of the trumpet to appear to come from the right loud-speaker.

Besides the spectral anomalies of comb filtering, other phase-related effects can result from spaced microphones. Some listeners consider these detrimental, but others find them beneficial. The most prominent of these *split personality* effects is an increase in the spaciousness of the sound. The general lack of precise imaging resulting from spaced microphones is another characteristic that some listeners find offensive; however, the slight increase in the overall loudness of the signal is an effect produced by phase anomalies that some listeners enjoy.

This dichotomy of listener preferences gives rise to numerous techniques for stereo recording. Referring back to chapter 4, there is no *right* way to record anything. The ultimate criterion is whether the illusion desired by the creative team (producer, performer, and engineer) is achieved and conveyed to the listener (Reference 9-7).

From the foregoing, it is evident that spaced microphones should be implemented with extreme caution. Instances occur when they are appropriate, however, like those with generally uncorrelated sound sources, such as pipe organ or outdoor ambiences. (They also can be advantageous when recording the surround channels of a multichannel recording, discussed in chapter 13.) When accurate stereo imaging is required, however, other techniques are better employed.

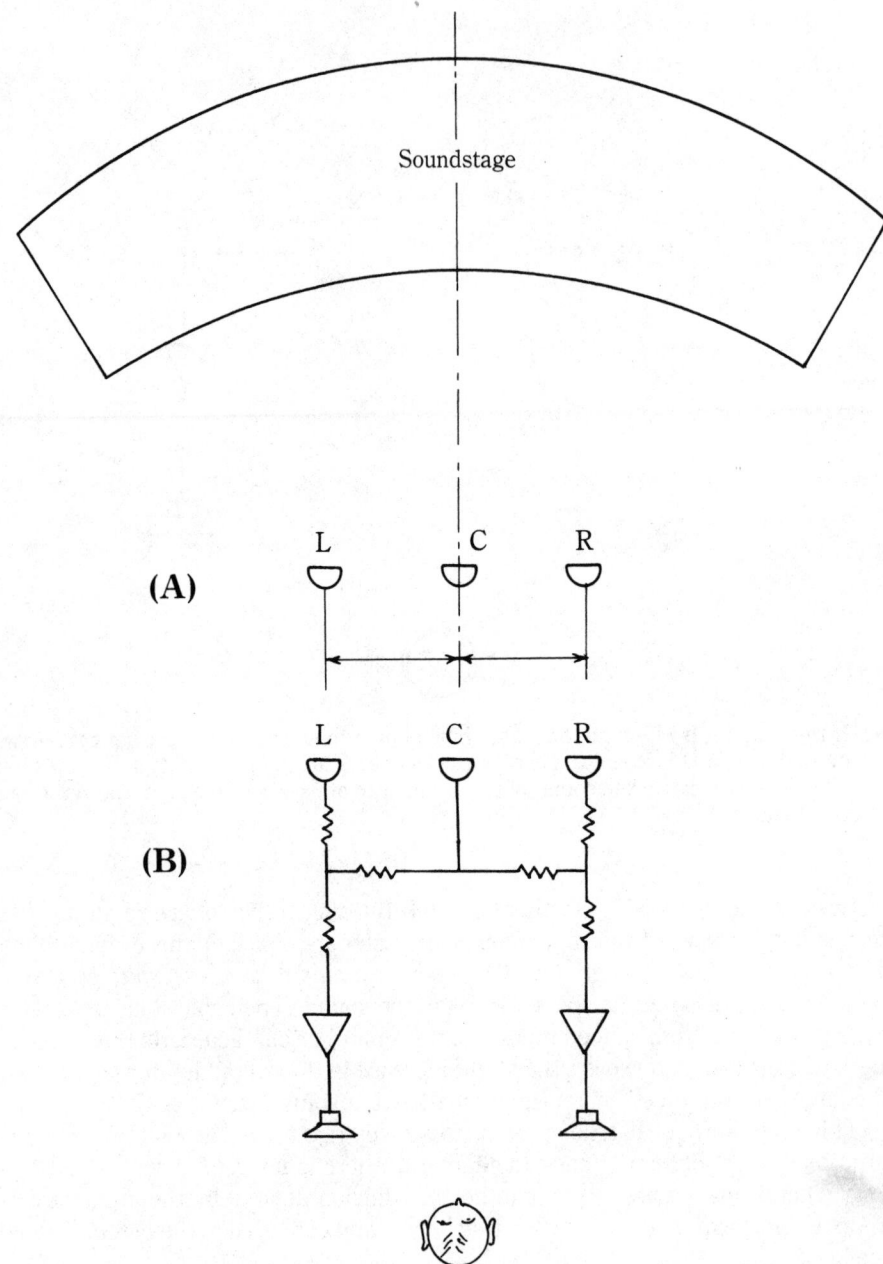

9-9 A center microphone is sometimes added to a spaced pair. Mixed equally into both channels, this will tend to fill-in the hole in the middle sometimes encountered when just two microphones are used.

Spaced omnidirectional microphones

Omnidirectional microphones are most often used to configure a spaced pair, because their pickup is theoretically unaffected by the angle of sound arrival. Careful examination of the polar response diagrams of actual microphones, however, reveals that most of these microphones become directional at higher frequencies. Therefore, when placing the microphones—whether on stands or suspended from above—it is best to aim their pickup axis toward the sound source instead of just letting them hang. Optimum response will result from this precaution.

Because the pickup of sound is equal from all directions, placement of a spaced pair of omnidirectional microphones is critical for maintaining a proper direct-to-ambient sound balance. It is generally best to position them high, in front of the soundstage. The separation between the microphones is determined by the width of the soundstage (Figs. 9-6 and 9-10). The actual distance in front of the soundstage, as with most microphone placement, is determined by critical distance (see chapter 5); the more ambient the space, the closer the microphones need to be. By placing the microphones high above the front of the sound source, the differential distance between them and the front and back of the stage will be minimized. This helps reduce acoustical imbalance between the nearer and more distant elements.

The extended low-frequency response inherent with omnidirectional microphones offers both advantages and disadvantages—all of which should be considered. Sounds with ample low-frequency information are reproduced well—often better than with any other microphone type. This is advantageous for pipe organ and orchestral music, as well as some environmental or sound effect recordings.

The omnidirectional microphone's extended response, however, also can have negative effects when excessive undesirable low-frequency noise is present from such sources as air conditioning systems, traffic, etc. Responsive only to pressure, omnidirectional microphones are relatively undisturbed by wind, which is primarily air motion or velocity energy. Thus, they are not as susceptible to the mechanical effects of wind noise as their directional counterparts. The excellent low-frequency response and lack of discrimination against off-axis sounds, however, allow omnidirectional microphones to pick up the low rumbling effects of wind, air conditioning systems, etc.

A final benefit of omnidirectional microphones is their complete lack of *proximity effect* (i.e., the artificial boosting of low frequencies when the microphone is placed close to the source of sound). Proximity effect, or *bass tip up* as it is known in the United Kingdom, is a common artifact with all directional microphones. Although a spaced microphone pair is not usually close enough to the sound source to encounter the proximity effect, situations might arise when this could occur, such as a system set relatively close to a piano or other musical instrument. In this case, the lack of proximity effect preserves the natural timbral balance of the instrument, without the need for external equalization.

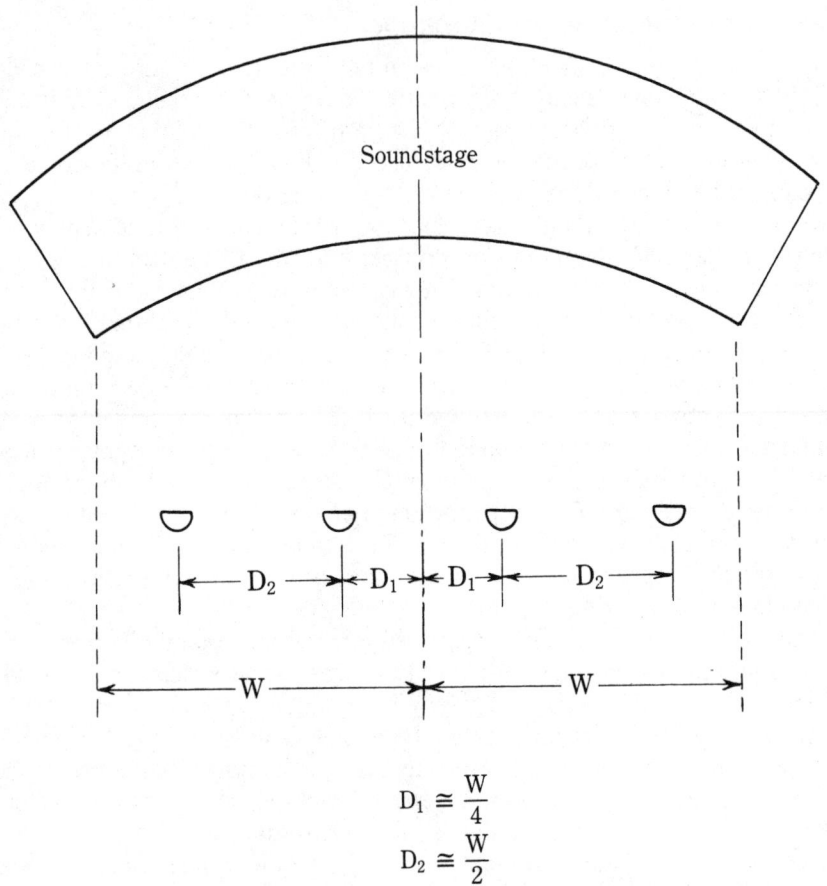

Soundstage

$$D_1 \cong \frac{W}{4}$$
$$D_2 \cong \frac{W}{2}$$

9-10 A stereo array using four directional microphones to pick up a large ensemble. The center microphone pair provides the principal stereo pickup, and the outer microphones help to cover the extremes.

Spaced directional microphones

If the recording environment is too noisy to allow the use of omnidirectional microphones, or when the microphones must be placed further from the sound source for visual reasons, directional microphones such as cardioids or hypercardioids must be used. In these situations, the spacing between the microphones still could be similar to the placement in Figs. 9-6 and 9-9, although they probably will need to be closer together. Frequently, two microphones are used on either side of center, as shown in Fig. 9-10. The distance factor of the microphones, together with the critical distance of the sound source in the environment, will dictate their placement to the sound source (see Fig. 7-13).

The aiming of directional microphones is more critical than with omnidirectionals, because all desired sound must be kept within the acceptable regions of the microphones' polar response patterns. The off-axis response of the microphones also must be considered, because it determines how they *color* the sound of the environment around them.

The effects of wind noise must be considered. Appropriate wind screening might be needed if the microphones are used outdoors or near air conditioning supply ducts.

More about interference problems

When a third or fourth microphone is added to the array, the amount of comb filtering is compounded; three microphones produce three sets of combs (Fig. 9-11), that combine to produce a complex set of response aberrations. Similarly, four microphones produce six sets of combs (Fig. 9-12).

Another problem with spaced microphones is the *duality of time cues* that results from two sets of lateral time cues presented to the listener (Fig. 9-13). Because the distance between the sound source and the microphones is generally different than the distance between the loudspeakers and the listener, the time cues are distorted on playback. For sounds equidistant from the microphones, this distortion could be minimized if the spacing between the loudspeakers is made the same as the spacing between the microphones; it would not, however, eliminate the problem for sounds not situated equidistant from the microphones. Trying to maintain such an equal spacing for microphones and loudspeakers is not practical. This is another reason why accurate stereo imaging is difficult to achieve with spaced microphone techniques.

The Decca Tree

Developed by the recording engineers of Decca Records, the *Decca Tree* was configured using three omnidirectional condenser microphones positioned at the ends of a T-shaped fixture. The spacing between the left and right microphones was approximately 2 m and the center microphone was in front of these by approximately 1.5 m (Fig. 9-14). The relatively close spacing provides sufficient intensity cues for good stereo imaging and sufficient phase information to produce an *open* sound. The middle microphone ensures a solid center for the stereo soundstage. (The use of Neumann M-50 microphones for the original Decca Tree provided it with its characteristic warm and enveloping sound—one still cherished by the London/Decca label, as well as many other recording engineers around the world.)

This technique is also favored by film scoring mixers, because of its ability to produce good stable stereo imaging, which will hold up through the application of the Dolby Surround Sound matrix system.

Flanking microphones

Occasionally, spaced microphones are used as *flankers* for a central main stereo pickup. The primary purpose of these microphones is to extend the breadth of the

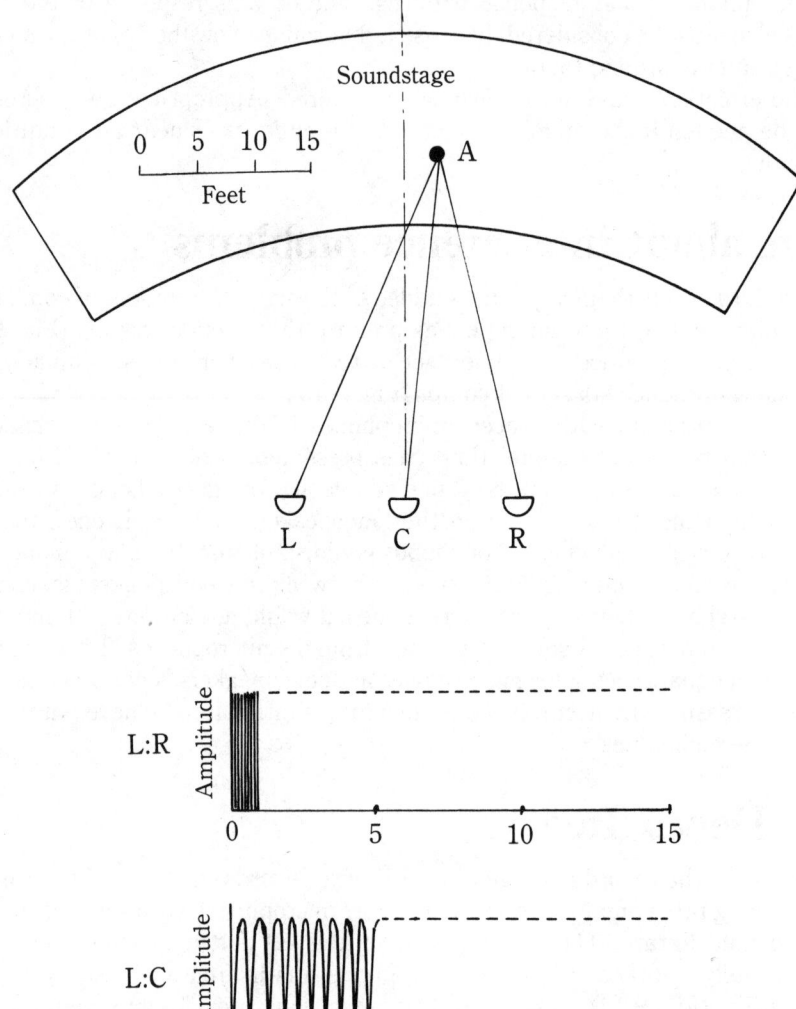

9-11 Comb filter effects occur between any two microphones in a three-microphone spaced array. The three response curves shown will combine into a complex comb filtered response.

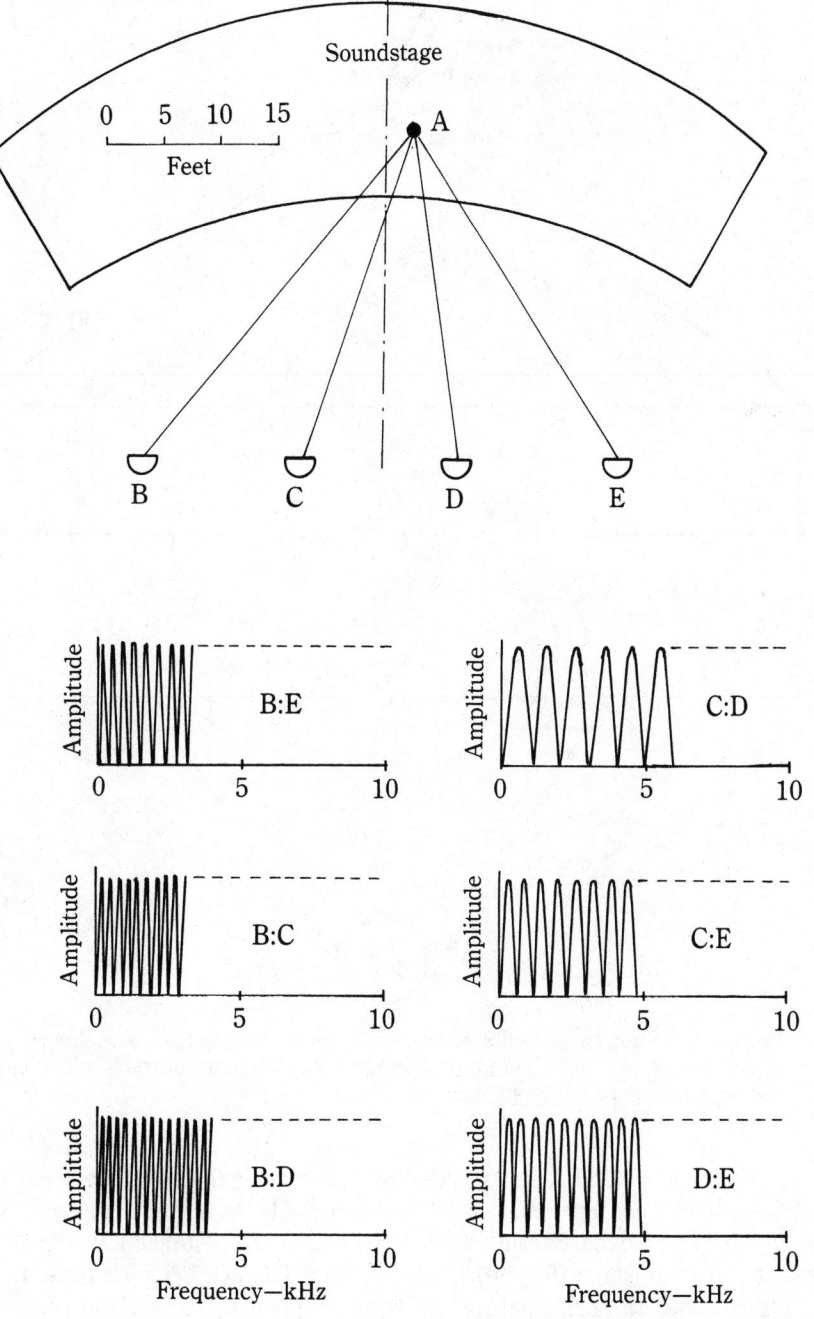

9-12 When four spaced microphones are used, six comb filter response curves are generated. These will combine to produce a highly colored frequency response, which can seriously affect the stereo signal. These effects are even more pronounced if the signal is summed to monaural.

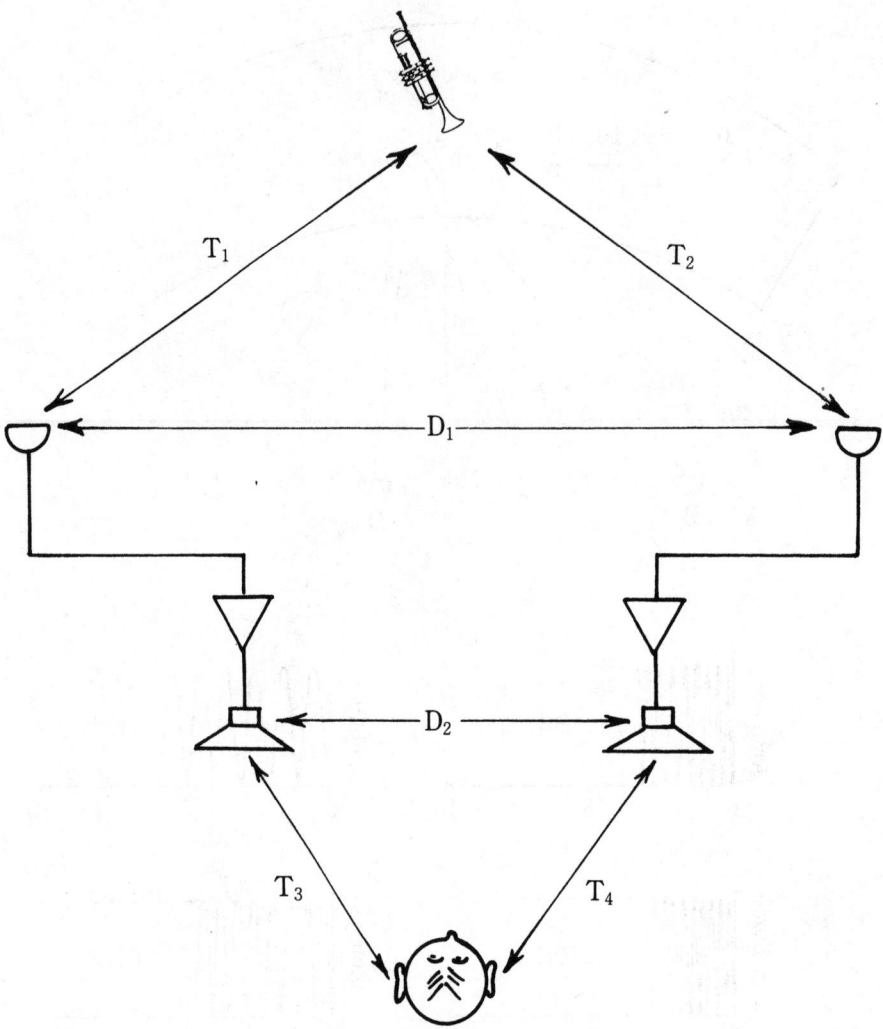

9-13   A duality of time cues results when the distance between the microphones is different than that between the loudspeakers. This leads to an unstable phantom center
image when spaced microphones are used.

stereo image and to lend support to the main stereo pickup. These are most often
omnidirectional microphones, placed symmetrically on either side of the main
pickup—spaced anywhere from a half to two-thirds the distance toward the edges
of the stereo soundstage (Fig. 9-15). The relative balance between these flanking
microphones and the principal pickup is determined by the overall sonic image
desired, but generally they are mixed at nearly-equal levels with the main pickup.
Their spacing is usually wide enough that the comb-filter effects become so ran-
domized that they do not seriously degrade the overall quality of sound for stereo
reproduction. Because they add a considerable amount of reverberation to the total

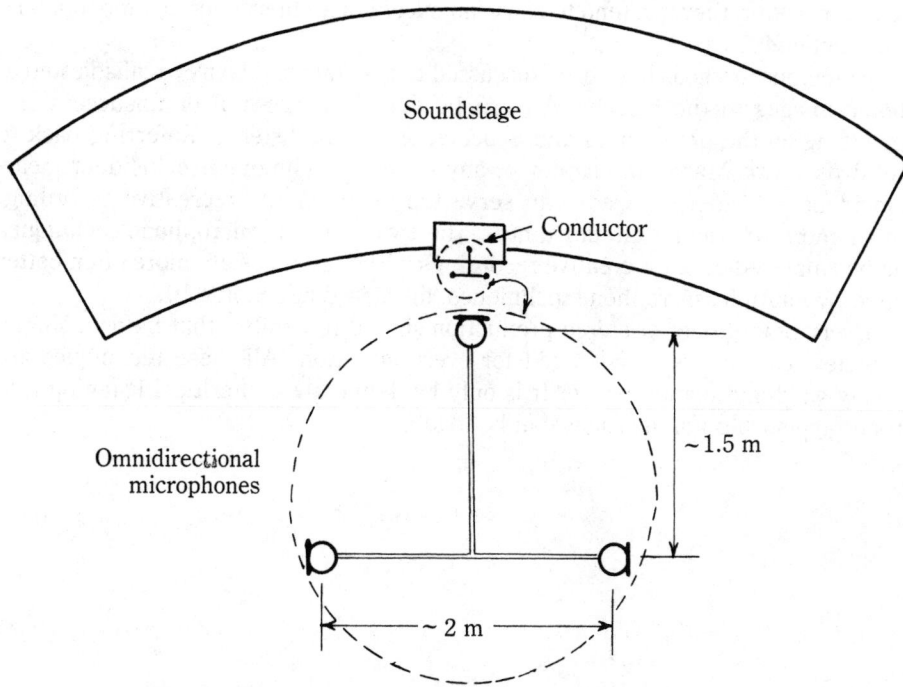

9-14 The Decca Tree is comprised of three omnidirectional microphones, placed at the ends of a T-shaped fixture. The array is generally located just behind, and a few feet above, the conductor's head. Traditionally configured with Neumann M-50 microphones, any omnidirectional microphone can be used.

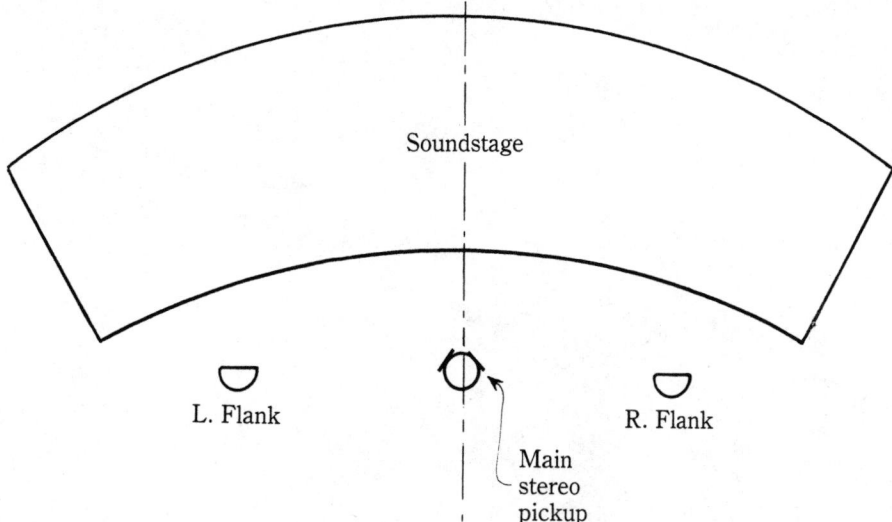

9-15 A stereo array showing a pair of omnidirectional microphones flanking a center coincident or near-coincident stereo pickup. The outer microphones are used to broaden the overall sound, and to cover the extremes of the sound stage.

pickup, however, they can tend to cause an excess of ambience for any monophonic reproduction.

Numerous methods have been discussed to generate and convey realistic stereophonic images to the listener. All can be equally successful or unsuccessful—depending on the preferences and expectations of the listener. Referring back to the Two-by-Two Matrix in chapter 4, any of these techniques—coincident, near-coincident, or widely spaced—can serve the needs of the recreative recording. Under more restricting circumstances, the two or three microphone techniques can be employed even for creative recordings, although these are more often better suited by multiple microphone techniques, discussed in chapter 10.

Every practitioner of stereo production should remember that no one, single, absolutely correct method is used for every situation. All these techniques are equally valid and inappropriate. It is only by deliberate and critical listening that proper and successful decisions can be made.

10
Multi-microphone techniques

THE FOCUS HAS THUS FAR CONCENTRATED ON THE MORE BASIC MICROPHONE techniques, i.e., those that involve a minimal number of microphones, and attempt to preserve the natural acoustical balance inherent in the original soundstage. The use of additional *spot* microphones to highlight or add extra *presence* to a particular element within the overall soundfield has been mentioned, but these microphones were considered supplemental to the principal stereo pickup.

Another radically different approach to microphone technique for the pickup of larger or more complex soundfields is the implementation of numerous microphones, each in essence a spot microphone, which are then mixed together to create a composite sonic image. The term *create* is used in the truest sense of the word, because the sonic image that results is solely the product of purposeful manipulation of the individual microphone signals. Performer, producer, and recording engineer must combine efforts to create the specific sonic illusion they desire the audience to hear. In this manner, the final product is the *mix*, as much as the *performance*.

Intensity stereo revisited

In chapter 7, intensity stereo was explained as relying on the differences in intensity between two coincident microphones to provide the sole determinant of the stereo image. Multimicrophone stereo is another manifestation of intensity stereo. The individual microphone signals are monophonic representations of one particular element of the soundfield, and all that contributes to any stereophonic imaging relies on the artificial, or electronic, placement of each of those elements within the defined stereo soundstage. The key tool that accomplishes this is the panoramic potentiometer, or *panpot*.

The panpot was developed by the engineers at the Walt Disney Studios in 1939 to create the spatial effects for their film *Fantasia*. William E. Garity, Disney's chief engineer, was asked to create the illusion of a sound moving back and forth across the screen. The engineers determined that by fading a signal between two loudspeakers a moving sound source could be simulated if the total level in the room remained constant. Simple ganging of potentiometers proved insufficient. The solution was a special two-gang volume control with complementary log attenuations where the sum of the attenuations, expressed as power ratios, equals a constant. This special control was nicknamed *The Panpot* (Reference 10-1).

The panpot

A panoramic potentiometer, or panpot, is a control that proportions an electrical signal between two outputs; it is essentially a variable voltage divider. Figure 10-1 shows how a panpot works. A signal is divided via a common voltage divider comprised of two fixed resistors, R_1 and R_2 (Fig. 10-1A). The amount of signal at the two outputs, 1 and 2, is directly proportional to the values of R_1 and R_2. The total resistance, R_T, is the sum of the values of R_1 and R_2. Because these are two fixed resistors, the amount of signal distributed to the two outputs is also fixed; it cannot be changed without altering the value of one or both of the resistors.

In Fig. 10-1B, a variable resistor, or potentiometer, is substituted for R_1 and R_2; its value is R_T. By moving the wiper up or down the relative amount of signal can be easily varied between the two outputs. This changes the level of the signal applied to the corresponding loudspeakers and the placement of the original signal in the stereo soundfield between the two loudspeakers.

The circuit shown in Fig. 10-1B is a simple variable voltage divider. In practice, a true panpot is a dual-gang potentiometer, as shown in Fig. 10-1C. Made of special, concentrically mounted log and reverse-log potentiometers, the total power output of the two stages remains constant, yet the signal is distributed evenly between the two outputs as the control is turned from one extreme to the other (Fig. 10-1D). At the center of rotation, the output of the two channels is only 50% of their full signal level, so no *center buildup* occurs when the panpot is centered. Whether this 50% factor is derived from a reduction of 3 dB, considered on a power basis, or a 6 dB reduction, considered on a voltage basis, it is somewhat controversial. Some panpots are constructed so the center point is down 4.5 dB, as a compromise between these two approaches.

The world of nonreal time

To show how the panpot plays a major role in the contemporary recording scene, an illustration of its use in the recording and mixdown process is shown in Figs. 10-2 and 10-3. A keyboard player might be recorded in a studio in Los Angeles and, because this is an electronic instrument, its signal could be fed directly into the mixing console—without the need for any microphone pickup (Fig. 10-2A). A microphone could be used to pick up the acoustical output from its loudspeaker, if desired; it is common practice to record both the direct and the acoustical output from such electronic instruments. The keyboard part establishes the basic track of the recording—setting the tempo, the style, and the overall feeling of the song. It is recorded to one (or more) tracks of a multitrack tape.

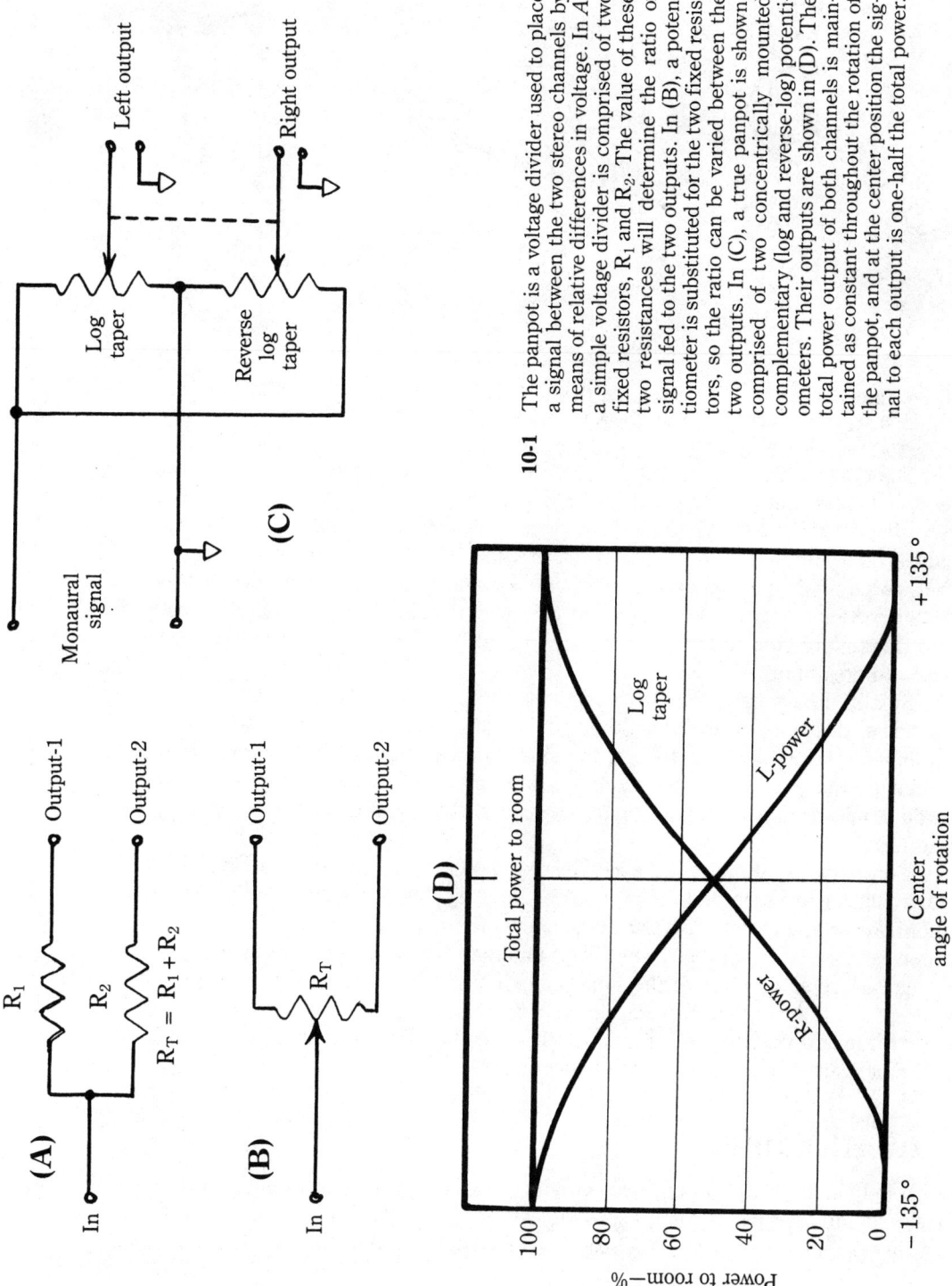

10-1 The panpot is a voltage divider used to place a signal between the two stereo channels by means of relative differences in voltage. In *A*, a simple voltage divider is comprised of two fixed resistors, R_1 and R_2. The value of these two resistances will determine the ratio of signal fed to the two outputs. In (B), a potentiometer is substituted for the two fixed resistors, so the ratio can be varied between the two outputs. In (C), a true panpot is shown, comprised of two concentrically mounted complementary (log and reverse-log) potentiometers. Their outputs are shown in (D). The total power output of both channels is maintained as constant throughout the rotation of the panpot, and at the center position the signal to each output is one-half the total power.

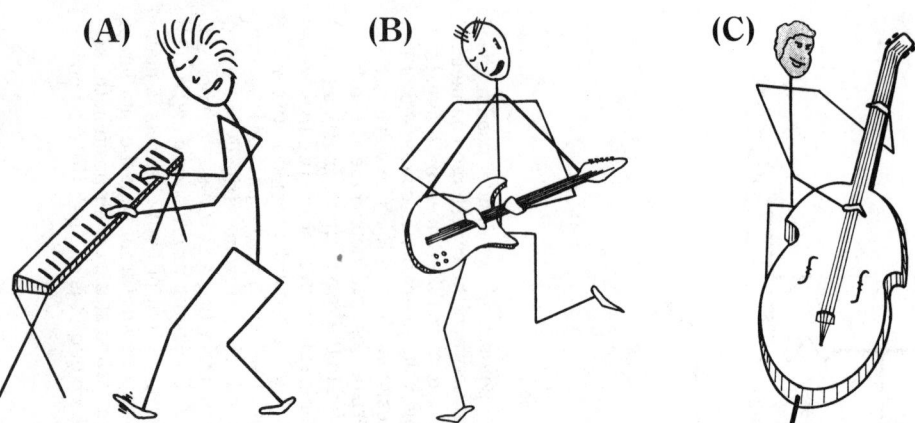

10-2   Three musicians, comprising the rhythm section, are each recorded independently on separate tracks of a multitrack recorder.

Next, a second instrument is recorded. In this example, a guitar part is recorded in a studio in Chicago (Fig. 10-2B). To do this, the tape from the previous recording is flown to the Chicago studio where the keyboard track(s) will be played back—via headphones—to the guitar player while he plays his part in synchronization with it. This new part is recorded on a separate track of the multitrack tape. As with the keyboard, the signal from the electric guitar could be taken directly into the mixing console, or a microphone could be used to record the acoustical output of its amplifier.

Finally, a bass part, Fig. 10-2C, is added to complete this rhythm section. In this case, the tape is sent to another studio, this time in New York, to record a prominent player there. As before, the musician will listen via headphones to the tracks of the two previous recordings and play in synchorization—this time through a microphone because this is an acoustic bass—onto another track on the multitrack tape.

Three tracks (or more, if the keyboard and guitar produced more than a single track apiece), are recorded thus far on the tape. Each track is essentially a monophonic-recording of its respective instrument. All are in synchronization with each other, so they later can be played back together—as though they had been performed in the same place at the same time. This is the essence of the multitrack system: a performance can be created in *nonreal* time. The beauty of this approach is that it makes possible a performance that, due to the limitations of time, space, and practicality, could never have come together otherwise.

The mixdown

With individual tracks on tape, the producer can create a stereo rendition of the basic rhythm section before recording additional instruments. To do this, the multitrack tape is returned to the studio in Los Angeles, where all of the individual (monophonic) tracks are mixed onto two new tracks that become the stereo rhythm tracks.

The producer's desired soundstage calls for the keyboard positioned on the left, the bass on the right, and the guitar in the center. To accomplish this, the mixing engineer turns the panpot for each instrument so their sounds emanate from those desired positions in the soundstage (Fig. 10-3). Finally, the playback level of each track is adjusted so a proper musical balance among the instruments is achieved.

10-3 By the use of panpots, the three musicians of Fig. 10-2 are placed within the stereo soundstage as indicated.

Sounds recorded and mixed this way pass for true stereo, even though the sonic image is comprised solely of individual, independently recorded monophonic signals placed into the stereo soundfield by totally artificial means. This process is not illegal, immoral, or even unethical. Rather, this method is a valid means of creating a stereophonic image. It is the primary means employed for most popular music recordings made since the mid-1950s, thanks in large part to the pioneering efforts of jazz guitarist Les Paul and his wife, singer Mary Ford. A satisfying lateral spread can be achieved using the panpot method. With the addition of artificial reverberation or other signal processing, a realistic sense of space can be generated around the performers. Only direct comparison to a more *conventional* stereo recording reveals some of the differences.

Basic rules of microphone usage

Whenever using microphones, certain basic constraints must be observed. The most important of these involve the advantages and limitations imposed by the polar response—frequency and sensitivity—of the microphones themselves. Proper knowledge of these factors becomes even more important when using multiple microphones to create a stereo recording. How the various microphones *hear* not only their intended subject but all of the sounds from other nearby instruments, or other sources, is of critical importance to the overall quality of the final product. Using the right microphone in the right circumstances makes the job of the recording engineer more enjoyable and successful. Using the wrong microphone—or even the right microphone in the wrong way—can only lead to disaster.

Directional patterns

In chapter 7, the common directional patterns found in most currently used microphones were surveyed. One of the most useful is the omnidirectional, which picks up sound equally well from all directions. When an omnidirectional microphone is not appropriate, however, knowledge of a microphone's directional response characteristics will allow its use to maximum advantage. All directional microphones have a primary area of pickup and one or more null regions where the response is minimal.

A properly used cardioid microphone, Fig. 10-4, has a fairly broad frontal pickup, with a reasonably even response as far as ±90° off-axis (at 90° and 270°) and a major null to the rear of the microphone (180° off-axis).

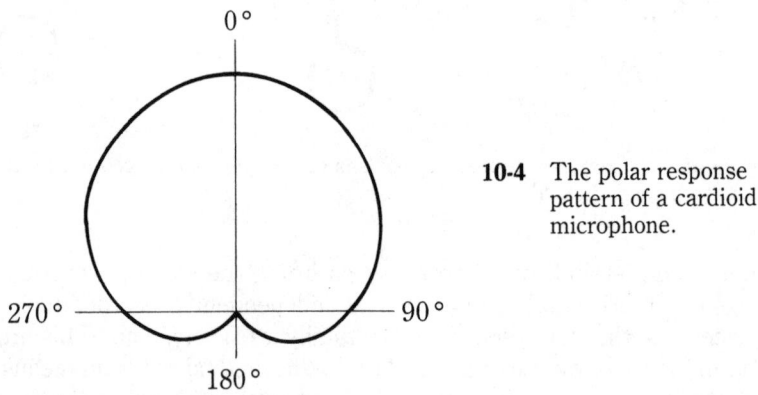

10-4 The polar response pattern of a cardioid microphone.

A hypercardioid or supercardioid microphone has a more narrow frontal pickup lobe and a rear lobe of lesser sensitivity; the polarity of the rear lobe is also reversed from that of the front lobe. Two null regions, at about ±120° to ±150° off-axis, comprise a *cone of rejection* region around the rear of the microphone (Fig. 10-5).

A bidirectional microphone has two lobes, one to the front and one to the rear,

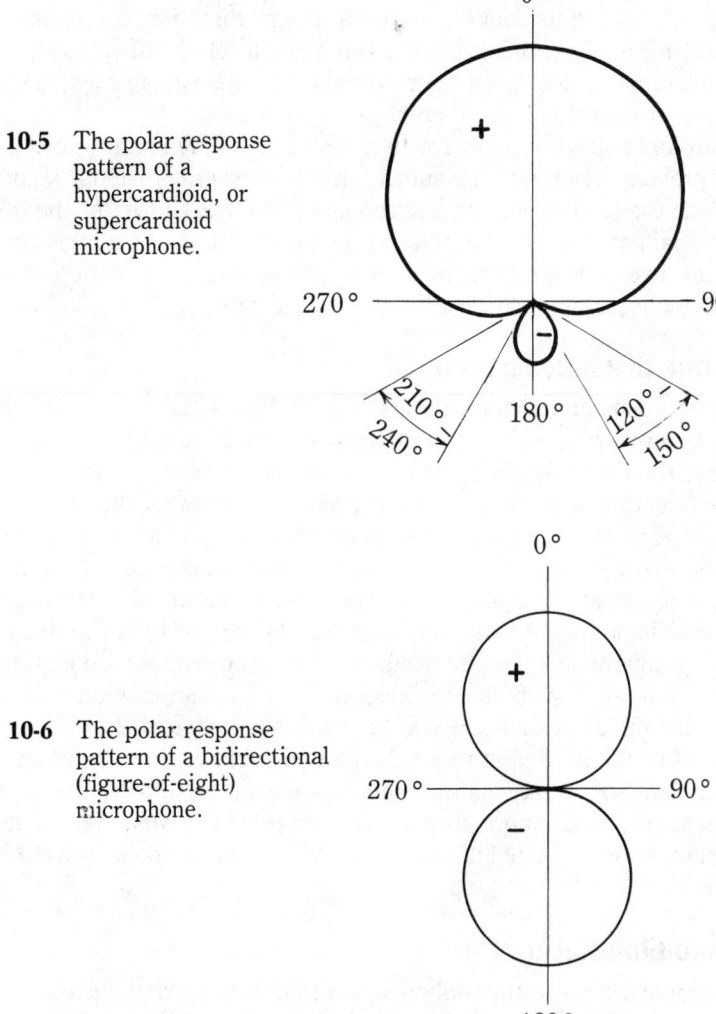

10-5 The polar response pattern of a hypercardioid, or supercardioid microphone.

10-6 The polar response pattern of a bidirectional (figure-of-eight) microphone.

of equal sensitivity but opposite polarity. The null plane (Fig. 10-6) bisects the microphone's pickup at ±90° (90° and 270°)

Referring back to Fig. 7-13, these common microphones are shown with their polar pattern, the polar equation that defines this pattern, and other factors describing the directional performance characteristics of each microphone type. The last two factors bear further discussion here: these are the random energy efficiency and the distance factor.

Microphone random energy efficiency

The random energy efficiency (RE) of a microphone is a measure of the degree to which it responds to the desired sound subject, relative to the totality of the sonic environment surrounding it (Reference 10-2). Because an omnidirectional micro-phone responds equally to sound arriving from any direction, its RE is defined as unity—or 1. (In Fig. 7-13, this is given a reference level of 0 dB.) Because they are intended to be more selective in their directional response, all other microphones are thus measured against this reference.

The cardioid pattern is shown with a RE of 0.333. Thus, for a given distance and sound pressure level from the subject, it responds only to about 1/3 of the total soundfield, as the omnidirectional microphone. The RE shown for the other com-mon directional patterns indicate that if rejection of ambient sound is the primary criterion, the use of a hypercardioid microphone is recommended, because its effective ambient pickup is lower than that of the cardioid.

Microphone distance factor

An omnidirectional microphone exhibits none of the off-axis polar response irregu-larities common with directional microphones. Thus, it would seem that for most applications, the omni should be the microphone of choice; however, because it offers little rejection of unwanted sounds arriving from other directions, its use is often unwise. A more directional microphone must be used to avoid problems such as feedback, extraneous noise pickup, visual interference, etc. From the random energy figures, a related guideline has been established to aid in the proper selec-tion of a directional microphone. The distance factor (DSF) is the distance from which a given microphone can be used, relative to an omnidirectional, to achieve the same random energy efficiency (Reference 10-2). If an omnidirectional micro-phone is undesirable because it would be visible in a camera shot, for example, a hypercardioid could be used at twice the distance and yet still maintain the same direct-to-ambient sound ratio as the omni. An even more directional microphone, the *shotgun* microphone—more properly termed the *differential-tube*—is most com-monly used for boom-mounted dialogue recording; many of these can achieve a RE of 0.1.

The Two-to-One Ratio

In his benchmark text on microphones, Lou Burroughs defined the *Two-to-One Ratio* (Reference 10-3). He stated that for the same signal level and direct-to-rever-berant sound ratio, a cardioid microphone can generally be used at twice the dis-tance from the sound source as an omnidirectional microphone. Although this is a somewhat loose generalization of the distance factor, the practical applications of the Two-to-One Ratio for microphone selection and placement are widely applied.

The Three-to-One Rule

This distance factor is also important to remember when using multiple micro-phones in a close proximity to one another, because it is the key to avoiding audible phase interference, or comb filter effects when creating the final stereo mix. Again, Burroughs penned a useful guideline, the Three-to-One Rule (Reference 10-4). This states that if two (or more) microphones are used to pick up two (or more) subjects, each microphone must be at least three times the distance from any other microphone as it is from its own subject.

To minimize the comb-filter effects resulting from leakage of an opposing subject into a microphone, its sound pressure level should be at least 10 dB lower in level than that of the intended subject. The inverse square law conveniently provides this required reduction, because a tripling of distance results in almost 10 dB reduction in sound pressure level.

An example of the three-to-one rule can be seen in Fig. 10-7, where two omnidirectional microphones are 6 inches from their respective subjects and 18 inches from one another. This 10 dB rejection also can be achieved using directional patterns, allowing the spacing between microphones to be somewhat reduced. With directional microphones, the response tends to become less directional at lower frequencies. In addition, the off-axis response of directional microphones must be considered, because off-axis coloration can sound unnatural and still contribute to phase interference effects later when the signals are mixed.

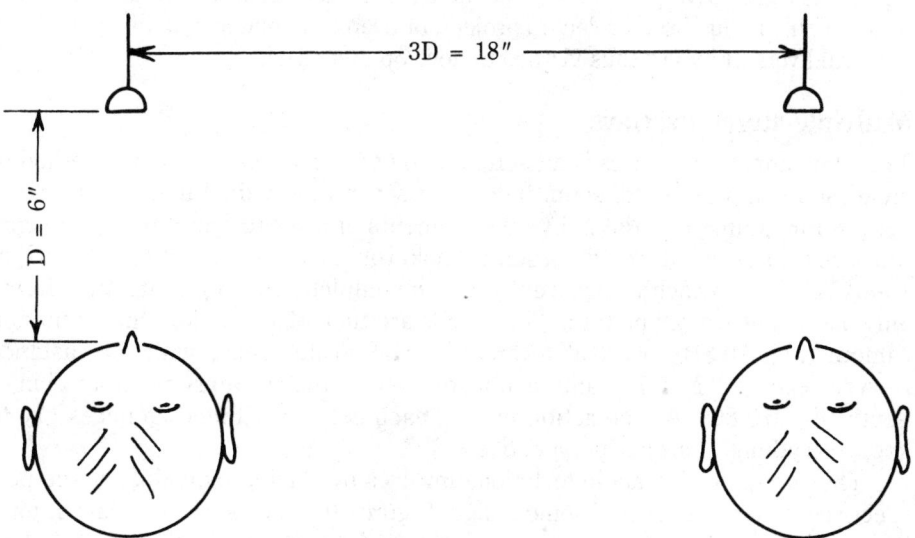

10-7 The three-to-one rule requires that the distance between any two microphones be at least three times the distance from either microphone to its respective subject.

Microphone sensitivity and sound pressure levels

Because multiple microphone techniques often result in microphone placement that is close to the source of sound, it is important to consider the effects of the sound pressure level on the microphones being used. Quiet musical instruments or sounds (such as ambient sounds, soft dialogue, stringed instruments, etc.) require microphones with high sensitivity and low self noise. (Self noise is the *noise floor* of the microphone itself—i.e., the minimum internal electrical noise level generated by the microphone even in the absence of an acoustical input signal.) Loud sounds, on the other hand, demand a microphone with a high overload characteristic, i.e., the ability to withstand high sound pressure levels without electrical or mechanical overload distortion. Knowledge of the sensitivity rating of the microphone helps minimize the unpleasant effects that might result from the compromises involved in microphone sensitivity, polar response, and placement.

Multiple-microphone concepts

In chapter 4, various approaches to the creation of the stereo illusion were introduced. Microphone techniques that tend to fall within the recreative column of Fig. 4-2 were discussed in chapters 7 and 9. Multimicrophone techniques generally fall on the more *creative* side of the matrix. Even so, the producer and recording engineer can choose from several ways to proceed when building the mix. In this realm, no hard and fast rules exist, however. Rather, the dictum is: "If it sounds right, it is right." Every producer has his/her own ideas of what sounds right, and these might change from project to project, or even from one day to the next. Flexibility and versatility are thus virtues to develop and cherish.

Multiple stereo overlays

The film animation process is a useful analogy for understanding our method of creating a complex stereo soundfield from several individual microphone pickups. In film animation, the individual elements of a scene are drawn onto separate cells: foreground, middleground, background, principal action, etc., (Fig. 10-8A). Although each transparent cell is a complete drawing in itself, it forms only part of the overall picture. These cells are then placed before the animation camera (Fig. 10-8B), overlaid to create a composite scene, with the distance between each cell and the camera adjusted to give the appropriate impression of depth (Fig. 10-8C). As the action moves, each cell is repainted as necessary to keep everything in proper perspective.

The corresponding audio technique involves overlaying individual stereo perspectives to create an overall sonic image. Figure 10-9 shows a typical layout for a large musical work, with chorus, orchestra, and four soloists. (Although recording this performance with a single pair of microphones might be possible, internal balances between the various musical elements makes this a difficult task to achieve.) A useful approach would be to pick up each major section as a semiindependent entity and then to combine the sections into one composite stereo image.

Figure 10-10 shows how this might be done. In Fig. 10-10A, four microphones are used to create a stereo pickup of the chorus. In Fig. 10-10B, a near-coincident stereo pair is used for the orchestra pickup. Finally, Fig. 10-10C shows that individual microphones are used for each of the four singers, each panned across the soundfield to create a stereo spread for the soloists to match their original positions on the stage. Three stereo pickups then exist—soloists, orchestra, and chorus— each focusing on just one element of the complete performance.

To give sense of perspective to the performance, two additional stereo pickups

A. Individual cells

Foreground   Action   Middleground   Background

B. Animation camera

C. Composite picture

10-8 Film animation techniques employ multiple overlays of individual drawings to create a composite image. In (A) individual cells are shown for the foreground, the principal action, the middleground, and the background of a scene. In (B) the drawings are arranged before the camera to create the illusion of depth seen in the composite picture (C).

are used, (Fig. 10-10D): a coincident stereo pair placed to give a reasonably good balance of the overall performance, and a second pair of spaced microphones to provide a feeling of ambience and reverberation. There are five stereo pickups in all.

To create the composite mix from these five pickups, the producer usually decides to use the overall pickup shown in Fig. 10-10D as the starting reference point. This is analogous to the middleground cell in the animation drawing. Next,

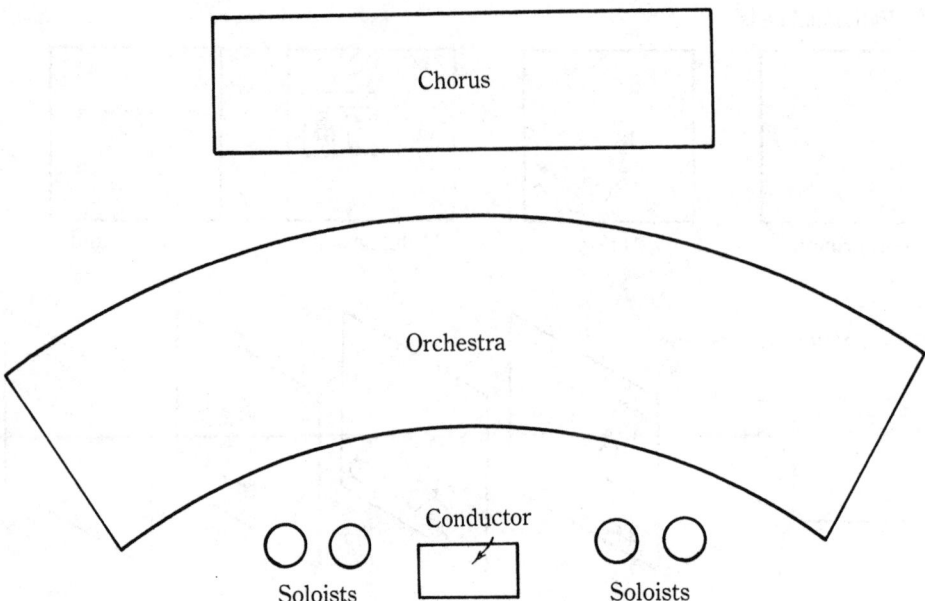

10-9 The typical concert setup for music requiring four soloists, chorus, and orchestra.

the soloists are placed *in front* of this by mixing them a little *forward* (i.e., louder); the chorus is mixed slightly *behind* the soloists, perhaps with a bit more emphasis on the side microphones to allow the soloists to occupy the center of the stereo soundfield. Finally, the ambience microphones are mixed in to provide a background environment for the performance—a feeling of space and reverberation. In all, 14 microphones generate five stereo pickups to form one composite stereo image. Although every situation requires its own specific microphone placement, the foregoing describes the concept of the overlay approach for creating a complex stereo perspective.

Multiple microphone stereo

At the beginning of this chapter, the concept of panpot stereo was introduced. This technique is also sometimes called *multi-mic mono* because each microphone produces a separate monophonic recording in itself. Individual recordings can be combined successfully to create a complex stereo illusion; this is equally true of monophonic and stereo elements. The concepts are similar; only the applications differ.

Referring back to Fig. 10-9, the performance can be broken down again into three basic elements—each one treated independently. Figure 10-11A shows that the chorus is again given four microphones, but this time they are placed to pick up each of the four sections (sopranos, altos, tenors, and basses). Figure 10-11B shows that a separate microphone is used to pick up each of the four soloists.

The major difference between this approach and that of Fig. 10-10 is in the treatment of the orchestra. In Fig. 10-11C, many more microphones have been used, as compared to Fig. 10-10B. There are two microphones for each section of the orchestra, with an extra *spot* mic over the tympani and one for the harp. Twenty microphones in all are used for the orchestra pickup. In practice, many modern recording sessions might employ even more microphones to pick up a large orches-

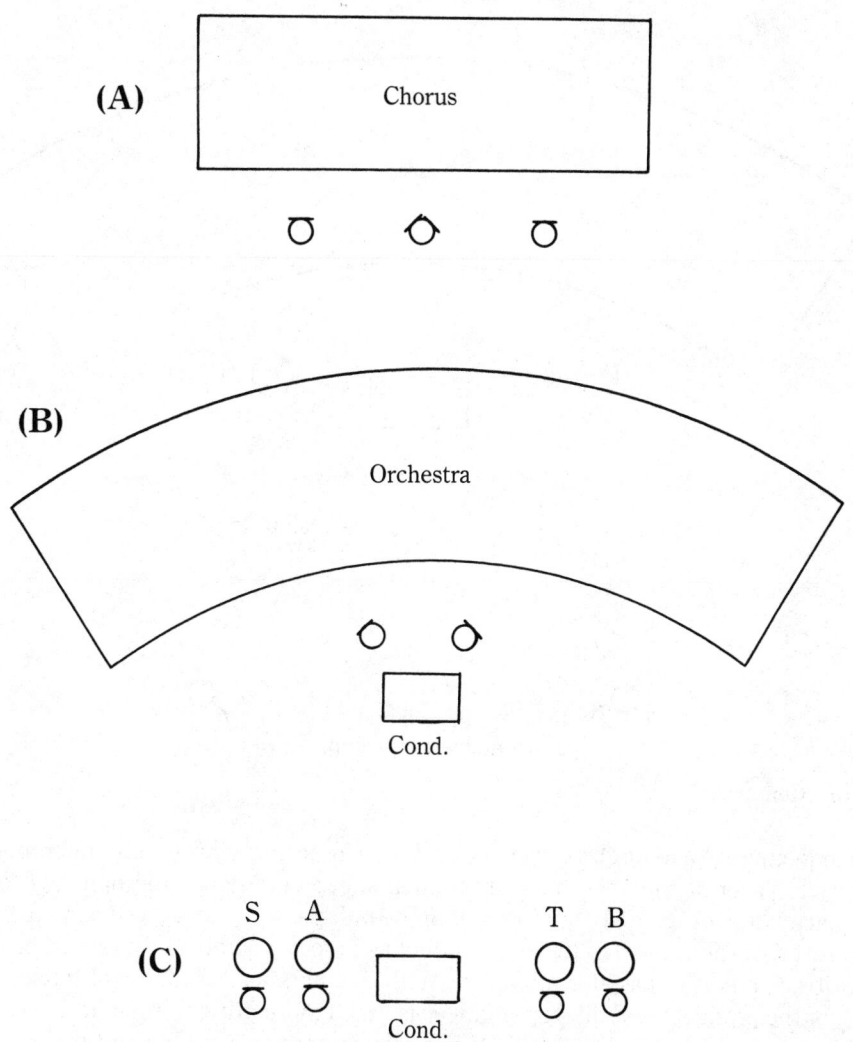

10-10 A simple microphone technique employing three stereo pickups to record the performance of Fig. 10-9. These will be overlaid to create a composite stereo image of the entire performance. In (A), the choral pickup consists of a coincident pair of microphones, flanked by two spaced microphones. In (B), a near-coincident pair of microphones is used as the orchestral pickup. In (C), an individual microphone is used for each of the four soloists. In (D) two additional stereo microphone systems are added to the preceding: a coincident XY pair to provide an overall perspective pickup of the performance, and a spaced pair to record the ambience and reverberation.

(D)

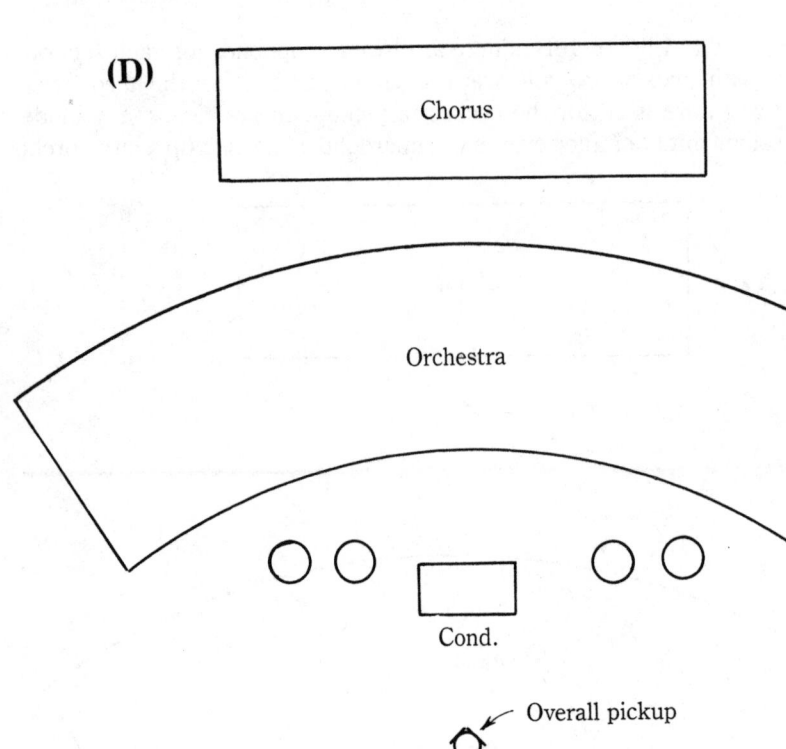

10-10 Continued.

tra: one microphone might be set for each pair of string players, one microphone for each player of wind and brass instruments, etc. Additional microphones could be placed, as in Fig. 10-10D, to record an overall perspective as well as ambience and reverberation. Each of these microphones is recorded on a separate track of a multitrack recorder for later mixdown. With this number of individual tracks, the task of the producer and mixing engineer is much more difficult than in the earlier example, in which there were only five stereo images to combine and the general balance within the sections was established by the conductor. Now, as many as 32 microphones must be balanced. The musical balance is entirely up to the producer and mixing engineer. They determine the balance heard in the final recording, and unless intimately involved in this crucial process, the conductor's only purpose is to keep the various performers playing together, nothing more.

The mixing process begins, as before, with the placement of the orchestral sound. This time, however, all the microphones need to be panpotted into the proper position and their levels adjusted, so the individual sections of the orchestra

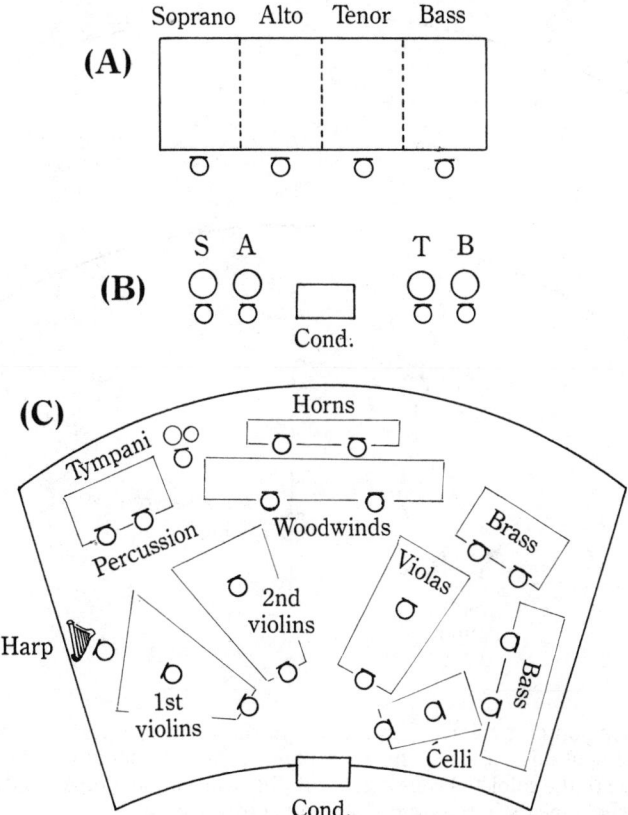

10-11 (A) A different approach to microphone placement for the chorus of Fig. 10-9; in this case one microphone is used to pick up each of the four sections. (B) As before, one microphone is placed for each of the four soloists of Fig. 10-9. (C) This time, several microphones are used to record the orchestra of Fig. 10-9. Each section of the orchestra is provided with two microphones, and extra spot microphones are placed for the tympani and harp.

achieve a correct musical balance; furthermore, this mix needs to be adjusted continually throughout the performance to maintain this balance.

Similarly, the microphones for the chorus and soloists need to be placed into the overall perspective. Finally, the ambience microphones are added, and perhaps some artificial reverberation as well, to *round out* the overall sound.

Placement of spot microphones

An important factor to remember when using spot microphones with any of the stereo techniques discussed so far—whether minimal microphone or multimicrophone stereo—is that the apparent spatial position of these accent signals must coincide exactly with the natural position of their subjects in the overall perspective.

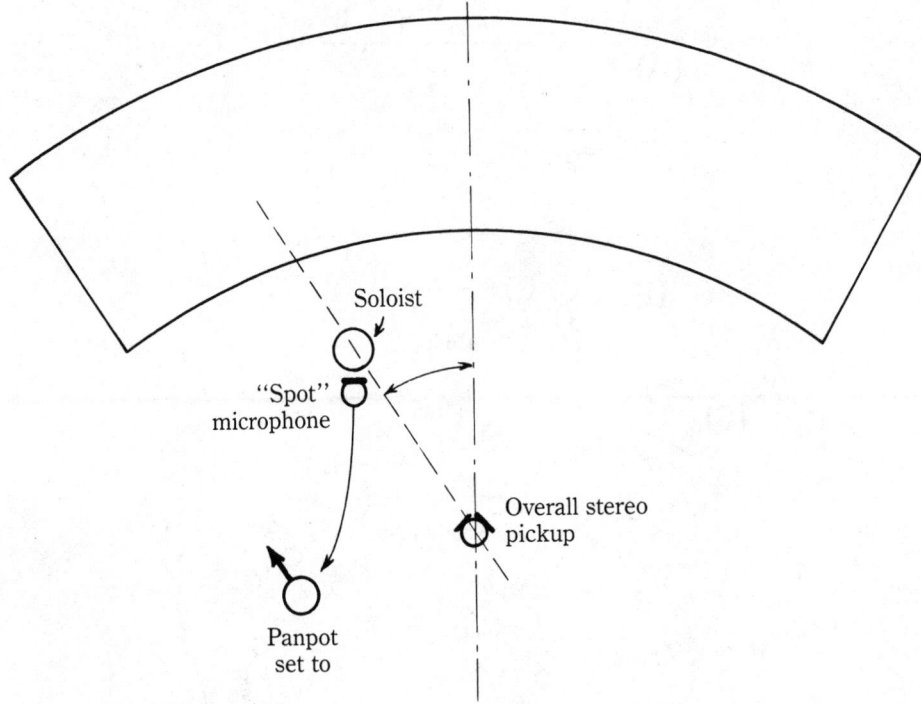

Soloist

"Spot"
microphone

Overall stereo
pickup

Panpot
set to

10-12 The position of a soloist with respect to the orchestra must be maintained when using a spot microphone. The microphone's panpot should be adjusted so that the position of the soloist is consistent with the same angle (i.e., a ° to the left of center) as he/she appears in the overall stereo perspective.

Figure 10-12 shows the example of a soloist with an orchestra. If an overall stereo pickup is used, the soloist will appear $a°$ to the left of center in the stereo image. If an accent microphone is used to provide a little additional presence to the soloist, its sound *must* be positioned with the panpot exactly coincident with the natural position of the soloist (i.e., $a°$ to the left of center). If not, the image of the soloist will tend to wander throughout the performance. When soft, the soloist will be favored by the accent microphone, and the sonic position will be determined by the setting of the panpot. When loud, the overall pickup will pull the soloist back toward the natural perspective. The psychological effect of this is annoying to the listener and should be avoided.

Creating the illusion

As indicated in the previous discussion, multiple microphone techniques are best suited when creating a stereo panorama from scratch. The classical approach to the placement of the various performing forces is shown in Fig. 10-9. Although this setup is typical of a concert performance, it need not dictate placement for a recording session. This traditional placement would likely make a good recording more difficult to achieve. Figure 10-13 shows one of many possible alternative layouts. This arrangement would provide the recording engineer with greater control of the balance between the various forces—orchestra, chorus, and soloists—yet still allow the conductor and performers the necessary ability to hear and coordinate with one another without having to resort to artificial means.

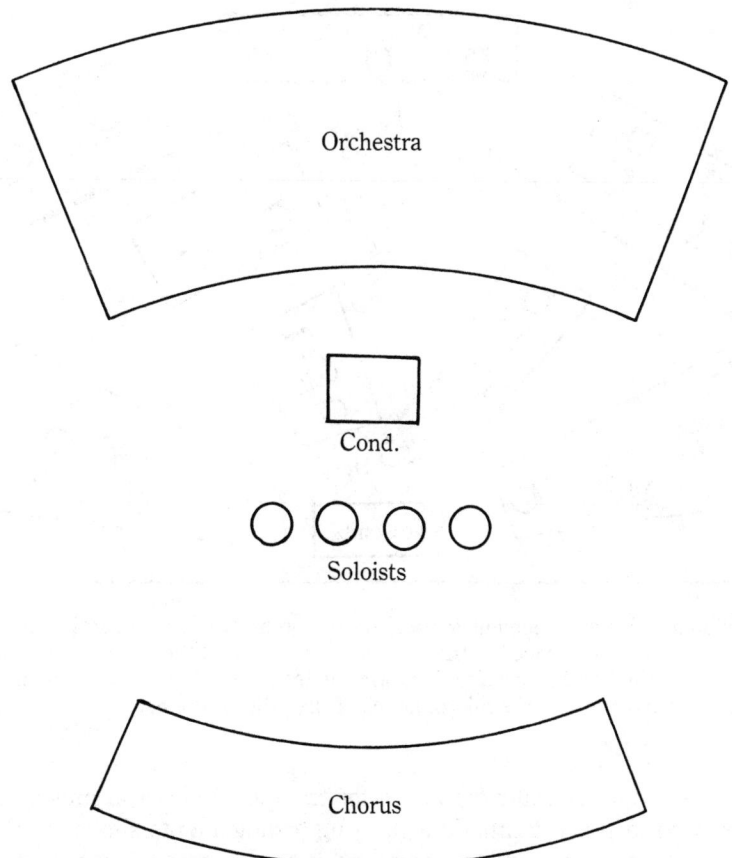

10-13 An alternative placement of the performers employed for recording the same music as Fig. 10-9. Because there is no requirement to serve an audience, the chorus and soloists can be placed facing the conductor and orchestra. This tends to improve the separation between the various forces.

Similarly, Fig. 10-14 shows one of many possible alternatives to that of Fig. 10-11C, for the setup of a large orchestra. To give more definition between the first and second violins, the latter are placed on the opposite side of the conductor, and the harp is directly in front to keep it away from the louder instruments. Note also the use of *baffles* (large, solid, acoustically treated barriers) between the percussion and brass, and between the brass and strings, to help control the leakage of these louder instruments into the microphones intended for pick up of the softer

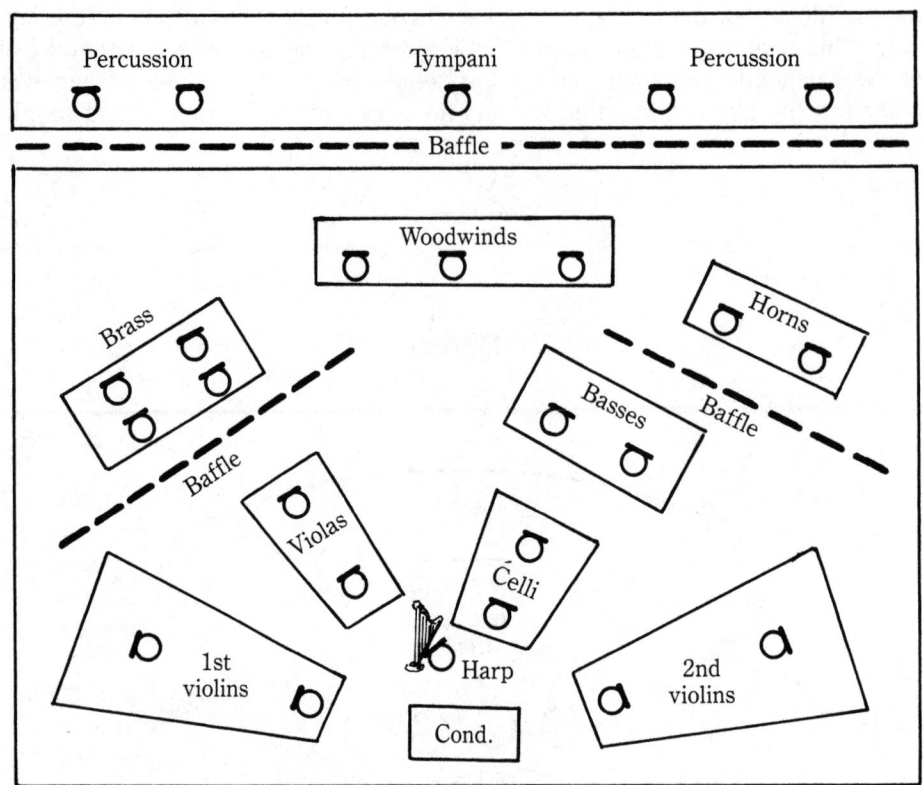

10-14 An alternative arrangement for seating the orchestra for a recording session. The second violins are placed to the conductor's right, and the harp is front and center. Acoustical baffles are used to decrease the leakage of the louder brass and percussion instruments into the microphones of the other sections.

ones. Although not generally employed for traditional classical music recording, and never used in concert situations, seating arrangements similar to this might frequently be found on scoring stages where motion picture music soundtracks are recorded. Placement of microphones and their balance, and position within the overall stereo soundfield are determined by the recording engineer and producer to create a specific aural image.

Selection of microphones

Some of the operating parameters of the various microphone types have been discussed. A thorough understanding of these principles is necessary in order to determine which microphone should be used in any particular situation. The differences between the polar response patterns and the resulting distance factor—overall sensitivity; susceptibility to wind, breath, or handling noise; proximity effect; general frequency response—are all factors that recording engineers must be thoroughly familiar with for every microphone available to them. Studying specification sheets that accompany microphones helps, but actual use and listening tests are essential to fully gain an appreciation of the character of each microphone.

Placement of microphones

When using multiple microphones, relatively close placement to their respective subject is common. This gives rise to a basic question: Where should the microphone be placed for proper pickup? Anyone who has listened to a musical instrument close up knows that it sounds quite different from various vantage points, but where does it sound *right*? This is a problem that has baffled recording engineers since the beginning of *recorded time* (pun intended), and several excellent texts were written to describe the sound spectra and radiation patterns of common instruments and ensembles (References 10-5, 10-6, 10-7).

The serious practitioner of recording engineering must understand how an instrument or ensemble produces its sound before the placement of the microphone(s) can be determined to properly capture their sound. Thorough knowledge of the theory of sound propagation, however, must also be supplemented by careful and experienced listening, because theory is always affected by circumstance: different instruments, performance attitudes and styles of playing, room acoustics, seating arrangements—all are factors that bear serious effects on the proper choice and placement of microphone(s) for recording. The same holds true for recording sound effects, dialogue, environments, ambiences, or whatever. Only by carefully listening and evaluation of a sound can the recording engineer determine precisely where to place the microphone(s) to capture it properly.

One from many

Although many possible roads can be taken, the journey must ultimately lead to one specific destination. This goal often can be reached by the most direct path. At other times, circuitous routes and numerous detours are necessary. As stated in chapter 4, the product of all the technology in the recording process is ultimately the creation of a unique listening experience. What will be its effect on the listener? Will it engender a sensation of pleasure or pain, joy or terror, relaxation or anxiety, tension or release? The goal is established by the producer. Determining what route will make the trip successful, however, is the job of the recording engineer. The two must work together to see that the goal is achieved and the journey is pleasant.

11
Pseudostereo

AT FIRST RECORDINGS WERE ALL MONOPHONIC. THEN CAME STEREO, AND many producers with inventories of mono recordings sought ways to reissue these recordings in *stereo* format to capitalize on the great interest in stereo. Numerous methods of changing mono signals to at least a semblance of stereo were proposed.

The most important point in studying the various methods of changing a mono signal to stereo is the realization that it is impossible to do so. The best that can be hoped for is a signal that has certain characteristics of a stereo signal. The stereo pickup system produces left and right channel signals that differ from each other in subtle ways. Because these subtle incoherencies are not picked up by the mono microphone, no mono-to-stereo device can precisely re-create them.

In addition to the current need to change mono recordings to stereolike form in numerous practical production operations, there is an instructional value in examining these mono-to-stereo systems. Each system underscores the delicate differences in the signals of the two channels of a true stereo recording. The deficiencies of pseudostereo emphasize the importance and uniqueness of the basic stereo signals (References 11-1 and 11-2).

Pseudostereo by frequency response differences

In 1948 Janovsky proposed that a 3-dimensional effect could be given to a mono recording by splitting it into two channels, which differ only in frequency response (Reference 11-3). He suggested that if the low-frequency content was reduced in the left channel and the high-frequency content was reduced in the right channel, the reproduced image would be spread between the two loudspeakers (Fig. 11-1). A certain broadening of the image can be achieved by this method, but anything resembling a true stereo effect is totally absent.

Interaural incoherence obtained by this method is at the expense of sound quality. The low-frequency energy of the signal is *rolled off* in one loudspeaker, and high-frequency energy is *rolled off* in the other. In the example of Fig. 11-1, the musical signal directly to the left ear contains little bass, but the signal to the right ear contains much bass and little else. The overall perception of full timbre in the music is lost. With real stereo, the full spectral quality of the music is not only perceived, but enhanced with the addition of spatial information.

Pseudostereo by reverberation chamber

Schroeder (1958) and Lockner and Keet (1960) proposed that a reverberation chamber be used to generate incoherency between the left and right channel signals as shown in Fig. 11-2 (References 11-4 and 11-5). The mono signal, radiated into the chamber by a loudspeaker, is picked up by microphones feeding left and right channels. If the microphones are close together, their signals will be essentially coherent. By changing their spacing and relative positions, the degree of incoherency can be varied, introducing a sense of *space* to the pseudostereo recording. The result is a more *open* recording, with a feeling of the *presence* of a music hall, but still no real stereo image is created.

Incoherency also can be generated between the two channels with a single microphone in the reverberation chamber (Fig. 11-3). If the output of the single microphone is fed to both loudspeakers, a phantom image will appear between the loudspeakers, but no image spread will occur because no incoherency exists between the channels. The introduction of a time delay in one channel provides the needed incoherency. Delays by approximately 50 ms are appropriate in this system.

Pseudostereo by signal delay

Incoherencies between left and right channels can be obtained without the reverberation room using nothing more than a time delay device as shown in Fig. 11-4. Attenuator A controls the level of the sound to the delay device. Attenuator B controls the relative distribution of the delayed signal between the right and left loudspeakers. Delaying the signal to the right channel results in the localization of the sound at the left loudspeaker by the law of the first wavefront. By manipulation of the two controls, the phantom image—with an adjustable amount of spread—can be moved to a point midway between the two loudspeakers (Reference 11-2).

Pseudostereo by complementary comb filters

Lauridsen in 1954 proposed a clever pseudostereo method that conserved a major part of the mono signal in both channels and introduced less distortion than the Janovsky method (Reference 11-6). He used complementary comb filters to give a stereolike spread to the reproduced sound (Fig. 11-5).

When a delayed replica of a signal is combined with the signal itself, interference takes place (see chapter 8). Constructive interference at some frequencies

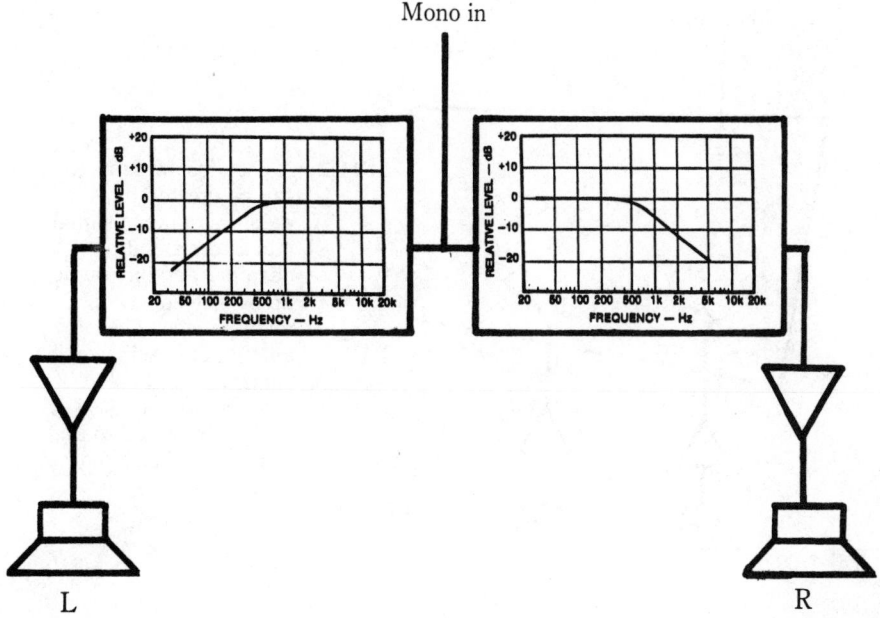

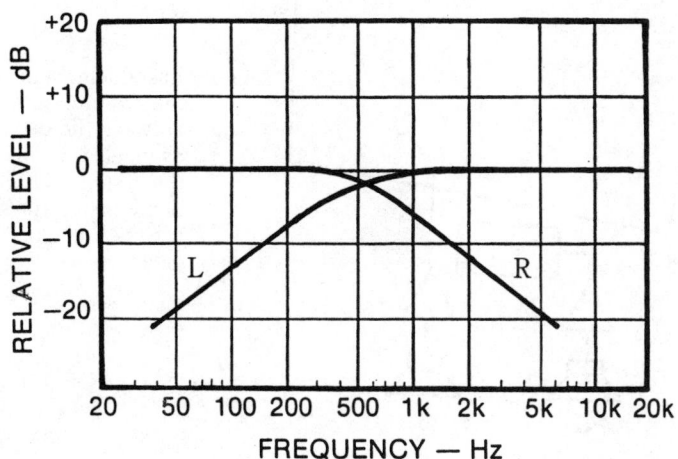

11-1 A mono signal can be given a certain *spread* between two stereo loudspeakers by treating the mono signal differently for the left and right channels. In this example, the low frequencies are rolled off in the left channel and the high frequencies are rolled off for the right channel. The incoherency thus created yields a far-from-perfect stereo effect.

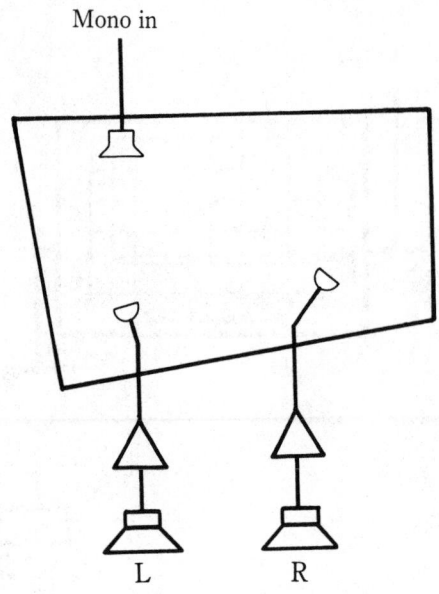

11-2 A pseudostereo image can be created by radiating a mono signal into a reverberation chamber and picking it up by spaced microphones. The amount of spacing controls the degree of incoherency. A sense of *space* is imparted to this type of pseudostereo signal.

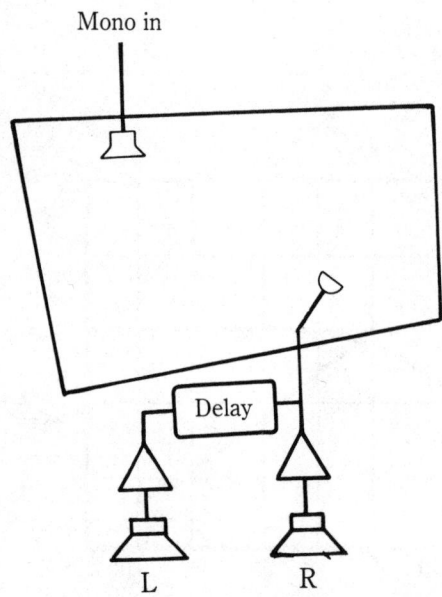

11-3 Introducing a delay of the order of 50 ms between the two channels is a variant of the system of Fig. 11-2. Some image spread results from such a delay.

results in an increased signal level by as much as +6 dB. Destructive interference at other interspersed frequencies results in response minima (theoretically, minus infinity). In this way, a uniform frequency response is changed to a series of peaks and dips throughout the audible spectrum.

Mono in

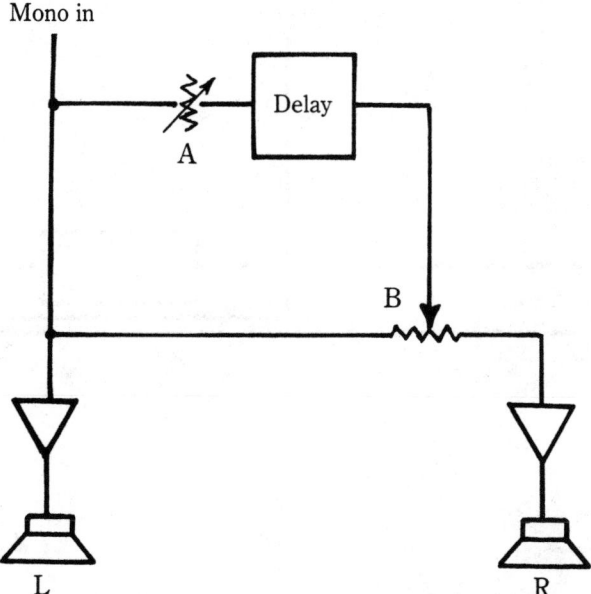

11-4 Incoherency between the left and right mono signals can be obtained by introducing a small delay between the two. Attenuator A controls the level of sound to the delay device. Attenuator B controls the amount of the delayed signal to each loudspeaker. By manipulation of these two controls, the phantom image with adjustable spread can be moved to its proper place between the two loudspeakers.

The staggering of peaks in one channel with minima in the other is accomplished by a complementary comb-filter arrangement. The complementary feature is produced by adding the delayed signal to the undelayed signal for one channel and subtracting the two for the other channel. By sending the sum signal to one channel and the difference signal to the other, the peaks of one channel occur at frequencies at which minima occur in the other channel. In this way, offset signals having similar spectra, or timbre, are radiated from both loudspeakers.

The comb filter peaks occur at frequencies $1/t$ apart, t being the delay in seconds. For example, a delay of 0.001 second (1 ms) places the peaks $1/0.001 =$ 1,000 Hz apart, which would result in a rather course spectrum. On the other hand, a delay by 0.050 of a second (50 ms) yields peak (or null) spacing of 20 Hz yielding a much finer spectrum. By adjustment of the amount of delay, the spacing between adjacent peaks (or adjacent minima) can be changed. By this control the interchannel incoherency might be varied in the trade-off between image spread and sound quality (i.e., the audibility of the frequency-response irregularities).

Lauridsen's method of producing pseudostereo from a mono signal gives a relatively uniform spectral quality in the two channels; however, it unfortunately also gives a definite coloration of the signal. The shorter the delay time, the greater the interaural incoherence and image spread but also the worse the sound quality. A balance must be reached between these conflicting factors.

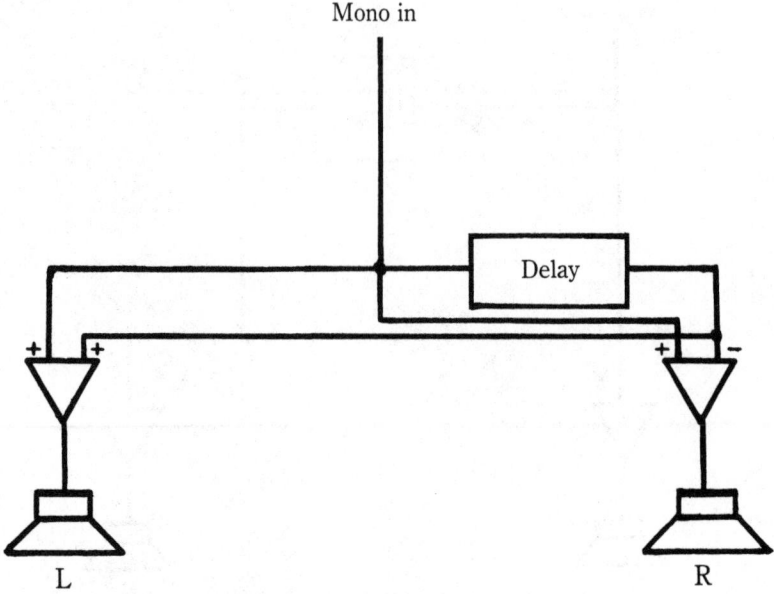

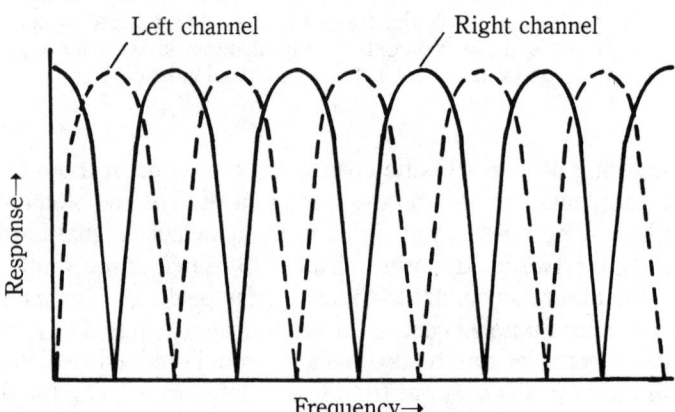

11-5 Pseudostereo left and right channel signals can result from complementary comb filters, obtained by adding the sum of direct and delayed components to one channel and the difference between the two to the other channel. This arrangement gives relatively uniform spectral quality to the two channels, but is still far from true stereo.

In 1956 two more papers on the subject of pseudostereo by complementary comb filters appeared (References 11-7 and 11-8). These offered minor changes from the Lauridsen approach. Figure 11-6 shows a circuit that achieves essentially the same thing as that of Fig. 11-5. The only difference is that a complementary comb filter is obtained by inserting a 180° phase shift in one channel. The staggered, complementary comb filter response results.

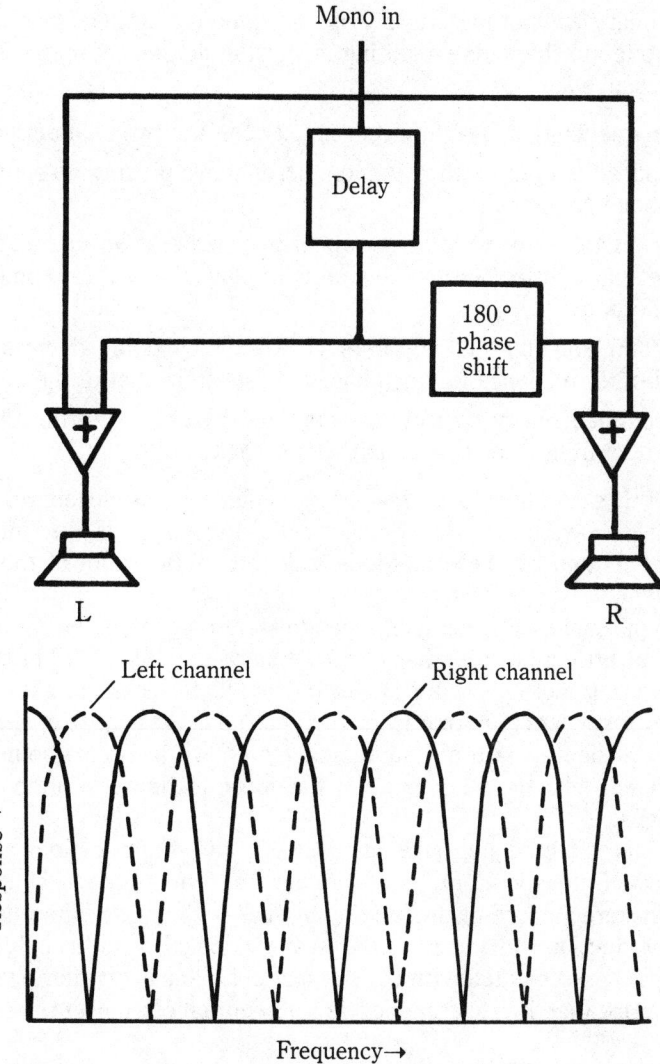

11-6 Another arrangement for production of sum/difference complementary comb filters for the two pseudostereo channels.

Pseudostereo by phase shifting

In 1961, Schroeder suggested an improved *quasi-stereophony* utilizing phase shifting instead of time delay (Reference 11-9). He made use of *all-pass* electronic circuits to generate the phase shift. The phase-shifted signal is added to and subtracted from the original mono signal creating the familiar peak alignment of one channel with minima of the other channel. This method produces results comparable to Lauridsen's time-delay method and is much cheaper to produce.

In summary, numerous ways exist to generate a degree of incoherency between two mono channels—resulting in varying degrees of image spread with a sense of presence and space:

- By frequency response differences between the two channels
- By spaced left- and right-channel microphones picking up sound in a reverberation chamber
- By a single microphone pick-up in a reverberation chamber to achieve some spatial effect, to which a signal delay is added for some comb-filter incoherency
- By complementary comb-filters generated by delay devices that give a comb-filter response for one channel offset from that of the other
- By complementary comb-filters obtained by phase-shifting that also yield offset comb-filter responses in the two channels.

None of these pseudostereo methods provides images closely resembling true stereo images, however, for the simple reason that the *brute force* interaural incoherencies generated by these methods lack the subtle detail of the true stereophonic system.

Other approaches of producing pseudo-stereo signals from mono have been proposed, but little innovation has occurred since the 1960s. All of these pseudostereo generating methods sound better on signals that change with time. Therefore, whatever success resulting from such methods is because speech and music signals are transient in nature. Commercial stereo synthesizers abound in the market today. These all use one or more of the above techniques, often with proprietary adaptions.

Pseudostereo techniques have found their greatest applications with regard to sound effects. Extensive libraries of mono sound effects have been brought into active use in stereo recording and mixing by such techniques. Their use in film and television production is made easier because the visual stimulus helps to reinforce the illusion of space created with the sonic effect. This is another example of how the senses work together to create overall perception of an event.

12

Auditory spaciousness

AN IMPORTANT ATTRIBUTE OF MUSIC IN THE CONCERT HALL IS THE QUALITY of *auditory spaciousness*, which involves the perceived broadening of a sound source so it seems to fill a greater space than that defined by the visual image. Auditory spaciousness would seem to embrace such terms as *ambience, enveloped by sound, source width, broadening of the image, diffusion*, etc. *Spatial impression*, however, is a more restricted term relating to the space rather than to the perception of the music source. While difficult to define, auditory spaciousness is readily identified by the untrained ear and eagerly sought after by those who appreciate high-quality sound. Blauert gave special attention to the subject of spaciousness in his work, which had a strong influence in this chapter (References 12-1, 12-2, 12-3).

As early as 1947, Maxfield and Albersheim began to expand beyond the catch-all word *liveness* in describing the subjective aspects of the acoustics of a space (Reference 12-4). They discovered a change in tone quality attributable to the space and a blending of the sounds from the various instruments of an orchestra. They also revealed an acoustic perspective perceived by the listener and evidence suggesting that the listener actually could sense the size of the space in which the music was played by listening to the sounds. Upon this early foundation research-ers erected a science of auditory spaciousness that expanded horizons to the extent that it is today—a primary consideration in the design of music halls.

For a person listening to a musical performance in a music hall, auditory spaciousness deals with the sound energy that reaches the listener's ears by paths other than the direct one, particularly lateral reflections (References 12-5, 12-6). All sound arriving at the position of the listener following the direct component is delayed in time with respect to the arrival of the direct sound.

Definition vs. auditory spaciousness

Definition is the quality of sound that enables a listener to distinguish its temporal details, whether music or speech. Definition suffers with an excess of indirect delayed sound. Spaciousness, on the other hand, depends entirely on indirect delayed sound. Superficially, it would seem the two are diametrically opposed to each other. A compromise between the two is possible by careful attention to the intensity and delay of the indirect, reflected sound. The right amounts of definition and spaciousness are important for good room acoustics.

Delayed sound and spatial impression

Sound could be delayed by an electronic device as in signal processing, or it might result from reflected energy in an enclosed space. Thus room acoustics and/or signal processing could vie with microphone selection and placement as the means of achieving and controlling the effect of auditory spaciousness.

Reverberation and spaciousness

Sound in an enclosed space dies away rather slowly because of the slow speed of sound (1,130 ft/sec). The various rays of sound emanating in all directions from an impulsive source take a certain amount of time to reach the boundaries of the room. Each individual ray then undergoes a series of reflections from different surfaces. Upon the cessation of the sound source, the combined sound field (composed of all the rays cut off in midflight), decays at a rate determined by the size of the hall, the characteristics of the reflecting objects, etc. *Reverberation time* is the time required for the average sound pressure level to fall 60 dB. Reverberation times of 1 to 4 seconds are common for music halls as well as ordinary places of assembly. For many years reverberation time was considered the chief factor in the acoustical quality of a space. It is now considered as only one of several such factors. Reverberation imparts information upon which a perception of the size of the hall is based and thus contributes to spaciousness.

Obtaining spaciousness through reverberation is limited by a detrimental defect. Reverberation, by nature, slurs speech and degrades the clarity of music. This is a high price to pay for spaciousness.

Baranek made a comprehensive study of music halls around the world, attempting to correlate physical measurements with subjective judgments of hall quality by trained and respected musicians (Reference 12-7). He found that in the superior halls the onset of the reverberatory decay of an impulsive sound followed the direct sound by about 20 ms, illustrated in the sketch of Fig. 12-1. He called this the *initial time delay gap*. Blauert calls it the *arrival-time gap*, which is shorter, somewhat more descriptive, and will be used henceforth. This gap subconsciously gives the listener the auditory spatial impression, or the sense of the size of the space. The importance of a gap of this general magnitude is further underlined by experience with artificial reverberation devices; the addition of such a delay results in a more natural-sounding artificial reverberation.

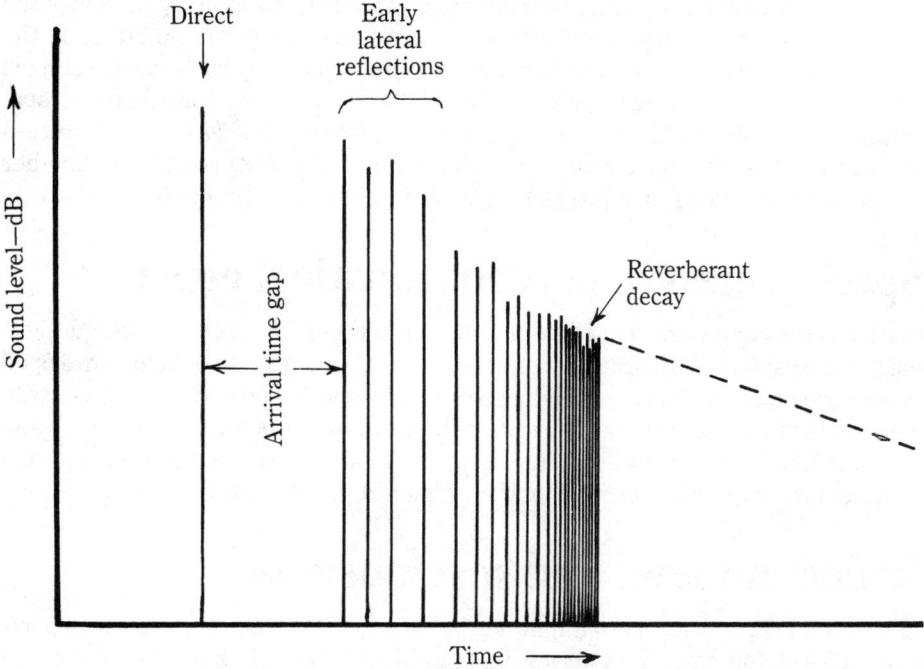

12-1 An *echogram* showing the typical components of the reverberatory decay of an impulsive sound in a large space. Between the arrival of the direct sound at a given seat position and the arrival of the early lateral reflections at that position is a period of quasi-silence called the *arrival time gap*. The human ear associates this gap with the perceived size of the space. The early lateral reflections contribute to the sense of *spaciousness* of the sound. The reverberant decay contributes to the richness of music produced in the space.

Spaciousness in mono

Monophonic systems are deficient notoriously in the sense of spaciousness resulting from reverberation. Without the stereo *spread*, the mono reverberation and direct sound from the subject are hopelessly confused, one on top of the other, so to speak.

Spatial impression by lateral reflections

Consider a direct sound from the soundstage followed by a single reflection from a side wall. The combination of the two at the listener's ear produces a comb-filter effect, which is normally not audible because the auditory system tends to inhibit it. The actual situation, however, is much more complicated. The most important cues for sound localization are interaural level and time of arrival differences at the two ears. These are constantly changing with time and frequency. The direct sound to the two ears establishes the direction of the sound source by the law of the first wavefront. The subsequent arrival of lateral reflections has no effect on the perception of direction; they are *locked out* psychoacoustically as far as direction is concerned. In this way the energy of later lateral reflections contributes to spaciousness without disturbing directional impressions. This *locking out* process holds true only for the spectrum of the direct sound. If another sound with another spectrum comes along, it will trigger a fresh perception of direction.

Spaciousness, a psychoacoustical effect

Spaciousness can be considered as the responsibility of the architect who designs the listening space. With spaciousness commonly occurs a sense of being enveloped in the sound and ambience, which makes spaciousness a vital and important attribute of the sound. Auditory spaciousness might stem from the shape of the space and the materials used in its construction, but in the final analysis the perception of spaciousness is a subjective response of the listener to the physical stimuli.

Reflection level and spaciousness

In a music hall, spaciousness might not be experienced when the orchestra plays at a low level, but it might be very evident at higher levels. Evaluating opinions on the spaciousness of different halls is suspect as long as this variable of sound level is not controlled. Until the relationship of spaciousness and sound level is thoroughly established, the prediction of the spaciousness of proposed structures cannot be made with certainty, and the only option is to resort to the judgement of experienced persons.

The relationship between the sound level of the delayed signal, or reflection, with respect to the level of the direct sound and delay is shown in Fig. 12-2. The field of this graph is limited at the lower levels by masking of reflections and at the upper levels by the production of echoes. Reflections having a level and delay above the reflection masking level and below the echo threshold are free of echoes and potentially usable as producers of spaciousness. Reflections delayed less than 5 ms that tend to shift the stereo image are exceptions to this rule.

Spaciousness does not depend on whether a single lateral reflection exists or multiple reflections occur. The combined energy of all the reflections is important, however, with respect to the total energy of the direct sound plus reflections. Auditory spaciousness can be evaluated by exciting the room with a short impulse and measuring this lateral-energy fraction at the position of the listener.

Reflection spectrum and spaciousness

Some people believe that low-frequency reflected energy, below about 1.5 kHz, is especially important to auditory spaciousness. Recent research, however, tends to indicate that all frequency components of the reflections contribute to spaciousness. Some experiments indicate that frequency components below 3 kHz contrib-

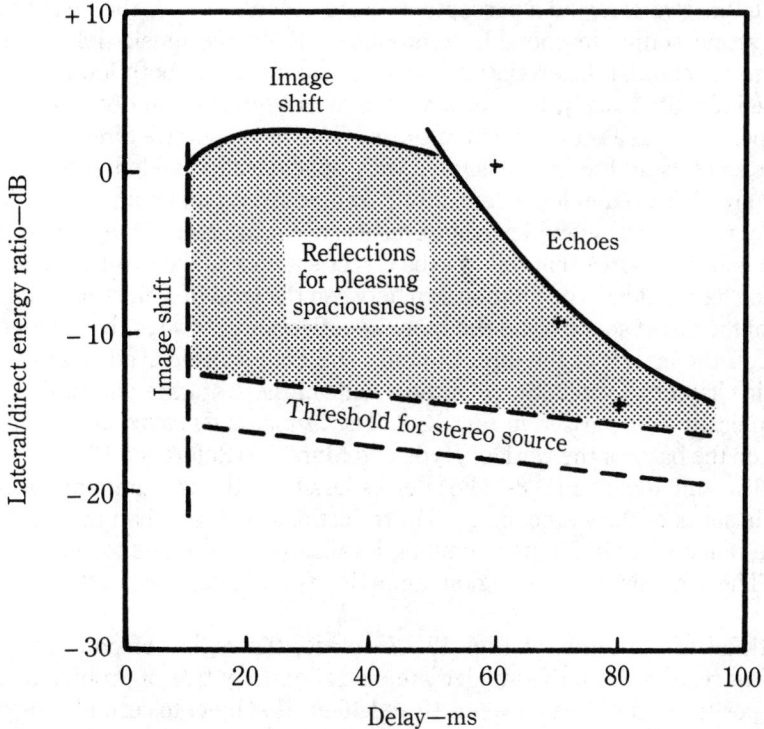

12-2 Reflections having level and delay that fall within the shaded area are most likely to contribute to the spaciousness of the sound. Reflections having level and delay that fall outside this area result in various defects. This area is bounded at the top by the Haas-effect curve, at the bottom by threshold limitations, on the left by shift of the stereo image and on the right by the production of discrete echoes. A composite of the work of Barron, Blauert and others.

ute to the perception of depth, and those above 3 kHz to the perception of width. In general, reflections should have a broad spectrum to aid the dimensional perception of the space.

The time window of spaciousness

Sending the white noise from one generator to the left headphone of a subject and the white noise from another generator to the right headphone elicits an in-head image of sound bunched near each ear, as chapter 3 describes for uncorrelated sound. If the same white noise from a single generator is sent to both ears, the correlated sound will be perceived in the center of the head. The interaural correlation in the first case is zero; in the second case it is maximum.

Next, the headphones are discarded and the subject sits in an anechoic space with loudspeakers hanging all around, which are driven with controllable signals. Music from the loudspeaker directly in front of the subject gives nicely correlated signals to the two ears and a perceptual image in the center of the head results. A second sound source to one side, reproducing the same music delayed 100 ms, results in substantial decorrelation of the music signal. If both loudspeakers are energized simultaneously, the decorrelation is still present and each loudspeaker will be perceived as a separate sound source from its respective direction. The subject does not hear the music signal with spaciousness added; the two sound sources are perceived independently, one from in front and another from the side. Similarly with a strong and lengthy reverberation, the reverberant sound tends to become another source that follows the direct sound and early reflections.

Many have studied the relationship between the level of reflections—compared to that of the direct sound—and the time the reflections arrive at the listener's position—after the arrival of the direct sound. The effects of delayed sound were discussed in chapters 3 and 8. Some of the results of these studies and those of others are graphically summarized in Fig. 12-2. The *threshold for stereo source* region was located on the basis of the work of Hyde and Marshall (Reference 12-8), but is similar to Olive and Toole's Fig. 8-1. For delays less than 10 ms, summing localization results in shifts of the stereo image. For reflections stronger than the direct signal over the range of 10 to 50 ms, summing localization also tends to shift the stereo image. The echo disturbance region limits the use of reflections in the 50 – 100 ms region.

With all of the limits of Fig. 12-2 in place, the region of potentially useful reflections results. Even this shaded area is not entirely free of problems, because the left portion of this area between 10 and 40 ms is subject to certain distortions of timbre. Lateral reflections falling in this shaded area, especially later than 40 ms, are responsible for a pleasing effect of spaciousness.

The amount of delay tolerated without echo depends on the type of music and the reflection level. Blauert gives the following conditions as typical upper limits for classical-romantic music to avoid creating echoes:

Reflection level same as direct	60 ms
Reflection level 10 dB down	70 ms
Reflection level 15 dB down	80 ms

These three points are plotted as crosses in Fig. 12-2. The strongest reflection falls somewhat over the echo limit, but the other two fall in the shaded area. The upper limit of delay depends strongly on the kind of signal decoded as well as its reflection level.

Interaurally decorrelated sound does not always result in auditory spaciousness. Our auditory system has a time window during which reflected sounds must be received. Figure 12-2 indicates that early lateral reflections must arrive within a time window of about 10 to 80 ms of the direct signal to achieve spaciousness. This figure varies somewhat with type of music and level of the reflected sound.

Designing for spaciousness

Designing music halls for spaciousness is a relatively new concept in the music scene. The advancing knowledge of the psychoacoustics of auditory spaciousness has made it mandatory for designers of music spaces, designers of electroacoustic devices, and recording engineers to apply the criteria of spaciousness.

Computer modeling and scaled physical models of proposed spaces has made actual listening judgments possible before construction. Listening in a scale model is accomplished by *scaling* the sound. For example, in a physical model built to a 1:20 scale, a 20 Hz – 20 kHz band would be translated to a 400 Hz – 400 kHz band radiated in the model and picked up by special microphones; then it would be translated back to a 20 Hz – 20 kHz band for listening.

Perception of distance to source

Many cues can contribute to sensing distance to the source of sound. For familiar sounds, intensity might give a crude idea of the distance to a sound source. The spectrum (timbre) of familiar sounds might give a clue as to distance to the source; for example, the distant sound of a marching band is different from its closer sound. The curvature of the wavefront of sound from a nearby source is compared to that of a distant sound source and could be perceived as interaural differences. These cues apply more to outdoor sound than to sound in an enclosure.

Listening to sound sources indoors involves reflected sound. The perception of apparent distance to the source of sound depends on a subjective comparison of the relative levels of direct sound and sound from the environment. As the distance to the source of sound increases, the level of the direct sound decreases, but the level of reverberant sound remains essentially constant. The perception of distance to the source thus rests on the direct/indirect ratio. In the 5 – 30 ms region the inaudible *echo* still can be used to sense distance. Just as the perception of direction depends on several cues, judgments of distance appear also to depend on many different physical cues.

Another important factor in distance estimation is based on the arrival time gap—the time between the arrival of the direct sound at the listener's position and the arrival of the reflected sound. In a concert hall or auditorium of normal shape, the arrival time gap decreases with distance from the source.

The perception of distance to the source of sound has not yet attracted the interest of psychoacousticians like some of the other subjective aspects of hearing. In the context of the study of spaciousness, however, the perception of distance depends on many of the same cues, such as direct sound, reflections, and reverberance.

13
Multidimensional and surround sound systems

FROM THE EARLY DAYS OF RECORDED SOUND, A CONSTANT STRIVING FOR an improved sense of realism has progressed. Initially, all recordings were monophonic, with only one channel of recording or reproduction. In the early 1930s Alan Blumlein in England and Bell Laboratories in the United States began developing what has become stereo as we know it today, although initially these experiments were specifically intended for use in the motion picture industry (see appendix). The goal was a multichannel, multiloudspeaker system that would enhance the spatial imaging capabilities of the playback system and/or create a soundfield that could surround the listener with direct sound from the front (and for effect, from the sides) as well as ambient sound from all directions. The first significant commercial realization of a truly multichannel sound system was the Disney Studios production of *Fantasia* in 1939.

Fantasound

Building on the research of Bell Laboratories and working in collaboration with the recording engineers at RCA Victor records, the Disney Studios sound department developed a scheme whereby three primary audio channels—screen left, screen center, and screen right—could be recorded as discrete signals on optical sound tracks. On playback in the motion picture theater, the sound-head projector reproducing these soundtracks was synchronized via a fourth track, a control track, with the projector showing the picture, which also bore a synchronizing control track on the film. This is the heart of the *Fantasound* system developed specifically for *Fantasia*. The first showing appeared in New York City, on November 13, 1940.

The three discrete audio signals were not all that was heard by the audiences, however. Various elements of the musical soundtrack were manually routed to several loudspeakers that surrounded the audience. The signals for these were taken directly from the basic left and right audio tracks. Eventually, the control track (called tone-operated gain-adjusting device, or TOGAD) was also used to control the playback levels of all the audio tracks and surround loudspeakers. In a limited showing, special notches were cut into the edge of the film; these notches triggered additional control devices that routed the sound to as many as 100 loudspeakers throughout the motion picture theater. Due to the complexity of this system and the onset of World War II, *Fantasound* was short lived and not used for any other commercial motion picture releases. The technology and innovations that were developed, however, ultimately found their way into other sound recording and reproduction applications (Reference 13-1).

Three-channel stereo

In the 1950s, the three discrete screen channels first used for *Fantasia* became common and are the basis for all motion picture sound production today. Some early experiments in consumer stereo also used this format, with the recordings distributed on three-channel magnetic tape. This format did not last long, however, because it was too inconvenient and expensive for the consumer. All of the dialog in this format is confined to the center loudspeaker, although occasionally it might be panned to one side of the screen or the other for special emphasis or effect. Music, background ambience, and special sound effects are spread in stereo across the screen. Because the center loudspeaker provides a real as opposed to a phantom center image, the three-channel format provides a solid, stable, and repeatable sonic illusion, which the producers can rely on to enhance the overall experience for all viewers/listeners, irrespective of seating location within the audience.

The best localization for these three screen channels can be achieved when loudspeakers with a controlled, fairly narrow dispersion pattern are used. These loudspeakers provide optimum articulation for dialog and help separate it from the background music and sound effects.

Rear-channel sound

Renewed attempts to provide sonic information that can surround the listener began with simple rear-channel ambience effects. These were derived from the difference signal between the left and right channels (i.e., the L minus the R signal). This difference signal, which contains all information that is not common to the two channels, is essentially the spatial component of the stereo program. It is directly comparable to the side signal information of the MS stereo system described in chapter 7.

Figure 13-1A shows the simple three-channel system (left, right, and rear) proposed by David Hafler in the early 1970s. This system requires only the addition of a single loudspeaker behind the listener to enhance the sense of spatiality of a conventional stereo program. For a more effective enhancement, a second rear loudspeaker can be added (Fig. 13-1B). In this system, the two surround loudspeakers are placed somewhat to the sides, yet still behind the listener. This tends to provide more side information to increase the sense of spaciousness. Loudspeakers with a fairly broad dispersion pattern should be used to create the best effect, because the more diffused sound produced by these speakers is less likely to be localized by the listener.

For the home listener, the primary advantage of this approach is that, in addition to requiring only a little extra wire and two loudspeakers, it is fully compatible with all conventional stereo program material and distribution formats. It is a simple two-channel, multidimensional system that demands no special recording techniques or playback equipment.

In the motion picture industry more control of the surround effect was desired, so this rear channel information was provided by a discrete fourth soundtrack

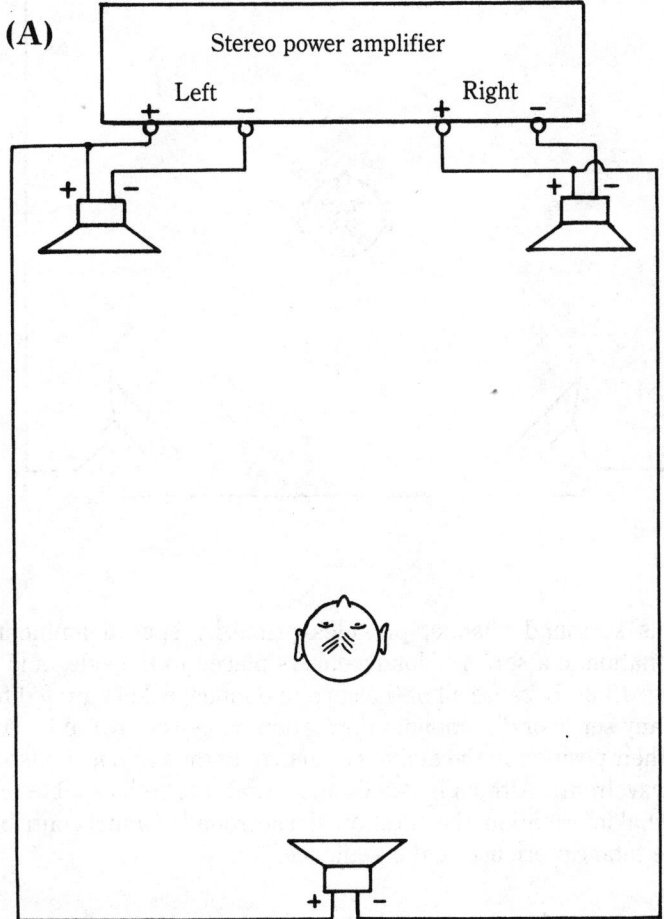

13-1 (A) Single loudspeaker employing the *Hafler System*, using the difference signal (left minus right) of conventional stereo program material to derive the rear channel information. (B) Increased spatial envelopment can be achieved by using two loudspeakers. The signals produced by the two rear loudspeakers are out of phase with each other.

(B)

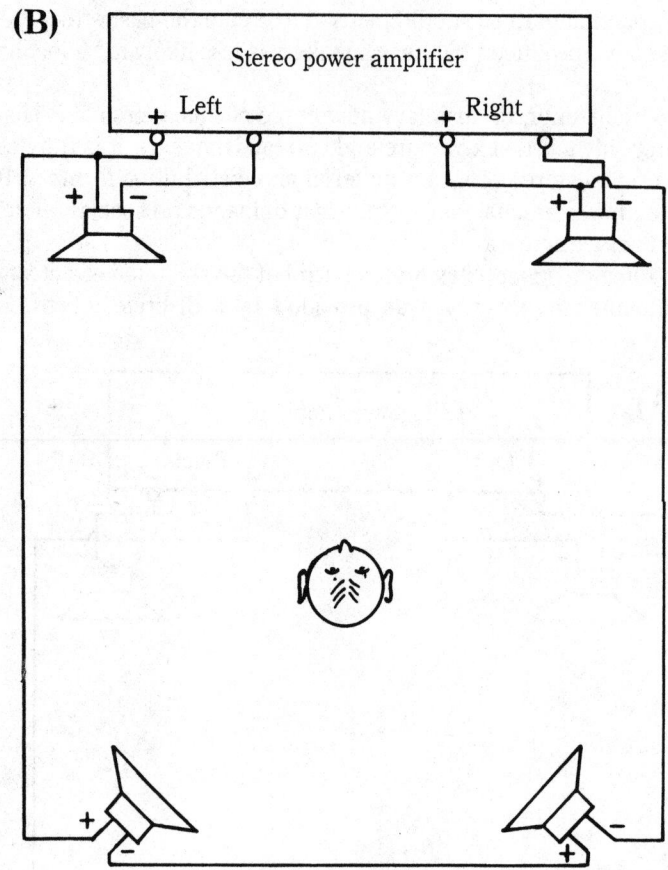

13-1   Continued.

channel. This surround channel provides primarily special ambient or sound effects information to a series of loudspeakers placed to the sides and behind the audience (Fig. 13-2). Because all of the surround loudspeakers are fed from a common signal, any sense of directional information perceived by the listeners results solely from their position in the audience relative to the various loudspeakers (law of the first wavefront). Although strictly monaural, hence incapable of conveying truly directional information, the addition of a surround channel contributes significantly to the total experience of the audience.

Four-channel surround systems

In the 1970s, the quest for full surround sound systems for the home rose to new heights, and by the latter part of the decade several competing systems were devel-

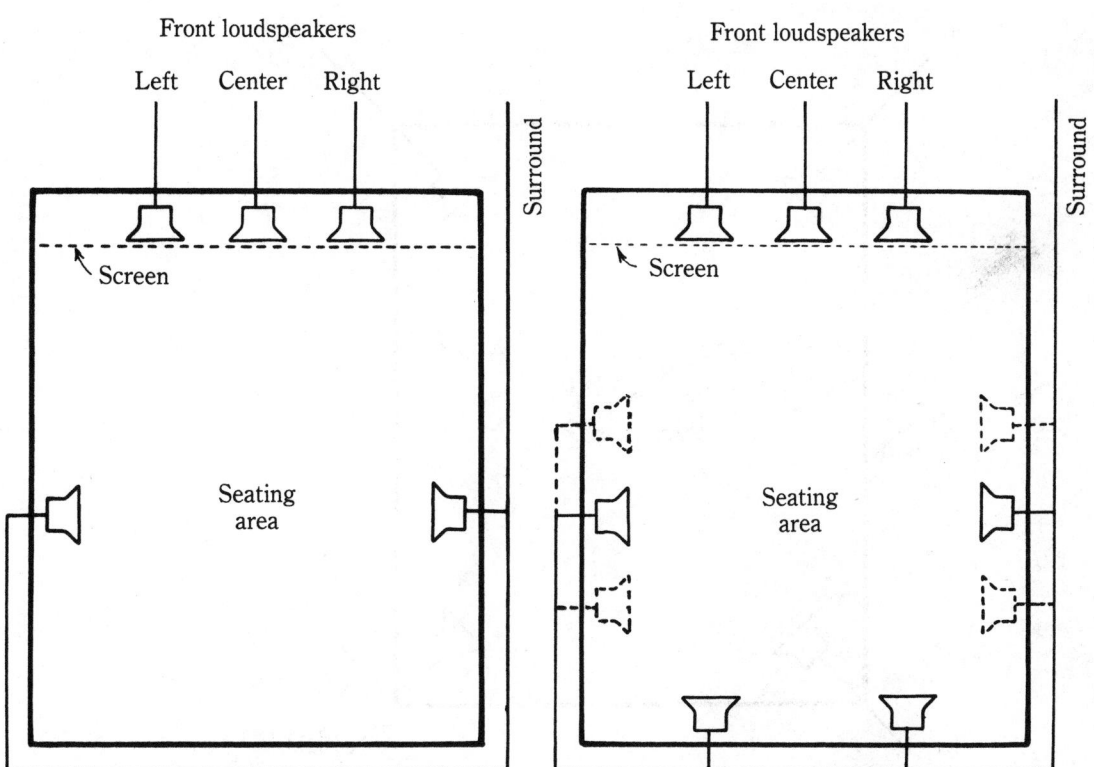

13-2 Arrangement of loudspeakers for conventional motion picture theater sound system. The surround loudspeakers are driven by a common signal.

oped. Because compatibility with existing stereo systems and recordings was also a concern of the proponents of many of these systems, various methods of encoding the surround information were proposed. Most required the addition of two rear or surround loudspeakers, as well as using a special interface device to direct the signals to all four loudspeakers. A few systems eschewed the restrictions of compatibility and offered four discrete channels of sound.

What all of these systems did agree upon, however, was the basic loudspeaker configuration in the listening room. Loudspeakers were placed in the four corners to provide conventional front, left, and right speakers for normal stereo listening, and to add rear, left, and right loudspeakers to reproduce the new *quadraphonic sound* recordings (Fig. 13-3). This loudspeaker arrangement, however, was just about all the various systems held in common. Recording techniques and what sonic perspective the listener should be given were widely debated topics. The methods of recording and reproduction were even more hotly contested because of the several commercial interests involved.

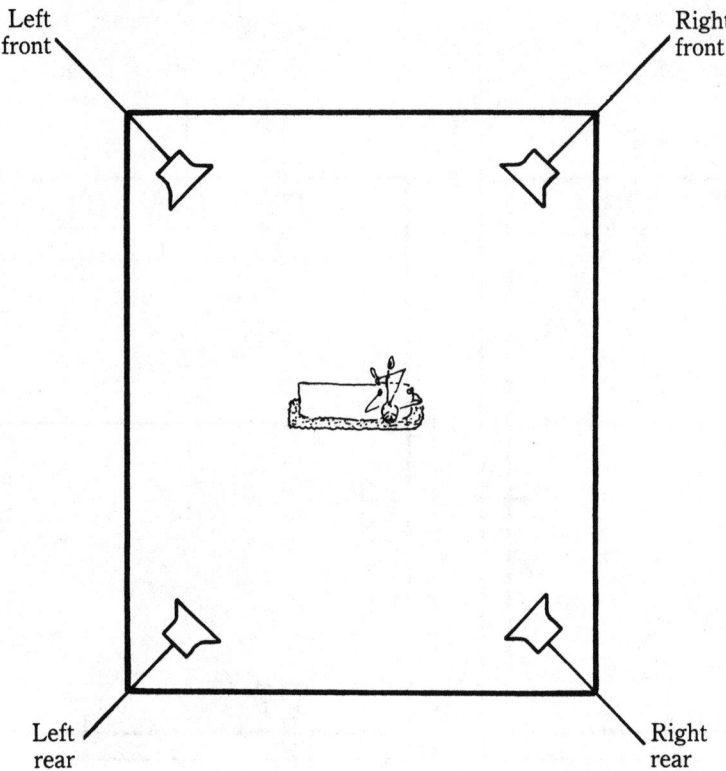

Left front

Right front

Left rear

Right rear

13-3 Loudspeaker arrangement for the Quadraphonic sound systems common in the late 1970s.

Matrix *quad* systems

The most direct method of recording and distributing quad was via four-channel magnetic tape (shades of the 1950s). Although this held great appeal for the audiophiles who prized the quality of their open-reel tape recorders, the average consumer did not favor this approach. The consumer wanted something that was compatible with, and could be played on, conventional record turntables and cassette recorders—devices that are inherently only two-channel. The FM stereo stations also lobbied for a system that could be broadcast to their audiences.

To meet these demands, numerous matrix systems soon appeared and competed to win the rapidly growing consumer audio market. Each developed some scheme to reduce four discrete channels into two—for recording onto phonograph disc or cassette tape, or broadcast—and then reexpand these into four channels in the listener's homes. Although the technical processes were different from one manufacturer to the next, they all relied on some form of specific electronic matrix encoding during recording or production, and a complementary matrix decoding during playback. Figure 13-4 shows the basic concept employed by these 4:2:4 matrix systems. Several commercial systems incorporated the matrix encoding

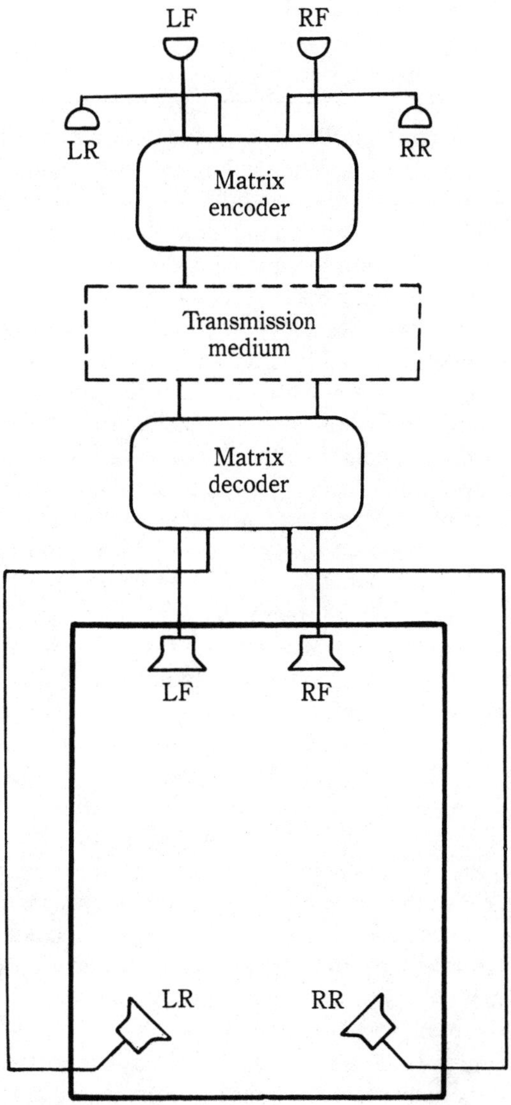

LF   RF

LR   RR

Matrix
encoder

Transmission
medium

Matrix
decoder

LF   RF

LR   RR

13-4 Matrix encoded 4:2:4
four-channel sound
recording and
reproducing system.
Four discrete channels
are encoded into two
transmission channels
(i.e., stereo) and then
decoded back into four
channels during
playback.

work of Peter Scheiber, a pioneer of this technology (References 13-2 and 13-3).
The two primary competing commercial systems were the SQ Matrix (promoted
by CBS Records, Sony Corporation, et al.) and the QS Matrix (promoted by the
Warner Records Group, Sansui, et al.). Except for the two additional loudspeakers
and associated channels of amplification, a special matrix decoding unit was the
only other equipment required to reproduce these recordings. Therefore, the consumer could use his existing stereo equipment as the basis for his new surround
sound system.

These systems had some success in reproducing discrete sounds via these additional channels, and many recordings were made specifically to exploit the particular characteristics of each system. A further advantage claimed by both of these systems was the ability to create surround signals from existing conventional stereo recordings. This was achieved by phase manipulation of the stereo signal inherent in the matrix decoding process. When properly encoded, this manipulation extracted the directional information as originally recorded for the surround channels. With conventional stereo recordings, this manipulation derived the surround signals from the difference information of the stereo program material (the L minus R component).

A serious drawback of these matrix systems was the instability of the surround image and the inability to localize anything solidly in the rear center. These problems resulted from both the encoding/decoding process and instabilities of the recording matrix. Because the matrix process was so reliant on the phase manipulation of dual signals from the stereo media, it was subject to any of their limitations— distortion in the record groove, phase errors resulting from poor tape alignment in cassette players, and radio propagation problems. Center rear imaging was virtually impossible because the difference information (L minus R) formed the electrical basis of this signal. To achieve a phantom center between the two rear loudspeakers, the left-rear and right-rear signals must be equal. If these signals are equal however, L-R minus R-R equals zero, and no signal results. For these reasons, and others not so technical, matrix systems found little favor with consumers.

A third system, claiming to provide more *discrete* surround signals than conventional matrix systems, was developed by RCA Records and its subsidiary, the Japanese Victor Company. Named CD-4, it required special phonograph playback equipment to extract the coded information from the records. This was both its blessing and its curse. The special stylus, phonograph cartridge, and decoding processor were capable indeed of improved separation between the four electronic signals, so the rear channel sound image was more stable and defined than that of other matrix systems. The information encoded into the record grooves, however, was fragile and after repeated playing, or even one or two playings by a conventional stereo phonograph, the groove had worn sufficiently so the rear channel signals were no longer stable.

To its disadvantage, the CD-4 system was incapable of being broadcast; thus radio stations did not support it. Further, because it provided no enhancement for conventional stereo recordings, it offered no additional incentives to consumers to use it with their existing record collections.

The experiment into quad sound systems was short lived, barely surviving into the 1980s. This had little to do with the technical capabilities of the systems themselves, however. The ultimate problem was that the industry, and therefore the consumer, could not decide on one system; all three fought hard to win in the marketplace and, by so doing, killed themselves and each other. Record companies, if not aligned with one particular system, were unable to decide which system to use; those companies that did adopt one system lost the record buyers who favored another. Record stores had to stock multiple copies of any recording that was released in more than one format. The most critical factor in the demise of Quad, however, was that all systems were incompatible with each other. To listen to any recordings one might want to buy, the consumer would have to own all three competing systems and their associated decoding equipment. Thus, consumer dissatisfaction eventually proved the death knell for all of these quad systems, and prevented a resurgence of widespread interest in surround systems until the late 1980s when an outside influence provided a new impetus.

Audio-follow-video

By the mid-1980s, the concept of the home entertainment center was fostered by the development of large screen television sets with stereo television sound (BTSC), the widespread sales of videotape players, and the rampant growth of neighborhood video rental shops. What had once been the sole province of the motion picture theater now was finding its place into family rooms throughout society; movies, shown on *large* screens and accompanied by multichannel sound systems were becoming commonplace.

These home theater sound systems initially adopted the time honored format shown in Fig. 13-2, using a simple decoder to realize the four audio channels from the stereo soundtrack on the tape or broadcast and two surround loudspeakers. These decoders, however, soon began to embody some of the improvements that were developed specifically for motion picture theaters, such as the Dolby Stereo, Dolby Pro Logic, and THX systems that incorporated more sophisticated encode/ decode processes and highly specific loudspeaker arrangements (Fig. 13-5 and References 13-4, 13-5, 13-6, and 13-7).

Surround sound and ambience enhancement systems

As the listeners' sophistication broadened, so did their demands for enhancements to their home sound reproduction systems. They were no longer satisfied with surround sound merely for watching movies; they also wanted the enhancements to improve the spatial qualities of their music listening. This gave rise to renewed development of signal processing techniques that could extract spatial information from existing stereophonic material and distribute it to surround the listener. Earlier research into the psychoacoustics of spatial perception and phase manipulation of stereo signals, coupled with improved digital signal processing capabilities, enabled designers to incorporate this spatial processing into the decoders intended for home use. Among the first commercial units, the Yamaha model DSP-1 provided signal processing and side loudspeakers to simulate the lateral reflections so important to spatial imaging.

More recently, David Griesinger strove to find out just what is involved in listening to recorded sound, and to identify the characteristics of sound and spatial hearing that maximize listening pleasure. He then strove to use digital technology to bring these characteristics to the home. No one technique works in all situations, but many, both old and new, can make a significant contribution to home lis-

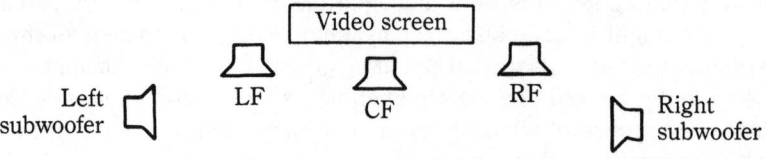

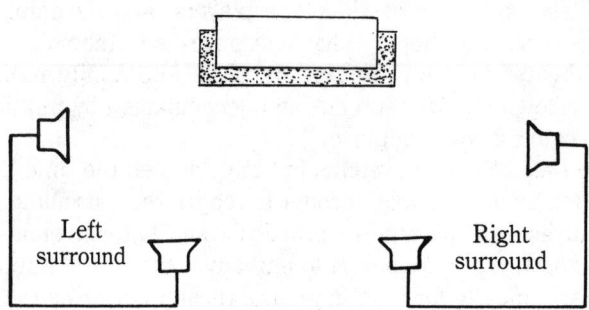

13-5   Typical home theater surround sound system layout. The center loudspeaker is situated either directly above or below the video screen. (Smaller systems use only two surround speakers and one subwoofer.)

tening. All the techniques have a common thread; they raise the lateral sound energy in the listening room. (Reference 13-8). Griesinger's system therefore provides discrete signals directed to two side loudspeakers, in addition to the surround speakers (Fig. 13-6). In addition to a mode for conventional processing of film soundtracks, Griesinger's device also includes several processing modes for creating various spatial effects with conventional stereo material. Reverberation and time delay can be added to simulate the acoustical properties of various concert halls in the listeners' living room. Also included is a *binaural* mode, which creates the spatial effects of binaural sound via the several loudspeakers. Several other manufacturers have developed similar surround sound processors, each with its own set of parameters for generating spatial imaging from stereo source material. Other systems, involving more discrete recording formats, are also being revived in the continuing search for true 3-dimensional spatial perception.

Ambisonics

In the early 1970s, Michael Gerzon, British recording engineer and mathematician, developed a process for recording the spatial information present in the entire soundfield (Reference 13-9). His premise was that only by capturing the actual acoustical signals present in the concert hall can proper spatial imaging be re-

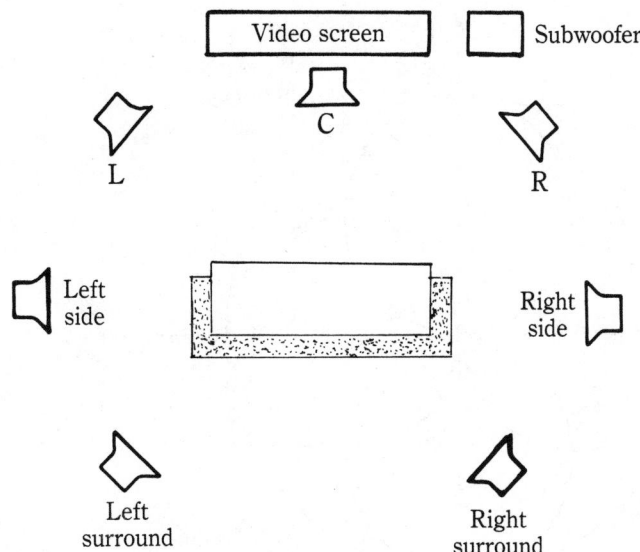

13-6 Surround sound system suggested by Griesinger employing left and right side loud-speakers in addition to the rear surround loudspeakers. All signals are discrete out-puts from the surround sound processor. After Griesinger, Reference 13-8.

created in the listening room; other techniques using multiple microphones or arti-ficial reverberation devices to create surround channels could not convey a sonic image that was faithful to the original performance.

Gerzon's process focused on the acoustical components that define the sound-field: the absolute sound pressure, and the three pressure gradients that define the cardinal directions—left/right, fore/aft, and up/down (Fig. 13-7). By accurately preserving these four components, all information needed to recreate any point in the soundfield could be recorded and later reproduced precisely. Recording the pressure component posed no problem, because an omnidirectional microphone is a pressure response pickup and would serve the purpose perfectly. Similarly, the three pressure gradient components also could be recorded using three bidirec-tional microphones, each oriented in the appropriate direction. The real problem involved the configuration of these microphones as a point in space to capture the proper relationship of the four components, and then how to reproduce the signals to give proper perceptions to the listener.

The process that Gerzon developed through appropriate application of higher level mathematics was ultimately called *Ambisonics*. (References 13-10 and 13-11) It is a fully systematic approach comprising four stages: transduction of the four sound components of the original soundfield, encoding this information into a con-ventional transmission medium, decoding this information at playback, and repro-ducing the soundfield via appropriately positioned loudspeakers. For the sake of compatibility with existing stereo formats, the four original signals preferably were encoded into two channels that could be listened to as a conventional stereo program.

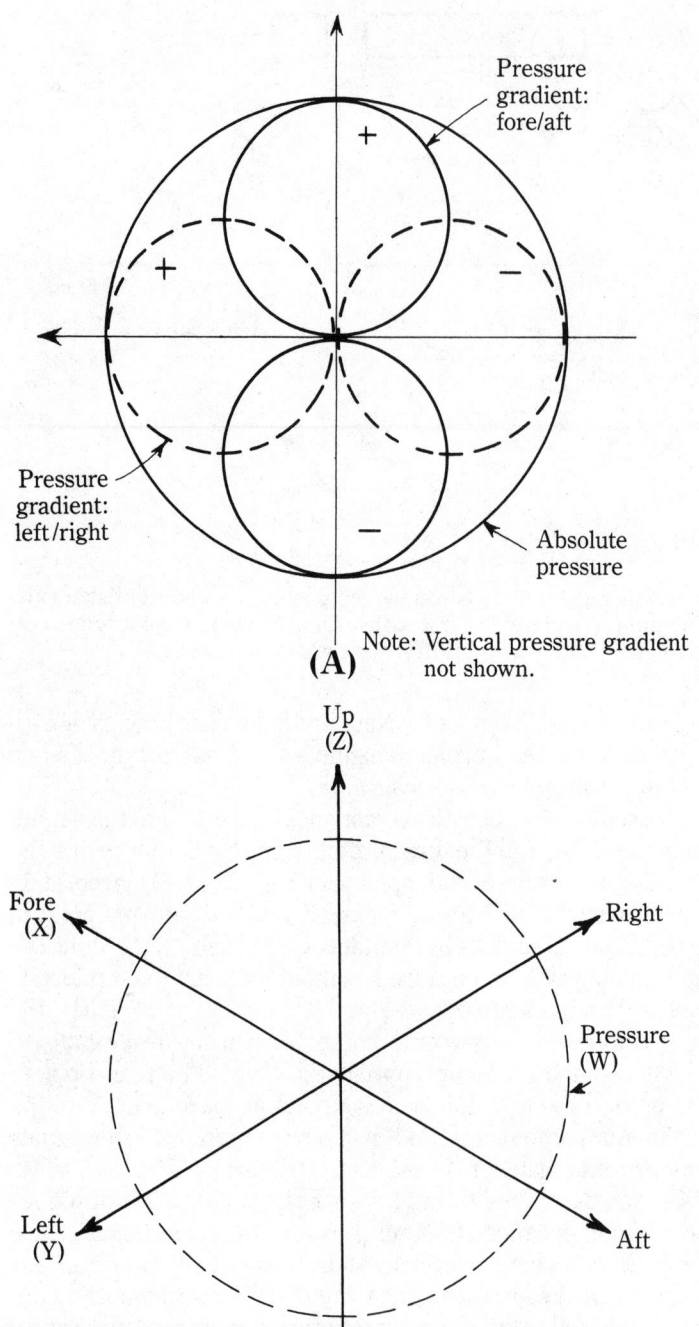

Pressure gradient: fore/aft

+

+

−

−

Absolute pressure

Pressure gradient: left/right

Note: Vertical pressure gradient not shown.

(A)

Up
(Z)

Fore
(X)

Right

Pressure
(W)

Left
(Y)

Aft

Down

(B)

13-7   (A) The basic components that describe a soundfield are the measure of absolute pressure (omnidirectional) and three pressure-gradient (bidirectional) vectors: two horizontal—fore/aft, and left/right—and the vertical—up/down. (The vertical component is not shown in this diagram.) (B) A different view of the four basic components of the soundfield: the absolute pressure, *W*; the fore/aft pressure gradient, *X*; the left/right pressure gradient *Y*; and the up/down pressure gradient *Z*. After Farrar, Reference 13-12.

The soundfield microphone system

To facilitate the ambisonic process, a special microphone system called the *Soundfield Microphone* was developed in England by Calrec Audio Ltd. (Reference 13-12). The microphone head is comprised of four subcardioid transducers mounted on the faces of a regular tetrahedron—a regular four-sided pyramid with equilateral triangle sides (Fig. 13-8). Although these four microphone signals, called the A-format signals, are aimed to record four equal regions of the soundfield, they are not the four components described in Fig. 13-7, nor do they even form a truly coincident *point in space*. By critical electronic combining and manipulation, these A-format signals are processed into four B-format signals: a coincident and precise representation of the absolute pressure (termed the W signal), fore/aft pressure gradient, X, left/right pressure gradient, Y, and vertical pressure gradient Z (Fig. 13-9). It is these B-format signals that define the soundfield and are used for further recording purposes.

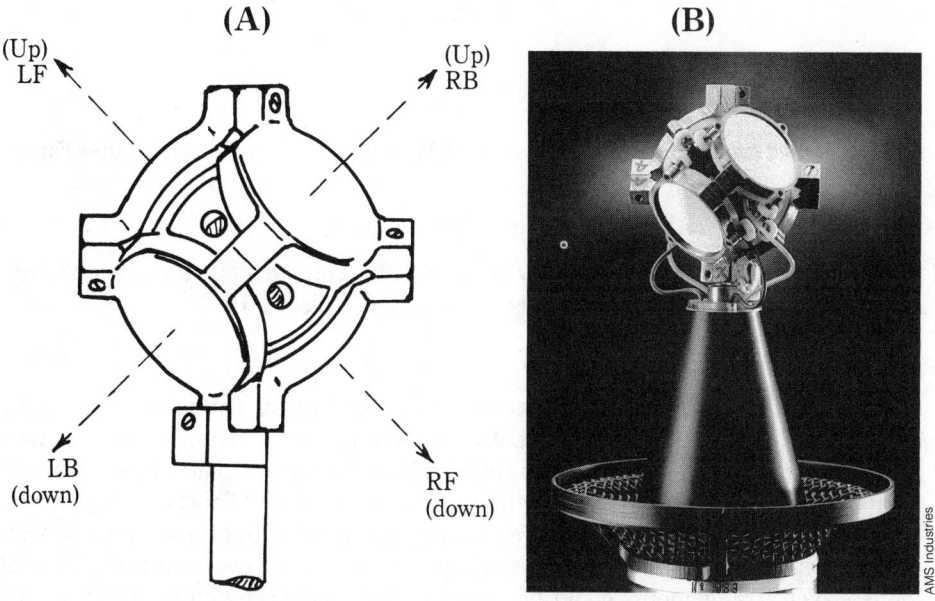

(A)

(Up)
LF

(Up)
RB

LB
(down)

RF
(down)

(B)

AMS Industries

13-8 (A) Schematic view of capsule arrangement of Soundfield Microphone showing the A-Format orientation of microphone capsules on the four sides of a regular tetrahedron. After Farrar, Reference 13-12. (B) Internal view of Soundfield Microphone.

Using the Soundfield Microphone, the B-format signals could be recorded as four discrete channels on a multitrack tape for later manipulation. It is also possible, using a 4:2:4 matrix process developed by the BBC, and known as UHJ (Reference 13-13), to distribute the B-format signals via compatible stereo program material for later surround sound decoding by the listener at home. The Soundfield Microphone's controller also allows these B-format signals to be further processed into conventional two channel stereo, providing the recording engineer an

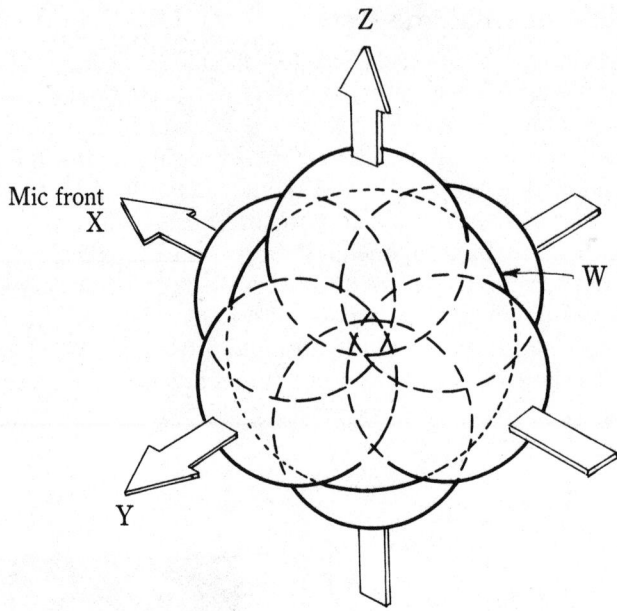

13-9 *B-Format* signals produced by Soundfield Microphone after processing. After Farrar, Reference 13-12).

unparalleled ability to electronically steer the microphone's apparent orientation, directional characteristics, and stereo perspective. (Fig. 13-10)

Ambisonic playback

Arranging four loudspeakers at the corners of a tetrahedron, complementary to the arrangement of the microphone capsules, would reproduce the microphone signals accurately and re-create a complete soundfield, however, it would be necessary to locate the listener precisely in the center of the tetrahedron. This is not a practical situation (Fig. 13-11). Instead, the ambisonic surround sound process uses common perceptual principles of loudspeaker placement to achieve its effects. Several loudspeaker arrangements could be implemented, depending on whether the listener wants to re-create simply a left/right, front/rear (i.e., horizontal) soundfield or include height (i.e., vertical) information as well.

According to P.B. Fellgett: "Ambisonic reproduction in which vertical directional information is preserved may be called periphonic, and ambisonic reproduction with only horizontal information pantophonic. Pantophonic reproduction geometrically requires a minimum of three loudspeakers, since the triangle is the minimal figure able to enclose space in a plane. Similarly, a minimum of four loudspeakers are geometrically necessary to surround the listener in three dimensions and give periphonic reproduction. To satisfy the psychoacoustic criteria sufficiently well, however, the practical minimum is four loudspeakers for pantophonic reproduction and six for periphony." (Reference 13-11)

AMS Industries

13-10 The complete Soundfield Microphone system, comprised of the microphone head unit and processing control unit.

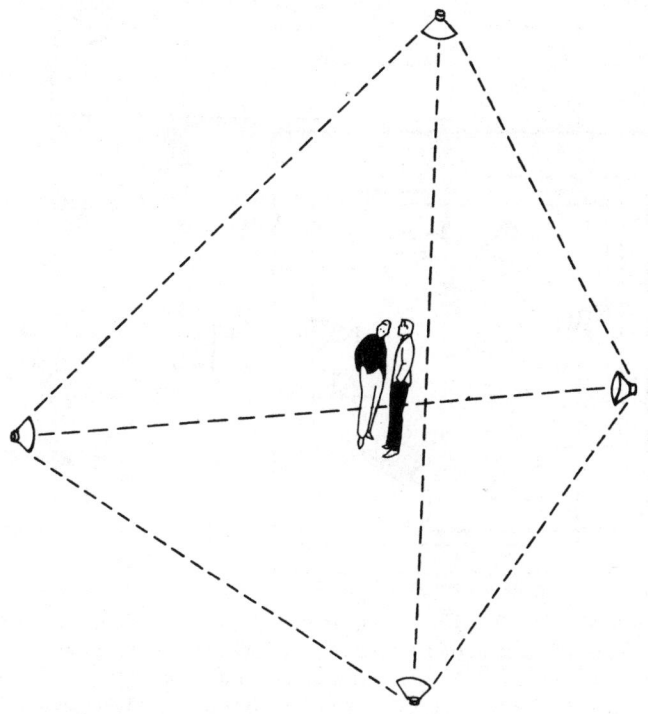

13-11 Concept of ambisonic soundfield reproduction showing loudspeakers located at the four corners of a regular tetrahedron. The listening position is located precisely at the center of the enclosed space.

Thus, for pantophonic reproduction, several loudspeaker arrangements can be employed, as shown in Fig. 13-12. As few as four loudspeakers can be used, although six tend to provide more even coverage throughout the listening area with less likelihood of the listener localizing on any individual loudspeaker. The law of

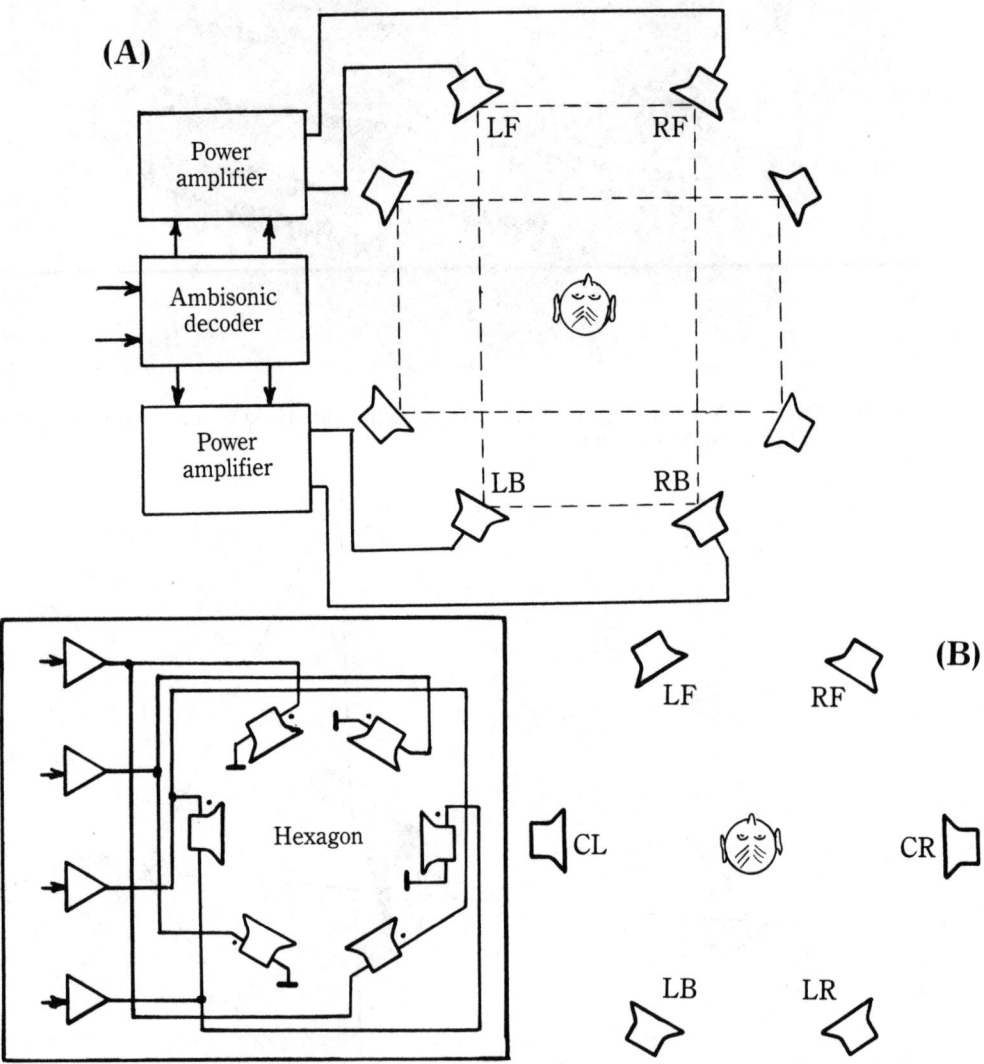

13-12 (A) *Pantophonic* soundfield reproduction, utilizing four loudspeakers. The placement of the loudspeakers can be arranged to accommodate the shape of the listening area. After Farrar, Reference 13-12. (B) *Pantophonic* soundfield reproduction system utilizing six loudspeakers arranged in a hexagonal pattern. Side loudspeakers increase the spatial impression by providing discrete lateral imaging for the listener. After Furness, Reference 13-10. (C) *Pantophonic* soundfield reproduction system utilizing six loudspeakers arranged in a different hexagonal pattern. Center-front and center-rear loudspeakers eliminate any ambiguity that might result from phantom centers. After Furness, Reference 13-10.

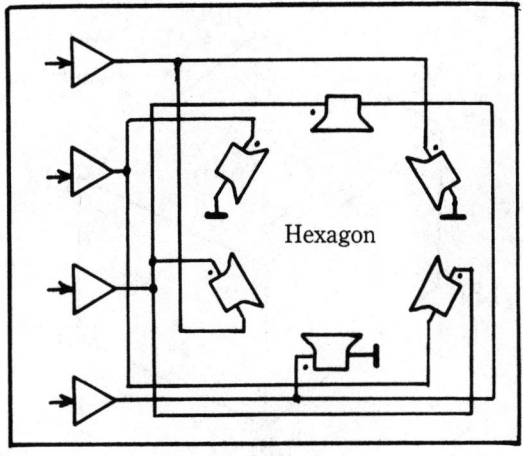

Hexagon

(C)

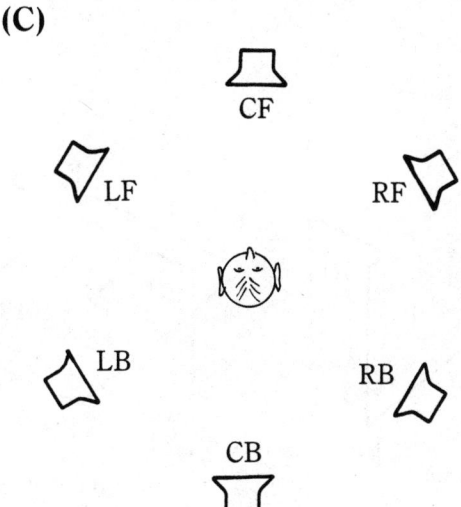

CF

LF

RF

LB

RB

CB

13-12 Continued.

the first wavefront still applies, however, so this listening area remains somewhat restricted. For periphonic reproduction, three possible loudspeaker arrangements are shown in Fig. 13-13.

Despite the complex technical nature of ambisonics, it is capable still of being encoded via the UHJ system into two audio channels so that it remains fully compatible with stereo and monaural transmission and playback systems.

The ambisonic system presents discrete, or nearly discrete, signals into the listening space and each is as important as any other. Unlike many of the less complex surround sound systems that allow lower powered amplifiers and loud-

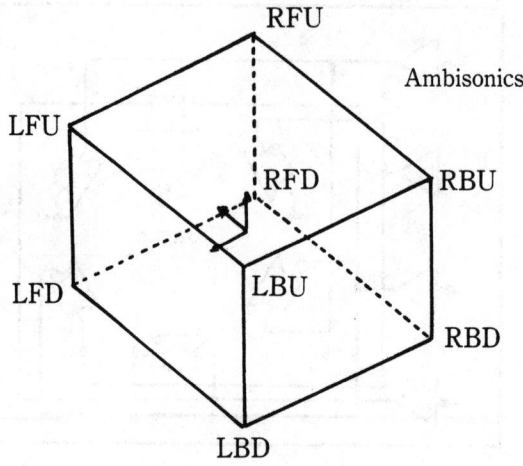

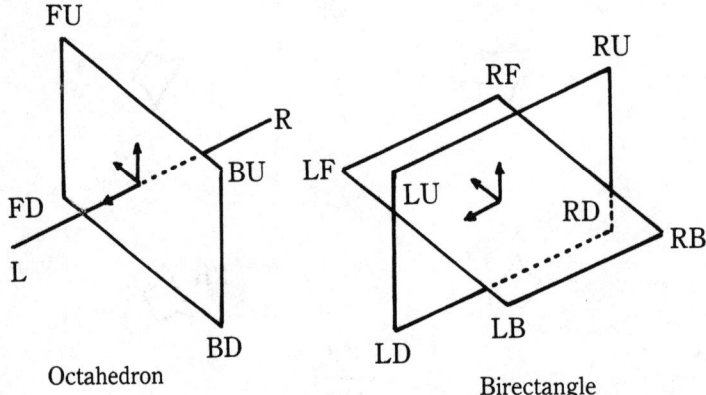

13-13   *Periphonic* soundfield reproduction systems provide full spherical imaging, i.e., vertical as well as horizontal information. Loudspeaker designations: F = front; B = rear; L = left; R = right; U = up; D = down. After Furness, Reference 13-10.

speakers to be used for the rear channels, ambisonics requires all loudspeakers and their associated amplifiers to be of equal quality.

Ironically, the technical complexity that provides ambisonics with its unique ability to localize sonic images in 3-dimensional space is also the cause of its relative failure in the commercial audio marketplace. Its rather stringent requirements on the decoding of the signals and the placement of both loudspeakers and listeners has relegated the ambisonic system to the homes of only its most dedicated adherents.

Binaural systems revisited

In chapter 6, binaural sound was discussed as a means for re-creating a complete soundfield via headphone reproduction. Although the results are not fully convincing, recent developments in digital signal processing, together with improved binaural head design, have reopened experimentation into binaural as a means of providing surround sound via loudspeakers as well (References 13-14, 13-15, 13-16, and 13-17). Experiments in *transaural* recording and reproduction rely heavily on new methods for critical analysis of the transfer functions of the pinna and ear canal, (see chapter 6). These experiments are further aided by improved techniques for processing the signals fed to the two, or more, loudspeakers in order to cancel the crosstalk that ordinarily occurs when each ear hears both loudspeakers (References 13-18 and 13-19).

Production techniques for surround sound

In the earliest days of stereo records, locomotive trains passed through many living rooms until the novelty wore off. Similarly, when the first quad records appeared on the store shelves, discrete antiphonal brass choirs and circularly arranged symphony orchestras were not uncommon. Happily, for all concerned, these recordings were short-lived.

The concept of surround sound recording can assume many guises, depending on the context of the project. One fundamental feature is simply the enhancement of the primary stereo musical material by providing an added degree of spatial perspective; the ambience and reverberation of the original performance can envelop the listener, rather than come from the same two loudspeakers as the music itself. Recording antiphonal music also is a valid application of these techniques. With the widespread growth of high-quality audio with pictures, however, it is the special effects and environmental sounds or *actualities* that serve as the principal material for surround channels today.

Ambience recording

In conventional two-loudspeaker stereo, the reverberation is reproduced from the same direction as the music, and therefore does not have the same effect on the listener as it would in a concert hall. By recording only the reverberation and reproducing this through the surround speakers, the illusion of *being there* is enhanced greatly.

The key to successfully recording ambience is to keep as much of the direct soundfield out of the ambience microphones as possible, as this should come only from the front loudspeakers. The first rule is to place ambience microphones beyond the critical distance. Second, these microphones should have a smooth off-axis (diffuse field) polar response, because they are primarily responding to sound coming from all directions. It is common to place a pair of omnidirectional microphones far back in the concert hall to record the ambience and reverberation of the hall (Fig. 13-14). The microphones should be fairly high in the air on tall stands or

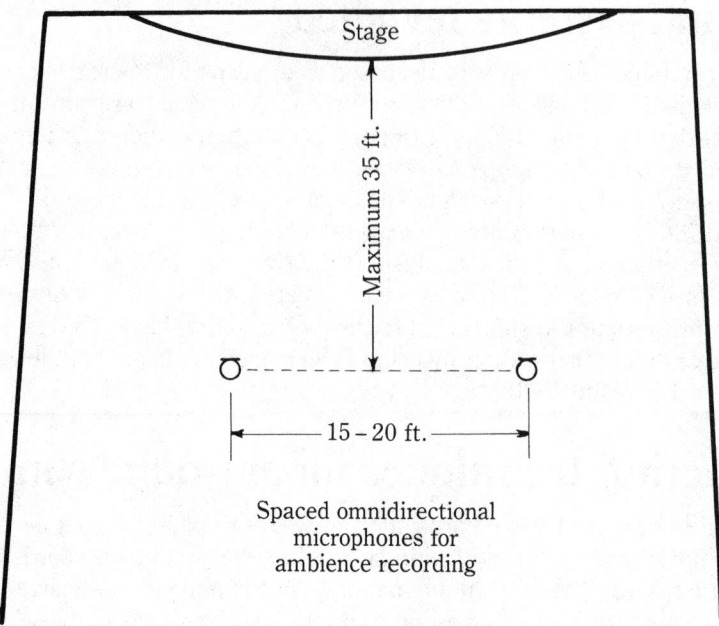

13-14 Ambience recording microphone placement showing two omnidirectional microphones situated in the audience area. To minimize the possibility of echoes that might result from mixing the signal from these acoustically delayed microphones with the direct signal of the principal stereo microphones, their distance from the stage should not exceed 35 feet. The spacing between the two ambience microphones is limited to 15 – 20 ft, to minimize comb-filter effects between them.

suspended from the ceiling. Because they are omnidirectional, precise aiming is not essential and as long as the spacing between the two microphones is reasonably wide, 15 to 20 ft., any time-delay effects or comb-filter between them will be negligible.

One problem can arise, however, from this technique: echoes might result due to the delayed arrival of the direct sound into these microphones when it is combined with the signals from the primary microphones. To minimize this, the reverberant microphones should not be more than 35 ft. behind the principal stereo pickup, as this will keep the signals from these microphones well within the echo-free region discussed in chapter 3.

A different approach to ambience recording involves using bidirectional microphones for the reverberation pickup. By aiming their null plane at the stage, the pickup of direct sound is minimized (Fig. 13-15A and B). Orienting the principal axes of the microphones so they are aimed diagonally across the reverberant field (i.e., are aimed at the opposite wall/ceiling intersection) will help randomize any reflections from the walls or other hard surfaces of the hall and reduce any specific echoes that might otherwise result to near inaudibility. These microphones should be at least 15 ft. away from any hard reflecting surface to minimize comb-filter effects. As with omnidirectional microphones, suspending these microphones or placing them on tall stands high above the seating area reduces their pickup of noise from the audience, if recording live concerts.

Enhanced ambience recording

John Eargle, a well-known recording engineer and author, employed a unique method for the artificial enhancement of natural ambience through the use of digital reverberation devices. Instead of feeding an *auxiliary mix* of all the principal microphones to this device, Eargle suggested using the reverberant field microphones to provide its input signal. Then, the output of the digital reverberator is used to *create* the ambience around the recording; the direct output of the reverberant microphones is not used. The purpose of this is to provide absolute control over the sound quality of the reverberation and simultaneously maintain a feeling of proper perspective for the reverberation. When the primary stereo or accent microphones are used to feed the reverberation device, their signal provides false cues; the signal is too close up to sound natural.

Whatever techniques used, providing ambience to the surround loudspeakers can greatly enliven the music listening experience.

(A) Proscenium

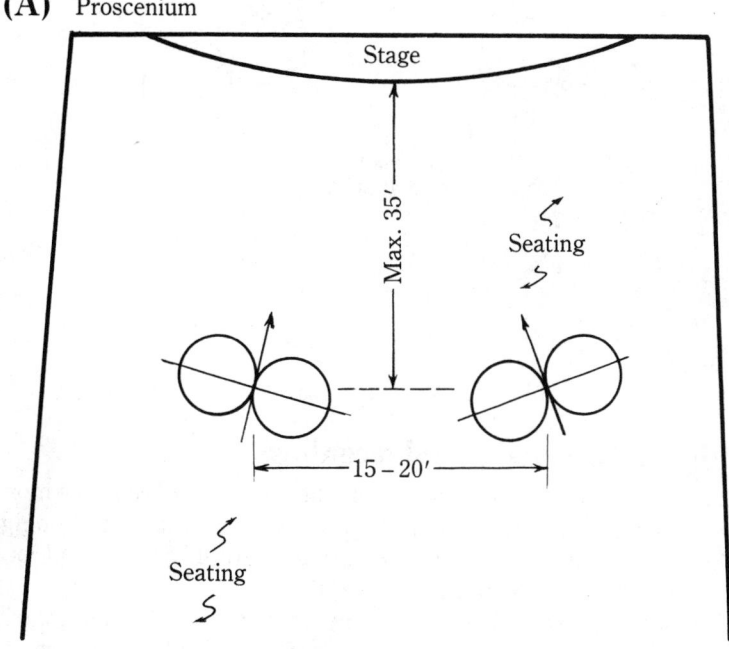

13-15 (A) Two bidirectional microphones used for recording ambience. Shown in plan view, their null-axis is oriented toward the stage (the direct sound source) so the pickup of the microphones is primarily of nondirect sound, reflected from the walls of the auditorium. As in the earlier example, their distance from the stage is no more than 35 ft, and the spacing between them is 15–20 ft. (B) Shown in elevation, these two microphones are aimed diagonally across the auditorium, so each microphone is *looking* at the intersection of the opposite side wall and ceiling.

(B)

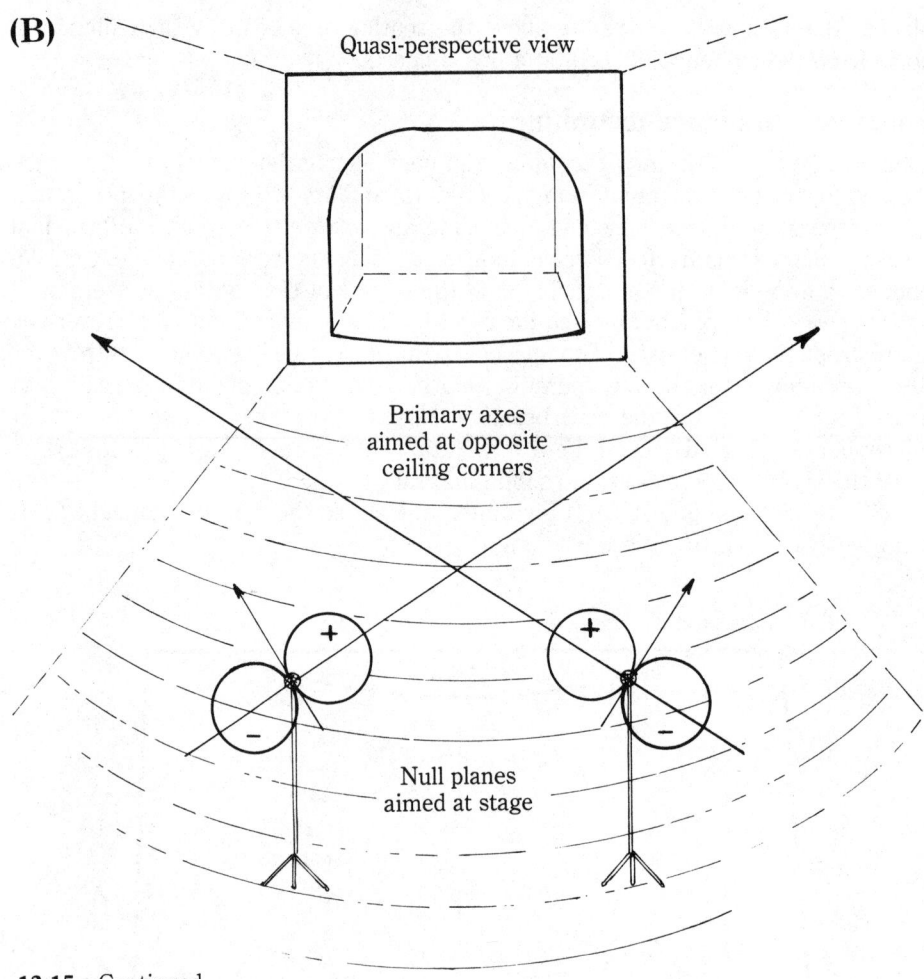

Quasi-perspective view

Primary axes
aimed at opposite
ceiling corners

Null planes
aimed at stage

13-15 Continued.

Localization in surround sound recordings

The discrete placement of sounds in the surround soundfield requires more critical microphone placement and production techniques. In addition, positioning of loudspeakers for playback might need to be controlled carefully if pinpoint localization is required in the surround soundfield.

Because modern surround sound systems rely on some form of matrix encoding/decoding process, precise localization might be difficult to achieve. The common microphone techniques employed for making stereo recordings are not always suited to the particular requirements of surround sound productions. Coincident microphone techniques, for example, do not convey sufficient phase-difference information to provide a full spread between the left-front and right-front loudspeakers; the matrix tends to collapse coincident recordings into the center channel. This might not be a problem with dialogue recording, because this is usually kept close to the center channel anyway. To provide music scoring and sound effects with a full stereo spread through matrix systems, near-coincident, or even spaced microphone techniques, generally are more appropriate. For example, the Decca Tree described in chapter 9 provides an excellent starting-point for music scoring with enough phase information to retain good stereo spread with the Dolby Surround matrix system. One caveat, however, is if too much phase-difference information occurs in the front channels (left, center, or right), it tends to *pull toward the surrounds*. There is a fine line between too little and too much phase-difference information when recording for matrix surround systems.

Similarly, coincident techniques do not reproduce well over the surround channel(s) because they provide little or none of the difference information necessary for encoding into the surround channel (Reference 13-20). Again, near-coincident or spaced microphone techniques work best through the matrix. With the exception of multichannel techniques employed with some of the larger film formats, all surround loudspeakers are fed from a common audio signal—unlike the earlier quad systems that employed two separate surround channels. The only sense of directionality is determined by the listener's position relative to the various loudspeakers. Thus, the best that can be achieved in this context is the surround effect can be related to one or the other of the front channels so it can be pulled to one side or the other by the effect of interaction with that channel (chapter 2).

Monitoring surround sound recordings

It is an axiom of any recording technique that the final result is only as good as the monitoring system used when making the recording. The more accurately the recording engineer can hear throughout the process, the better the final result will be. This is important with stereo imaging and is absolutely critical when producing recordings for surround sound reproduction. The difference between creating too little or too much signal for the surround channel is precise. There is no way to guess what will happen; the only way is to listen to the recording through the complete process, including the decoder and surround loudspeakers. For this reason, manufacturers of surround sound systems usually recommend that both the encoder and decoder should be inserted into the production and monitoring signal chains during the recording and/or mixing process (Fig. 13-16 and Reference 13-21).

The illusion of reality

At the very beginning of this book, we defined stereophonics as *the science of three-dimensional sound*. Our discussion has come a long way since then, covering various ways in which we perceive, record, and reproduce sound. Scientific analysis and complex technical processes notwithstanding, however, the realization must be that it is the listener who, in the final conclusion, decides whether what is heard seems *real* or not. Sound recording is still an art which happens to be enveloped in science. Whatever the means employed—whether it involves two or more microphones, transmitted via two or more audio channels and reproduced via two or more loudspeakers—on this "illusion of reality" rests the ultimate success or failure of the entire recording/reproduction process.

(A)

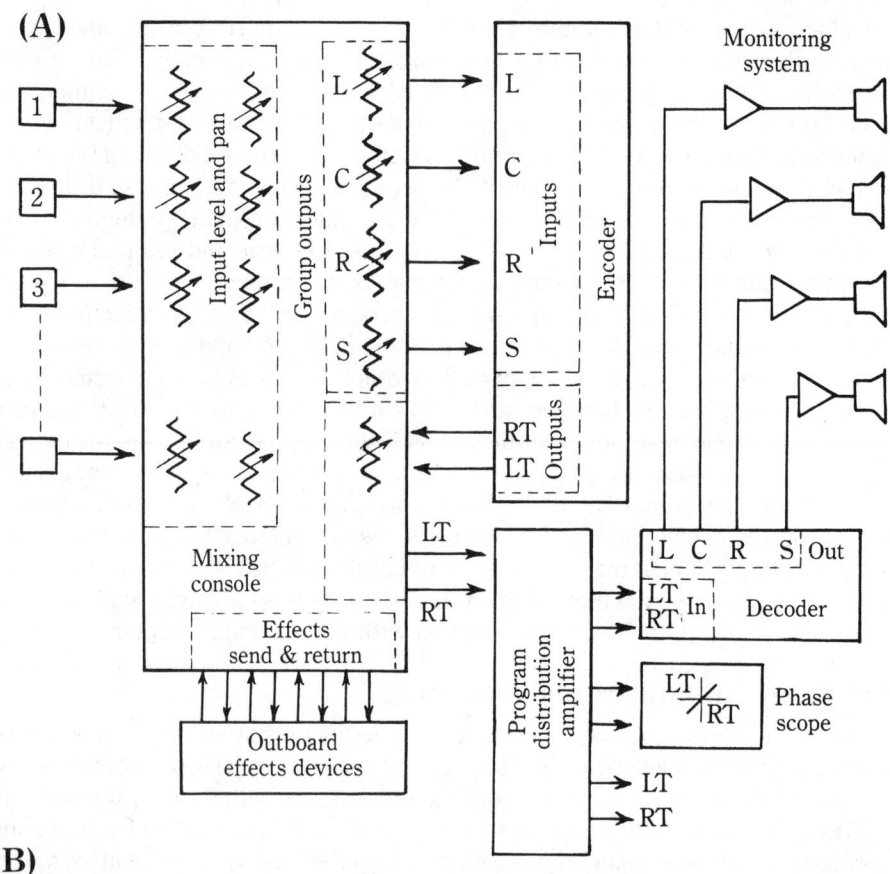

(B)

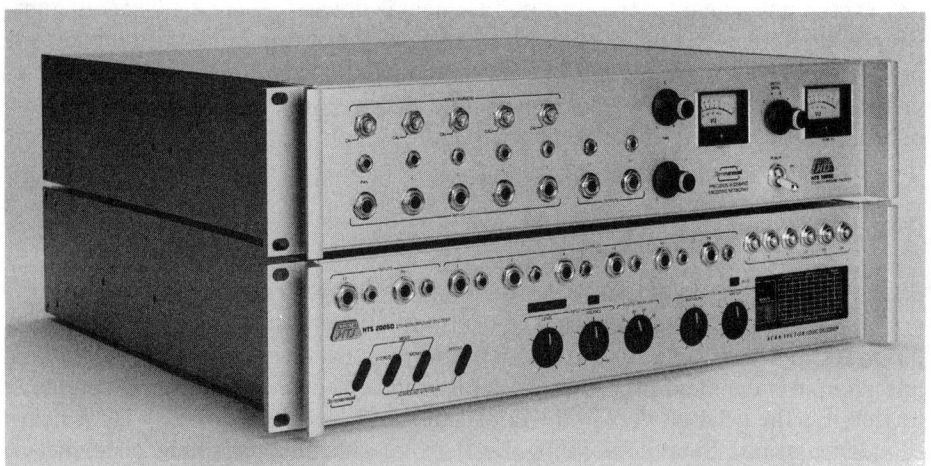

13-16 (A) Matrix surround sound system production block diagram, showing mining console, matrix encoder, matrix decoder, and monitoring system. After Schulein, Reference 13-21. (B) Shure HTS Stereosurround™ Encoder (top) and Decoder (bottom).

14
Optimizing the listening environment

GOOD LISTENING IS A CHAIN OF THREE LINKS: THE AUDIO REPRODUCTION equipment, human perception, and room acoustics (Fig. 14-1). The audio industry has lavished attention on playback equipment, amplifier, and loudspeaker quality. Human auditory perception and room acoustics, however, seem to be less accessible to the average audio consumer. Human perception remains a reasonably consistent, but complex link. The acoustics of the listening room is a vital and highly variable element that cries for the attention it deserves. By removing some of the mystery surrounding acoustics, it can be made to contribute to the goal of superior reproduced sound (Reference 14-1).

Long ago a child defined salt as "something that makes potatoes taste bad if you don't put any on." Acoustics makes music sound bad if nothing is done to correct it.

Assuming that the other two links of the audio reproduction chain are in good working order, good acoustics can be expected to contribute the following to the quality of reproduced sound in a room:

- Sharply defined stereo image and good depth of soundfield
- Clean and crisp dynamics of music and speech with natural attack and decay of impulsive sounds
- Smooth and uniform frequency response of the room
- Listening quality reasonably independent of position in the room
- Freedom from interfering noise
- Satisfactory reverberation and ambience

Confinement of sound in an enclosure

A loudspeaker far removed from any reflecting surfaces can radiate sound in any direction like a point source in free space. The sound from this truly *outdoor* loud-

219

14-1 Good listening is depicted as a chain of three links: the quality of the audio reproduction equipment, human perception, and the acoustics of the space. Equipment quality is usually high. The study of auditory perception is a fast growing scientific field yielding valuable insights, but our understanding of human hearing is still rudimentary. Room acoustics is a mature science, but misunderstood by many audio practitioners.

speaker is perceived as dead and flat. The soundfield produced by the same loudspeaker in an enclosed space would be infinitely more complex and, with the same input at the same distance, would sound louder. Understanding the effect of the reflecting surfaces on the sound in an enclosed space allows one to manipulate the surfaces to his/her advantage (Reference 14-1).

The audible spectrum is commonly taken as 20 to 20,000 Hz. These 10 octaves span such a tremendous range that it is necessary to treat the low-frequency response of a room differently than the high-frequency response. For the low frequencies, sound must be considered as waves; for the higher frequencies it is easier to consider sound as rays traveling in straight lines. No specific frequency of transition exists from one to the other, but there is a region in which both effects are present in reduced amounts.

For sound below a few hundred hertz, the volume of the room must be considered as a resonant chamber, because most listening rooms have dimensions comparable to the wavelength of sound. For example, consider a living room or a studio 20 × 15 ft with a ceiling height of 8 ft (Fig. 14-2). This acoustical chamber resonates at many frequencies determined by the dimensions of the room. These resonances can result in unequal distribution of bass sound energy. The secret is to distribute the resonances to avoid troublesome *holes* or *hot spots* in the room's low-frequency response, at least near the listening area.

Axial mode resonances

Any pair of opposite, parallel surfaces constitutes a resonant system. For example, if two ends of a rectangular room are 20 ft apart, they are resonant at a frequency of 1,130 divided by twice the distance (1,130/40 = 28.3 Hz). The 1,130 ft/sec is the speed of sound; the sound must make one complete round trip at the resonance frequency.

The two side walls spaced 15 ft resonate at a frequency of 1,130/30 = 37.7 Hz, and the floor/ceiling surfaces spaced 8 ft resonate at 1,130/16 = 70.6 Hz. In this

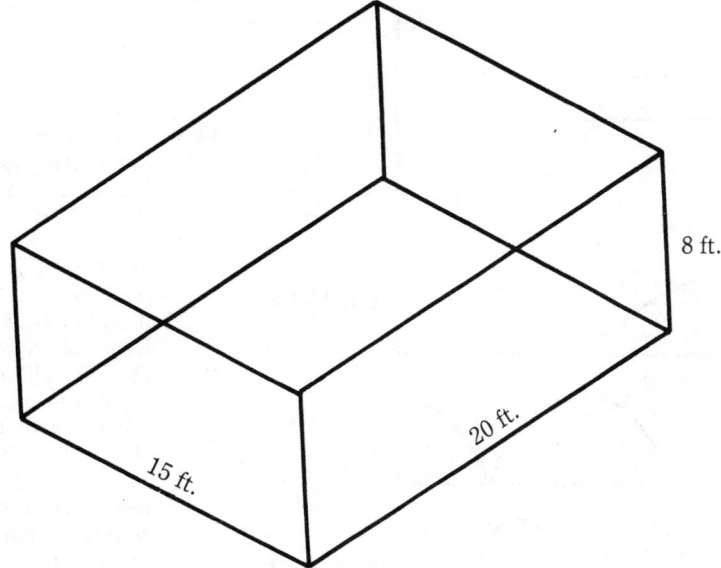

14-2   The dimensions of a typical music/living room that is to be studied as an enclosure having many natural resonances (modes) affecting the low-frequency response.

way the rectangular room resonates simultaneously at 28.3, 37.7, and 70.6 Hz, called the *axial modes* of the room. If stopping at this point were possible, life would be simple. Each set of plane, parallel surfaces also resonates at multiples of the same frequencies (Fig. 14-3). Thus the two end walls are resonant not only at 28.3 Hz, but also at 2, 3, 4, . . . etc. times 28.3 Hz. In other words, these two surfaces are just as resonant when the sound makes a second, third, or fourth round trip as they were for the first round trip (neglecting successive reflection losses). A series of resonance frequencies exists for each pair of surfaces (Table 14-1). Each series is terminated at about 300 Hz because few axial mode problems are found above that frequency (Reference 14-2).

In a practical sense, if the room is energized by feeding a 28.3 Hz signal to a loudspeaker, a sound level meter would show a maximum sound pressure at each end wall and a null in the center of the room (Fig. 14-3). If the frequency is shifted to 56.6 Hz, two nulls would be detected with a peak at the center of the room and at the walls. Energizing the room at three times the basic resonance frequency, 84.9 Hz, three nulls would be found. Sound pressure is always maximum (particle velocity zero) at the reflecting surfaces.

The resonance frequencies for the length, width, and height of the room are plotted on a linear frequency scale in Fig. 14-4, as well as a combination of the three. Both length and width are resonant at 113.0 and 226.0 Hz. A similar situation occurs at 141.3 and 282.5 Hz. These coincidences result in the excessive buildup of energy at these frequencies, which can result in severe colorations of the sound. The arrows indicate frequencies at which these coincidences appear.

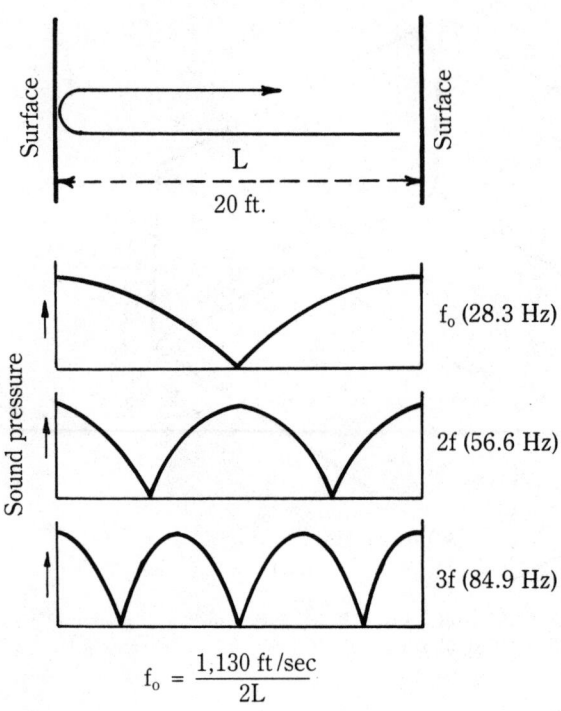

$$f_o = \frac{1{,}130 \text{ ft/sec}}{2L}$$

14-3 The two end walls of the music/living room of Fig. 14-2 constitute a system that has a frequency of resonance found by dividing the speed of sound (1,130 ft/sec) by twice the length of the room, or 28.3 Hz. These two end walls spaced 20 ft are also resonant at 2, 3, 4, etc. times 28.3 Hz. A similar series of resonances is associated with the height of the room (floor/ceiling) and another with the width (side walls).

Table 14-1.
Frequencies of axial modes
for
room: 15 × 20 × 8 ft

Length	Width	Height
28.3 Hz	37.7 Hz	70.6 Hz
56.5	75.3	141.3
84.8	113.0	211.9
113.0	150.7	282.5
141.3	188.3	353.1
169.5	226.0	
197.8	263.7	
226.0	301.3	
254.3		
282.5		
310.8		

Listen carefully for the possibility of sound colorations in the music at these coincident frequencies.

No easy way exists to avoid these coincidences completely, but selecting favorable room proportions during the construction stage can minimize their effect. The coincidences of Fig. 14-4 are directly traceable to a 3:4 ratio of length to width dimensions. Techniques have been developed to determine room dimensional ratios that give favorable distribution of these resonance frequencies. These are of interest primarily when considering new construction, before room dimensions or shape are fixed (Reference 14-3A).

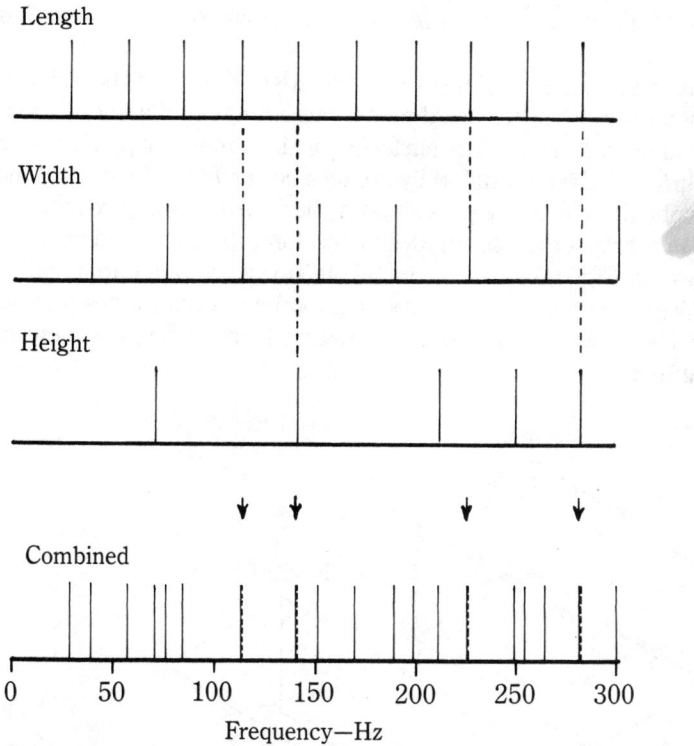

14-4 Plotting these three series of axial mode frequencies on a linear frequency scale and combining them makes possible an evaluation of the evenness of distribution of low-frequency sound energy in the room. Both length and width are resonant at 113.0 and 226.0 Hz. These coincidences result in excessive buildup of energy at these frequencies that can result in colorations of the sound. The arrows indicate frequencies at which colorations are most likely to appear.

For existing spaces, the usual approach is to first examine the resonance frequencies for coincidences. If any are found, use them as guides in the search for frequencies at which audible colorations of the sound might be discovered. Corrections can then be made by introducing absorption at the offending frequencies. For a *rifle* approach, this absorption must be placed at strategic points in the room where the sound pressure at a given frequency is high. A much easier *shotgun* approach is to introduce absorbing material or devices effective in that particular frequency region and move it around until the offending coloration is gone.

Tangential and oblique modes

The spacing of modal resonance frequencies in Fig. 14-4 could be greater than desired. Each mode is effective over a narrow frequency region of approximately 5 Hz. It would be good for room response if all modes were close enough to overlap. Independent action of single or coincident modes well spaced from neighbors often leads to audible colorations of the sound. Guilford came to the conclusion that spacings greater than 25 Hz were especially prone to sound colorations (Reference 14-2).

Fortunately, many modal resonances exist other than the axial modes. Figure 14-5 illustrates not only an axial mode, but a tangential and oblique mode as well. Tangential modes involve four surfaces for their round trip; oblique modes involve all six surfaces. Even though they are less powerful than the axial modes, tangential and oblique modes help to smooth the low-frequency response of a room as they fill in between the axial modes. Therefore, the combined axial modal frequencies shown in Fig. 14-4 are not the whole story; the tangential and oblique modes help make the response of this room smoother. Axial modes dominate, however, and consideration of them alone is usually sufficient for treatment of the average listening room.

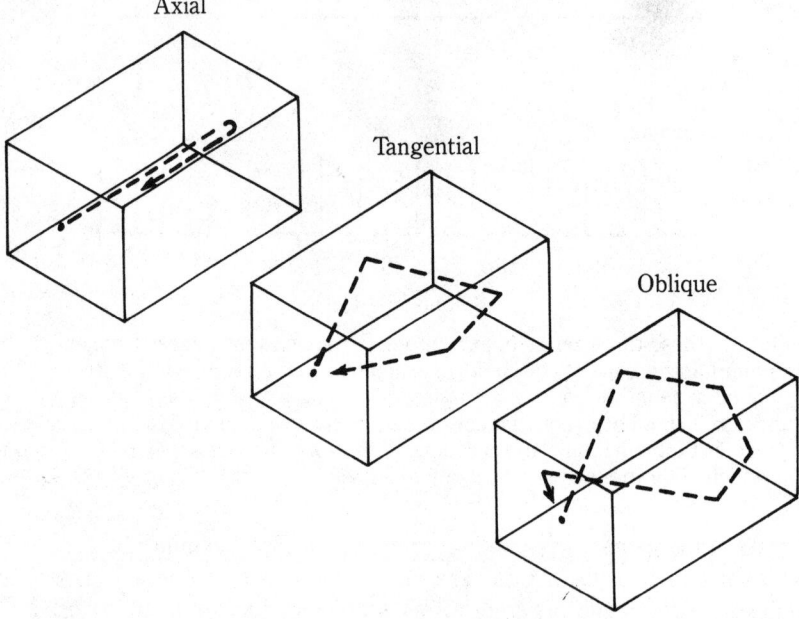

14-5   In addition to the system of axial modes, tangential and oblique modes occur of lesser strength, which are helpful in filling in between the axial modes for a smoother room response.

Low-frequency sound absorbers

Few commonly available acoustic materials have significant absorption at the low-modal frequencies. Carpets, drapes, acoustic tile, and sculptured foam are excellent absorbers of sound in the mid-to-high frequency region, but are close to worthless at lower frequencies. At these low frequencies, such absorbers as glass fiber are effective only if the thickness is 6 inches or more.

Resonant structures can be used to *trap* this low-frequency energy. One such device is known as the Helmholtz resonator and can be made effective at these low frequencies. A bottle is a good example of such a resonator (Fig. 14-6). The mass of the air in the neck of the bottle vibrates against the springiness of the air in the body of the bottle, absorbing some energy in the process. A common *soda pop* bottle has very high absorption at about 185 Hz, but the absorption peak is only effective over a narrow sliver of the frequency spectrum, so it is worthless in practical situations.

Practical Helmholtz low-frequency absorbers can be made with perforated or slat facings over an air space, as shown in Fig. 14-6. The air in the perforation or slit vibrates against the springiness of the air in the cavity below providing a peak of absorption. The losses provided by the glass fiber in the cavity in this case are sufficient to create a peak wide enough to be useful. The design of Helmholtz resonators is covered in References 14-3B and 14-4.

In Fig. 14-3 the pressure of each mode is maximum at the wall reflecting surfaces. Resonant modes of all rooms terminate in the corners; hence this is the most effective position for such absorbers.

Building construction is also an important factor. A considerable amount of low-frequency absorption is built into frame construction. For example, walls and ceilings of gypsum board (drywall) and frame floors are good absorbers of low-frequency sound energy. Such surfaces vibrate as diaphragms, absorbing sound in the process due to the frictional resistance in the materials.

To improve the acoustics of a space devoted to music listening, first make sure the resonances of the room are under control. In a frame structure the built-in low-frequency absorption of the surfaces of the room possibly could suffice in the control of modal resonances. If coincidences of modal frequencies are found, they should be taken as a warning of possible audible colorations at those frequencies. *Muddy* or *boomy* sound quality usually indicates the need for bass absorption for the control of room resonances.

Mid-high frequency region and delay effects

Above 300 – 500 Hz, sound could be considered as rays that travel in straight lines and geometric acoustics can be applied. In this mid-high frequency range, reflections of sound from the room boundaries are dominant and the angle of incidence is equal to the angle of reflection.

Sound reflected from room surfaces reaches the ear of the listener later than the direct sound because of the greater distance traveled, and at reduced amplitude, because of inverse square and reflection losses (Fig. 14-7). Delayed sound reflections open up a Pandora's box of psychoacoustical effects: the law of the first

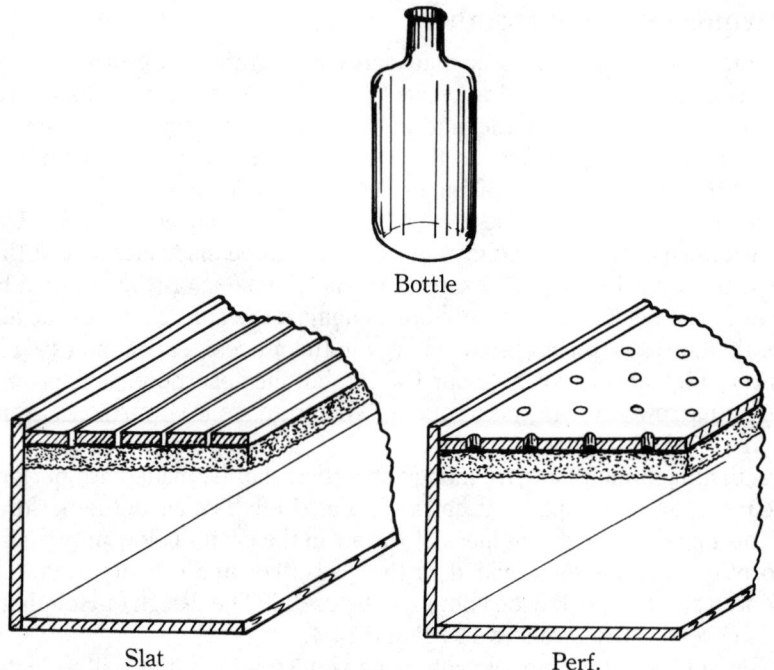

Bottle

Slat

Perf.

14-6 Ordinary acoustical materials, such as foam, carpets, and glass fiber are ineffective in absorbing sound at the low audible frequencies of room modes unless they are used in impractical thicknesses. Tuned Helmholtz resonators are both practical and effective at these low frequencies. A bottle resonates at a certain frequency determined by the mechanical vibration of the air in the neck of the bottle reacting with the springiness of the air in the body of the bottle. The air in the slits or holes of Helmholtz resonators similarly reacts with the springiness of the air below, absorbing sound at the frequency of resonance. The width of the band of absorption can be increased by adding the friction of the glass fiber layer. Such Helmholtz resonators are easy to design and build (References 14-3, 14-4).

wavefront (the precedence effect), echoes, and comb-filter distortion. The effects of combining a sound with its delayed replica are discussed in chapter 8. A simplified consideration of reflections in typical listening arrangements provides a basis for evaluating the acoustics of listening rooms in the mid-high frequency region.

The word *replica* was used to describe a reflected signal. It implies a close to perfect reflection that can be realized only with a perfectly smooth and a massive reflecting surface. Most practical reflecting surfaces alter the frequency response of sound rays impinging upon them. Thus, reflected sound reaching the ears of the listener differs from the direct sound. The sounds are *coherent*, but not *identical*. As a benefit, a modest amount of interaural incoherence resulting from reflections can contribute to the spaciousness of the reproduced sound (see chapter 12). The difference, however, between conserving the spaciousness on the record and adding listening-room spaciousness to it should be recognized.

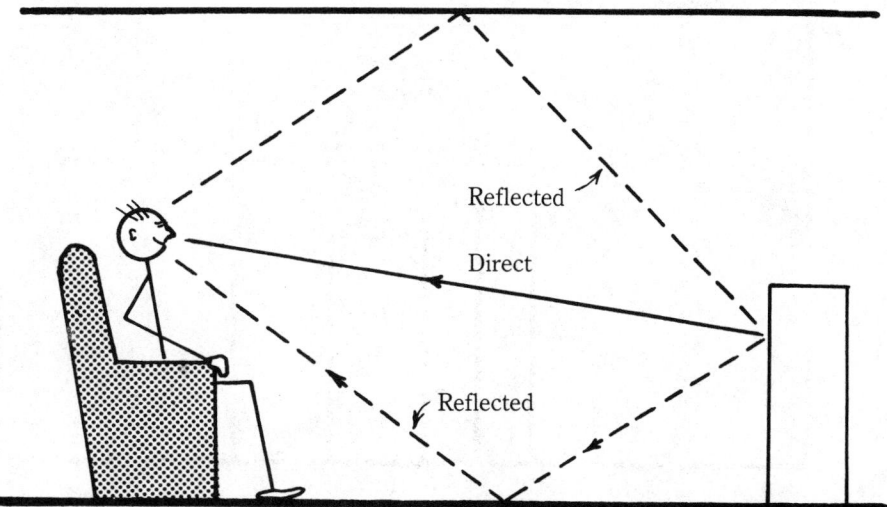

14-7   Direct rays arrive at the listener's ears first because they travel the shorter path. Shortly after the arrival of the direct ray the *early reflections* arrive, such as from the floor and the ceiling.

Reflections on and in the listening room

Figure 14-8 illustrates some of the first-order reflections in a typical listening arrangement. Only the direct ray travels from source to listener without reflection. The earliest reflections arriving at the ears of the listener are bounced from the floor, the ceiling, and the side walls. The wall behind the loudspeaker also yields a reflection that arrives soon after the direct ray.

These early reflections are followed by a host of later arrivals that have had two, three, four, or more reflections from the front surfaces of the room. Many single and multiple reflections from the rear wall and other surfaces in the rear of the room arrive even later.

Reflections and the auditory system

The time graph of Fig. 14-8 shows early reflections spread out in time. The auditory apparatus does not delineate individual early reflections; rather a composite sound is perceived that is louder and more pleasant than the direct sound alone (such as what might be heard outdoors). A host of such early reflections of various amplitudes and delays merged together is perceived as ambience and spaciousness and, at greater delays, as reverberation. If the delay exceeds 40 – 50 ms, however, a reflection is perceived as a bothersome discrete echo, which is not a problem in the average listening room.

Effect of early reflections

Are early reflections beneficial to the perceived sound? The answer is *yes* and *no* (see chapter 8). The overall effect of these early reflections is often a deteriora-

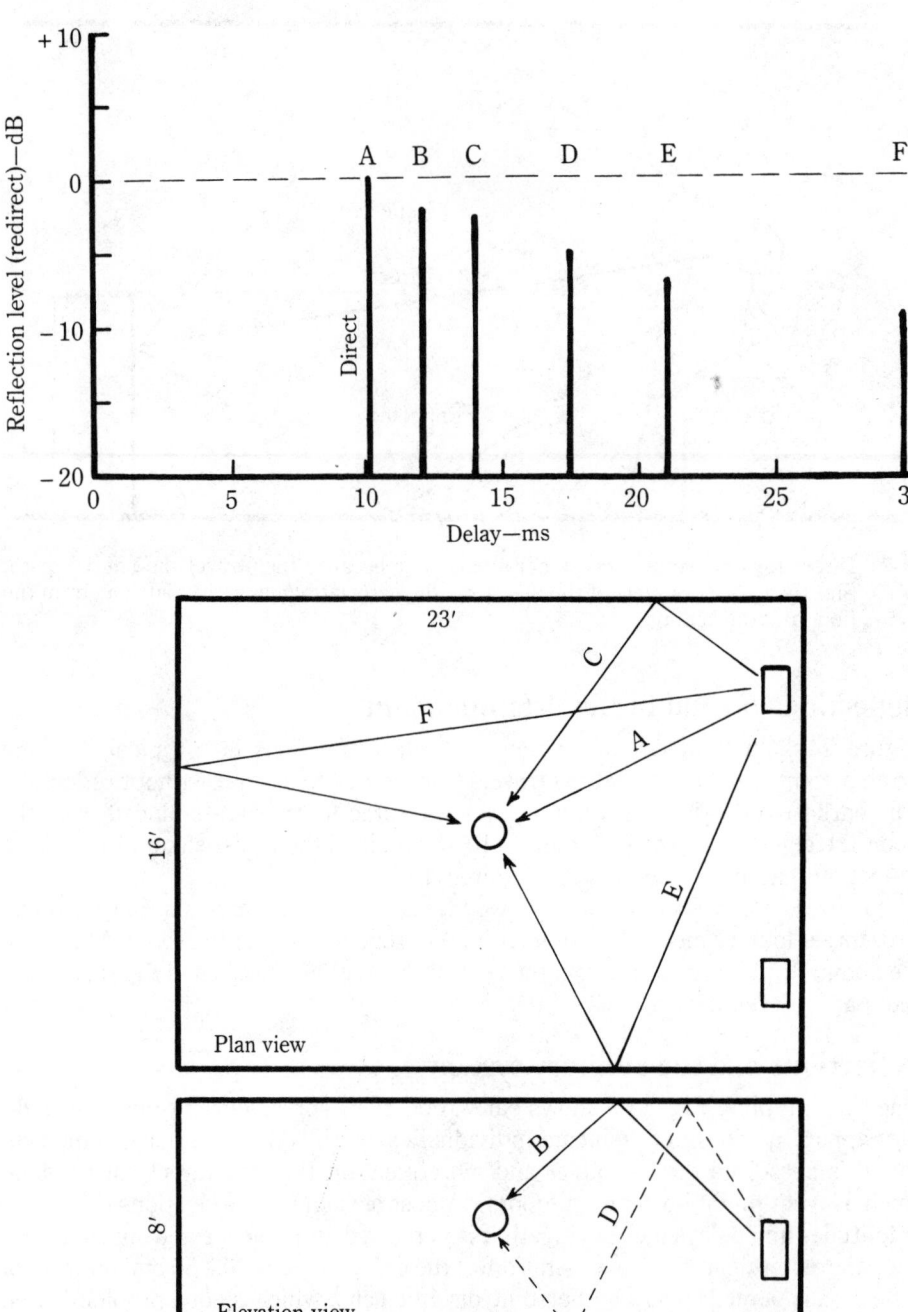

14-8   Plan and elevation sketches of a listening room having dimensions of 16 × 23 × 8 ft. By knowing the speed of sound, the relative time of arrival at the listener's ears can be determined. A simple calculation based on spherical propagation estimates the amplitude. An *echogram* can thus be built up.

tion of the timbre of the program material and of the stereo image; they need to be controlled.

Diffusion of sound

Reflecting surfaces and acoustical absorbing materials and structures have been the primary materials the acoustical designer has had to work with. Diffusion has always been earnestly sought through the use of nonsymmetrical rooms, splayed surfaces, and geometrical protuberances of various shapes; however, only modest diffusion resulted, and most of that occurred at mid-high frequencies. For an object to diffuse sound, it must be considerably larger than the wavelength of the sound. The old polycylindrical diffuser, which graced so many early studios, is still viable today. Their convex surfaces add mid-high frequency diffusion along with appreciable low-frequency absorption.

A completely different approach to diffusion was suggested by Schroeder, based on the application of number theory (Reference 14-5). He pointed out that a wall with regular grooves and depths varying according to certain number theory codes would act like a sonic-diffraction grating, diffusing sound uniformly in all directions. The diffusing action of such diffraction-grating diffusers is illustrated in Fig. 14-9. A ray of sound arriving perpendicular to the surface of the diffuser is scattered uniformly throughout the plane of that ray. If the wells are perpendicular, the diffraction is horizontal. By orienting the wells of a diffusing unit horizontally, the diffusion will be vertical, thus providing a hemisphere of diffused sound. Combination units are available that scatter sound in both horizontal and vertical directions. Proprietary units are available for mounting on ceilings and walls, in corners and freestanding.

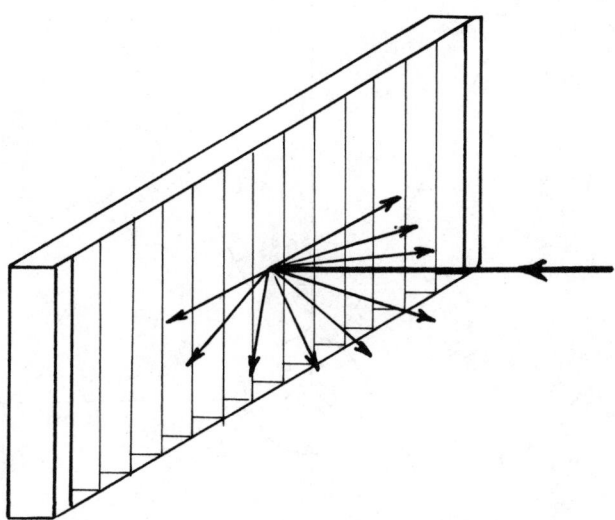

14-9 The sonic diffusion grating, based on number theory, diffuses sound arriving horizontally throughout the horizontal half-plane. Orienting the wells of some diffusors at right angles to the wells of others, diffuses sound throughout the entire hemisphere.

One commercial application of this theory, quadratic residue diffraction-grating diffusers, is presently used in many major recording studio control rooms around the world; their use in recording studios is fast growing. They are also widely used in music halls and churches. Their wide application in professional and home listening rooms gives much promise. Weighing the true value of highly-diffuse soundfields in informal listening situations, against the high cost of the diffusing units, is an issue to be addressed.

Stereo geometry

A general consensus is that a roughly equilateral triangle should be used to position the two loudspeakers and the listener (Fig. 14-10). Locating the listener on the centerline gives the best stereo image because sound arrives from both loudspeakers at the same time. Off this centerline, the sound from the closer loudspeaker arrives earlier and sound appears to come from that loudspeaker, the law of the first wavefront. Many also believe the loudspeakers should be spaced 6 to 10 ft apart and should be kept 2 or 3 ft from the front and side walls. The

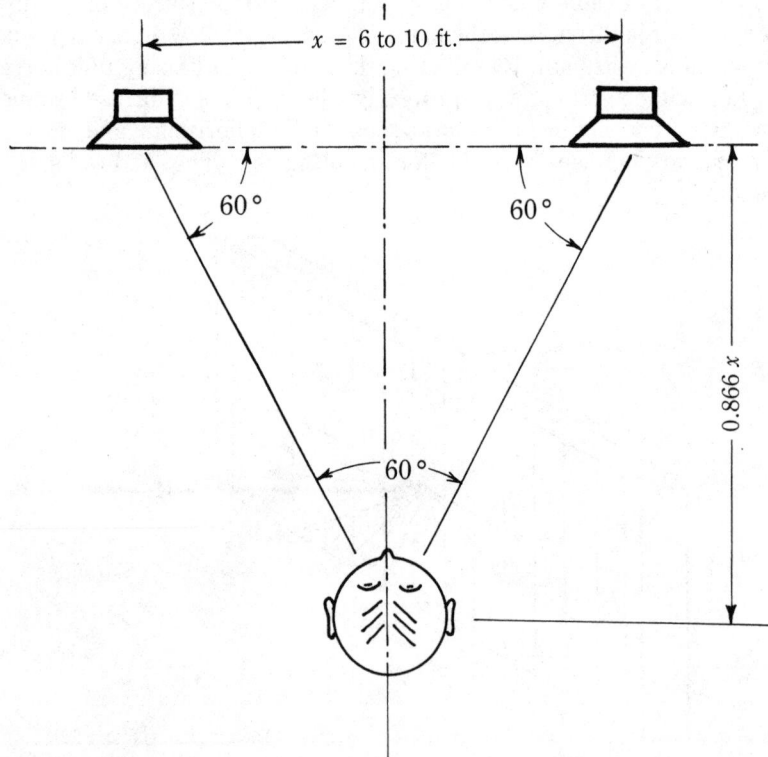

14-10　The *classic* stereo geometry based on an equilateral triangle. The listener position is often chosen a bit closer or a bit farther from the *sweet spot* to broaden the favorable area.

spacing determines the distance of the optimum listening position from the line joining the two loudspeakers. If the equilateral triangle plan is implemented and x is the spacing of the loudspeakers, the basic listener position is approximately $(x)(\sin 60°)$, or $(0.866)(x)$. The listening position is placed often a foot or so behind or in front of the basic position.

Deviations from this time-honored configuration might be desirable to realize more uniform low-frequency room response. Nulls and peaks of the prominent axial modes determine such response.

Low-frequency reflections from nearby surfaces

The low-frequency response of the loudspeaker is a function of its proximity to reflecting surfaces, as illustrated in Fig. 14-11. If a loudspeaker is placed close to a single, flat reflecting surface, the energy is radiated into a half sphere instead of a sphere (Fig. 14-11A). Thus the sound pressure at a standard distance from the loudspeaker is increased 6 dB in the low-frequency region. If the loudspeaker is placed at the intersection of two such reflecting surfaces, the sound pressure is increased 12 dB in the lows as the energy is confined to a quarter sphere (Fig. 14-11B). A loudspeaker placed at the intersection of 3 reflecting surfaces restricts the energy to an eighth sphere, and the sound pressure is increased 18 dB (Fig. 14-11C). In other words, the location of the loudspeaker can cause a significant rise in its bass response. At higher frequencies the directivity of the loudspeaker tends to direct the radiated energy away from these nearby reflecting surfaces.

Approaching the problem analytically, detail in the response of the loudspeaker can be obtained (References 14-6, 14-7). Using the dimensions of Fig. 14-12, an example is shown in Fig. 14-13. (The interference of the reflections from the boundaries so calculated assume a point source radiator and mutually perpendicular walls.) Such interference can result in major effects on the power response of the loudspeaker. Moving the loudspeakers away from reflecting surfaces does not minimize this interference effect. It just moves the interference notch to a lower frequency and succeeding notches closer together—making them less detrimental to the overall audible spectrum.

Size of the listening area

It is desirable to have a favorable listening area as wide and as deep as possible. As the listener moves back from the *sweet spot*, a general broadening of the stereo soundstage can be noticed. Experimentation will delineate the acceptable limits of the preferred listening area.

Room treatment: bass region

What should be done to an untreated room to guard against serious room resonance effects? First, a critical listening test should be made with a recording rich in bass to see if serious *boominess* exists at certain positions. If troublesome spots are found, a few calculations probably can identify the specific axial mode causing the problem. As this listening test is conducted, remember the locations of resonance

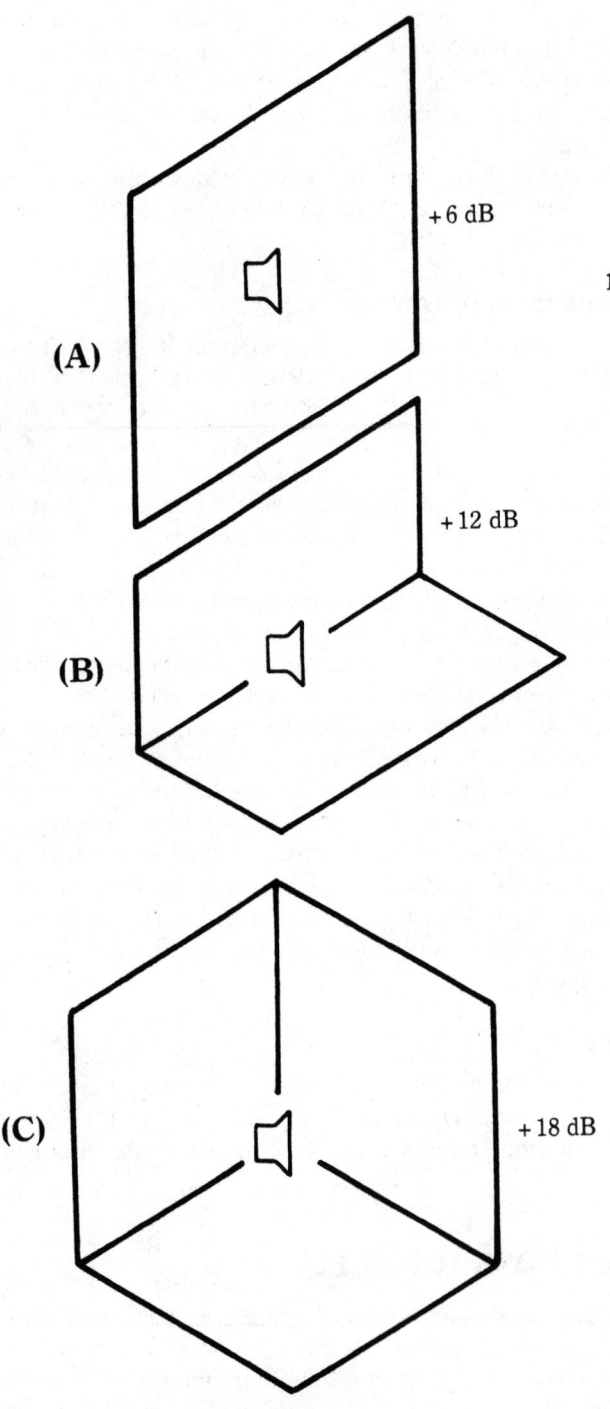

(A)

+6 dB

(B)

+12 dB

(C)

+18 dB

14-11 At low audio frequencies loudspeakers are not very directional. The proximity of loudspeakers to reflecting surfaces can radically affect their low-frequency response. The sound pressure at a fixed distance from a loudspeaker placed close to a wall will show a 6-dB bass rise as the power is confined to a hemisphere. Placing the loudspeaker at the intersection of two surfaces results in a bass rise of 12 dB as the energy is confined to a quarter sphere. Placing a loudspeaker at the intersection of three surfaces ($\frac{1}{8}$ sphere) gives a bass rise of 18 dB. A good rule to follow is to keep loudspeakers at least 2 or 3 ft from reflecting surfaces.

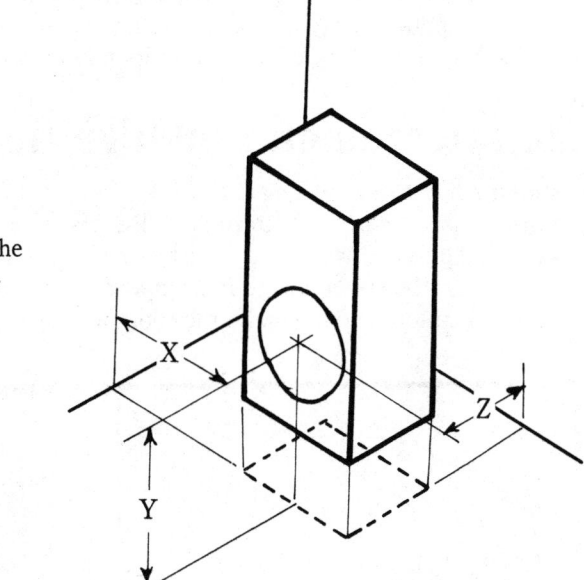

14-12 Dimensioning for the calculations of Fig. 14-13.

peaks are frequency dependent. Move around the room and listen for them. Peaks far removed from the choice listening area could be neglected at this stage.

The frame structure itself might supply enough low-frequency absorption to control room resonances. If some low-frequency control is required, home-made absorbers, such as those shown in Fig. 14-6, can be employed. It is possible that the effects of a particular mode could be minimized by equipment equalization, by

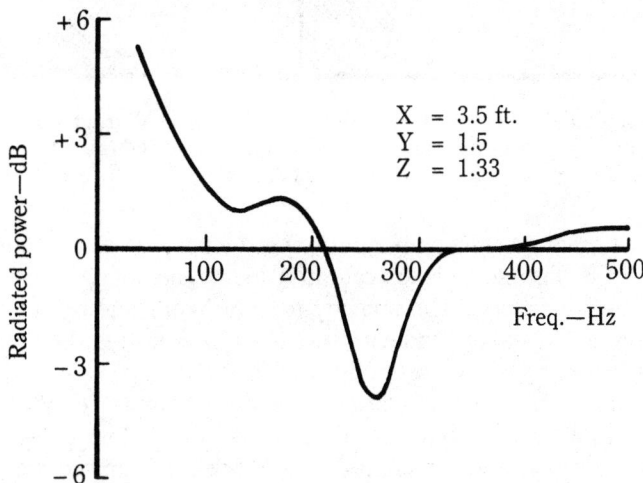

14-13 Calculations for a loudspeaker spaced from three intersecting surfaces as shown in Fig. 14-12. Moving the loudspeaker farther from reflecting surfaces does not eliminate the interference dip; it moves it to a lower frequency and succeeding notches closer together, reducing their detrimental effect. After Berger, Reference 14-7.

repositioning the loudspeakers or listening position, or by brute-force efforts to absorb some of the energy in that particular mode. The latter requires a knowledge of its frequency and the location of its maximum pressure points.

Room treatment: mid-high frequency region

One sure method of minimizing early reflections in the mid-high frequency region is to place sound absorbing material on all surfaces in the front of the room (Fig. 14-14). This approach was suggested by Davis and Davis (Reference 14-8). The improvement in the stereo image in such a room is immediately recognized; however, the absorption tends to make the room too dead for the enjoyment of music.

14-14 Early midband reflections can be reduced by treating all front surfaces of the listening room with absorbing material. This might make the room too *dead* for best listening. After Davis and Davis, Reference 14-8.

There is a great advantage in identifying the specific early reflections as was done in Fig. 14-8. The secret is to accurately locate the points on the room surface that reflect the sound rays. The analogy to light is our cue to success. First, the location of the loudspeakers and the listening position must be established (Fig. 14-15). This can be done with reference to Fig. 14-10.

Consider next the floor reflection from the left and the right loudspeakers (Fig. 14-16). A helper is required for these tests. The helper lays a mirror on the floor and moves it until the person in the listener's seat can see the tweeter of the left loudspeaker; this spot is temporarily marked. The procedure is repeated for the tweeter of the right loudspeaker. The marks on the floor locate the points for the two floor reflections. A rug covering these spots will reduce the floor reflection to manageable proportions.

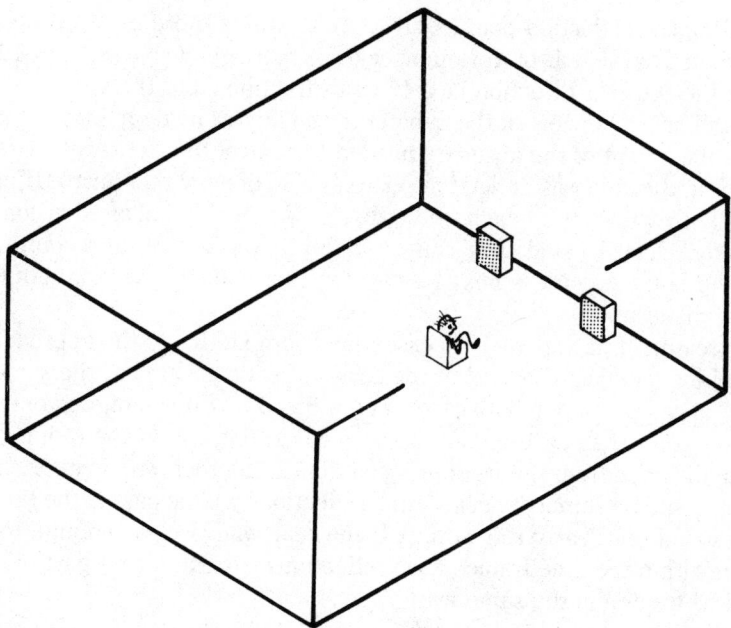

14-15 In this step-by-step study of reduction of early reflections in a listening room, the beginning is a classical stereo arrangement of loudspeakers and listening position.

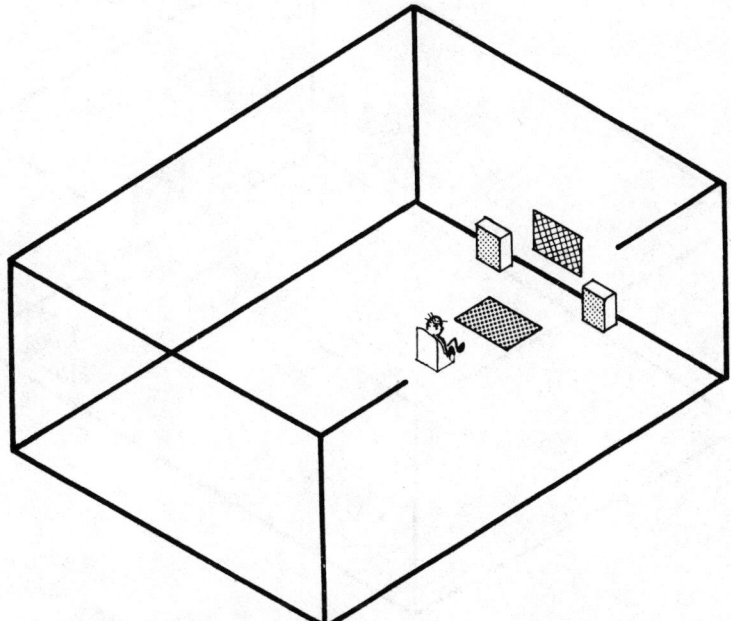

14-16 With the aid of a mirror, the floor-reflection points of the right and left loudspeakers are located and covered with absorbing material. The front wall reflection areas are similarly located and treated.

Locating the reflection points on the front wall is more involved because the sound radiated to the rear of the loudspeaker is more extensive (Fig. 14-16). Sound is radiated to the rear direction largely by diffraction from the edges of the loud-speaker cabinet. The view of the cabinet in the mirror held against the front wall identifies the extent of the absorber needed to control the front wall reflection.

Locating the side wall reflection points is also done with a mirror (Fig. 14-17). There will be two points on each side wall, one for the left and another for the right loudspeaker. Once located they can be amply covered with absorbing material. The ceiling bounce point is next located for each loudspeaker and covered with absorbing material.

The treatment of Fig. 14-17 is essentially comparable to the approach used in Fig. 14-14 for reducing the level of the early reflections. In fact, the same absorbing material can be used in both cases, but in Fig. 14-17 it is mounted only where it is needed, rather than covering all the surfaces at one end of the room.

If the distance from the listener's position to the rear wall is appreciable this procedure could be skipped, because the reflections will be part of the reverberant/ambient sound—not early reflections. If the rear wall is close enough to return a reflection within the time frame of the reflections from the front part of the room, it should be treated in the same way.

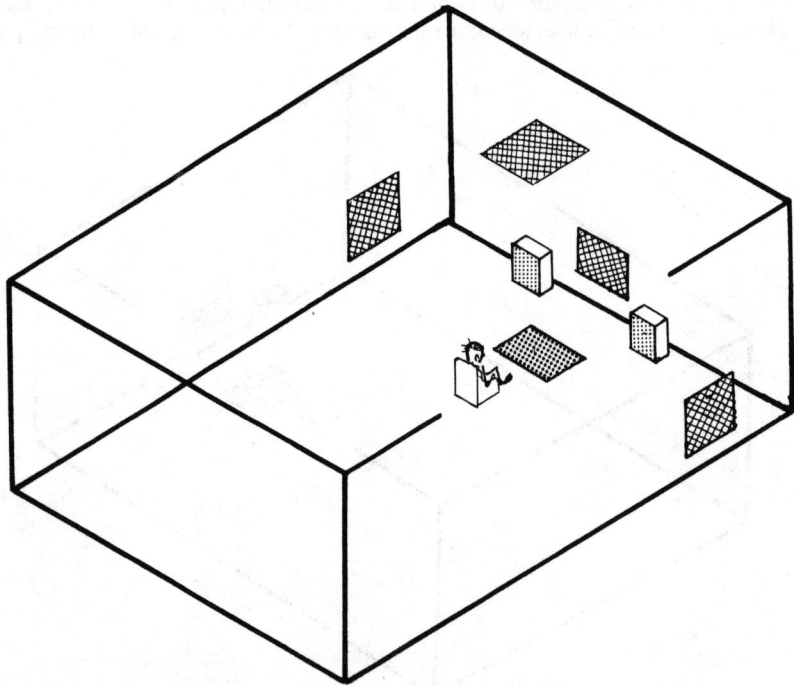

14-17   The side-wall and ceiling reflection points are also located with the help of a mirror and the points covered with absorbing material.

Summary

The principles discussed should help the serious audiophile upgrade the acoustical environment of his/her listening room. In summary, this would involve the following steps:

Low-frequency response of the room, dominated by axial mode resonances, should be evaluated by critical listening to music with high bass content in various positions in the room. If it is a frame structure, much low-frequency absorption could already be built into the structure. If major standing wave defects still are heard, specialized absorbing devices might be placed first in room corners and then, if necessary, at certain high-pressure points to control specific, known modes.

Early reflection points can be located on the floor, front wall, side walls, and ceiling by the mirror method. Listening for sound quality changes can be checked at each step. Ordinary glass fiber, sculptured foam, rugs, or drapes can be used to treat the reflection points.

At this point, an evaluation of the reverberant character of the room must be made by listening to music of various types. Is the space too live? Too dead? Furnishings of the average room (carpet, furniture, drapes, etc.) will usually provide the needed general absorption. Additional absorbing material might be introduced, if necessary, to control early reflections.

Appendix
Introduction to Blumlein's Patent

Alan Dower Blumlein was introduced in chapter 1 where his early accomplishments in the development of stereophonic sound recording and reproduction were detailed. It is difficult to overstate the importance of Blumlein's contribution to the history of audio, for in his patent he detailed much of what has become the foundation for all stereophonic theory and practice today. The purpose of reproducing this portion of Blumlein's patent disclosure is to underscore the magnitude and importance of this work and, at the same time, reveal a sense of Blumlein's genius.

To relate sections of the patent to the preceding text, paragraph numbers were inserted. This is not intended to serve as an extensive cross referencing, but rather as a guideline to assist the reader in understanding how Blumlein's work has subsequently been manifested in contemporary production techniques.

Improving the spatial illusion

Beginning with paragraph 3, (and again in his summation beginning with paragraph 78) Blumlein discusses the concept of "conveying to the listener a true directional impression." Although his discussion focuses primarily on sound with pictures, his concepts are "...not, however, limited to use in connection with picture effects, but may, for example, be used for improving the quality of public address, telephone or radio transmission systems, or for improving the quality of sound recordings."

Spatial perception

Paragraphs 4 through 11 detail the mechanisms in the human hearing process that lead to the perception of direction and spatial perspective. From this material, Blumlein logically develops a method for converting the acoustical cues present in *the original sound* into electrical signals that will ultimately be reproduced by two or more loudspeakers.

Microphone techniques

The techniques Blumlein proposes for the pickup of the stereo soundfield are discussed in paragraphs 15 through 17, and 22 through 45. Because he was originally working only with omnidirectional microphones, Blumlein addresses the concept of using *directionally sensitive* microphones, beginning in paragraph 50. In this, he details the development of the mid/side and crossed-bidirectional microphone techniques, as well as some methods for processing these signals during transmission and reproduction.

Surround sound

Paragraph 57 begins a discussion of methods for reproducing height information and a lateral spread that surrounds the listener. In this, he lays the groundwork for the Soundfield microphone developed decades later. Here the emphasis is specifically directed toward improving the effectiveness of sound for motion picture presentation—an emphasis that gained a strong resurgence in the decade of the 1970s.

The stereo phonograph record

Twenty years before the commercial realization of stereo for the home, Blumlein specified a means for recording stereo information in a phonograph record groove. The method he proposed was identical to that later *reinvented* by Western Electric, which became known as the *45/45 cutter head*. Although never realized in his lifetime, this system was eventually adopted as the standard for producing stereo records throughout the world. These details begin in paragraph 62.

Stereo radio transmission

Paragraph 77 outlines a proposal for a method of transmitting stereo over the radio. The mathematical models he described give a strong indication of the innovative genius that was manifest in Alan Dower Blumlein.

Acknowledgment

We acknowledge, with thanks, permission given by the Controller, HMSO, to reproduce the "Complete Specification" of Blumlein's patent #394,325. The "Provisional Specification" and 70 enumerated claims are not included. The paragraph numbering, not in the original patent document, has been added for convenience of reference.

British Patent # 394,325
Application Date: Dec. 14, 1931
Complete Accepted: June 14, 1933

COMPLETE SPECIFICATIONS
Improvements in and relating to Sound-transmission,
Sound-recording and Sound-reproducing Systems

(1) We, Alan Dower Blumlein, of 57 Earl's Court Square, London, S.W.5, a British subject, and ELECTRIC AND MUSICAL INDUSTRIES, LIMITED, of Blyth Road, Hayes, in the County of Middlesex, a company registered under the laws of Great Britian, do hereby declare the nature of this invention and in what manner the same is to be performed, to be particularly described and ascertained in and by the following statements:

(2) This invention relates to the transmission, recording and reproduction of sound and is more particularly directed to systems for recording and reproducing speech, music and other sound effects. It is applicable in particular, although not exclusively, to systems associated with picture effects as in talking motion pictures.

(3) The fundamental object of the invention is to provide a sound recording, reproducing and/or transmission system whereby there is conveyed to the listener a realistic impression that the intelligence is being communicated to him over two acoustic paths in the same manner as he experiences in listening to everyday acoustic intercourse and this object embraces also the idea of conveying to the listener a true directional impression and thus, in the case in which the sound is associated with picture effects improving the illusion that the sound is coming from, and is only coming, from the artist or other sound source presented to the eye.

(4) The invention is not, however, limited to use in connection with picture effects, but may, for example, be used for improving the qualities of public address, telephone or radio transmission systems, or for improving the quality of sound recordings. When recording music considerable trouble is experienced with the unpleasant effects produced by echoes which in the normal way would not be noticed by anyone listening in the room in which the performance is taking place. An observer in the room listening with two ears, so that echoes reach him with the directional significance which he associates with the music performed in such a room. He therefore discounts these echoes and psychologically focuses his attention on the source of sound. When the music is reproduced through a single channel the echoes arrive from the same direction as the direct sound so that confusion results. It is a subsidiary object of this invention so to give directional significance to the sounds that when reproduced the echoes are perceived as such.

(5) In order that the physical basis of the invention can be appreciated and the stages of its development understood, known and established facts concerning the physical relations between sound sources, sound waves emitted thereby, and the human ears will be briefly summarised.

(6) Human ability to determine the direction from which sound arrives is due to binaural hearing, the brain being able to detect differences between sounds received by the two ears from the same source and thus to determine angular directions from which various sounds arrive. This function is well known and has been employed to considerable extent for example in sub-

aqueous directional detection in which two microphones are connected by headphones, one to each ear of an observer, the two channels between the microphones and the two ears being kept entirely separate.

(7) With two microphones correctly spaced and the two channels kept entirely separate e.g., by using headphones it is known that this directional effect can also be obtained for example in a studio. If, however, the two channels are not kept separate (as, for example is the case in previously proposed arrangements for recording and/or reproducing sound, in which sounds picked up by a plurality of pressure microphones are led to loudspeakers which take the place of headphones) the effect is almost entirely lost and such systems have therefore not come into common use since they are quite unsatisfactory for the purpose. The present invention contemplates controlling the sound emitted for example by such loudspeakers, in such a way that the directional effect will be retained.

(8) The operation of the ears in determining the direction of a sound source is not yet fully known but it is fairly well established that the main factors having effect are phase differences and intensity differences between the sounds reaching the two ears, the influence which each of these has depending upon the frequency of the sounds emitted. For low frequency sound waves there is little or no difference in intensity at the two ears but there is a marked phase difference. For a given obliquity of sound the phase difference is approximately proportional to frequency, representing a fixed time delay between sound arriving at the two ears, by noting which the brain decides the direction from which the sound arrives. This operation holds for all frequencies up to that at which there is a phase difference of π radians or more between sounds arriving at the two ears from a source located on the line joining them: but above such a frequency if phase difference were the sole feature relied upon for directional location there would be ambiguity in the apparent position of the source. At that stage however the head begins to become effective as a baffle and causes noticeable intensity differences between the sounds reaching the two ears, and it is by noting such intensity differences that the brain determines direction of sounds at higher frequencies. It has been stated that the frequency at which the brain changes over from phase- to intensity- discrimination occurs at about 700 c.p.s. but it must be understood that this may vary within quite wide limits in different circumstances and from person to person, and that in any case the transference is not sudden or discontinuous but there is considerable overlap of the two phenomena so that over a considerable frequency range differences of both phase and intensity will to some extent have an effect in determining the sense of direction experienced.

(9) From the above considerations it will be clear that a directional effect is to be obtained by providing impressions at the two ears of low frequency phase differences and it would appear that in reproducing from two loudspeakers the differences received by the two microphones suitably spaced to represent human ears would give this effect to a listener if each microphone were connected only to one loudspeaker. It can be shown however that phase differences necessary at the two ears for low frequency directional sensation are not produced solely by phase differences at the two loudspeakers (both of which communicate with both ears) but that intensity differences at the speakers are necessary to give an effect of phase difference: while initial intensity differences from the sources necessary for high frequencies are not sufficiently marked when the sounds reach the ears, and to produce suitable effects therefore the initial intensity differences must be amplified. It is for this reason that the aforementioned methods previously proposed (wherein only pressure microphones were used) are not successful in achieving the desired effect, these necessary alterations not having been understood or in any way attained in those prior arrangements.

(10) It will be seen therefore that the invention consists broadly in so controlling the intensities of sound to be, or being, emitted by a plurality of loud speakers or similar sound sources, in suitable spaced relationship to the listener, that the listener's ears will note low frequency phase differences and high frequency intensity differences suitable for conveying to the brain a desired sense of direction of the sound origin. In other words, the direction from which the sound arrives at the microphones determines the characteristics (more especially, as will become apparent hereafter, the intensities) of the sounds emitted by the loud speakers in such a way as to provide this directional sensation.

(11) It must be understood that the manual control by an observer of intensities of a plurality of loud speakers spaced round a motion picture screen has previously been proposed but this method suffers considerably from the defects indicated above, and in any case is very difficult and inconvenient to operate. No novelty for mere intensity control per se is however claimed, except insofar as the nature of the control is such as to provide the necessary relative phase and intensity difference sensations.

(12) If in accordance with the invention the sound is first recorded and subsequently reproduced from the records, the control may be wholly effected either during the recording or during reproduction, or may be partially carried out in each stage. It must be understood that wherever throughout this specification the words "sound transmission" are employed (more especially in the claims specified below), they cover (unless the context otherwise requires) not only the case in which impulses pass directly from the microphones to the loud speakers, but also those arrangements embodying an intermediate process or system of recording; and in the latter cases the said words apply to either, or both, the passages of impulses from the microphones to the recording system, and from the reproducer to the loud speakers.

(13) More specifically, the invention consists in a system of sound transmission wherein the sound is picked up by a plurality of microphone elements and reproduced by a plurality of loud speakers, comprising two or more directionally sensitive microphones and/or an arrangement of elements in the transmission circuit or circuits whereby the relative loudness of the loud speakers is made dependent upon the direction from which the sounds arrive at the microphones.

(14) The invention also consists in a system of sound transmission wherein the sound is received by two or more microphones, wherein at low frequencies difference in the phase of sound pressure at the microphone is reproduced as difference in volume at the loud speakers.

(15) The invention further consists in a system of sound transmission in which the original sound is detected by two or more microphones of a type such as velocity microphones whose sensitivity varies with the direction of incident sound, and in which the dependence of the relative responses of the microphones to the direction of an incident sound wave is used to control the relative volumes of sound emitted by two or more loud speakers.

(16) The invention also consists in a system of sound transmission wherein impulses from two microphones transmitted over individual channels are adapted to interact whereby two sets of impulses are further transmitted consisting in half the sum and half the difference respectively of the original impulses, said impulses being thereafter modified to control the relative loudness of loud speakers whereby the sound is to be reproduced.

(17) The invention also consists in a system of sound transmission wherein the sound is picked up by two directionally sensitive microphones which are so spaced and/or with their axes of maximum sensitivity so directed relative to one another and to the sound source, that the relative loudness of loudspeakers which reproduce the impulses is controlled by the direction from which the sound reaches the microphones.

(18) The invention also consists in a system as set forth above wherein two sets of impulses are mechanically recorded in the same groove.

(19) The invention also consists in a system as set forth above wherein the impulses are transmitted by radio telephony.

(20) The invention also consists in a system as set forth above in combination with means for the photographic recording or transmission and/or reproduction of pictures.

(21) The word channel, as employed herein, means an electric circuit carrying a current having a definite form depending upon the original sounds in the studio. Thus two channels may be different not only because the average intensities or types of current in them differ but also because they originate from two microphones in different positions in the studio.

(22) The nature of the invention will become apparent from the following description of various methods and modes of carrying it into effect but it must be understood that the different forms described are given merely by way of example and do not impose any restrictions upon the scope of the invention or manner and means whereby it may be accomplished.

(23) The description will be more readily understood by reference to the accompanying drawings, wherein Figure 1 represents diagramatically the assembly of one system according to the invention:

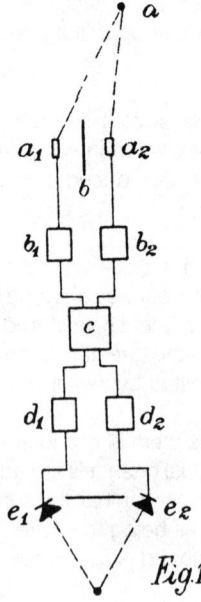

Fig.1.

(24) Figure 2 represents a microphonic arrangement for use according to one form of the invention.

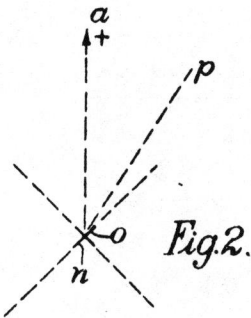

Fig.2.

(25) Figure 3 represents a transformer arrangement employed in one form of the invention: and

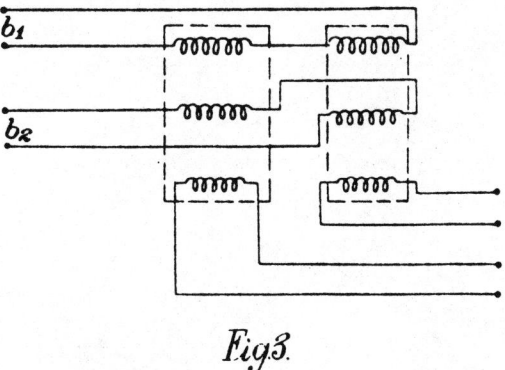

Fig3.

(26) Figure 4 shows a symbolic representation of the arrangement shown in Figure 3.

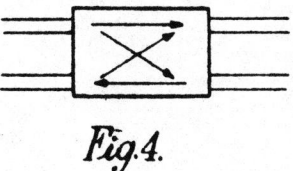

Fig.4.

(27) Figures 5, 6 and 7 represent various circuit arrangements applicable to various forms of the invention, while

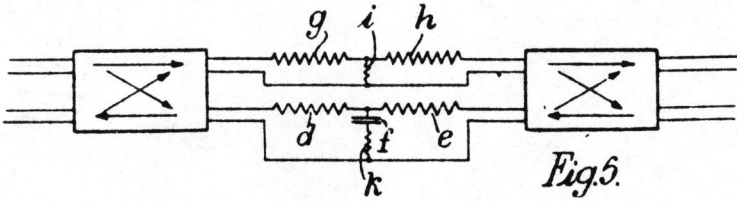

Fig.5.

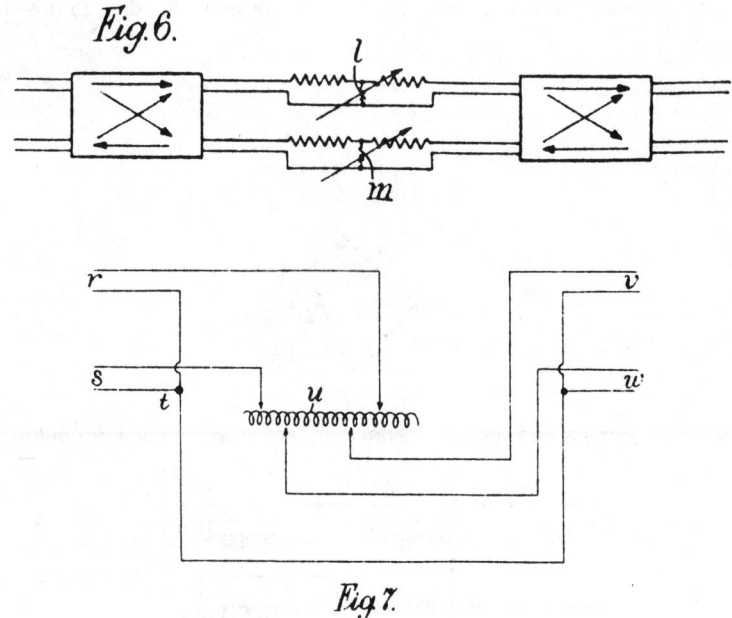

Fig.6.

Fig 7.

(28) Figures 8, 9, 10 and 11 represent different forms of sound recorders which may be employed.

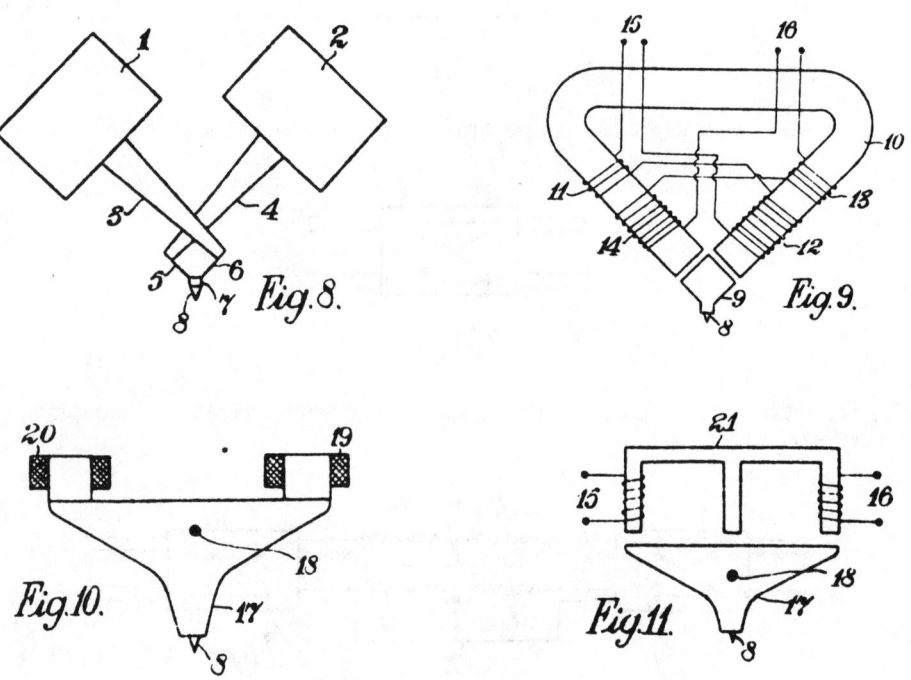

Fig.8.

Fig.9.

Fig.10.

Fig.11.

(29) It will be clear that the invention is particularly applicable to talking motion pictures and the following description will therefore be given with reference to this application. In one form of the invention convenient for this purpose shown in Figure 1 the sounds to be recorded and reproduced with the pictures may be received from a source a by two pressure microphones a1, a2, mounted on opposite sides of a block of wood or baffle b which serves to provide the high frequency intensity differences at the microphones in the same way as the human head operates upon the ears as indicated above. The outputs from the two microphones are after separate amplification by similar amplifiers b1, b2, taken to suitably arranged circuits c comprising transformers or bridge or network circuits which convert the two primary channels into two secondary channels which may be called the summation and difference channels. These are arranged so that the current flowing into the summation channel will represent half the sum, or the mean, of the currents flowing in the two original channels, while the current flowing into the difference channel will represent half the difference of the currents in the original channels.

(30) One convenient transformer arrangement for this purpose is shown in Figure 3 wherein input currents from amplifiers b1, b2, are separately fed each to two primary windings, one on each of two transformers, the secondary winding of each transformer providing a "sum" or "difference" output current on account of the senses in which the primary coils are wound as shown. A diagrammatic representation of a sum and difference arrangement (which may consist of a transformer similar to that of Figure 3 or any other suitable arrangement of circuit elements) is shown in Figure 4.

(31) In accordance with the form of the invention being described the two outputs from the sum and difference arrangement are modified in order to obtain subsequently the desired sound effects and one convenient circuit arrangement for effecting this is shown in Figure 5 which represents the portion of the circuits indicated by c in Figure 1. Assuming the original currents differ in phase only, the current in the difference channel will be $\pi/2$ different in phase from the current in the summation channel. This difference current is passed through two resistances d and e in series between which a condenser f forms a shunt arm. The voltage across this condenser f will be in phase with that in the summation channel. By passing the current in the summation channel through a plain resistive attenuator network composed of series resistances g, h and a shunt resistance i, a voltage is obtained which remains in phase with the voltage across the condenser f in the difference channel. These two voltages are then combined and reseparated by a sum and difference process such as previously adopted so as to produce two final channels. The voltage in the first final channel will be the sum of these voltages and the voltage in the second final channel will be the difference between these voltages. Since these voltages were in phase the two final channels will be in phase but will differ in magnitude. By choosing the value of the shunt resistance i in the summation channel and the shunt condenser f in the difference channel for a given frequency, any degree of amplitude difference in the final channels can be obtained for a given phase difference in the original channels. For the low frequencies it can be shown that the phase difference between the waves will, for a given obliquity of the sound source, vary proportionately with frequency, being very small for a very low frequency. Thus for a given obliquity of the sound the current in the difference channel will be increasingly great compared with that in the summation the higher frequency. Hence the use of a shunt condenser f in the difference circuit will have the effect of producing a fixed intensity difference in the final channels for a given obliquity at all low frequencies.

(32) For the higher frequencies as indicated above it is not necessary to convert phase shifts into amplitude differences, but simply to reproduce amplitude differences. The shunt con-

denser f in the difference circuit is therefore built out with a resistance k whose value is substantially equal to that of resistance i.

(33) In building this circuit the capacity of the condenser f is of such value that its impedance is small compared with that of the series resistances d and e over the whole working range, while the value of resistance k is such that it equals the reactance of the condenser at approximately the frequency above which it is desired not to convert phase differences into amplitude differences. The value of k is in general equal to that of i, in which case the amplitude differences for high frequencies are passed on without modification.

(34) It may be found necessary to employ more complex circuits than the shunt resistance k and the condenser f in the difference circuit and shunt resistance i in the summation circuit, which however form the basic arrangement. However it must be understood that the circuits employed may be considerably modified as required without departing from the scope of the invention.

(35) The outputs from the modifying circuit c (Figure 1) are passed to amplifiers d1, d2 and thence to loudspeakers e1, e2, suitably disposed on each side of a picture screen. It is to be understood that Figure 1 merely traces the passage of intelligence from the source a to a recipient and no recording or reproducing system has been shown. Such may however be inserted anywhere along the electrical circuit such for example as between amplifiers b1, b2 and modifying assembly c, or between assembly c and amplifiers d1, d2.

(36) In the latter case the impulses transmitted through the two channels as indicated above may for example be recorded on two sound tracks on a film by any suitable or known means, each of which records may comprise either a sound track of constant density and variable width (e.g., an oscillograph record) or a sound track of constant width and variable density (e.g., a light valve record). Alternatively both records may be made on a single track comprising a combination of the variable width and variable density forms of recording.

(37) Such a record may be reproduced by passing light from the same slit through the two tracks, separating the beam into the two record portions by means of prisms or like optical means and employing the outputs from two photo-electric cells, excited by these separate parts of the beam (after amplification) to operate two loudspeakers disposed one on each side of the screen upon which the cinematograph pictures are projected.

(38) From the above description it will be clear that obliquity of the direction of sound wave propagation relative to the microphones a1, a2 will produce differences of intensity at the loudspeakers so as to give an impression to an observer of oblique sound incidence,

(39) If two very small microphones are used and placed very close together it may be found possible to obtain microphone outputs which do not differ appreciably in amplitude but only in phase for all working frequencies. In this case the modifying circuit may be arranged to convert phase differences into amplitude differences throughout the entire frequency range. The phase differences dealt with at the low-frequencies however may be so small that in this case slight differences would have to have large effects. On this account microphone spacing of the same order as that of the human ears is most suitable.

(40) It will be appreciated that the amount of modification necessary to the impulses transmitted through the summation and difference channels as indicated above depends upon a

number of factors, including the relative spacing of the microphones and of the loudspeakers, and the size and positioning of the screen. It can be shown that for low frequencies the degree of modification required in the difference channel as compared with the modification in the summation channel is given by:

$$K = \frac{2v}{j\omega} \bullet \frac{y}{\theta k} \bullet \frac{s}{\chi}$$

where

v = velocity of sound.

y = fraction of half picture film width which the image of the sound source is off centre.

θ = angle of obliquity, in radians, of the source from the median plane between the microphones.

k = effective distance apart of the microphones.

s = width of screen of theatre.

χ = distance apart of loudspeakers in theatre.

(41) This expression in effect gives the impedance of the shunt capacity f in the difference channel in terms of the resistance i in the summation channel. It holds for all frequencies where k is small compared to the wavelength, and is based on the assumption that the θ is small and that χ and s are small compared with the distance of the listener from the screen and loudspeakers.

(42) The portion $y/(\theta k)$ is a factor of the recording, and is constant for a given arrangement if either the camera is in line with the microphones and the centre of the picture, or the action does not move appreciably to or from the microphones and camera. When recording, the relative distances of camera and microphones and the focal length of the lens may be adjusted to maintain this factor a constant.

(43) The expression s/χ is a constant for the theatre, as regards low frequencies only, the distance apart of the speakers need not exceed the screen width, but should certainly not be closer than 70 percent of the screenwidth. The closer the loudspeakers the greater the necessary power handling capacity, but the less the troubles introduced by formation of stationary waves.

(44) For the high frequencies no definite expression can easily be obtained, and the modification, if any, used will probably have to be gauged empirically by trial and error.

(45) The arguments and formula given above are based on a direct wave analysis and may have to be considerably modified in order to allow for reflection or other acoustic effects. It is preferred therefore to introduce the modifications it is proposed to employ, at the theatre since all factors will then enter into consideration. It will be clear that, as indicated above, the modifying networks and channel arrangements may be employed between the microphones and the film during recording, or between the record and the loudspeakers during reproduction, and the latter course, in addition to allowing of adjustment of the arrangements to suit the particular theatre as indicated above, has the additional advantage that the sound film can be reproduced by a single reproducing head or channel if, for example, one of the dual arrangements breaks down, or in a theatre which, having one installation, does not wish to go to the expense of installing a second apparatus.

(46) In order to employ successfully a system of the kind described above it is necessary to carry out preliminary experiments to determine the most suitable value of modifications to be employed for each recording, and it is also necessary to standardise various factors entering into every recording. In the preliminary experiments, before recording, volume indicator measurements may be made with a standard sound source placed at the extremes of the "set". i.e., the space within which recording is to be effected, and from these the proposed modifying network laid out. A further experiment may also be effected to standardise phase angles on the film. At the theatre a simple adjustment may be provided to check and balance the input to the two channels, a length of test film being used for this purpose. It will thus be seen that the total theatre equipment necessary is very simple and consists in a transmission modifier (comprising two or four transformers, for example, artificial line resistances and the control network, which may be no more than a condenser and a resistance) and two normal sound-reproducing heads or pick-ups, or one specially designed head or pick-up adapted to separate the two recordings to two complete reproducing channels. There is no reason why the second channel used should not be the "stand-by" channel now often installed for safety since if, as indicated above, one of the channels breaks down reproduction may be continued without serious consequences on the other channel only.

(47) In connection with the standardisation indicated above, while the binaural "transfer" (from phase- to intensity- discrimination) need have no definite significance in recording, since it is a function of the human brain, it is nevertheless necessary to fix a change-over frequency from high- to low-frequency working for recording, since this frequency fixes the values of the elements in the modifier and thus the form of modification to be used, the distance apart of the microphones and the form of baffle between them. Any convenient frequency may be chosen as standard after experience has decided which is most suitable. Instead of standardising it may be possible from the preliminary experiments to allow electrically for variation of microphone positions and/or of microphone spacing (although the latter would be extremely difficult) and it must be understood that this arrangement falls within the scope of the invention.

(48) The above analysis is based upon considerations which take no account of sound reflections or interference during reproduction. The reflected sound waves which arise during recording will be reproduced with a directional sense and will sound more natural than they would with a non-directional reproducing system. If difficulties arise in reproduction they may be overcome by employing a second pair of loudspeakers differently spaced and having a different modifying network from the first pair: or a row of speakers may be used with a composite, progressive modifying network to supply them: or the two speakers may be placed comparatively close together.

(49) In this last arrangement the sense of direction of the apparent sound source will only be conveyed to a listener for the full frequency range for positions lying between the loudspeakers; but if it is desired to convey the impression that the sound source has moved to a position beyond the space between the loudspeakers the modifying networks may be arranged to reverse the phase of that loudspeaker remote from which the source is desired to appear, and this will suffice to convey the desired impression for the low frequency sounds. With this arrangement of loudspeakers close together, however, it would not be possible to effect a similar illusion in connection with high frequencies.

(50) The system so far described employs to receive the sound waves two non-directional microphones, e.g. pressure microphones. Directionally sensitive microphones may also be employed spaced a small distance apart, the outputs being modified as indicated so that the

relative outputs of the loudspeakers are controlled both by difference in phase and differences in magnitude of the microphone outputs. Such directionally sensitive microphones may be, but are not necessarily, of the type known as velocity microphones, and preferably provided with movable conductor elements so light as to move substantially as the surrounding air.

(51) Velocity or moving conductor microphones (e.g. moving strip microphones) are very suitable for any system according to the invention and in addition to use with circuit arrangements described above: they may also be employed with various alterations in the circuits. These microphones give a response varying as the cosine of the angle of incidence of the sound relative to the direction of normal or optimum incidence, and they therefore have the advantage that a certain degree of loudspeaker output separation may be obtained without a phase-conversion or like network modifications.

(52) Three general arrangements employing velocity microphones are possible, and in all cases the microphones are placed as near together as possible instead of being spaced as artificial ears, as in the case of pressure microphones.

(53) (1) Two velocity microphones are placed one with its axis of maximum response directly facing in the direction of the centre of the scene, and the other with its axis at right angles to that direction. Both moving strips are in line, and arranged so that this line is vertical, whereas the sound source moves in a horizontal plane. A performer speaking from the middle of the scene will affect only the face-on microphone, but if he moves to one side both microphones will provide outputs, while if he moves the other way similar outputs are provided but the phase of the edge-on microphone is reversed. Since the microphones are close together no phase differences are experienced between them and if their outputs are summed and differenced after a suitable amount of relative amplification the two final channels differ in magnitude in the correct manner for operating the loudspeakers to give the desired directional effect. Such sum and difference arrangement differs from the modifying network employed with pressure microphones in that the pressure type provide phase differences (whereby direction is determined) which have to be converted, whereas with the velocity type the edge-on microphone provides an output proportional to the obliquity of the source. A suitable modifying arrangement for this form of the invention is shown in Figure 6. This is substantially identical with that shown in Figure 5 except that the shunt condenser f and resistance k in series, and the shunt resistance l are replaced by shunt resistances, m which are preferably variable as shown. These lines therefore form artificial attenuators and by altering their relative attenuation the intensity differences in the two lines corresponding to a given obliquity of sound is controlled.

(54) (2) Two velocity microphones or microphone elements, may be placed with their axes perpendicular to one another and each axis at 45 degrees to the direction of the centre of the screen. This arrangement is represented diagramatically in Figure 2 wherein n and o represent two velocity, or directionally sensitive microphones one above the other arranged perpendicular to one another and at equal angles at 45 degrees to the direction of the centre of the field from which the sound is to be received. It will be clear that movement of the sound source a laterally to a position p removed from the centre of the field will result in the sound waves striking o at a more acute angle than they strike n and differences in the microphone outputs will result. The microphones are sufficiently close together to render phase differences of the incident sound negligible and the output amplitudes therefore differ approximately proportionally to the obliquity of the incident sound. They may therefore be amplified

similarly, and supplied directly to the loudspeakers to which they will give the correct amplitude differences for the desired directional effect provided the relationship between the various dimensions of the recording and reproducing "lay-outs" are correct. If it is desired to accommodate any differences between the "lay-outs" the outputs may be modified by networks, in the manner described, suitably to increase or decrease the differences between them. An arrangement such as shown in Figure 6 is suitable for this purpose, and such an arrangement may of course also be employed even if the lay-out is correct if it is desired for any reason to control or modify the amplitude differences of the loudspeaker outputs.

(55) (3) Two microphones may be arranged with the two axes lying symmetrically to the direction of the centre of the field and with an angle between them of say θ degrees, so that sound from a performer at the centre subtends an angle of $\theta/2$ degrees to each microphone. If θ is small a small movement of the performer to one side is sufficient to make one microphone "edge-on" and to reduce its output to zero, while if θ is large a large movement of the performer is necessary to do this. By making θ adjustable different "lay-outs" may be accommodated without the modification indicated under (2) and it will be clear also that this provides a method of directional sound transmitting, recording and reproduction which avoids the necessity of combining and reseparating the two channels.

(56) The microphone elements in any of the above cases may be enclosed in a single casing if desired for convenience, and may also be positioned in a single magnetic system common to both.

(57) Two velocity microphones set in a line with one another and with their axes of maximum response symmetrically inclined to the direction of the centre line of the scene, may, if placed one above the other, be employed also to provide significance of vertical as well as horizontal movement of the sound source in a plane perpendicular to the axis of maximum response of the microphone system. Such vertical displacement of the source will in this arrangement give phase differences to the outputs while lateral displacement gives amplitude differences, and these can be separated, the phase differences converted to intensity differences by modifying networks, as described, and the resulting impulses employed to operate four or more loudspeakers distributed round the screen. The transmission in such a system occupies only two channels (one leading from each microphone) up to a point in the system where each of these channels is divided into two parallel channels in all at this point. Two channels, one from each parallel pair of these divided channels, are connected to one modifying network adapted to deal with phase differences, and the other two channels, one from each pair, connected to another modifying network adapted to augment intensity differences. Each modifying network operates a plurality of loudspeakers providing a directional sensation in one direction, and in this manner directional senses in two directions at right angles can be obtained. It will be seen that in such an arrangement the transmission and/or recording (which is the most expensive and difficult operation of the system) may be effected over only two channels although directional sensations in two perpendicular directions are subsequently obtained. A similar effect may be obtained with a plurality of pressure microphones by employing suitable modification previous to transmission.

(58) In obtaining a complete directional "sound picture", i.e. both horizontal and vertical directional effects, the invention is not limited solely to the use of two microphones. A plurality may be employed and their outputs suitably collected, modified and separated to transmit suitable differences of impulses to a plurality of loudspeakers. The general feature is that two transmitting channels, receiving impulses from two or more microphones for example, com-

municate impulses which can be modified and separated to provide two directional senses at right angles to one another, the sounds whereby this is done being provided by a plurality of loudspeakers. It will moreover be clear that if the sound source moves away from or towards the microphones the overall intensity of the combined loudspeaker propagations will vary and thus provide indication of the position of the source along that axis. Full three dimensional location of the source is thus obtained by this arrangement.

(59) It will be seen that while with pressure microphones it is preferred to transmit phase differences rather than amplitude differences and convert from one to the other as late as possible prior to reproduction, with velocity microphones it is more convenient to transmit the two channels in phase but at different amplitudes, the only modification then necessary being an increase or decrease of the amplitude differences should the reproducing "lay-out" differ from the recording "lay-out" or should more than two loudspeaker positions be used.

(60) There is a simple method by which modifications for increase or decrease of differences between channels may be effected if no conversion of phase differences into amplitude differences is required. The method is particularly useful for the operation of more that two loudspeakers, and is also useful for working into high impedances such as the grid impedance of a thermionic valve. The arrangement is shown diagramatically in Figure 7. If the transmission is effected in the form of two channels r, s of similar phase but different amplitudes, an alteration of these amplitude differences may be effected by connecting one wire of each channel r and s together at t and connecting a choke u between the other two wires of the two channels. The outgoing channels v and w whose difference is to be a modification of the original difference, are connected by one wire each to the common point t of the original channels, and by their other wires to tappings along the choke u. If the differences are to be increased, the tappings at which the output channels are connected lie outside the tappings to which the input channels are connected, so that the choke operates in effect as an auto-transformer amplifying the difference voltages. Similarly, for a reduction of differences, the output channels are tapped intermediately between the two input channels. Modifications of the arrangement in which the devices are balanced about earth, etc. may be arranged, but the chief advantage is that the modification is varied entirely by altering tappings along a transformer or choke, and that no great power loss is involved.

(61) This arrangement of a choke or transformer is well suited to working a number of loudspeakers for binaural reproduction. In this case, the two outputs from power valves are fitted to a choke such as u along which the loudspeakers are tapped. The position of the loudspeaker tappings can be adjusted to suit their relative positions, and it can be arranged that the valves are working into their best impedances. Transformers may be used to ensure the speakers taking their correct fraction of the output.

(62) While, in connection with the above described systems, it is suggested that when it is desired to record the sounds for subsequent reproduction this may be done upon a film, the invention is not limited to that medium since the recording may if desired be effected on discs or cylinders of suitable material. In carrying out the invention in this manner the two channels may if desired be recorded in separate grooves but it is preferred that they be recorded in the same groove having a hill and dale and also a lateral cut movement. For the purpose of television previous proposals have been made whereby a wax disc has a sound record as a hill and dale cut and a picture record as a laterally V-shaped groove at the bottom of the hill and dale groove, or vice versa. Such records appear unsuited for separate and distinct sound recordings since undoubtedly considerable cross-talk between the two recordings would

occur. They can however be used for two channels of the kind contemplated in the present invention, one being only slightly different from the other, since a certain amount of cross-talk in this case does not matter, or can be allowed for. Furthermore, the records now proposed are distinguished from those previously known in that both channels may be recorded as separate cuts in one groove and may be recorded by a single recording tool (either of moving iron or moving coil type) and be reproduced therefrom by a single reproducing device or pick-up.

(63) If the two channels being recorded are directly picked up from two microphones or are intended to work unmodified into two speakers, that is with intensities and qualities similar to those of the original sounds received, it is preferred not to cut one track as lateral cut and the other as hill and dale, but to cut them as two tracks whose movement axes lie at 45 degrees to the wax surface, or at some other convenient angle dependent on the relative available intensities from lateral cut and hill and dale respectively. If, however, the two channels recorded are such as summation and difference channels, it is preferred to separate them completely into pure hill and dale and pure lateral cut, i.e. to make the recording axes normal and tangential to the wax surface.

(64) The result in the two above suggested cases is very similar since channels recorded at 45 degrees to the wax surface give their sum and difference as the effective lateral and hill and dale amplitudes.

(65) It will be appreciated that a record cut as a combined hill and dale and lateral, may be reproduced if desired as two skew direction cuts, the basic principle being that the groove has amplitude in any direction in the plane at right angles to the direction of wax movement, and the recording and reproducing directions may be chosen as any pair of axes lines, not necessarily at right angles, in this plane.

(66) It would appear that for such a record, a material other than that now used for lateral cut records, would be desirable, and a material of the nature of cellulose acetate is indicated.

(67) The track section is preferably adapted to work with a sapphire and have a sufficiently fine angle to give lateral as well as vertical control to the sapphire.

(68) The recorder whereby both channels may be cut by a single tool on the same groove may take various forms, the underlying feature being that light stylus is pulled into two directions at right angles to one another and each preferably at 45 degrees to the wax surface.

(69) Figure 8 shows schematically a recorder of this kind suitable for producing records having complex cuts. 1 and 2 represent the driving elements of the two recorders normally adapted for cutting lateral cut records. These driving elements drive arms 3 and 4 about axes at right angles to the plane of the paper within 1 and 2. The ends of these arms are connected by ligaments 5 and 6 to the end of a reed 7 which extends backwards along an axis perpendicular to the paper to supports not shown. This reed carries a cutting sapphire 8. Movements of the recording arms 3 and 4 produce movements in the end of the reed 7. Thus currents in movement 1 will cause the reed 7 to move along an axis approximately 45 degrees to the vertical rising from left to right across the figure. Similarly, currents in movement 2 will produce movement of the reed 7 in an axis at right angles to the former axis, while currents in both movements will of course result in vertical movements of the reed.

(70) Another such form of recorder shown in Figure 9, representing a moving iron recorder,

may consist in a short reed 9 mounted close above and parallel with the wax track and carrying the cutting sapphire 8. This reed 9 may extend backwards perpendicularly to the paper to supports (not shown) which join the top of a laminated pole system 10 to complete a polarising magnetic system therewith. The two laminated arms of the pole piece 10 extend down towards the free end of the reed 9. These arms form two poles adjacent to a square portion of the reed at its free end, each pole being adapted to pull the reed in a direction at 45 degrees to the wax surface. The reed may be suitably damped, e.g. by a rubber line, and have a resonant frequency at the top of, or above, the working range. The two pole pieces may be wound with speech coils, and the energisation of one of these moves the sapphire in an upward direction at 45 degrees to the wax surface. The terminals 15 of one channel are connected to main winding 12 and compensating winding 11. The terminals 16 of the other channel are connected to main winding 14 and compensating winding 13. Current in either channel will pull the reed towards the pole carrying the main winding, the purpose of the compensating winding being to prevent movement of the reed away from the other pole due to the flux drawn away from this pole by the main winding. With the winding shown, currents in either channel will cause the reed to cut a track at approximately 45 degrees to the vertical. By a suitable rearrangement of windings, or by a suitable transformer connection between the channels and the terminals of the recorder as shown, any other movement axes may be obtained. Thus for example the tool may have one movement by torsion of its supporting reed and another by flexure thereof.

(71) An alternative moving coil design which may employ electromagnetic damping may consist of a moving member in the shape of a T as shown in Figure 10. The recorder sapphire 8 is supported on a light T member 17, which is supported at 18 by elastic means such that it may rotate about this point and may also translate vertically, though it is resistant to horizontal movements in the plane of the paper. The device is driven by moving coils, e.g. speech coils 19 and 20 which are freely located and immersed in the steady magnetic field provided in angular gaps in a magnetic system, not shown. Current in one of the moving coils tends to both rotate and translate the device so that the sapphire 8 moves along an axis at approximately 45 degrees to the vertical. The movement of this device may be damped and equalised along the lines described in British Patent Specification No. 350,998. As before any required axes of movement may be obtained by suitable interconnection of the two driving coils. Such a movement preferably has the same natural frequency for both rotation and translation. Further the distribution of mass is preferably such that a small instantaneous force applied at one coil produces no movement at the other.

(72) Figure 11 shows another form of recorder similar in principle to the one shown in Figure 10 except that a moving iron drive is employed. The member 17 moving about axis 18 is constructed of magnetic material, or has a magnetic upper portion. The "E" shaped member 21 is polarised either by being partially permanently magnetised, or having a magnetising winding on it, so that the central pole is of opposite polarity to the other two outer poles. Speech windings on the outer poles are brought out to terminals 15 and 16 to which the two channels are connected.

(73) In all the devices described above, the angles of the axes defining the movements of the sapphire can be altered by suitably connecting the speech windings; for instance, axes which are normally inclined at 45 degrees to the wax surface can be converted into pure hill and dale and lateral cut axes by arranging that the speech windings are in series aiding for one channel and opposing for the other channel. In like manner any axis conversion can be effected by suitably combining the channels through transformers.

(74) In designing an electric pick-up to reproduce both channels care must be taken that the inertia is kept as low as possible, and with this in mind a very light replica of any of the above described recorders may be employed. Preferably, a moving system in the form of a T following the lines of the moving iron recorder shown in Figure 11 is employed as best suited for the purpose. Since the fundamental resonant frequency of a pick-up appears to be of no critical importance as regards its characteristic, it may not be necessary to adjust the resonant frequency of the two modes to the same value, which should simplify the design. Adjustments for sensitivity in the two modes may be made by suitably connecting coils wound on the two limbs of the magnetic circuits. As in the recorder design the distribution of mass in the reproducer is preferably such that forces producing motion in one direction (e.g. lateral movements) leave it substantially undisturbed in its reproduction by motions in another direction (e.g. hill-and-dale).

(75) A good binaural effect may be obtained by giving directional significance to only a limited range of frequencies. For example, although good reproduction requires the transmission of all frequencies up to, say, 10,000 c.p.s. yet a good directional effect is obtained from frequencies up to, say, 3,000 c.p.s. This would assist disc recording of the binaural impulses since the lateral cut which represents the sum of the two channels to the speakers might have a frequency range extending to 10,000 c.p.s. whereas the hill- and-dale cut need transmit frequencies no higher than 3,000 c.p.s. This would considerably simplify the design of the recorders and pick-ups in that low inertia would only be required for the lateral cut and design would thus be greatly simplified.

(76) These frequencies are given merely by way of example, and are not necessarily the optimum frequencies for design of this character, which will be determined by other considerations.

(77) In transmitting the two channels indicated in the various systems above described, instead of employing line transmission, radio transmission may if desired be employed. Each channel may be separately transmitted or preferably the two channels may be sent as different modulations of the same carrier wave. Thus one channel may be transmitted as an amplitude modulation and the other as a phase or frequency modulation of the same carrier wave. Alternatively the two channels may be transmitted as amplitude modulations of different carrier waves which are 90 degrees out of phase, the two waves being radiated from the same aerial in combination as a single wave propagation. Various systems for the transmission and reception of duplex radio signals along these lines are known and any one of such or similar arrangements may be used in connection with the invention described herein according to its applicability or convenience in the circumstances under consideration. It must be understood that with such a system of duplex radiation, it is possible, if desired, to perform one of the summing and differencing processes in the radio link. For example, by demodulation at the receiving end with two carrier waves 90 degrees out of phase, which carrier waves are 45 degrees out of phase with the original modulating carriers, the resultant low frequency channels are the sums and differences of the original low frequency channels at the transmitter.

(78) The hereindescribed system while being especially applicable to talking pictures is not limited to such use. It may be employed in recording studio quite independently of any picture effects and in this connection (as well as when used in cinematograph work) it seems probable that the binaural effect introduced will be found to improve the acoustic properties of recording studios and to save any drastic acoustic treatment thereof while providing much more realistic and satisfactory records for reproduction. Furthermore, the system may clearly

be employed when the microphone outputs are led to the loudspeakers instead first of being recorded, and such an arrangement may for example be employed in public address systems in which directional sound effects are desired. In general the invention is applicable in all cases where it is desired to give directional effects to emitted sound. Also in all cases, both when the impulses are fed to the loudspeakers without recording and when they are recorded for subsequent reproduction the total modification and/or interaction of the channels may be accomplished in more than one stage. For example, using pressure microphones, the low frequency phase differences may be augmented, the medium frequency phase differences converted to amplitude differences, and the high frequency amplitude differences augmented in a first stage of modification; the low frequency phase differences may then be converted to amplitude differences in a later stage of modification. One or both of these stages may occur either before or after the sound has been recorded. In this manner the very low frequency phase differences are augmented before they are amplified, so avoiding troubles due to small low frequency phase shifts in amplifiers.

(79) Moreover, the various devices employed for carrying the invention into effect must be understood not to be limited to their use with other devices in the systems also herein-described since clearly many parts, such for example, as the dual track record prepared by a single cutter, and the multi-strip direction-detecting microphone, are clearly of wide use in such systems separately from one another. Such uses in binaural systems as herein described fall within the scope of this invention.

(80) It must finally be understood that the invention is not restricted solely to the details of arrangements of the forms of the invention described above since various modifications may be introduced in order to carry the invention into effect under different conditions and requirements which have to be fulfilled without departing in any way from the scope covered thereby.

References

Chapter 1

1-1. Snow, William B., "Basic principles of stereophonic sound," J. Soc. *Motion Picture and Television Engineers*, 61 (1953), 567 – 589.

1-2. Hertz, Bent F., "100 Years with stereo: the beginning," *J. Audio Eng. Soc.*, 29, 5 (1981), 368 – 372. Reprinted from *Scientific American* 3 December 1881.

1-3. Blumlein, Alan Dower, "Improvements in and relating to sound transmission, sound-recording and sound-reproducing systems," British Patent Specification 394,325. Applied: 14 Dec 1931, Issued: 14 June 1933. Reprinted *J. Audio Eng. Soc.*, 6(2) (1958), 91. Partially reproduced in the Appendix of this book.

1-4. Benzimra, B.J., "A.D. Blumlein electronic genius," *Electronics & Power*, 13 (June 1967), 218 – 224.

1-5. Fletcher, H., et al, *Bell Labs Record,* 11 (May 1933), 254 – 261, 12 (Mar 1934), 194 – 213.

1-6. Fletcher, H., et al, *Electrical Engineering*, 53 (Jan 1934), 9 – 31, 214 – 219.

1-7. Fletcher, H., et al, *Bell System Technical Journal*, 13 (Apr 1934), 239 – 308.

Chapter 3

3-1. Shaw, E.A.G., "Transformation of sound pressure level from the free field to the eardrum in the horizontal plane." *J. Acous, Soc. Am.*, 56, 6 (December 1974), 1848 – 1861.

3-2. Fletcher, H., "Auditory patterns," Ref. *Mod. Phys.*, 12 (1940), 47 – 65.

3-3. Moore, Brian C.J. and Brian Glasberg, "Suggested formulae for calculating auditory-filter bandwidths," *J. Acous. Soc. Am.*, 74, 3 (September 1983), 750 – 753.

3-4. Chernyak, R.L. and N.A. Dubrovsky, "Pattern of the noise images and the binaural summation of loudness for the different interaural correlation of noise," Proc. 6th Int. Congress on Acoustics, 1, Tokyo, 4-3-12. Cited by Blauert.

3-5. Mehrgardt, S. and V. Mellart, "Transformation characteristics of the external human ear," *J. Acous. Soc. Am.*, 61, 6 (June 1977), 1567 – 1576.

3-6. Olive, Sean E. and Floyd E. Toole, "The detection of reflections in typical rooms," *J. Audio Eng. Soc.*, 37, 7/8, (1989), 539 – 553.

3-7. Meyer, E. and G.R. Schodder, "On the influence of reflected sound on directional localization and loudness of speech," (in German) Nachr, Akad. Wiss., Göttingen, Math. Phys. Klasse IIa, Vol. 6 (1952), 31 – 42.

3-8. Haas, H., "The influence of a single echo on the audibility of speech," *Acustica*, 1, 2 (1957), 49 – 58. An English translation of Haas' dissertation by Dr. Ing. K.P.R. Ehrenberg has been published by J. *Audio Eng. Soc.*, 20, 2 (1972), 146 – 159.

3-9. Ando, Y., "Concert Hall Acoustics," 1985, Berlin, Springer-Verlag. Cited by Toole, Reference 10.

3-10. Toole, Floyd E., "Loudspeakers and rooms for stereophonic sound reproduction." Proc. 8th International Conference of *Audio Eng. Soc.*, 1990, 71 – 100.

3-11. Muncie, H., "The acceptability of speech and music with a single artificial echo" *Acustica*, 3 (1953), 168 – 173.

3-12. Bloom P.J., "Creating source elevation illusion by special manipulation," *J. Audio Eng. Soc.*, 25 (1977), 560 – 565.

3-13. Blauert, Jens, *Spatial Hearing*, Cambridge, MA, 1983, MIT Press.

Supplemental reading

Wiener, Francis M., "On the diffraction of a progressive sound wave by the human head," *J. Acous. Soc. Am.*, 19, 1 (January 1947), 143 – 146.

Shaw, E.A.G. and M.M. Vaillancourt, "Transformation of sound pressure level from the free field to the eardrum—presented in numerical form," *J. Acous. Soc. Am.*, 78, 3 (September 1985), 1120 – 1123.

Clark, David, "Measuring audible effects of time delays in listening rooms," *J. Audio Engr. Soc.*, presented at 74th Convention 8 – 12 October 1983, New York, preprint 2012.

Everest, F. Alton, "The filters in our ears," *Audio,* 70, 9, (September 1986), 50 – 59.

Chapter 5

5-1. Schroeder, Manfred R., "Models of Hearing," *Proc. IEEE*, 63, 9, (1975), 1332 – 1350.

Chapter 6

6-1. Bock, Timothy M. and D.B. Keele, Jr., "The effects of Interaural Crosstalk on Stereo Reproduction and Minimizing Interaural Crosstalk in Nearfield Monitoring by the Use of Physical Barrier," presented at 81st Convention of *Audio Eng., Soc.,* Los Angeles (1986), preprint #2420 A&B.

6-2. Atal, Bishnu S. and Manfred R. Schroeder, "Apparent Sound Source Translator," U.S. Patent #3,236,949. Appl. 19 Nov. 1962, issued 22 Feb. 1966.

6-3. Schroeder, M., "Models of Hearing," *IEEE*, 63 (1975), 1332 – 1350.

6-4. Bauer, B.B., "Stereophonic Earphones and Binaural Loudspeakers," *J. Audio Eng. Soc.*, 9, 2 (April 1961), 148 – 151. Reprinted in *Stereophonic Techniques Anthology*, published by *Audio Eng. Soc.* (1986), 373 – 376.

6-5. Damaske, P., "Head Related Two-Channel Stereophony With Loudspeaker Reproduction," *J. Acous. Soc. Am.*, 50, 4 (1971), 1109 – 1115.

6-6. Cooper, Duane H. and Jerald L. Bauck, "Prospects for Transaural Recording," presented at 85th Convention of *Audio Eng. Soc.,* Los Angeles, 1988, preprint #2734.

6-7. Toole, Floyd E., "The Acoustics and Psychoacoustics of Headphones," presented at the 2nd. International Conference of the Audio Engr. Soc., Anaheim, CA (1984), preprint #C1006.

6-8. Streicher, Ron, "Binaural Monitoring Sound Reinforcement Applications," Sound and Communications (July 1988) 21.

6-9. Burkhard, M.O. and R.M. Sachs, "Anthropometric Manikin for Acoustic Research," *J. Acous. Soc. Am.,* 58, 1 (July 1975), 214 – 222.

6-10. Gierlick, H.W. and K. Genuit, "Processing Artificial-Head Recordings," *J. Audio Eng. Soc.,* 31, 1/2 (Jan/Feb 1989), 34.

6-11. Genuit, Klaus and Wade R. Bray, "The Aachen Head System-Binaural Recording for Headphones and Speakers" *Audio,* 73, 12 (December 1989), 58 – 66.

6-12. _____, "A Special Calibratable Artificial-Head-Measuring System for Subjective and Objective Classification of Noise," Inter-Noise Conference, Cambridge, MA, (July 1986), 1313 – 1318.

6-13. Genuit, K., "Investigation and Simulation of Vehicle Noise Using the Binaural Measurement Technique," Noise and Vibration Conference, Traverse City, Mich. (April 1987), 97-104.

6-14. Greisinger, David, "Binaural Techniques For Music Reproduction," Proceedings of the 8th International Conference, Audio Eng. Soc., Washington D.C. (1990).

Chapter 7

7-1. Dooley, Wes, and Ron Streicher, "MS Stereo: A Powerful Technique for Working in Stereo," *J. Audio Eng. Soc.,* 30, 10, (1982), 707 ff.

7-2. Streicher, Ron and Wes Dooley, "Basic Stereo Microphone Perspectives - A Review," *J. Audio Eng. Soc.,* 33, 7/8, (1985), 548ff.

7-3. Griesinger, David, "New Perspectives on Coincident and Semi Coincident Microphone Arrays," presented at the 82nd Convention of the Audio Eng. Soc. (1987), London, Preprint #2464.

7-4. Griesinger, David, "Spaciousness and Localization in Listening Rooms and Their Effects on the Recording Technique," *J. Audio Eng. Soc.,* 34, 4, (1986), 255 ff. Subsequent issues of JAES contain comments and responses to this article.

7-5. Lipshitz, Stanley, "Stereo Microphone Techniques: Are the Purists Wrong," *J. Audio Eng. Soc.,* 34, 9, (1986), 716 ff.

Additional references

"Stereophonic Techniques," an anthology of reprinted articles on stereophonic techniques, published by the Audio Eng. Soc., (1986).

The Sound of Audio, Proc. of the 8th International Conf. Audio Eng. Soc., May, 1990

Peus, Stephan, "The MS Recording Technique for the Stereophonic TV and Movie Sound," presented at the 3rd Regional Convention of the Audio Eng. Soc., Melbourne (1988), Preprint #2674

Eargle, John, *Handbook Of Recording Engineering,* New York, Van Nostrand Reinhold Company, Second Edition, (1992).

Woram, John, *Sound Recording Handbook,* Indianapolis, Howard W. Sams Company, (1989).

Bartlett, Bruce, *Stereo Microphone Techniques,* Boston, Focal Press, (1991).

Chapter 8

8-1. Olive, Sean E. and Floyd E. Toole, "The detection of reflections in typical rooms," *J. Audio Eng. Soc.,* 37, 7/8 (1989), 539 – 553.

8-2. Toole, Floyd E., "Loudspeakers and rooms for stereophonic reproduction," Proc. 9th International Conference, Audio Eng. Soc., 71 – 91.

8-3. Schubert, P., "Die Wahrnehmbarkeit von Ruckwurfen bei Musik," Z. Hochfrequenz-tech. Electroakust., 78 (1969), 230 – 245, cited by Olive and Toole, Ref. 1.

8-4. Bartlett, Bruce, "A scientific explanation of phasing (flanging)," *J. Audio Eng. Soc.*, 18, 6 (1970), 674 – 675.

8-5. Blauert, Jens, *Spatial Hearing*, 1983, Cambridge, MA, MIT Press, 325 – 326.

Chapter 9

9-1. *Stereophonic Techniques—an Anthology*, published by the Audio Eng. Soc., New York, (1986).

9-2. Jecklin, Jürg, "A Different Way to Record Classical Music," *J. Audio Eng. Soc.*, 29, 5 (1981), 329 ff.

9-3. The SCHOEPS KFM 6 U stereo microphone shown in Fig. 9-5 was developed largely following the research of Gunther Theile, et al. An important paper on this technique is *On the Naturalness of Two-Channel Stereo Sound*, Proc. of the 9th International Conference of the Audio Eng. Soc., Detroit (1991), 143 ff.

9-4. Billingsley, Michael, U.S. Patent no. 4,658,931; trademark of Crown International, Inc.

9-5. Bartlett, Bruce, and Michael Billingsley, "Boundary Stereo Microphone Array - Theory," *J. Audio Eng. Soc.*, 38, 7/8, (1990), 543 ff. [This article is well worth reading for its overall discussion of stereo perception, microphone techniques, and the extensive list of references cited.]

9-6. Long, E.M., and Wickersham, R.J., U.S. Patent #4,361,736, "Pressure Recording Process and Device," The term *Pressure Zone Microphone*, abbreviated PZM, is now a Trademark of Crown International, Inc.

9-7. Toole, Floyd, "Loudspeakers and Rooms for Stereophonic Sound Reproduction," Proc. of the Audio Eng. Soc. 8th International Conference, Washington, D.C., (1990), 71 ff.

Chapter 10

10-1. Klapholz, Jesse, "Fantasia, Innovations in Sound," *J. Audio Eng. Soc.*, 39, 1/2, (1991), 68 ff.

10-2. Eargle, John, *The Microphone Handbook*, Plainview, NY, Elar Publishing, (1981), 28 ff.

10-3. Burroughs, Lou, *Microphones: Design and Application,* Sagamore Publishing Co., Plainview, NY, 1974, p. 171.

10-4. Ibid., pp. 105 ff.

10-5. Olson, Harry, F., *Music, Physics, and Engineering,* New York, NY, Dover Publications, (1967), Chapters Five and Six.

10-6. Hall, Donald E., *Music Acoustics*, Pacific Grove, CA, Brooks/Cole Publishing Co. (1991), Chapters 9 – 14.

10-7. Eargle, John, *Music, Sound, and Technology*, New York, NY, Van Nostrand Reinhold (1990), Chapters 4 – 10.

Chapter 11

11-1. Blauert, Jens, *Spatial hearing*, MIT Press, Cambridge, MA (1983). Translated from the German by John S. Allen.

11-2. Eargle, John, *Handbook of recording engineering*, Van Nostrand Reinhold, New York, NY (1986).

11-3. Janovsky, W.H., *An apparatus for 3-dimensional reproduction in electroacoustical presen-*

tations, (in German), German Federal Republic Patent No. 973570 (1948). Cited by Blauer, Reference 11-1.

11-4. Schroeder, M.R., "An artificial stereophonic effect obtained from a single audio signal," *J. Audio Eng. Soc.*, 6 (1958), 74 – 79.

11-5. Lockner, J.P.A. and W. deV. Keet, "Stereophonic and quasistereophonic reproduction." *J. Acous. Soc. Am.*, 32 (1960), 393 – 401.

11-6. Lauridsen, H., "Nogle forsoq med forskelliqe former rumakustik qenqivelski," *Ingenioren*, 7 (1954), 906. Cited in Schroeder Reference 4 and Blauert, Reference 11-1.

11-7. Schodder, G.R., "Simulation of an acoustical impression of space," *Acustica*, 6 (1956), 482 – 488.

11-8. Lauridsen, H. and F. Schlegel, "Stereophony and directionally diffuse reproduction of sound," (in German), Gravesaner Blatter, 5 (1956), 28 – 50. Cited by Blauert, Reference 11-1.

11-9. Schroeder, M.R., "Improved quasi-stereophony and 'colorless' artificial reverberation." *J. Acous. Soc. Am.*, 33 (1961), 1061 – 1064.

Chapter 12

12-1. Blauert, Jens, "Some fundamentals of auditory spaciousness," a chapter in *Perception of reproduced sound*, Gammel Avernaes, Denmark (1987), 33 – 40.

12-2. Blauert, J., "Auditory spaciousness. some further psychoacoustic analysis," *J. Acous. Soc. Am.*, 80 (1986), 533.

12-3. Blauert, Jens, *Spatial hearing*, MIT Press, Cambridge, MA (1983).

12-4. Maxfield, J.P. and W.J. Albersheim, "An acoustic constant of enclosed spaces with apparent liveness," *J. Acous. Soc Am.*, 19 (1947), 71 – 79.

12-5. Barron, M., "The subjective effects of first reflections in concert halls—the need for lateral reflections." *J. Sound Vib.*, 15 (1971), 475 – 494.

12-6. Barron, M., and A.H. Marshall, "Spatial impressions due to early lateral reflections in concept halls: the derivation of a physical measure," *J. Sound and Vib.*, 77 (1981), 211 – 232.

12-7. Baranek, L.L., *Music, acoustics, and architecture,* New York, John Wiley & Sons (1962).

12-8. Hyde, J.R. and A.H. Marshall, "Requirements for successful concert hall design: need for lateral and ensemble reflections," I.E.E.E. International Conference on Acoustics, Speech, and Signal Processing, Paper A24 (April 1980).

12-9. Rasch, R.A., and R. Plomp, "The listener and the acoustic environment," Chapter 5 in the *The Psychology of Music,* by Diana Deutsch, Academic Press, New York (1982).

Chapter 13

13-1. Klapholz, Jesse, *Fantasia,"* *J. Audio Eng. Soc.*, 39, 1/2, (1991), 66 ff.

13-2. Scheiber, Peter, *Quadrasonic Sound System,* U.S. Patent 3,632,886, 1972.

13-3. Scheiber, Peter, *Multidirectional Sound System*, U.S. Patent 3,746,792, 1973.

13-4. Holman, Tomlinson, "Surround Sound Systems Used with Pictures in Cinemas and Homes," Proc. Audio Eng. Soc. 8th International Conference, Washington, D.C., (1990), 191 ff.

13-5. Gilbert, Mark, and Robert Schulein, "Stereosurround™ A Compatible Multichannel Encoding/Decoding Process for Audio and Audio Video Applications," presented to the 87th Convention of the Audio Eng. Soc, and published by Shure HTS, Evanston, IL, 1989.

13-6. Jusltrom, Stephen, "A High Performance Surround Sound Process for Home Video," *J. Audio Eng. Soc.*, 35, 7/8, (1987), 356 ff.

13-7. Holman, Tomlinson, "New Factors in Sound for Cinema and Television," presented at the 89th Audio Eng. Soc. Convention, Los Angeles (1991), preprint #2945.

13-8. Griesinger, David, "Theory and Design of a Digital Audio Signal Processor for Home Use," *J. Audio Eng. Soc.*, 37, 1/2, (1989), 40 ff.

13-9. Gerzon, Michael, "The Design of Precisely Coincident Microphone Arrays for Stereo and Surround Sound," Proc. of the 50th Audio Eng. Soc. Convention, London, (1975).

13-10. Furness, Roger, "Ambisonics—an Overview," Proc. of the Audio Eng. Soc. 8th International Conference, Washington, D.C., (1990) 181 ff.

13-11. Fellgett, P.B., "Ambisonic Reproduction of Directionality in Surround Sound Systems," Reprinted by permission from Nature vol. 252 Copyright (C) 1974 MacMillan Magazines Ltd. *Nature*, 252, (1974).

13-12. Farrar, Kenneth, *Soundfield Microphone: The Design and Development of the Microphone and Associated Control Unit*, Calrec Audio Ltd.

13-13. Gerzon, Michael, "Ambisonics in Multichannel Broadcasting and Video," presented at the 74th Audio Eng. Soc. Convention, New York, (1983), preprint #2034.

13-14. Kotorynski, Kevin, "Digital Binaural/stereo Conversion and Crosstalk Canceling," presented at the 89th Audio Eng. Soc. Convention, Los Angeles, (1990), preprint # 2949.

13-15. Genuit, K., H.W. Gierlich, and W. Bray, "Development and use of Binaural Recording Technique," presented at the 89th Audio Eng. Soc. Convention, Los Angeles, (1990), preprint 2950.

13-16. Cohen, Elizabeth, "Technologies for Three Dimensional Sound Presentation and Issues in Subjective Evaluation of the Spatial Image," presented at the 89th Audio Eng. Soc. Convention, Los Angeles, (1990), preprint #2943.

13-17. Burkhard, M., W. Bray, K. Genuit, and H.W. Gierlich, "Binaural Sound for Television," Proc. of the 9th Audio Eng. Soc. International Conference, Detroit, (1991), 119 ff.

13-18. Cooper, Duane, and Jerald Bauck, "Prospects for Transaural Recording," *J. Audio Eng. Soc.*, 37, 1/2, (1989), 3 ff.

13-19. Griesinger, David, "Equalization and Spatial Equalization of Dummy-head Recordings for Loudspeaker Reproduction," *J. Audio Eng. Soc.*, 37, 1/2, (1989), 20 ff.

13-20. Woszczyk, Wieslaw, "A review of Microphone Techniques Optimized for Spatial Control of Sound in Television," Proc. of the 9th Audio Eng. Soc. International Conference, Detroit, (1991), 133 ff.

13-21. Schulein, Robert, "Television and Audio/Video Production Techniques using the Stereosurround Audio Production Format," Proc. of the 9th Audio Eng. Soc. International Conference, Detroit, (1991), 151 ff.

Chapter 14

14-1. Toole, Floyd E., "Loudspeakers and rooms for stereophonic sound reproduction," Proc. 9th Internat. Conf., Audio Eng. Soc., Washington, D.C., (1990), 71 – 91. An excellent overall treatment.

14-2. Guilford, C.L.S., "The acoustic design of talks studios and listening rooms," *Proc. Inst. Elect. Engrs.*, 106, Part B, 27 (1959), 245 – 258. Reprinted in *J. Audio Eng. Soc.*, 27, 1/2, (1979), 17 – 31.

14-3. Everest, F. Alton, *Acoustic techniques for home and studio*, 2nd. Ed. (1984), Blue Ridge Summit, PA., TAB Books. (A) Chapter 7, *Diffusion of sound*: (B) Chapter 9, *Acoustical materials and structures*.

14-4. Everest, F. Alton, *The master handbook of acoustics, 2nd. Ed.* (1989), Blue Ridge Summit, PA., TAB Books. Chapter 10, *Absorption of Sound*.

14-5. Schroeder, M.R., "Diffuse sound reflections by maximum-length sequences," *J. Acous. Soc. Am.*, 57, 1 (1975), 149 – 150.

14-6. Allison, R.F., "The influence of room boundaries on loudspeaker power output," *J. Audio Eng. Soc.*, 22 (1974), 314 – 319.

14-7. Berger, Russell E.II, "Speaker/boundary interference response." *Mix*, 8, 8, (August 1984).

14-8. Davis, Chips and Don Davis, "(LEDE) live-end-dead-end control room acoustics" Recording Engr/Prod, 10, 1, (Feb 1979), 41.

Glossary

ambience   That portion of the background sound in a music hall, auditorium, or listening environment other than that resulting from reflected program sound. Ambience includes intrusion of natural environmental noise inherent in the location, air-conditioning noise, audience noise, etc.

ambisonics   Method of recording the spatial information of the entire soundfield as defined by absolute sound pressure and three pressure gradients of the cardinal directions (left/right, fore/aft, up/down).

amplifier   Most commonly an electronic circuit or other device that increases the signal level by increasing voltage or current. Buffer amplifiers isolate one part of a circuit from another. Impedance matching amplifiers could actually decrease level. Preamplifiers are designed to handle small voltages, such as microphone signals. Power amplifiers are designed to drive loudspeakers.

amplitude   Another term for signal level. Measured often in decibels above a standard reference level.

analysis of sound   A process of determining the energy distribution of a signal with respect to frequency. A narrow filter is swept throughout the frequency range of interest to determine the spectral distribution.

anthropomorphic manikin (dummy head)   A manikin having head, shoulders, and upper torso with average human dimensions and with surface characteristics and pinna convolutions conforming closely to those of humans. High-quality microphones, commonly located in the concha region, record sounds encoded with directional information. A two-channel binaural signal results (German, *kunstkopf*).

attenuator   A device for reducing or adjusting signal level. A resistance with a sliding contact.

audio frequency   The range of human hearing is commonly accepted as 20 Hz to 20 kHz in audio work. Psychologists would use slightly different figures. (Hz = cycles per second)

auditory canal (auditory meatus)   The canal extending from the concha to the eardrum.

auditory filters   (See critical bands.)

auditory perspective   Early experiments in stereophonics at Bell Laboratories were considered analogous to sight and the term auditory perspective was used because of the spatial dimension added to sound.

auditory system   The hearing system composed of the outer ear (pinna, concha, auditory meatus, and tympanic membrane), the middle ear (ossicles: malleus, incus, stapes), and the inner ear (cochlea), and the brain.

axial modes   Acoustical resonance effects between two spaced, parallel surfaces such as side walls of a room, end walls, and floor/ceiling.

baffle   Barriers to provide some acoustical isolation between microphones assigned to specific instruments in a musical group (aka *Gobo*).

balance control   A potentiometer on a stereo set by which the relative level of the left and right loudspeakers can be adjusted.

basilar membrane   One of the cochlear partitions whose vibrations are involved in the analysis of sound in the auditory system

bass   The low-frequency portion of the audible spectrum.

bidirectional   A bidirectional microphone pattern, also known as *figure-of-eight*, provides sensitivity in two opposite directions.

binaural   Having or involving the use of two ears.

biphonic   A listening system providing a separate microphone/amplifier channel for each earphone.

Blumlein technique   A stereophonic microphone arrangement in which two bidirectional, coincident microphones are arranged so that their principal axes are 90° to one another. Named for Alan Dower Blumlein.

BMLD (Binaural Masking Level Difference)   The measured improvement in audibility resulting from the unmasking effect of incoherency between the two ears.

cardioid   A heart-shaped microphone directivity pattern that is sensitive primarily to sound from the forward direction and rather insensitive to the rear. The sensitivity to the sides is approximately half that of the forward direction.

channel   Path of a single signal from microphone, through amplifiers via the medium (radio or record/reproduce), to more amplifiers and loudspeaker. Mono uses a single channel, stereo uses two or more channels.

cochlea   The inner ear; the sound analyzing part of the auditory system connected to the brain by the auditory nerves.

Cocktail Party Effect   A name given to the ability of the human auditory system to hear a desired sound by suppressing the noise interfering with it. This is a binaural function requiring both ears.

coherence   The degree of similarity between two sounds.

coincident   Two microphones are said to be coincident if their diaphragms are as close together as physically possible.

coloration of sound   A deterioration in the spectrum of an audio signal. If the spectrum of a sound is altered, it is colored, analogous to light, which is colored as its spectrum is changed.

comb filter, combing Alteration of the frequency response of a system as a result of constructive and destructive interference between a signal and a delayed version of the signal. Plotted on a linear frequency scale, such a comb-filter response looks like the teeth of a comb.

compatibility Mono compatibility is the quality of a stereo signal that allows its summed reduction to mono without serious comb-filter distortion.

compression A sound wave traveling in air is made up of alternating cycles of crowding air particles together, compression, and spreading of air particles apart, rarefaction.

conceptual A mental impression or image.

concha A resonant cavity of the outer ear between the pinna and the ear canal.

condenser (capacitor) microphone A microphone using the vibration of one plate of a capacitor (condenser) to transduce the air pressure fluctuations of the sound wave to a usable signal voltage. A polarizing voltage is required.

correlation coefficient A coefficient that expresses the degree of similarity between two functions.

critical bands The frequency resolving power of the auditory system can be considered as the result of bandpass filters. Such filters have been measured extensively by masking techniques and have become known as critical bands.

critical distance The distance from a source of sound at which the total energy of the direct sound level equals the total energy of the reverberant soundfield.

crosstalk Listening to binaural (dummy head) signals over stereo loudspeakers is unsatisfactory because of the unwanted leakage of sound from the right loudspeaker to the left ear, and the unwanted sound from the left loudspeaker to the right ear. These unwanted components are called crosstalk.

***dead* acoustics** A term applied to a space with little reverberation, or a space with too much sound absorbing material in it. Music quality suffers more than speech quality in such a space.

DECCA Tree A configuration of three omnidirectional microphones, positioned in a T-shaped frame, noted for its warm and enveloping sound.

decibel, dB A unit of measurement defined as the logarithm of a ratio of two powers. Although defined in terms of a power ratio, it can also be computed from voltage and current ratios because of their relationship to power. One element of the ratio is usually a standard reference value, such as 1 mW for power, 1 V or 20 micropascals for sound pressure. The extremely wide ranges of sound pressure encountered, for example in audio work, are conveniently expressed in dB. .

decoding Directionally encoded sounds falling on the human ear are decoded by the brain. Directionally encoded sounds picked up by a microphone yield voltage fluctuations that must be decoded before they are used to drive loudspeakers (see encoding). Also, en electronic process of recovering encoded information from a stereo signal and reconstructing a surround soundfield.

definition The definition of a musical sound, for example, is a measure of the clarity and purity by which small changes and nuances are conveyed.

delay A measure of the time separation between two events. Examples from the field of audio include: the time separation between a direct signal and a reflection of it, and the delay of a signal in electronic circuits or in loudspeakers. Audio signals are often purposely delayed by digital delay devices to achieve certain effects.

diaphragm   There are diaphragms in ears (eardrum), microphones, loudspeakers, etc. Their purpose is to increase the efficiency of sound energy transfer to and from a tenuous medium, such as air.

diffraction   The scattering of sound. (See diffraction grating.)

diffraction grating   Diffraction gratings in optics scatter light into its spectral (frequency) components. In acoustics, theoretically similar devices are used to scatter or diffuse sound. In acoustical treatment of spaces, such gratings add diffusion to previously available tools of absorption and reflection.

diffuse field   A sound field composed of sound arriving in random directions.

digital delay   An electronic circuit capable of delaying an audio signal a controllable amount with high fidelity.

distance factor   A comparison of the sensitivity of a directional microphone to that of a omnidirectional microphone in any given direction.

distortion   Any difference between the input and output signal as it passes through a device (amplifier, loudspeaker, microphone) is distortion attributed to the device.

dummy head   (See anthropomorphic manikin.)

dynamic microphone   The vibration of the diaphragm in a dynamic microphone causes an electrical conductor to move in a magnetic field. A signal voltage corresponding to the air pressure variations acting on the diaphragm is generated in the conductor by magnetic induction.

dynamic range   The extremes between loud and soft. All audio systems are limited on the low end by circuit and other noise, and on the high end by distortion. The usable range in between is called the dynamic range of the system.

ear canal   (See auditory canal.)

eardrum   (See tympanic membrane.)

early reflections   Those reflections reaching a listener after the arrival of the direct sound, but before the arrival of reverberation sound resulting from late reflections. The early reflections give rise to a feeling of spaciousness in the music hall, but in the typical listening room they tend to confuse the stereo image, giving rise to coloration of sound due to combing.

echoes   If a reflected or delayed sound arrives at the listener 50 or more milliseconds after the arrival of the direct sound, a discrete echo can be heard.

electret microphone   A condenser or capacitor microphone with the element permanently charged so no external polarizing voltage is necessary.

encoding   1. As related to auditory perception, the process by which sound arriving at a listener's ears is encoded with directional information through the action of pinna reflections, head diffraction, and reflections from shoulders and torso. 2. An electronic process for reducing the several channels of a surround sound system into a compatible stereo transmission medium. Encoding processes in surround sound include 4:2:4, matrix, Dolby N.R., etc.

ensemble   1. A group of musicians performing together. 2. The ability of musicians to hear each other.

equalization (EQ) The use of filters to alter the frequency response of a system. Commonly arranged with filter spacings of one octave, $1/3$ octave, etc.

eustachian tube The tube between the middle ear and the pharynx that serves to equalize air pressure on both sides of the eardrum.

filter A device that attenuates or increases certain portions of the audio frequency spectrum. A bandpass filter passes signal energy only in a specified band and attenuates all others. A highpass filter attenuates energy below a certain cutoff frequency. A lowpass filter attenuates signal energy above a certain frequency.

flanging or phasing The utilization of comb filters for generating certain special sound effects.

frequency The number of cycles in a periodic wave per second; measured in hertz (Hz).

gobo (See baffle.)

Haas effect (See precedence effect.)

Helmholtz resonator A reactive, tuned, sound absorber usually employing slats or perforated facing over a cavity.

Hertz The unit of frequency replacing the term **cycles per second**, abbreviated Hz.

hole in the middle Stereo systems sometimes fail to yield a strong phantom image between the two loudspeakers. This is called a hole in the middle.

hypercardioid A combination of omnidirectional and bidirectional microphone patterns produces a family of directional patterns, one of which is the hypercardioid that has appreciable sensitivity in the rear direction.

impedance The opposition to the flow of electrical or acoustical energy, measured in ohms.

incoherence The degree of difference between two signals.

incus One of the three ossicles that convey eardrum vibrations to the cochlea (see ossicles).

inner ear The cochlea; the sound analyzing portion of the ear.

intensity Commonly implied as the amplitude of an acoustical signal. In acoustics, intensity is the sound energy flux per unit area.

intensity stereo Stereo dependent only on the relative amplitude (intensity) of signals in the two channels.

interaural The response of the two ears to a given stimulus.

interference The combining of two or more signals resulting in constructive or destructive interaction as in the comb-filter effect. The word is also used to denote undesired signals.

inverse square law The intensity of sound diverging spherically as from a point in free space decreases inversely as the square of the distance. Sound pressure, the commonly measured parameter, varies as the first power of the distance. Thus sound pressure decreases 6 dB with each doubling of the distance in free space.

law of first wavefront The first sound to strike the ear determines the perception of direction.

live acoustics   A space is considered live if there is little absorption so that reverberation effects dominate hearing.

loudness   A subjective term for the sensation of the intensity of a sound.

magnitude   (See amplitude.)

malleus   One of the three ossicle bones that conduct the vibrations of the eardrum to the oval window of the cochlea (see ossicles).

masking   The process by which the threshold of audibility of one sound is raised by the presence of another masking sound.

matrix   1. An array of elements comprising a multidimensional subject. 2. An electronic circuit designed to accomplish a specific task, such as encoding or decoding spatial information from a microphone.

meatus, auditory   (See auditory canal.)

median plane   The vertical plane equidistant from the two ears bisecting the head.

medium   1. Sound is transmitted through media such as air, liquids, or solids. 2. A transmission format, such as recording (tape or disc), broadcast, film, etc.

microphone   A device that transduces air vibrations into corresponding electrical signals.

microphone distance factor   (See distance factor.)

middle ear   The portion of the ear between the eardrum and the cochlea.

mid-side   A stereo microphone arrangement comprised of two microphones by which one directional microphone contributes the principal pickup of an ensemble and the other, a bidirectional, contributes the lateral information.

mixdown   The process by which a multichannel recording is combined into one, two, or more channels.

modes   The low-frequency resonances (modes) prominent in small rooms.

monaural   A single channel recording or reproducing system arranged for one-eared listening.

mono   A contraction of monophonic (or, less frequently, monaural).

mono compatibility   The capability of a stereo recording to be reduced to a monophonic recording with low distortion.

monophonic   A single channel recording or reproducing system arranged for two-eared listening.

noise floor   The circuit or system noise that establishes the lowest signal level usable.

noise, pink   Random noise having equal energy per octave, commonly used for evaluating and calibrating sound reproduction systems.

noise, random   An undefined blend of all audio frequencies, heard as a hiss.

noise, white   Random noise with a uniform distribution of energy throughout the entire audible spectrum, analogous to the electro-magnetic spectrum of white light.

N.O.S. technique   An arrangement of two cardioid microphones set at an angle of 90° with a capsule spacing of 30 cm (from the Netherlands).

objective   Without bias or prejudice; detached; impersonal.

oblique modes   Those normal modal resonances of a room that involve all six surfaces of the room.

octave   The interval between two frequencies having a ratio of 2:1.

omnidirectional   A microphone with uniform sensitivity to sound arriving from all directions is said to have an omnidirectional pattern.

O.R.T.F. technique   An arrangement of two cardioid microphones whose principal axes are angled 110° and with capsules separated 17 cm (from France).

ossicles   The three bones of the middle ear (malleus, incus, stapes) providing a mechanical linkage between the eardrum and the oval window of the cochlea.

OSS technique (Optimum Stereo Signal)   Utilizes a pair of omnidirectional microphones separated 16.5 cm with an acoustically opaque baffle between them. (Jecklin Disk)

outer ear   (See pinna.)

oval window   A membraneous window of the cochlea to which the stapes ossicle is attached.

panoramic potentiometer (panpot)   A variable resistance control by which a mono signal might be placed anywhere between the two channels of the stereo field.

perception, percept   The faculty of consciously perceiving. A recognizable sensation or impression received through the senses.

perceptual   Involving perception.

periodic   A signal having a regularly repeating pattern, i.e., a tone as opposed to speech, noise, or music signals.

phantom image   The image appearing between two stereo loudspeakers driven with a stereo signal.

phase   The time relationship between two signals.

phase coherency   Two coincident microphones are in phase coherency if they yield primarily intensity cues and minimize all phase (time) cues. *Phase integrity* might be a better phrase to avoid confusion with interaural coherency.

phasiness   Audible combing distortion.

phasing   (See flanging.)

pinna   The outer ear. Directional cues result from the reflection of sound from the folds of the pinna.

pitch   The subjective perception of frequency.

polar pattern   A graphical representation of the sensitivity of a microphone in a horizontal plane through 360°.

polarity, absolute   A sound wave compression moving outward can arbitrarily be considered as positive. The concept of absolute polarity can be maintained by making a positive electric wave conform to positive acoustic waves (and vice versa). This can be done by adjustment of polarity of electrical equipment and loudspeakers.

potentiometer   A variable voltage driver or a resistance with an adjustable slider by which voltage can be varied between two outputs.

precedence effect (Haas effect)   If two loudspeakers in normal stereo arrangement are energized with the same signal and a small time delay is introduced in one of them, the sound from the earlier one will determine the localization of the sound. This is the Haas or precedence effect. Haas found that delays within a certain range could be compensated by intensity changes. A 10 ms delay requires a 10 dB adjustment to return the phantom to the center. This fusion or integration zone persists up to about 30 or 35 ms delay. Delays greater than this result in discrete echoes.

presence Speech can be given *presence* and made to stand out from a music background by an equalization boost of 2 – 4 dB at a frequency of 2 – 3 kHz. Sounds in this region tend to be coded for arrival from the front.

pressure gradient The ribbon microphone is called a pressure gradient microphone in that the force acting on the diaphragm is proportional to the differences between the pressures on both sides of the diaphragm. This type of microphone is also called a *velocity* microphone because its output depends on the air particle velocity at the diaphragm or ribbon.

pressure microphone An omnidirectional microphone that responds only to the fluctuations of air pressure at the diaphragm.

pressure sound Small fluctuations of air pressure above and below the static atmospheric pressure carry acoustic information. Sound pressure can be measured by common sound level meters.

psychoacoustics The study of the interrelationships between the human hearing mechanism and acoustics.

quadratic residue diffuser A sound diffuser based on a sequence of numbers derived from number theory.

random energy efficiency A measure of the degree to which a microphone responds to the desired sound relative to the total sonic environment surrounding it.

random noise (See noise, random.)

rarefaction The negative portion of a sound wave in which the air particles are spread apart.

reflection, early (See early reflections.)

refraction The bending of sound rays usually resulting from stratification of the medium.

Reissner's Membrane With the basilar membrane, Reissner's Membrane divides the cochlea into three longititudinal chambers.

resonance Acoustical resonance in a room results from the combination of a foreward-going wave with a backward-going wave resulting from reflections between two opposite, plane, parallel surfaces.

reverberation A temporal extension of acoustical events in a space generated by multiple sound reflections.

ribbon microphone A microphone whose diaphragm is a metallic ribbon stretched in a magnetic field so that its movement by sound waves induces a signal voltage between its ends. It operates on the differential of pressure between its two sides that results in a figure-eight pattern.

room tone Similar to ambience.

round window A window of the cochlea opening into the middle ear that acts as a pressure release on the fluid of the inner ear.

S.A.S.S.™, (Stereo Ambient Sampling System) A mono compatible, near-coincident array of microphones designed to give highly localized stereo imaging for loudspeaker reproduction.

self noise (See noise floor.) The noise floor of the microphone itself.

sensation The feeling resulting from a stimulus.

shotgun microphone A microphone utilizing differential phase interference to achieve its highly directional pattern. Used for speech pickup at a distance from the subject.

simple harmonic motion A vibratory motion in which the moving object sweeps back and forth over the same path.

sine wave A combination of simple harmonic motion and uniform linear motion. Called a sine wave because the displacement is proportional to the sine of the angle.

sonic Pertaining to sound.

soundfield microphone™ A microphone composed of four subcardioid capsules mounted on the face of a tetrahedron. After electronic combination they yield absolute pressure, as well as the fore/aft, left/right, and vertical pressure gradients.

sound pressure level A sound pressure referred to a standard level; expressed in dB; abbreviated SPL.

spaciousness The sense of envelopment that is created in music halls by early lateral reflections from a variety of different horizontal directions.

spatial Having to do with space.

spectrum The spectrum of a signal is the distribution of its energy throughout the audible spectrum. Related to timbre.

speed of sound (velocity of sound) Approximately 1,127 ft/sec at normal air temperature and normal atmospheric pressure.

spherical divergence (See inverse square law.)

spot microphone A microphone placed close to a performer to augment that performer's sound in the overall recording.

standing wave A room resonance in the low-frequency region that results in uneven distribution of sound energy in the room.

stapes (See ossicles.)

stereo seat That position giving the optimum listening conditions.

stereo The Greek word carries the meaning of *solid*, i.e., with depth, breadth, and height implied.

stereoscopic Pertaining to the visual ability to perceive depth. Judgments of direction to a sound source utilize information from two ears.

stimulus Something that incites a sensation.

supercardioid (See hypercardioid.)

super stereo A phrase applicable to a recording/reproducing system that would accurately convey all spatial information with true fidelity, via only two loudspeakers.

sweet spot (See stereo seat.)

synthesis of sound The act of artificially building up a sound from component parts.

tangential mode The room resonance that involves four of the six surfaces of a room.

Three-to-One Rule A practical rule for avoiding comb-filter distortion; keep adjacent microphones at least three times as far apart as the distance between any microphone and its sound subject.

threshold   The point at which a stimulus is just strong enough to be perceived or produce a response.

timbre   The perceived tonal quality of a sound based on the pitch and the relative mix of fundamental and harmonic frequencies.

tone   A sound that is distinct and identifiable by its constant pitch.

transducer   A device that converts one form of energy into another. In audio the most common examples are the microphone and loudspeaker.

transfer function   Description of a function in terms of its frequency and phase (time) response.

treble   Tones of higher frequency.

Two-to-One Ratio   For the same signal level and direct-to-reverberant sound ratio, a cardioid microphone can be used generally at twice the distance from the sound source as an omnidirectional microphone.

tympanic membrane   The eardrum. The tympanic membrane is actuated by the vibration of air in the ear canal. These vibrations are transferred to the chain of ossicles in the middle ear, which in turn mechanically transmit them to the oval window of the cochlea.

unidirectional   A microphone whose sensitivity is primarily in one direction.

unmasking   The application of certain interaural incoherencies to achieve a release from masking.

velocity of sound   (See speed of sound.)

wall of sound   A theoretical concept employed by early workers in stereo at Bell Laboratories; a two-dimensional wavefront.

wave form   The shape of a signal wave.

wavelength   The distance between successive similar points on a sound wave. Easily computed by dividing speed of sound by the frequency.

XY stereo   The arrangement of two directional microphones in a coincident stereo pickup.

Index